October, 2000

To Wendy –
with much affection –
we will talk about its point –
Janice.

Youth and Coping in Twelve Nations

What are the problems that concern young people today? How do young people cope? This book presents the findings of a team of international researchers, including both social scientists and practitioners, who have surveyed more than 5,000 youth in twelve countries in order to find answers to these vital questions.

The book is arranged into five key sections:

- Part I outlines the innovative research methods and theories underpinning the study, including the central 'intervention research paradigm'.
- Part II offers a composite portrait of concerns and coping strategies across the survey, examining trends by socio-economic status and gender.
- Part III provides detailed case-studies from Brazil, Canada, China, England, Greece, India, Israel, Japan, Russia, the USA and Venezuela.
- Part IV examines special youth populations, both immigrant and impoverished.
- Part V draws conclusions and implications for theory and practice, and offers a basis from which helping professionals can develop successful interventions and practices.

Youth and Coping in Twelve Nations is an innovative work of cross-cultural research that offers a wealth of empirical research material, as well as important new conclusions and recommendations for practice. It will be of vital interest to all sociologists and social psychologists, as well as youth and social work professionals.

Janice Gibson-Cline is Professor Emeritus of Developmental Psychology, University of Pittsburgh. She has served as Fulbright Research Professor in Greece and the Philippines, National Academy of Science Exchange Professor in the former Soviet Union and Visiting Research Professor in the People's Republic of China. Her previous publications related to *Youth and Coping* include *Adolescence: From Crisis to Coping* (Routledge 1996).

Routledge Research International Series in Social Psychology

Edited by W. Peter Robinson, University of Bristol, UK

This series represents a showcase for both the latest cutting-edge research in the field, and important critiques of existing theory. International in scope, and directed at an international audience, applied topics are well represented. Social psychology is defined broadly to include related areas from social development to the social psychology of abnormal behaviour. The series is a rich source of information for advanced students and researchers alike.

Routledge is pleased to invite proposals for new books in the series. In the first instance, any interested authors should contact:

Professor W. Peter Robinson
Department of Experimental Psychology
University of Bristol
8 Woodland Road
Bristol BS8 1TN
E-mail: P.Robinson@bristol.ac.uk

Routledge Research International Series in Social Psychology

1 Cooperation in Modern Society
Promoting the welfare of communities, states and organizations
Edited by Mark van Vugt, Mark Snyder, Tom R. Tyler and Anders Biel

2 Youth and Coping in Twelve Nations
Surveys of 18–20-year-old young people
Edited by Janice Gibson-Cline

3 Responsibility
The many faces of a social phenomenon
Hans-Werner Bierhoff and Ann Elisabeth Auhagen

Also available in the International Series in Social Psychology, now published by Psychology Press

Children as Consumers
A psychological analysis of the young people's market
Barrie Gunter and Adrian Furnham

Adjustment of Adolescents
Cross-cultural similarities and differences
Ruth Scott and William Scott

Social Psychology and Education
Pam Maras

Making Sense of Television
The psychology of audience interpretation
Sonia Livingstone

Stereotypes During the Decline and Fall of Communism
Gyorgy Hunyady

Understanding the Older Consumer
The Grey Market
Barrie Gunter

Adolescence: From Crisis to Coping
A Thirteen Nation Study
Edited by Janice Gibson-Cline

Changing European Identities
Social psychological analyses of social change
Edited by Glynis M. Breakwell and Evanthia Lyons

Social Groups and Identities
Developing the legacy of Henri Tajfel
Edited by Peter W. Robinson

Assertion and its Social Context
Keithia Wilson and Cynthia Gallois

Children's Social Competence in Context
The contributions of family, school and culture
Barry H. Schneider

Emotion and Social Judgements
Edited by Joseph P. Forgas

Game Theory and its Applications
In the social and biological sciences
Andrew M. Colman

Genius and Eminence
Edited by Robert S. Albert

The Psychology of Gambling
Michael Walker

Social Dilemmas
Theoretical issues and research findings
Edited by Wim Liebrand, David Messick and Henk Wilke

The Theory of Reasoned Action
Its application to AIDS-preventive behaviour
Edited by Deborah Terry, Cynthia Gallois and Malcolm McCamish

Youth and Coping in Twelve Nations

Surveys of 18–20-year-old young people

Edited by Janice Gibson-Cline

London and New York

First published 2000 by Routledge
11 New Fetter Lane, London EC4P 4EE

Simultaneously published in the USA and Canada
by Routledge
29 West 35th Street, New York, NY 10001

Routledge is an imprint of the Taylor & Francis Group

Typeset in Garamond
by Curran Publishing Services Ltd, Norwich
Printed and bound in Great Britain
by MPG Books Ltd, Bodmin

British Library Cataloguing in Publication Data
A catalogue record for this book is available
from the British Library

Library of Congress Cataloging in Publication Data
Youth and coping in twelve nations: surveys of 18–20-year-old young people / Janice Gibson-Cline (editor).
pp. 15.6 x 23.4 cm
Includes bibliographical references and index.
1.Adolescent psychology -- Cross-cultural studies. I. Gibson-Cline, Janice, 1934–

BF724.Y69 2000
305.235`09..dc21 00-038245

ISBN 0-415-21715-6

To my American family who learned together with me how to cope in this exciting and rapidly changing world – and my international family who worked with me to explain the process.

Thank you

Contents

Figures

Tables

Contributors

David Acres (England) Counsellor, supervisor, consultant trainer, Fellow of the British Counselling Association, and faculty member of the College of St Mark and St John at the time of this study. His book, *Passing Exams Without Anxiety* (5th edn) was published in 1998.

Anna Adaskina (Russia) Faculty member, Moscow State University.

Carol E. Baker (USA) Director of the Office of Measurement and Evaluation at the University of Pittsburgh. Provided data analysis and interpretation for *Youth and Coping*.

William A. Borgen (Canada) Professor of Counseling Psychology, University of British Columbia. President of the International Counseling Association. Authored articles and books on career development.

Qi Chen (China) Professor, Department of Psychology, Beijing Normal University. Research and publications in fields of learning and instruction, information technology, values of Chinese youth, teacher education.

Maria Dikaiou (Greece) Associate Professor of Social Psychology at the University of Thessaloniki. Research publications deal with psychological problems of minorities, migrants, refugees and gypsies.

Rachel Erhard (Ethiopian immigrants) (Israel) Head of Graduate Program in Counseling, Tel Aviv University and R&D Unit, Psychology and Counseling Services, Israel Ministry of Education. Research publications in 'mental hardiness', counselling and intervention.

Maria Eugenia Felce DiPaula (Venezuela) Past Chief of Clinical Psychology, Military Hospital of Ft. Tiuna; Associate Professor and Head, Educational and Family Counseling, Simon Rodrigues University. Dr DiPaula died in June 1998.

Gueorgui Emelianov (Russia) Faculty member, Moscow State University.

Kevin Feaviour (England) Chair, Community and Youth Studies, College of St Mark and St John; Senior Associate, Trust for the Study of Adolescence;

Coordinator, Young People at Risk, Plymouth Centre for Educational and Social Research.

Fengchun Miao (PRC) Ph.D. candidate, Department of Psychology, Beijing Normal University. Employed by the Department of Educational Psychology and Information Technology in Education and Beijing Normal University Press. Research deals with counselling and problem-based-learning within hypermedia environments.

Mika Haritos-Fatouras (Greece) Professor of Clinical Psychology, University of Thessaloniki. Publications include cross-cultural and cross-national studies of refugees and migrants, behavioral psychotherapy and counselling.

Janice Gibson-Cline, Editor (USA) Professor Emeritus of Developmental Psychology, Univeristy of Pittsburgh. Fulbright Researcher in Greece, PRC, the Philippines and Yugoslavia. Academy of Science Professor in USSR. Ten previous books and numerous research articles on cross-cultural and cross-national research.

Keiko Honda (Japan) Adjunct Professor of Education, Tamagawa University. Counselor, International Christian University, Tokyo. Author of textbooks on school counselling and cross-cultural counselling for Japanese youth returning from abroad.

Lina Kashyap (India) Professor and Head of Department of Family and Child Welfare, Tata Institute of Social Sciences. Serves on Executive Boards of a number of governmental and non-governmental agencies.

Lisa Maccarelli (USA) University of Pittsburgh doctoral candidate in counselling psychology employed at the Western Psychiatric Institute of Pittsburgh at the time of this study.

Louise Martinson (Canada) High school counselor and sessional instructor in counselling psychology, University of British Columbia. Work includes peer programs and group counseling for adolescents and young adults. Co-author, article on group process for 'at risk' teens and their parents.

Elisabete Monteiro de Aguiar Pereira (Brazil) Professor of Curriculum Studies, Assistant to Vice-Chancellor for Graduate. Studies at the University of Campinas and counsellor. Most recent book dealt with university teachers as researchers in post-modernity.

Benjamin Shafrir (Israel) Student at l'Ecole des Hautes Etudes Sociales, Paris. Co-Director, Tokayėr Children's Home; Founder/Director, Special Education Institute, Kibbutz Givat Haim Ichud, currently Chairman of Board; Senior Consultant, Takam Kibbutz Movement Child and Family Guidance Clinic. Lecturer; Published *To Be Involved* (1985). Recipient, 1996 Israeli Presidential Outstanding Life Achievement Award in Education

Brenda J. Shaw (Canada) Researcher on career identity formation and transition from high school, University of British Columbia. Private practitioner on women's issues and childhood abuse. Worked in areas of gender-fair counselling, developmental psychology, and abuse dynamics and effects.

Nina F. Talyzina (Russia) Professor and Past Chairperson, Department of Psychology, Moscow State University. Active for many years in cross-national research. Bibliography includes books and articles, written in Russian and translated into English.

Additional contributors of data used in *Youth and Coping*

David Botwin (USA) University of Pittsburgh

Tatiana Gabay (Russia) Moscow State University

Isaura R. F. Guimaraes (Brazil) Campinas State University

Ishu Ishiyama (Canada) University of British Columbia

Xin Lu (USA) graduate student, University of Pittsburgh in 1989

Gundalina Velazco (Philippines) DeLaSalle University

Acknowledgements

The author members of our Multinational Research Team acknowledge with gratitude the assistance of the University of Pittsburgh in providing computer services for the analysis of our data and secretarial services that allowed us to prepare our quarterly *Newsnote* used to communicate with research team members.

We also thank Hans Z. Hoxter, President of the International Round Table for the Advancement of Counseling during the years of our project for inviting us to hold our seminars during IRTAC annual meetings, permitting us not only to begin our work together and to meet on regular bases to continue it, but also to share ideas annually with eminent scholars participating at the IRTAC meetings.

Finally, we wish to thank David Lane, President of the Professional Development Foundation in London, for the Foundation's support in providing internet access for team communication and David McDonald of Curran Publishing Services for his perseverance in copy-editing.

Preface

This book about young people, their problems and their coping strategies is a collaborative work by social scientists and practitioners from twelve countries. The group first came together at the University of Calgary during a 1988 meeting of the International Round Table for the Advancement of Counseling (IRTAC). It was the beginning of twelve years of cross-cultural collaboration which resulted in our first book, *Adolescence: From Crisis to Coping* (a multinational study of 13–15 year olds) and now Youth and Culture (an investigation of 18–20 year olds). These two books stand as testimony both to the cross-cultural understanding we have developed of the problems and coping of young people and to the empathetic relationships developed in the twelve years of working together that transcends national, cultural and religious boundaries. Our team members became an international family as well as an international research team.

The author-members of our team present *Youth and Coping* as an multicultural work of love. We have created a database in our two books of the concerns and coping strategies of more than 10,000 young people from countries across the world. It is our hope that, through the words of our subjects, we will help bridge the gap between generations so as to ease the difficult transition to adulthood in what might otherwise be an uneasy beginning to the new century.

Youth and Coping is presented in five parts:

I Introduction (Chapters 1 and 2): Our methodology and the concepts and theories that underlie our understanding of young people.

II The multinational study (Chapter 3): A composite of the concerns and coping of our 18–20 year old subjects, examining concerns and coping trends across the two years of survey by socio-economic status and gender.

III National studies of advantaged and non-advantaged youth (Chapters 4 –14): The concerns and coping strategies of Brazilian, Canadian, Chinese, English, Greek, Indian, Israeli, Japanese, Russian, American and Venezuelan youth set in their own cultural backgrounds and with interpretation and suggestions for intervention by our researchers from those cultures.

IV Special youth populations (Chapters 15 and 16): A sampling of populations that are changing the faces of countries across the world today: immigrants – Ethiopians in Israel – and poverty populations from Brazil, England and the Philippines.

V Conclusions and implications for theory and practice (Chapter 17): An assessment of our multinational findings to provide a basis for developing effective interventions to help youth make the difficult transitions to adulthood.

The research findings reported in these chapters appear in terms of highlights only. Since it would have taken volumes to reply to all the questions that could be answered from our collected data, we have provided full statistical results in Appendices III and IV in formats that permit 'picking and choosing' desired material. We invite readers to use this data to answer questions of concern to them that we have not covered in this book.

Janice Gibson-Cline
Stinson Beach, California, USA
June 2000

Foreword

The publication of this book signifies the culmination of twelve years of intensive collaboration for the *Youth and Coping* team of the International Research Seminar. This is an amazing accomplishment that may be attributed both to the International Round Table for the Advancement of Counselling that fathered the child and to its infatigable mother, Dr Janice Gibson-Cline, who all these years acted as the co-ordinator of the team and editor of its publications. This book follows a number of earlier articles published in the *International Journal for the Advancement of Counselling* and the book, *Adolescence: From Crisis to Coping* (Routledge 1996), the first major publication of the team.

Cross-cultural research of this nature is rare. That is no wonder because the problems that have to be overcome in this kind of endeavour are gigantic. To my knowledge, one of the few successful cross-cultural researches related to the subject of young people was the *International Educational Achievement Project* sponsored by the UNESCO Institute in Hamburg (Germany) and carried out by a group of universities in different parts of the world (1967 and after). Even though educational achievement may be easier to measure than the psychological problems of young people, the researchers in that study faced issues that were hardly surmountable.

The *Youth and Coping* team is an informal group of psychologists, counsellors, counsellor educators and researchers who met once a year at Round Table conferences and decided not only to talk but to do things together. Their resources were minimal, but their enthusiasm was without limits. This being said, it must be realized that enthusiasm *per se* does not solve all the problems that face cross-cultural research. Procedures must be developed, logistics have to be solved (nowadays helped by the Internet!), contents have to be determined, and instruments must be chosen or developed so that they are valid for the study purpose. Of course, cultural differences and linguistic diversity play their parts, and nobody can expect a study like this to achieve the methodological strictness required from small-scale local studies. That would be unfair. Hence it should not come as a surprise that we find heterogeneity in the samples, both in terms of composition and size, and that in some chapters, comparisons with the first study were possible while they were not in others. Poverty subjects, although widespread in the world, could be studied in only three countries, Brazil, the Philippines and England, where the last sample was very small. It is quite understandable, therefore, that the editor sometimes cautions us not to overrate some of the results. This may be one of the drawbacks that stems from the informality and minimal resources of the group.

Acknowledging these problems does not diminish the importance of the book and its findings in comparing youth in twelve nations. The study reported in this book used, for the most part, the same approach as did the first study published in 1996, and the findings are consistent with those reported earlier, even though the subjects questioned were some years older. Here again, cross-cultural awareness is important when interpreting results, as is shown in two vignettes about an Indian and a North-American young woman who both talk about their concerns regarding future marriage. Such vignettes, found throughout the book, add a qualitative flavour that not only makes reading more pleasant but also provides important information. It might be worthwhile for researchers to focus future work in this area on similar qualitative interviews with small, carefully selected samples.

It struck the editor and authors that some obvious problems that young people across the world face today, such as the possibility of AIDS, drug addiction, sexual abuse and incest, were not, or were only marginally mentioned by the subjects of this study. Why? Both the editor and authors question this phenomenon. Were the subject samples atypical? Was the lack of reporting a by-product of the questionnaire method or, as some authors suggest, a matter of culturally-given hesitation that comes to the fore with these types of concerns? Even worse, might subjects' lack of reporting be due to a genuine lack of concern on the part of young people? Unfortunately, this study is unable to prove which, if any, of the possible explanations the authors offer are correct. The various possibilities, however, may provide a challenge to the *Youth and Coping* team to develop other innovative research approaches within the possibilities available to the group.

Research is not meant to please or displease political bodies with the power to establish or abandon counselling services. Nonetheless, this book presents a strong case for the advancement of counselling services in forms and methods that fit local cultures. The approach used by the team has the wisdom of defining the counselling needs of young people without prescribing how the required counselling must be offered. Here we find one of the fundamentals of multicultural work: respect for the cultural identity of the partner. In this sense this book means a significant step forward. The authors and the editor deserve congratulations and admiration. I am proud and honoured to be the first in line to express these feelings.

Nathan Deen
Emeritus Professor of Guidance and Counselling, Utrecht University, the Netherlands
Former editor of the *International Journal for the Advancement of Counselling*

Part I

Introduction

> 'I want to solve my problems myself . . . I don't want anyone else to decide what I should do.'

What are the problems that concern young people today? How do they cope? Do males and females have similar – or different – concerns and coping strategies? Do youth of different national or socioeconomic backgrounds worry and act in similar – or different manners? How do the answers to these questions affect the ability of youth to make successful transitions to adulthood?

Chapter 1 explains the collaborative model designed by our international research team to produce culture-fair answers to these questions, detailing the steps from development of research questions to publication of this book. It describes the methodology used to survey our 5,156 subjects who grew up in Brazil, China, Canada, England, Ethiopia (our Ethiopian subjects were imigrants living in Israel at the time they were surveyed), Greece, India, Israel, Japan, the Philippines, Continental USA and Venezuela. Equally important, it provides the limitations of this cross-cultural research to ensure the reader is aware of what studies of this type can – and cannot – tell.

Chapter 2, intended for readers with a variety of professional backgrounds, explains the behaviour of youth from various theoretical positions from traditional phychoanalytic to modern social constructivist, the former focusing on age-and-stage related factors and the latter on ability to cope with support provided from the environment.

1 Our study and its methodology

Janice Gibson-Cline, Carol E. Baker, University of Pittsburgh and Maria Dikaiou, University of Thessaloniki

From *Youth and Coping in Twelve Nations*:

'I'm afraid of being unemployed.'

Marcela, an impoverished young man from Brazil:
'I'm terribly afraid of {losing my job and} being unemployed. What do I do about it? I try to forget as much as possible about the problem. What else is there to do?'

'I worry about the future of my country.'

Anjana, an advantaged young woman from India:
'I want to help my country. My plan {after I finish my schooling} is to work towards making our people literate. Only with a literate population can my country move ahead.'

'I worry that there is no hope for peace.'

Joel, a male army recruit from Israel:
'I feel a terrible sense of injustice and despair, as if Rabin's assassin, by killing the Prime Minister, killed the chance for peace as well.'

PROLOGUE

Young people are an important commodity. Whatever roles they play as adults, from leaders of countries to individuals who require help simply to stay alive, this population will one day determine national, political, economic and educational policies throughout the world. Today, youth everywhere are beset by increasingly complex and intense problems that threaten their futures. How can we, as researchers and helping practitioners, assist them to become worthwhile and productive citizens? If we are even to begin helping young people who have difficulty coping with what they now face in their lives, we need to know first what their problems and coping strategies are. We also need to explore the underlying causes of their problems, whether these be cultural, social, environmental, developmental or all of these and, finally, we need to find the differences between youth who cope successfully in their environments and those who do not.

This book provides a first step of a monumental task by compiling a series of pictures of what youth from different national, cultural and socio-economic backgrounds have to say about their problems and coping. We use their responses as well as information regarding their social and physical environments to suggest possible causes of their problems and suggest ways to improve the help that we now provide.

The research project was not an easy one to design or conduct. In the first place, designing and conducting a multinational study in which the collected data is not compromised by cultural bias of the researchers requires specialists in research design as well as specialists in human service practice who have experience in working with youth and who understand their backgrounds. Unfortunately, human service practitioners whose job it is to help youth and social science researchers are normally employed in different settings and only rarely have opportunity to work together or even communicate. (See Bryant *et al.* 1992; Edwards *et al.* 1990.) To make use of the knowledge of groups, our *Youth and Coping* research team utilized an exceptional group of researchers and practitioners willing to share their expertise. We chose as our first step learning what young people perceive as their problems and how they respond to them. Our next step was to share our expertise to use this information as a basis for developing practical steps to help change the situation. We call this approach an 'intervention research paradigm': a scheme that involved researchers, practitioners and young people themselves as participants in a process of creating scientific understanding of youth problems and, at the same time, setting the groundwork for developing interventions.

One of our underlying assumptions was that problem-coping and help-seeking methods are best understood in terms of ongoing transactions with the environment rather than simply as static events. This position is supported by both earlier theories of stress and coping (Lazarus 1976; Lazarus and Folkman 1984) as well as more recent views on social constructivism (Hoskins 1998), and will be discussed in further detail in Chapter 2.

Another assumption was that human problems and coping strategies vary across time and situations. We know, for example, that the same person may use two different coping strategies for the same problem at two different points in time. Individuals may cope inappropriately, as for example, denying reality, to deal with one problem and use another strategy, such as individual coping, quite appropriately when dealing with a different concern. If our findings are to be socially relevant for psychosocial interventions, it follows that they must address phenomena that are, themselves, capable of change (Lazarus and Folkman 1984). For this reason, it is far more effective to study youth problems and coping in different time periods and situations than in one point of time and one particular socio-environmental or cultural context.

In order to provide a firm basis for development of intervention strategies, and taking these two assumptions into consideration, we decided on a study of male and female youth from different socio-economic backgrounds and nationalities and in two time periods: 1997 and 1989. The same team members who gathered data worked together to suggest practical interventions.

Theoretical premises of our 'intervention research paradigm'

In utilizing the 'intervention research paradigm', our team engaged in a dynamic process of development. Everyone – researchers, practitioners and subjects – worked together, beginning with the creation of research questions by our team members, continuing with provision of answers to these questions by our young subjects and concluding with proposals for providing solutions to youth problems constructed through the joint interactive participation of all participants. This process, which abandoned the classic scheme of 'doing research and using the results to propose models of help', created what we believe intervention research should be: that is, a research process designed to:

- set the ground for developing interventions and to involve research participants in various phases of the process
- use the natural cultural context in which individuals operate as the appropriate context for conducting research and development
- enhance the possibility of developing new theories based on both the research findings and on the accumulated practical and applied knowledge of the research team members. (Most *Youth and Coping* team members have been involved in various attempts to solve specific individual or social problems.)

YOUTH AND COPING: A BRIEF HISTORY

Youth and Coping was born in the late 1980s when a multinational group of researchers and practitioners first came together to discuss the problems of young people. Knowledge that client concerns do not always match helping professionals' assumptions (see p. 6), together with a paucity of information describing what youth themselves actually view as their problems, convinced us that we needed to go directly to youth for help. We needed youth to tell us in their own words what *they* perceived as problematic issues and coping solutions, and planned to use this information as the basis for developing effective helping strategies. Our first step was to outline the 'intervention research paradigm' described earlier: a process in which a most important component was our subjects and in which participants worked together to develop proposals, design research instruments, contact subjects and interpret findings.

We began in 1988 by planning a multinational survey on two age groups: 'adolescents' (13–15-year-olds) and 'youth' (18–20-year-olds). We designed our research paradigm to set the groundwork for developing interventions. We emphasized the natural cultural context by surveying our subjects in their national as well as socio-economic settings, so that we could not only study our male and female subjects' responses by cultural context but could also arrive at separate conclusions regarding intervention procedures useful to subjects of different backgrounds. Since most of our team members have worked professionally as individual researchers and practitioners at solving individual or social problems, we utilized to best advantage their accumulated practical and applied wisdom.

Data collection was begun in 1989, using two groups of subjects, whom we called 'adolescents' and 'youth'. Our first book, *Adolescence: From Crisis to Coping* (Gibson-Cline 1996), presented answers obtained in 1989 from adolescents in thirteen countries, compared them by nationality, socio-economic status (SES) grouping and gender of subjects and used this information to suggest helping strategies likely to be most effective.[1]

Our second book, *Youth and Coping*, which you are now reading, focuses on 18–20-year-olds in twelve countries, using survey results from both 1989 and 1997.[2] In this book, we compare our subjects' answers not only by nationality, SES grouping and gender, but, for nine countries in which the study was conducted in both 1989 and 1997, by year of survey.[3] We work with what our informants have told us, once again, to suggest helping strategies.

METHODOLOGICAL GROUNDWORK

Our reseach approaches

Our 'research intervention paradigm' makes the assumption that a person who experiences a given situation may interpret it differently from another person, and that professional helpers' inaccurate interpretations of the perceptions of their clients might lead them to choose ineffective helping strategies. Llewelyn (1988) and Wark (1994) suggested that this problem results when therapists work from their own 'world view' which emphasizes teaching of self-knowledge as a major part of therapy, whereas clients tend to believe that successful therapy should help them solve immediate problems. To insure that that we were examining the perceptions of our subjects and not those of help-providers, we directed our survey directly to our subjects. To increase our objectivity, we used the research approaches described next.

Cross-cultural collaboration

In order to prevent cultural bias, we took direction from previous cross-cultural researchers such as Berrien (1970); Triandis (1972); Hofsted (1984); Herr (1987); Ivey (1990) and others. Rather than designing our project in one country and collecting subjects' responses in the various countries and socio-economic groups, research team members from every country of the study shared equally in all aspects of the project. This began with selecting the research problem, designing survey questions and planning the study procedures and continued with the conveying of subjects' responses into numerical codes to make group comparisons and interpret the results.

We reduced communication difficulties across professions by having social scientists (academics/ researchers) and practitioners (human service providers) work together as one problem-solving team, with each having equal input into all aspects of the study.

Cross-sectional data-gathering

Lazarus (1976), Lazarus and Folkman (1984) and others suggested that coping behaviour is dependent on a variety of situational and other factors outside the subject's control and can be best understood in terms of ongoing interactions with the environment rather than as static events.[4] For this reason, it is not always possible to draw meaningful conclusions from one incident of data-gathering alone. To make our findings more meaningful and to enable us to track trends as well as discrepant results, we used the same survey instrument with subjects in both 1989 and 1997, and compared the results.

RESEARCH QUESTIONS

The specific questions we asked in our 1997 study were:

- What did our 1997 male and female subjects from advantaged, non-advantaged and poverty populations tell us about the concerns that caused them stress, how they coped and the helpers to whom they went for help?
- For those countries in which responses were collected in both 1997 and in 1989, how did our 1997 subjects' answers compare with those of their 1989 youth peers? How did they compare with the composite picture of subjects in our 1997 Multinational Study?
- What do the answers to these questions suggest as to helping strategies most likely to be effective for given nations, SES groups and genders, and what generalizations might we make concerning what creates an effective intervention?

METHODOLOGY

Our subjects and their backgrounds

The *Youth and Coping* study includes surveys of 5,156 young people.[5] Of these, 3,193 subjects were surveyed in 1997 and 1,963 were surveyed in 1989. Subjects were grouped by year of survey, national and cultural backgrounds, socio-economic status, and gender and immigrant status. Each of these descriptors are described below, together with a brief summary of what researchers suggest is their relationship to coping.

National and cultural backgrounds

Research concerned with coping and national background suggests that the type of national background may affect coping behaviour. For example, Emmite and Diaz-Guerrero (1983) pointed out that young people in highly industrialized nations such as the United States or Britain tend to use more active modes of coping than youth in agricultural societies such as Mexico. An earlier study by Mar'i and Levi (1979) also demonstrated considerable differences in coping behaviour between different ethnic groups. More recent studies by Bosma and Jackson (1990) and by our own 1989 research team survey of young adolescents suggested that cultural differences are not so apparent. In our 1989 research team study, although few coping strategies seemed to be situation-specific and idiosyncratic to specific national backgrounds (Gibson-Cline *et al.* 1996: 267), young adolescents appeared to cope actively with their problems most frequently and to use defence mechanism or denial far less often. The true meaning of these findings cannot be determined, however, without consideration of the influence of socio-economic status of subjects.

Our 18–20-year-old subjects were surveyed in 1997 in Brazil, Canada, China, England, Greece, India, Israel, Japan, the Philippines, Russia, USA and Venezuela. Subjects of same age group were surveyed in the same sites in 1989 in Brazil, China, Greece, Israel, Japan, Russia, the Philippines, USA and Venezuela. To determine possible relationships of findings to socio-economic status, subjects in both surveys were described in terms of their 'advantaged', 'non-advantaged' or 'poverty' statuses as listed in the next section.

Socio-economic status

Pearlin (1989) suggested that it is likely that individuals who interact with one another on regular bases and share important life circumstances and problems are likely to share coping strategies. Earlier research has also suggested that individuals with higher socio-economic status tend to be more actively involved in solving their problems (Pearlin and Schooler

1978, Hallahan and Moos 1987, Billings and Moos 1981). Impoverished peoples, by contrast, have been reported to use passive, defensive strategies. If these are true differences in coping strategies, they may be due to individual choices of how to best adapt to problems when given restricted resources (Bond and King 1985, Alva 1995, Howard 1996, Rosella and Albrecht 1993, Fitzpatrick 1993, Rosella 1994). Our research team decided to explore this issue by grouping our subjects by their socio-economic backgrounds.

There are no international scales available that describe socio-economic status across all the countries of our study. Because conditions usually used to define SES vary so greatly across nations, we developed our own definitions taking into consideration the norms regarding what is accepted within each of our respective countries. In general, researchers agreed that important variables in their country that were related to SES included education and career expectations, type and location of residences, and employment and income. While specific descriptions varied by country, 'advantaged' subjects were rated as above the mean and 'non-advantaged' below the mean for these variables in their countries. Poverty subjects were not only below the means

Advantaged → Parents: literate; well educated per national norm; employed in skilled professions earning average-to-high incomes for that country.
Residence: average-to-wealthy neighbourhoods.
Educational aspirations: usually higher education.

Non-advantaged → Parents: not all literate; below average educations per national norm; non-skilled jobs earning average-to-below average income for that country.
Residence: average-to-below average economic areas.
Educational aspirations: usually secondary school.

Poverty → Parents: often non-literate; educations below average per national norm; unemployed or lowest paying jobs in that country.
Residence: poverty area; less-than-adequate housing.
Educational aspirations: usually primary school.
Other: food and medical coverage not always adequate to meet basic needs.

Figure 1.1 Characteristics of advantaged, non-advantaged and poverty populations used to describe our subject groups

of their countries but did not always meet their basic needs. Figure 1.1 (page 9) provides detailed descriptions of our SES groups.

Advantaged and non-advantaged subjects surveyed in 1997 tended to be students, the former studying in universities or colleges, and the latter more often in technical schools. Poverty youth, by contrast, tended to work at low paid occupations or were searching for work. While some were studying in government night-schools that provided remedial education, they were working or seeking work at low-skill jobs at the same time and the purpose of their attending night school was to increase their employment opportunities in order to meet basic needs. Although some few subjects might have been in counselling at the time of the surveys, they were not selected on the basis of their being in any type of treatment.

The 1997 survey included 1,846 advantaged subjects. Table 1.1 shows the distribution of subjects by socio-economic grouping.

Gender

Most studies of youth and coping have found that males and females tend to cope with their problems in different ways. Studies have shown, for example, that females tend to seek help from others and to elicit (or offer) physical contact, while males act out more aggressively and tend to seek attention (Whiting and Whiting 1975, Broman 1987, Bosma and Jackson 1990) Females, who have been shown in some studies to worry more about personal relationships than their male peers, appear also to be more emotionally expressive in dealing with their concerns (Macoby and Jacklin 1974). Such differences, when found, have been attributed to gender-specific behaviours as well as societal expectations and reinforcements.

A more recent study conducted by our research team on the coping of young (13–15-year-old) adolescents showed that the effects of gender on coping are complex (Gibson-Cline 1996: 31–4). In addition to typical gender differences found in interpersonal interactions in this study, the research team found that, regardless of their SES status, young adolescent females responded in some ways more like subjects from lower than higher SES groups, that is; they reported a lower percentage of school problems and a higher percentage of family problems than males and they chose to attempt solving their problems themselves less frequently than males. When grouped by SES status, subjects lower on the SES scale reported a

Table 1.1 Distribution of 1997 and 1989 subjects by SES grouping

	Advantaged	*Non-advantaged*	*Poverty*	*Non-classified*
1997	1846	983	163	201
1989	949	400	200	401

lower percentage of school and a higher percentages of family problems. Lower SES subjects also chose to attempt solving their problems themselves less frequently than higher SES subjects. This finding occurred in most of the thirteen countries explored.

To determine whether these results hold for 18–20-year-olds and, if so, whether they remain over time, the current *Youth and Coping* study compares youth by gender as well as by SES in both 1989 and 1997.

Immigrant and poverty status

Researchers have associated poverty, minority and immigrant status with passive coping strategies such as 'giving up' (Pearlin and Schooler 1978, Billings and Moos 1981, Dikaiou and Kiosseoglou 1994). 'Disengagement from the situation', another passive response, is reported to occur most frequently when both personal and contextual responses that ordinarily provide help are scarce (Hallahan and Moos 1987). Studies of immigrants to new cultures suggest that coping is affected by complex relationships between many factors. For new immigrants, these include ethnic, racial and national identity, general socio-emotional adjustment, competence to satisfy basic needs in the host culture, as well as what is considered the best choice of personal and social adaptation, all play roles in determining behaviour (Alva 1995). *Youth and Coping* includes one study of immigrants: the subjects of Chapter 15: 'Immigrant youth: Ethiopians in Israel' are included in the non-advantaged population of the Multinational Study.

Research instruments

The research team developed three instruments for the study: a questionnaire, a case study format designed for data gathering and a coding scale designed to convert data from each national study so that it could be compared with data collected in other countries.

Questionnaire

We agreed at the outset that both our standardized questionnaire designed for literate subjects and the standardized interview format designed for non-literate subjects should permit persons to answer our questions in their own words. For this reason and to avoid the prompting provided in 'multiple-choice' and 'yes–no' survey formats, we developed open-ended questionnaires and interviews as our data-gathering instruments.

Aware of the research literature that suggests that it is typical with the general range of outpatient clientele that that clients rarely enter counselling with a specific problem but instead report generalized dissatisfactions, malaise or demoralization and only after counselling is in progress begin to isolate their worries (Wills 1982), clinician-members of our team decided not to ask for one problem only, but instead asked five separate sets of questions three consecutive times, so that our subjects, in reporting their concerns, would have more opportunity to isolate the problem(s) that actually bothered them. Subjects thus were asked three times to list their problems, coping strategies and choices of helpers, helper qualities and modes of helping. Figure 1.2 lists the questionnaire items.

The introduction to the questionnaire solicited background data such as date of birth, gender and parental education and employment. The team prepared the initial questionnaire and standardized interview in English. Each researcher translated it for subjects whose native language was not English, using standard procedures that we developed for this purpose. Researchers usually administered questionnaires to groups of subjects in educational, occupational or, sometimes, recreational settings, with special versions developed for individual oral administration to subjects who were non-literate. Directions for administration were also standardized, with questionnaires usually administered in educational or career groups. For some subjects, when required, questionnaires were administered on a one-to-one basis or standardized interviews were used. This occurred most frequently with poverty populations. Directions included guarantees of anonymity to all subjects. (See Gibson-Cline *et al.* 1996: 18 for details as to both the development of the questionnaire and interview format, translation procedures and standardized procedures for administration.) To preserve subject anonymity, names were not requested.

Case studies

Because questionnaire responses do not supply as much information about subjects as other instruments, the team used standardized case study interviews to gain more understanding and to provide a stronger 'flavour' of our subjects' perceptions, concerns and coping strategies as well as the situations in which they lived. Details from these case studies appear in boxed off areas of each national chapter.

1 Concern: name one concern or problem that causes you to feel worried or pressured; please descirbe this concern in more detail.
2 Coping: when you have this concern, what do you do about it? If you do not do anything to solve the problem, what do you do to make yourself feel better?
3 Desired helpers: if you were to discuss this concern with anyone, who would that person be?
4 Desired helper qualities: what qualities of helpers allow them to help you?
5 Desired modes of helping: what would they say or do to help you?

Figure 1.2 Questionnaire items

Coding scale

Since the purpose of the study was to compare concerns and coping strategies across nations, socio-economic groups and time periods as well as genders, it was necessary to convert the written responses into data that we could use to make objective comparisons. Since an international scale of human concerns and coping strategies does not exist, the team prepared its own scale of possible responses, beginning by sampling responses collected from the countries of the study. Successive drafts were repeatedly disseminated to all team members for review and refinements until consensus was reached as to thirty-eight classes and 102 categories-within-classes of responses and to standardized procedures for use of the scale. (See Showalter (1990) for an analysis of this project.) Because there were far fewer classes than categories-within-classes and only a given number of responses by our subjects, we agreed to increase the reliability of categories-within-classes reported in our findings by limiting our tables to include only those categories into which more than 5 per cent of responses were coded.

Figure 1.3 lists the classes of the coding scales of the *Youth and Coping* manual. Appendix II provides a full listing of categories within each of these classes. Categories-within-classes listed in Appendix III include all categories into which more than 5 per cent of responses were coded by our researchers.

Coding reliability

Cultural backgrounds have important effects on thinking, often making it difficult for groups coming from different backgrounds to agree on the meaning of concepts important in their lives. Our study required researcher-authors from a variety of national and cultural backgrounds to develop a

1 Concerns: extreme poverty; war; catastrophe; material desires; family issues; schooling; personal identity/self concept; sexuality; courtship and dating; inter-personal/socialization; concerns about emotions; self-fulfilment; altruistic (societal) concerns; other.
2 Coping strategies: seeking or giving assistance; interpersonal strategies; individual problem-solving (involving subject only); stress management; crying; religious response; resignation; disengagement; antisocial responding.
3 Desired helpers: family member, non-family member; offender (source of problem); supernatural; animate creatures/inanimate objects.
4 Desired helper qualities: powerful; available; knowledgeable; appealing personal attributes (trustworthy, loyal, etc.); concern for others.
5 Desired helping mode: direct satisfaction of need (gives something); counsels (gives advice; attends to; exercises power (solves problem); intercedes with others; assists client to evade.

Figure 1.3 The five coding scales and classes within these scales

coding scale capable of portraying subjects' responses in a way that provided a reliable picture across the backgrounds of our subjects. Figure 1.4 describes the steps used to measure reliability of coding.

The full study results are reported in Appendix III in terms of percentages of coded responses falling into each class and category-within-classes. Highlights of findings and their interpretations are given in Chapters 3–16.

Study procedure

Preparation and administration of the questionnaire and case study format

Team members prepared the initial questionnaire and standardized interview in English. Each researcher then translated it for subjects whose native language was not English, using standard procedures that we developed for this purpose. Researchers usually administered questionnaires to groups of subjects in educational, occupational or, sometimes, recreational settings, with special versions developed for individual oral administration to subjects who were non-literate. Directions for administration were also standardized, with questionnaires usually administered in educational or career groups. For some subjects, when required, questionnaires were administered on a one-to-one basis or standardized interviews were used. This occurred most frequently with poverty populations. Directions included guarantees of anonymity to all subjects. (See Gibson *et al.* 1996: 18 for details as to both the development of the questionnaire and interview format, translation procedures and standardized procedures for administration.)

Coding of subject responses and measurement of the reliability of coding

Coding of subject responses took place only after researchers were trained in coding procedures and tested for reliability, as described in Figure 1.4.

1 Each researcher individually coded responses to the same sample set of answers to questionnaire items.
2 These coded responses were then compared with a 'standard' developed by the team members.
3 The percentage of coded responses that agreed with the 'standard' was determined. For *Youth and Coping*, the mean percentage of agreement for our coders (the authors of the national chapters) was 95% for classes and 85% for categories-within-classes: extremely high for a multinational study of human behaviour! We list reliability agreement percentages for each individual researcher in Appendix III.

Figure 1.4 The three steps used to measure reliability of coding

Coding was conducted by team members in their home countries; Results were sent to the University of Pittsburgh for central analysis.

THE NEXT STEP: WORKING TOGETHER TO DEVELOP HELPING STRATEGIES

Comparing results cross-nationally for use in developing helping strategies useful across countries requires communication. The author-researchers compared their findings, gave them interpretations and used them to suggest helping strategies through several means of communication: we met each year as a research team for face-to-face discussions as part of a pre-conference International Research Seminar held in conjunction with the annual meetings of the International Counseling Association (formerly the International Roundtable for the Advancement of Counseling). We also made use of modern technology, sharing within-country results and commentary from members of our group through a website provided by the Professional Development Foundation of London and by regular e-mail communication. Interestingly, while only five of the members of the 1989 research team had access to e-mail, every one of the members of the 1997 team was able to communicate on regular bases via this medium.

METHODOLOGICAL LIMITATIONS

The model developed by our team met important requirements for our research. At the same time it created limitations common to cross-cultural research. We list what we consider the eight most important below:

1 The use of open-ended questionnaires and interviews prohibited us from obtaining some personal information from subjects (see Maccarelli 1994). We believe, for example, that subjects may have been inhibited by our format from discussion of some very personal issues.
2 The same use of open-ended questionnaires and interviews prohibited us from making direct comparison with other research that uses more common approaches, such as ‘multiple-choice’ or ‘yes–no’ formats.
3 While asking our subjects to describe three rather than one concern may have increased the numbers of personal concerns cited, it prevented more elaborate statistical procedures we may have used and limited us to descriptive statistics.
4 Variances in sample sizes also limited us in statistical analysis. (See Table 1.1 for subject sample sizes for each country.)
5 In a very few samples, researchers were able to survey only a relatively

small number of subjects, making the results less reliable than the results of the other countries. In each of these, because of the importance of the particular populations surveyed, the data was included, but with notation of this limitation cited in the introduction to the study.

6 Even with as extensive and detailed a coding scale as we developed, there remained a small number of responses idiosyncratic to individual countries or time periods that our instruments were not sufficiently detailed to pick up. In the 1997 survey, for example, the authors of Chapter 12, 'Russia: university students in Moscow before and after Perestroika', chose to add new classes to describe the concerns of their subjects most accurately. While these were used in Chapter 12, they had to be 'collapsed' as categories into existing classes for comparison with results of other countries. (See Gibson-Cline *et al.* 1996 for discussion of this issue.)

7 It was not possible for our researchers who surveyed young adults in 1989 to conduct follow-up studies of the same young people in 1997, although the young adults surveyed in 1997 were selected for similarity in background to their predecessors.

8 Although some subjects might have been in some form of counselling at the time of the surveys, they were not selected on the basis of their being in or out of treatment. Since they may have responded to our survey in a different manner than if they had been selected on the basis of their being in treatment and had been surveyed at a clinic site, we cannot generalize the findings of this study to those of patients in therapy.

Even with these problems, we are pleased to report that we met Berrien's (1970) requirements for as ideal a multinational, multicultural research as was possible. Although this study was created by academic researchers, it has organized information useful to parents, educators, doctors, psychologists, sociologists, etc. It has successfully left the perception of 'young adults as a social problem' to consider them as what they are: capable of proposing action, formulating solutions, sustaining dialogues with other social actors and contributing to the solution of social problems. The greatest importance of our work thus lies in its recovery of human problems from the actor's perspective.

Notes

Thanks to Louise Martinson and Brenda Shaw for their carefully prepared and extensive editorial revisions of this chapter.

1 These comprise Australia, Brazil, China, Greece, India, Kuwait, the Netherlands, the Philippines, Russia, Turkey, the USA and Venezuela.
2 These comprise Brazil, Canada, China, England, Greece, India, Japan, the Phiippines, Russia, the USA and Venezuela.
3 These comprise Brazil, China, Greece, Israel, Japan, the Philippines, Russia, the USA and Venezuela.

4 In our study, cross-sectional data-gathering refers to research carefully repeated at different time periods using same-aged subjects in similar settings.

5 *Youth and Culture* does not examine minority status *per se* and the survey did not ask subjects to note minority status. However, subjects from minority backgrounds were included in most national studies and authors of studies describing more than one SES group have observed informally during surveys that the proportion of subjects from physically noticeable minority backgrounds was higher among lower SES populations. In Chapter 15, a description of Ethiopians who are immigrants to Israel and a non-advantaged population noticeably physically different from the majority population in terms of their skin colour, subjects reported feelings of discrimination as in minority groups.

References

Alva, S. (1995) 'Psychological distress and alcohol use in Hispanic adolescents'. *Journal of Youth and Adolescence* 24 (4): 481–97.

Berrien, F. (1970) 'A superego for cross-cultural research', *International Journal of Psychology* 5: 33–9.

Billings, A. and Moos, H. (1981) 'The role of coping resources and social resources in alternating the stress of life events', *Journal of Behavioural Medicine* 4: 139–57.

Bond, M. and King, A. (1985) 'Coping with the threat of westernization in Hong-Kong', *International Journal of Intercultural Relations* 9: 351–64.

Bosma, H. and Jackson, S. (eds) (1990) *Coping and Self-concept in Adolescence*, New York: Springer-Verlag.

Broman, V. (1987) 'Race differences in professional help-seeking', *American Journal of Community Counselling* 15: 473–89.

Bryant, F., Edwards, J., Tindale, R., Posavac, E., Heath, L., Henderson, E. and Suarez-Balcazar, Y. (eds) (1992) *Methodological Issues in Applied Social Psychology* 2, New York: Plenum.

Dikaiou, M. and Kiosseoglou, G. (1994) 'Identified problems and coping strategies: Gypsy minority *vs.* non-minority adolescents', *International Migration* 31: 473–95.

Edwards, J., Tindale, R., Heath, L. and Posavac, E. (eds) (1990) *Social Influence Processes and Prevention* 1, New York: Plenum.

Emmite, P. and Diaz-Guerrero, R. (1983) 'Cross-cultural differences and similarities in coping style, anxiety, success-failure on examinations', *Stress and Anxiety* 2: 191–206.

Fitzpatrick, K. M. (1993) 'Exposure to violence and presence of depression among low-income African–American youth', *Journal of Consulting and Clinical-Psychology* 61(3): 528–31.

Gibson-Cline, J. (ed) (1996) *Adolescence: From Crisis to Coping*, London: Routledge.

Gibson-Cline, J., Baker, C. *et al.* (1996) 'Methodology for a multinational study', in Gibson-Cline, J. (ed.), *Adolescence: From Crisis to Coping*, London: Routledge, 13–17.

Hallahan, C. and Moos, R. (1987) 'Personal and contextual determinants of coping strategies', *Journal of Personality and Social Psychology* 52: 946–55.

Herr, E. (1987) 'Cultural diversity from an international perspective', *Journal of Multicultural Counselling and Development* 15: 99–109.

Hofsted, G. (1984) *Culture's Consequences: International Differences in Work-Related Values*, Beverly-Hills, Calif.: Sage.

Howard, D. (1996) 'Searching for resilience among African–American youth exposed to community violence: theoretical issues', *Journal for Adolescent Health* 18 (4): 254–62.

Hoskins, M. (1998) 'Constructivism and child and youth care practice: visions for the 21st century', *Journal of Child and Youth Care* 11 (4): 83–92.

Ivey, A. (1990) *Developmental Counselling and Therapy*, Pacific Grove, Calif.: Brooks/Cole.

Jaccard, J., Turrisi, R. and Wan, C. (1990) 'Implications of behavioural decision theory and social marketing for designing social action programmes', in Edwards, J., Tindale, R., Heath, L. and Posavac, E. (eds), *Social Influence Processes and Prevention* 1: 103–42, New York: Plenum.

Lazarus, R. (1976) *Psychological Stress and the Coping Process*, New York: McGraw-Hall.

Lazarus, R. and Folkman, S. (1984) *Stress, Appraisal and Coping*, New York: Springer.

Llewelyn, S. (1988) 'Psychological therapy as viewed by clients and therapists', *British Journal of Clinical Psychology* 27: 223–37, cited in Borgen, W. (February 1999) 'Perceptions of clients and counsellors', Stinson Beach, Calif.: *International Research Seminar Newsnote.*

Maccarelli, L. (1994) *Problems Reported by Adolescents: A Comparison of Data Collection Methods*, unpublished Master's thesis, University of Pittsburgh.

Maccoby, E. and Jacklin, C. (1974) *The Psychology of Sex Differences*, Stanford, Calif.: Stanford University Press.

Mar'i, S. and Levi, A. (1979) 'Modernization or minority status: the coping style of Israel's Arabs', *Journal of Cross-cultural Psychology* 10: 375–89.

Pearlin, L. (1989) 'The sociological study of stress', *Journal of Health and Social Behaviour* 30: 241–56.

Pearlin, L. and Schooler, C. (1978) 'The structure of coping', *Journal of Health and Social Behaviour* 19: 2–21.

Rosella, J. (1994) 'Review of adolescent coping research: representation of key demographic variables and methodological approaches to assessment', *Issues in Mental Health Nursing* 15 (5): 483–95.

Rosella, J. and Albrecht, S. (1993) 'Toward an understanding of the health status of Black adolescents: an application of the stress-coping framework', *Issues in Comprehensive Pediatric Nursing* 16 (4): 193–205.

Showalter, S. (1990) *Making Sense of Cross-Cultural Data*, unpublished Master's thesis, University of Pittsburgh.

Triandis, H. (1972) *The Analysis of Subjective Culture*, New York: Wiley.

Wark, L. (1994) 'Therapeutic change in couples' therapy: critical change incidents perceived by therapists and clients', *Contemporary Family Therapy* 16: 49, cited in Borgen, W. (February 1999) 'Perceptions of clients and counsellors', Stinson Beach, Calif.: *International Research Seminar Newsnote.*

Whiting, B. and Whiting, J. (1975) *Children of Six Cultures*, Cambridge, Mass.: Harvard University Press.

Wills, T. (1982) 'Nonspecific factors in helping relationships', in Wills, T. (ed.), *Basic Processes in Helping Relationships*, N.Y.: Academic Press.

2 Concepts, theories and practices

Maria Dikaiou, University of Thessaloniki

INTRODUCTION

This chapter provides a brief survey of concepts, theories and practices used by clinical and counselling psychologists and counsellors from conceptions of the stage of life through which young people pass in their transitions to adulthood to various explanations of their strategies for coping with problems and effectiveness of various helping procedures. Intended especially for readers from a wide variety of professional backgrounds, it defines terminology used later in this book and provides psychological explanations for youth behaviour as well as current therapeutic approaches.

YOUTH PROBLEMS AND COPING

'My deepest worry'

'*My grade point average isn't high enough.*' (Venezuelan)

'*Pressure from my parents for me to succeed.*' (Filipino)

'*I won't ever be able to have the life I want.*' (Russian)

'*I will not be able to continue my studies and lose my opportunity for better employment.*' (Brazilian)

'*I have no time. I took supper at about 10 p.m. after I returned from my job. I sat up studying until 3 a.m!*' (Japanese)

'*I'm juggling a part-time job and school-work all at the same time and have no time for anything else! I need more hours to do everything I have to do.*' (Canadian)

Youth as a transition to adult life

Psychologists consider the period between 18 and 25 years of age as a time when young people prepare for adulthood. In Western societies, this traditionally has meant becoming socially and financially independent. Until the early 1980s, studies of this age group were monopolized by psychological, medical and psychiatric approaches that associated problem-behaviour and crisis with inability – or lack of desire – to take on tasks required by society. The notion that crisis was a critical part of this age helped to create images of disturbance and problematic behaviour that the public came to view as the 'problems of adolescence' (du Bois-Reymond *et al.* 1995).

The concept of youth as a stage of life separate from adolescence came slowly. Erikson (1968) defined the term simply as 'late adolescence', suggesting that this age is merely something 'less than adulthood'. Keniston (1972) pointed out, however, that many characteristics of youth differ significantly from those of adolescence. Young Western people of college age may no longer spend their energies rebelling against the adult generation, but often have trouble settling down the way their parents did, they are not ready to commit themselves to what are generally regarded as adult tasks. According to Keniston, youth have begun to sense who they are without having yet resolved their conflicts with society. For many young people, the question of whether to live their parents' lives or to what extent to do so, causes great concern. Keniston believed this stage of life is an environmental phenomenon caused by the horrific speed with which changes are taking place in technologies, institutions and values (Gibson 1983: 382–4). The changes that Keniston described were minuscule in comparison to those faced by each new generation of young people as we enter the next millennium.

Today, youth is a time of life when important decisions are made. In most western societies, this decision-making is complicated by a somewhat inconsistent process of social enfranchisement. In England, for example, people may join the army, marry and work-at the age of 16, drive a car legally at 17 and yet not vote until the age of 18. For many youth, this creates an uneasy transition:

> Legally I am not entitled to adult wages . . . and I'm not allowed to vote, drink, go to a club or do a number of other things. Yet, for some reason, I have to pay adult fares on buses, at the cinema and at swimming pools., etc . . . Can someone please tell me what age is required to become adult?
>
> (Plymouth, England: *Evening Herald* 5 March 1997)

In the early 1980s, sociologists and cultural anthropologists began to examine the transition from youth to adulthood, and portrayed the 'stage' of youth as a journey between preparation for adulthood (education, early employment, etc.) and adulthood (establishing new families and adult occupations). (See, for example, Galland 1995, Bourdieu 1980.) The important new dimension here is crossing of thresholds. Social scientists believe that many factors such as socio-economic background, gender and cultural meanings determine life courses. In this framework, youth problems bear less relationship to age than to thresholds passed or discontinuities in the passage (Chisholm 1995).

Because of the increased importance of advanced technology in modern societies, more 18–20 year olds, the age of *Youth and Coping* subjects, are in school longer than ever before, with many countries reporting a growing gap between the abilities of the wealthy and poor to cope adequately with new demands. For wealthy youth who can afford to follow traditional educational routes to employment, the transitional period includes quantitatively more time in school before adulthood (Coleman 1997). For the less fortunate, it includes not only more time, but lack of financial support. For the impoverished, it often includes barriers impossible to traverse. The subjects of our *Youth and Coping* study often were students whose concerns mirrored the pressures of this complex situation.

Most of our advantaged subjects were still dependent financially on their families in societies in which independence is considered a major developmental task of adulthood. Many non-advantaged subjects and most or all of our poverty subjects took on low-level outside jobs either to support themselves or their families. Some of these, including our non-advantaged Ethiopian immigrant sample (Chapter 15) and our Brazilian poverty sample (Chapter 16), grew up in cultures in which obtaining higher education was not a highly reinforced developmental task. The issues faced by these youth were quite different from those of their advantaged peers. One question raised by the *Youth and Coping* study is to determine whether they perceived these differences as their problems.

Youth needs, problems and stress

'How do I cope? What can I do?'

> 'My problems are unsolvable!' (Indian)
>
> 'It's all out of control! There is nothing I can do!' (Greek)

Needs and problems

The definition of what constitutes a 'need' or a 'problem' varies across disciplines and depends on the complexity of the situation under study as well as the theoretical perspectives used. Traditional psychology (expressed primarily by early psychoanalytic and cognitive behaviour approaches) was concerned with what goes on 'inside' individuals and had as its goal the explaining of behaviour and experience (problematic or not). In this sense, 'needs' and 'problems' were identified with 'intra-' or at the very most, inter-personal processes. Although there is a noble tradition from Adler to Laing which places the creation of 'problems' in society, most clinical and therapeutic practices are addressed to problems that deal with the internal state of individuals rather than the material and social environments in which they live.

In the 1950s, B. F. Skinner's behavioural approach to externalize 'needs' and 'problems' from the psyches of individuals in order to study human behaviour led to varieties of behaviour therapies which dealt only with what could be seen and measured 'scientifically'. From Skinner's behavioural psychology and earlier theories of classical conditioning, 'need' came to be considered 'a requirement that must be met for an individual to adjust optimally to the environment' with physiological requirements considered to be primary needs and psychological requirements to be secondary needs (Gibson and Chandler 1988: 496). It followed that 'problems' were the result of unmet needs.

Sociologists and social psychologists have refined these concepts by adding the notion that material and social characteristics of an environment can be reproduced in and through individual praxis. This approach suggests that negative characteristics of environments, as for example, poverty, can be translated into directly felt emotional distress.

More recently, scientists have suggested that what constitutes a problem is related to the time, place and context in which individuals operate so that external factors such as culture and potential for solutions actually predetermine what constitutes a problem for a given individual (Seidman and Rappaport 1986). Following this line of thought, they defined 'problems' as 'discrepancies between actual and ideal levels of behaviours or related conditions that society considers important' (Fawcett 1990). In this definition, if present opportunities do not meet peoples' expectations, the discrepancy may be considered a problem and the solution may be to change the discrepant conditions. According to Suarez-Balkazar *et al.* (1992: 27) 'issues become problems when they happen to be of importance to a community of interest and people's level of satisfaction with the issue is perceived as low.' This interpretation views problems as attributes of a dynamic person – environment relationship and the focus turns to cultural, contextual or environmental conditions that surround a particular problematic event.

'I'll Never Forget!'

> 'I was lighting a candle at the city square at a memorial for Rabin . . . in the same place where he was shot . . . when suddenly I looked up and saw thousands of young people just like me with candles in their hands, and I thought how sad it was that only pain and sorrow could unite a nation. I felt a terrible sense of injustice and despair.' (Israeli)

Stress

Theories of 'stress' take the social psychological concepts just described one step further: they suggest that problems result from circumstances that are either threatening or are perceived as threatening by subjects in situations in which resources required to reduce the threat are not available. (See Milburn and D'Ercole, 1991: 1162; Pearlin 1989; Rosella and Albrecht 1993.) In this sense, the 'problem of stress' resides in the interaction between an individual and a threatening situation. This approach makes it possible to conceptualize the youth problems explored in this study as either, one, potential outcomes of external pressures associated with the transition from youth to adulthood (changes in family status, peer relations, sexuality, gender roles, financial independence and employment, etc.) or two, specific external conditions that would make it difficult for them to acquire needed resources at any time.

'No one cares'

> 'I worry about the racism . . . How can I build a future?' (Ethiopian immigrant)
>
> 'I worry about the world we live in. Every day we see more new diseases, more children, more unemployment and violence . . . No one cares.' (Brazilian poverty subject)
>
> 'I worry about AIDS that kills million of young people and no one cares.' (Brazilian poverty subject)

'I'm overwhelmed!'

> 'I feel so stressed that I can't cope with it all!' (advantaged American)
>
> 'I don't feel that I can talk about my problems with anyone.' (Indian)

Youth coping

The term, 'coping', refers to the behaviours, cognition and perceptions in which people engage when solving problems. Coping is a central theme of psychoanalytic and cognitive-behavioural theory as well as of theories of developmental psychology and crisis-intervention. The 'coping process', as used in traditional theory, is situation-specific and not necessarily adaptive or maladaptive. More modern approaches have added to and changed this concept.

Social psychological theories

Social psychological research describes coping responses either as direct (acquiring resources, learning new skills, reframing the problem) or indirect (using thought or actions to relieve the emotional impact of stress (Lazarus 1966; Lazarus and Folkman 1984). They can be used individually, consecutively or in combination, although flexible access to a range of responses usually provides more positive results than any one response (Moos 1986). This perspective enlarges the traditional situation-specific view of coping by emphasizing the importance of individual, family and community resources. It takes the position that stressful experiences typically can be traced back to surrounding social structures and individuals' locations within these structures.

Systems theories

The systems theory approach, as outlined by Watzlawick *et al.* (1973), enlarges on that of social psychologists. This approach deals with coping by viewing the individuals or groups of individuals who cope as elements in a 'social system' which possesses an inherent tendency to maintain itself and to resist change. deWeerdt (1996: 165–6) described two alternative results of action by a 'system' when it is not possible to avoid change:

1 Coping by simply varying already existing elements within the system. This is usually done by intensifying the same earlier unsuccessful coping efforts so that the individual (or group of individuals) maintains a 'more of the same' scenario. In this case, the original problem is left unsolved and what is perceived by the system as the solution of a problem actually contributes to it.
2 Coping by looking at the broader problem and considering the system as one element in a larger collection of elements. This broadening of the concept of 'coping' to extend beyond numerous individual problems of the system has considerably different implications for helping interventions.

Freire (1983) took this position one step further by arguing that the highest priority of helping professionals should be to assist clients in 'reinventing' and 'transforming' their societies and the institutions they encompass. Freire's approach asserts that productive coping requires an initial 'critical' perspective of the 'true' cause of problems which he defined (for impoverished clients) as societal or political institutions, and that, when coping strategies do not work for individuals, the most productive strategy would be to change the situation. Although Freire's primary concern was to help impoverished peoples, his arguments can be applied to the counselling of more advantaged peoples as well.

Constructivist theories

A theoretical approach to coping that takes social psychological and systems approaches still another step by reconceptualizing the self and coping.

Constructivism makes four interdependent assumptions (Hoskins 1998; Mahoney 1996):

1 Order: all individuals participate actively in interpreting events, contexts and actions and, in doing so, create new and ongoing coping processes. We can best understand these processes by considering them in terms of their historical patterning rather than solely as static cause-effect relationships.
2 Activity: humans are best understood as 'self-organizing' systems that are in a continual process of patterning their experiences to achieve the best balance possible. Problems result when systems fall out of balance and resulting chaos cannot be eliminated.
3 Social-symbolic responses: the shaping of personal and social realities is usually accomplished through use of linguistic systems (words, images and other symbols of discourse) that permit individuals to communicate cultural norms and practices that influence the choices available to them.
4 Identity: identity of the self is best understood in terms of the social lives of individuals, the types and qualities of the relationships in which they are involved and the manner in which these relationships affect their images of themselves, rather than in terms of individual selves alone.

These assumptions recognize individuals as active agents in construing their worlds rather than objects predetermined by their social environments. They provide a view of coping as a fluid process affected continually by changes that buffet the individual and that require frequent redirection. This approach looks for the explanation of problems in the historic patterning of their clients' lives.

Social action approaches based on constructivist principles and paradigms of social action (Jaccard *et al.* 1990) attempt to reduce biased interpretations of client problems (blaming the victim for his problems) by involving clients in the process of defining their own needs and problems and utilizing clients, practitioners and other interested parties in the design of solutions. ('Interested parties' in this case emerge out of interactive processes between the actors and are not predetermined.) This approach departs from traditional types of 'us' (professional counsellors) designing actions for 'others' (clients) and constitutes a process designed to empower clients, focusing on need identification and analysing the contexts in which problems occur.

HELPING YOUNG PEOPLE

'When you go for help, what do you want your helper to do?'

> 'I want a helper who will let me decide myself what I want to do! I don't want anyone else to decide for me.' (Chinese)

> 'I think of independence [all the time] – doing what I want – [not what someone else wants me to want].' (English)

So long as human society has existed, humans have protected one another from adversity. As societies increased in complexity, sources of adversity and complexity of resulting problems also increased, the informal methods used by our ancestors within family groupings lost their effectiveness. In the past century, as the complexity of problems became too great to handle in these informal ways, helping professions throughout the world began developing the wide variety of formal methods of helping we have now. We now describe those methods that fall within the purview of professional psychology and counselling.

Traditional (formal) approaches to helping

Psychological counselling

A classic definition of the practice of psychological counselling was given by Hans Hoxter, President of the International Round Table for the Advancement of Counselling, as a process he described as:

> An interaction developing through the relationship between a counsellor and a person in a temporary state of indecision, confusion and distress, which helps that individual to make his own decisions and choices, to resolve his confusion or cope with his distress in a personally realistic and meaningful way, having consideration for his emotional and practical needs and for the likely consequences of his behaviour.
>
> (Hoxter 1981: viii)

Initially a one-on-one approach, this type of counselling is used today by many practice-based helping professionals who work with youth, including physicians and other health care workers, social workers, teachers and others devoted to helping. The term 'counselling' as we use it in *Youth and Coping*, refers to this process, regardless of who provides the assistance or what approaches are used. It includes the formal approaches listed below as well as informal methods still used in family and other settings by nonprofessional relatives and friends.

Psychoanalytic or psychodynamic approaches

This approach has traditionally provided clients with one-on-one counselling in which personality organization and defense mechanisms are examined in relationship to the developmental stage of clients. The primary contributors to its application in the helping of young people, Erik Erikson and Anna Freud, held that youth need to respond to problems common to their age group and that the appropriate role of the therapist is to help them do so.

Current adaptations emphasize helping clients to determine their self-identities , reduce anxiety and maladaptive defences and act out of problems in socially acceptable ways (Erikson 1968; Jaffe 1991).

Behavioural and cognitive-behavioural therapy

Behavioural and cognitive-behavioural approaches teach productive coping strategies using environmental reinforcers, looking to the client's environment to determine what constitutes effective reinforcement. Behavioural therapy, pioneered by followers of B. F. Skinner, was designed initially to increase appropriate behaviour and decrease inappropriate behaviour. Systematic desensitization, in which feared objects are paired gradually with positive reinforcers is used frequently to decrease conditioned fear responses. Cognitive-behavioural therapy adds thought processes to the equation, and is designed to help clients deal with 'maladaptive' thought processes in addition to behaviour. Assertiveness training uses these techniques and has been effective in some situations (Meichenbaum 1977).

Non-directive client-centred therapy

This approach, based on the work of psychologist Carl Rogers and his disciples (1966), utilizes the 'curative' power of client-helper relationships to change behaviour and attitudes. Rather than considering 'maladaptive' thoughts or behaviours, non-directive counsellors assume that any positive changes that occur after their interventions are caused by the empathy, congruence and unconditional regard they give their clients.

Group counselling

This approach to helping, in which a helper works with more than one person at a time, has been used with many of the above approaches and is an increasingly frequent method of helping young people today. Common types of group counselling include group psychotherapy offered by trained mental health specialists; occupational, dance or art therapy in which clients are encouraged to act out their feelings in ways that do not require them to express their emotions verbally; encounter and sensitivity training groups that provide clients who have had little experience interacting with people from other backgrounds to interact intensively with such people in close encounters; and self-help and mutual-help groups in which clients interact with others with the same problem. All of these approaches have been offered in recent years in a variety of settings from mental health facilities to private homes. They are far less expensive than one-on-one counselling, and, for this reason, are increasing in popularity. Evidence of effectiveness needs to be gathered independently for the separate types of group approaches in terms of their efficacy of helping various types of clients deal with various presenting problems.

Current approaches to helping

Most approaches to helping today as in former years, are identified with psychological support, treatment or other types of assistance. Today, help providers frequently utilize eclectic combinations of traditional methods to work with specific populations or in specific situations. (See, for example, Perschy 1997; Crow and Crow 1997; Gibbs *et al.* 1995.). We have grouped these approaches in general terms, with knowledge that some methods overlap others, as:

1 direct forms of interpersonal counselling in which counsellor and client are involved in face-to-face interactions and
2 indirect forms of counselling in which trained specialists prepare other individuals such as parents, teachers, friends or other specialists, to help young people deal with specific youth problems.

Direct helping approaches

Helping as a one-on-one direct interpersonal act is addressed normally today in situations involving

1 psycho-social problems (Hibbs and Jensen 1996; Newton 1995; Linfoot 1994)
2 difficult social-environmental conditions (Richman 1993; Appelstein 1993; Eisner 1993; Furstenberg and Hughes 1995)
3 developmental problems (McAdams and Aubin 1998); behavioural problems (Rose 1998; Mattaini and Thyer 1996)
4 group problems (Wolf *et al.* 1996).

The emphasis in all of these approaches is working with individuals.

Sociological and social-psychological approaches to helping

Unlike behaviour and cognitive-behavioural therapy, sociological approaches take the position that intervention should be based on caring communities that focus on action rather than on psychological defenses and drive states. This action may take the form of developing strong social support systems to enhance the 'social capital' of youth (Coleman 1988) as well as developing empowerment strategies such as those offered through the teaching of democratic values (Prilleltensky *et al.* 1997).

Systems theory approaches

The systems approach of Watzlawick *et al.* (1973) described earlier (p. 24) also suggests helping professionals look to the larger picture and consider all of the factors involved in the situation. deWeerdt (1996: 166–7) gave an example of how this approach might be used to help young people, using a group of Dutch adolescents who felt helpless to solve their school problems. These youngsters needed to learn better study techniques, and counsellors at their school were trained to teach them. However, the youngsters were uncomfortable going to the counsellors for help and turned instead to peers who were concerned and ready to listen. deWeerdt suggested that, in this case the first step needed was to help counsellors develop ways to show the concern that the youngsters wanted. Then and only then could they succeed in teaching the needed study lessons.

Followers of Freire (1983) suggest that productive coping requires an initial 'critical' perspective of causation of problems and that helping professionals should begin with 'macro' realities such as the 'real' causes of the problems their clients face as well as their perceptions of these problems. Building on these premises, counsellors and clients should work together actively with counsellors serving in the process as models for their clients and both prepared to engage in a struggle for the betterment of society.

Constructivism

By recognizing that individuals are active agents in construing their worlds and that successful coping is a fluid process, constructive therapy encourages clients to participate in developing new ways to perceive their lives. Constructivist youth-care practitioners take into consideration the historic patterning of clients' lives, including outside factors such as relationships and cultural norms that affect choices with the goal of creating new types of decision-making). With many youth having difficulty in interpersonal relationships, counsellors frequently helps clients learn to understand the patterns underlying their social relationships and to develop new strategies to create change. The counselling process, like the coping process, is dynamic, unpredictable and locally situated with the counsellor joining youth in their worlds, not vice versa (see p. 25).

Social action counselling (p. 25), based on constructivist principles, involves clients in a counselling process in which clients, counsellors and others work together to define needs, problems and solutions in a process designed to empower clients.

Drug therapies

A very different direct approach not discussed elsewhere in this chapter, but one used with increasing frequency in many countries, is drug therapy. This is used with clients seriously disabled by certain mental illnesses and other serious problems, as for example, attention-deficit disorders in school children, for which traditional counselling approaches alone have proved less helpful. To the best of our knowledge, while counsellors in many countries today work with other mental health professionals (psychiatrists and other medical doctors, psychiatric nurses, psychologists and social workers) to provide a wide variety of prescription-drug treatments, drugs are prescribed in the countries of our study only by physicians. The extent of the role played by professional counsellors varies from country to country. In China, for example, where counsellors are certified with very little formal training, hospital psychiatrists are the sole personnel legally using this type of therapy. In other countries which provide more stringent certification procedures, such as the USA, Canada and Israel, counsellors work together with other mental health professionals on diagnosis and medical personnel are required for the writing of prescriptions. In the USA, psychiatric nurses are involved in ongoing efforts of organized nursing to expand currently restricted prescription privileges, including psychotropic medications. American psychologists currently are lobbying for the legal right to prescribe some drugs for some problems. Although drug therapy itself is listed here as a direct helping approach, it is often used together with therapies provided in other settings, as for example, self-help programmes.

Indirect helping approaches

Indirect helping ('help-to-help') approaches have been developed primarily for use at interpersonal, group, and social levels, the latter referring usually to community services. All may take the form of training individuals to give advice for dealing with specific problems (as, for example, the dangers of sexually transmitted diseases), to provide psychological and emotional support, and to screen serious problems for further attention. (McKeever 1998; Phillips and Straussner 1997; Noble and Gibson 1994; Bagley *et al.* 1994; Fitzgerald 1994; Furlong and Smith 1994.)

The following are just a few of the uses to which indirect helping has been found useful:

1 Peer and paraprofessional counselling in which young people (peers of those seeking help) or paraprofessionals (other individuals whose role it is to interact regularly with youth but have not been trained as counsellors) are trained on how to advise young people, to provide social and emotional support, and, most importantly, to recognize problems of sufficient severity that suggest the need of intervention by a specialist. Peer and paraprofessional counselling can play extremely important roles in crisis situations in which problems are severe and few professionals are available to assist clients. (The editor of *Youth and Coping*, Janice Gibson-Cline, worked in one such situation: a refugee camp in which there were 5,000 refugees who had experienced severe psychological and emotional trauma, and one psychiatrist-counsellor. In this case, refugees were chosen on the basis of their ability to learn how to interview, provide advice and screen for those most serious problems that required

immediate action of a specialist.) Peer and paraprofessional counselling is also particularly effective in getting help to prospective clients who are afraid to confide in professionals. (For examples of peer and para-professional counselling, see Appelstein 1993; Gibbs *et al.* 1995.)

2 Crisis intervention approaches vary according to crisis. For example, counsellors and trained para-professionals work as team members with other specialists to provide immediate on-site assistance to victims of catastrophes caused by natural events such as earthquakes to those caused by man-made events such as violence or war. Counsellors have also worked in many countries to establish telephone hotlines that provide youth in crisis with immediate one-on-one confidential attention and counselling. Hotlines are usually staffed by trained para-professionals, although professional counsellors sometimes staff these posts. Because of an increasing incidence of crisis among youth in countries, more and more countries are providing this service. Hot-lines are advertised in most countries in youth centres, in telephone books and other places where they can be found easily by young people. (Chapter 12 describes a hot-line programme for young people in Russia. See Bagley *et al.* 1994 for a description of para-professional counselling.)

3 Self-help programmes in which clients interact with one another in discussing their problems, normally under the supervision of a specialist. Some self-help programmes, such as Alcoholics Anonymous, have proven extremely effective in helping clients solve their problems . Because of this as well as the low cost of the approach, it is a very popular approach in many countries.

4 Prevention programmes designed to help at-risk youth before they are in difficulty. These include programmes for students as well as programmes for parents provided by schools, church institutions and community centres as well as at helping centres for youth, usually dealing with problems common to this age group, such as violence, aggression, physical and mental health issues dealing with grief. Included in these services are programmes related to physical and health as well as well as family values, education and employment. (See Corvo 1997; Furlong and Smith 1994; Newton 1995; Noble *et al.* 1994; Perschy 1997; Shelton 1995; Tan 1994 for examples of programmes.)

A SUMMARY OF FORMAL HELPING

Counselling procedures used today have their roots in the helping methods of the past, with each generation of professionals adding new approaches appropriate to the important issues of the time, often combining new techniques with old to meet new needs (See. p. 28) Traditional psychoanalytic therapies in use for most of this century have provided help for an 'elite' group of consumers and deal with intimate issues regarding self-identities, anxieties and 'maladaptive' defenses. Scientific interest in the effects of environment on behaviour led, in the 1950s, to behavioural, cognitive-behavioural and non-directive approaches, which added the new dimension of utilizing environmental factors to change behaviour. Twenty years later, concern regarding specific effects of social environments led helping professionals to add psycho-social approaches to their inventory. More recently, systems theory approaches which consider problem situations in terms of the larger picture of affecting factors and constructivism, which focuses on the coping as a fluid and changeable process have been added to the counselling repertoire. Today, counselling approaches are still enlarging on these perspectives as they consider new concerns to society. Today's approaches take into consideration a far wider spectrum than ever before, including psycho-social, environmental and social problems facing citizens of the modern world as well as internal issues personal to individual members of society. Group techniques and para-professional counselling, as well as self-help programmes, make help available to larger numbers of youth with new and different problems. On the eve of the twenty-first century, helping professionals are exploring with their clients the wide range of diversity we know exists among youth groups, including variations due to socio-economic circumstances and situations that are outside the 'norm' of youth behaviour or age expectations.

Just as the world is changing, so must the roles of helping professionals if they are to respond effectively to new challenges. The twenty-first century will require that individuals face new political and cultural issues such as cultural diversity within countries, already increasing throughout the globe through war, migration, etc. Fortunately, new psycho-social theories and approaches, such as social construction (discussed in Chapter 17), provide new possibilities to create needed helping strategies.

Note

The author is grateful for the assistance of E. Pereira in providing material for the discussion of Freire; K. Feaviour for his contribution to the discussion of youth as a transition to adult life; S. Harris, C. Falz, R. Kemerling, L. Martinson, B. Shafrir and B. Shaw for their assistance in developing the discussion of drug therapies; and N. Eythimia and S. Parthena for their survey of counselling research literature.

References

Appelstein, C. (1993) 'Peer helping peer: duo therapy with children in residential care', *Residential Treatment for Children and Youth* 10 (4): 33–53.

Bagley, C., Tse, J. and Hoi, W. (1994) 'Suicidal adolescents in Hong Kong: peer counselling strategies', *Journal of Child and Youth Care* 9 (4): 71–87.

Bourdieu, P. (1987) 'The excellence and value of the French system', in Miceli, S. (ed.), *The Economics of Symbolic Changes*, São Paulo: Perspective, in Portuguese.

Bourdieu, P. (1980) 'Youth is but a word', in *Sociological Questions*, Paris: Editions de Minuit: 143–54, in French.

Chisholm, L. (1995) 'Youth transitions in the European Union', in Coulby, D., Jones, C., Bash, L. and Green, A. (eds), *Youth, Education and Work. World Yearbook of Education*, London: Kogan Page.

Coleman J. (1997) *Key Data on Adolescence*, London: Trust for the Study of Adolescence.

Coleman, L. (1988) 'Social capital in the creation of human capital', *American Journal of Sociology* 94 (Suppl.95): S95–S120.

Corvo, K. (1997) 'Community-based youth violence prevention: a framework for planners and funders', *Youth and Society* 28 (3): 291–316.

Crow, G. and Crow, L. (1997) *Helping Parents Cope with Children's Adjustment Problems: An Advice-giving Guide for Professionals*, Springfield, Ill.: Charles C. Thomas.

deWeerdt, P. (1996) 'The Netherlands study', in Gibson-Cline, J. (ed.), *Adolescence: From Crisis to Coping*, London: Routledge: 153–68.

du Bois-Reymond, M., Diekstra, R., Hurrelmann, K. and Peters, E. (eds) (1995) 'Coping strategies and status transitions in adolescence', *Modern Youth in Germany and The Netherlands*, Berlin/New York: de Gruyter.

Eisner, Z. (1993) 'Cultural diversity and intervention planning', *Journal of Child and Youth Care* 8 (4): 21–28.

Erikson, E. (1968) *Identity: Youth and Crisis*, New York: Norton.

Fawcett, S. (1990) 'Some emerging standards for community research and action: aid from a behavioural perspective', in Tolan P., Keys, C., Chertok, F. and Jason, L. (eds), *Researching Community Psychology* 64–75, Washington D.C.: American Psychological Association.

Fitzgerald, M. (1994) 'Resistant attitudes and behaviours of adolescents in residential care', *Child and Youth Care Forum* 23 (6): 365–75.

Freire, P. (1983) *Pedagogy for the Oppressed*, Rio de Janeiro: ed. Paz e Terra, in Portuguese.

Furlong, M. and Smith, D. (eds) (1994) *Anger, Hostility and Aggression: Assessment, Prevention, and Intervention Strategies for Youth*, Brandon, Vt.: Clinical Psychology Publishing.

Furstenberg, F. Jr. and Hughes, M. (1995) 'Social capital and successful development among at-risk youth', *Journal of Marriage and the Family* 57 (3): 580–92.

Galland, O. (1995) 'Changing family transitions: young people and new ways of life in France' in Chisholm, L., Büchner, P., Krüger, H. and du Bois-Reymond, M. (eds), *Growing Up in Europe*, Berlin/New York: Walter de Gruyter.

Gibbs, J., Potter, G. and Goldstein, A. (1995) *The EQUIP Programme: Teaching Youth to Think and Act Responsibly Through a Peer-Helping Approach*, Champaign, Ill.: Research Press.

Gibson, J. (1983) *Living: Human Development through the Life-Span*, NewYork: Random House.

Gibson, J. and Chandler, L. (1988) *Educational Psychology: Mastering Principles and Applications*, Needham Heights, Mass.: Allyn and Bacon.

Hibbs, E. and Jensen, P. (eds) (1996) *Psycho-social Treatments for Child and Adolescent Disorders: Empirically-Based Strategies for Clinical Practice*, Washington, D.C.: American Psychological Association.

Hoskins, M. (1998) 'Constructivism and child and youth care practice: visions for the twenty-first century', *Journal of Child and Youth Care* 11 (4): 83–92.

Hoxter, H. (1981) *The Forms, Methods and Techniques of Vocational and Educational Guidance: International Case Histories*, Paris: UNESCO.

Jaccard, J., Turrisi, R.and Wan, C. (1990) 'Implications of behavioural decision theory and social marketing for designing social action programmes', in Edwards, J., Tindale, R., Heath, L. and Posavac, E. (eds), *Social Influence Processes and Prevention* 1: 103–42, New York: Plenum.

Jaffe, C. (1991) 'Psychoanalytic approaches to adolescent development', in Gold, J. (ed.), *Adolescent Psychotherapy*, Washington, D.C.: American Psychiatric Press, 11–40.

Keniston, K. (1972) 'Youth: a 'new' stage of life', *American Scholar* 109–27.

Lazarus, R. (1966) *Psychological Stress and Coping Paradigm*, New York: McGraw-Hill.

Lazarus, R. and Folkman, S. (1984) 'Coping and adaptation', in Gentry, W. (ed.), *Handbook of Behavioural Medicine*. New York: Guilford, 44–8.

Linfoot, K. (ed) (1994) *Communication Strategies for People with Developmental Disabilities: Issues from Theory and Practice*, Sydney: Paul H. Brookes.

Mahoney, M. (1996) 'Connected knowing in constructive psychotherapy', in Goldberger, N., Tarule, J., Clinchy, B. and Belenky, M. (eds), *Knowledge, Difference and Power* 126–47, New York: Basic Books.

Mattaini, M. and Thyer, B. (eds) (1996) F*inding Solutions to Social Problems: Behavioural Strategies for Change*, Washington, D.C.: American Psychological Association.

McAdams, D.and De Aubin, St. (eds) (1998) *Generativity and Adult Development: How and Why We Care for the Next Generation*, Washington, D.C.: American Psychological Association.

McKeever, B. (1998) *Hidden Addictions: A Pastoral Response to the Abuse of Legal Drugs*, New York: Haworth.

Meichenbaum, D. (1977) *Cognitive Behaviour Modification: An Integrative Approach*, New York: Plenum.

Milburn, N. and d'Ercole, A. (1991) 'Homeless women: moving towards a comprehensive model', *American Psychologist* 46 (11): 1161–9.

Moos, R. (1986) *Coping with Life Crises: An Integrated Approach*, New York: Plenum.

Newton, M. (1995) *Adolescence: Guiding youth through the perilous ordeal*, New York: Norton.

Noble, D. and Gibson, D. (1994) 'Family values in action: family connectedness for children in substitute care', *Child and Youth Care Forum* 23 (5): 315–28.

Pearlin, L. (1989) 'The sociological study of stress', *Journal of Health and Social Behaviour* 30: 241–56.

Perschy, M. (1997) *Helping teens work through grief*, Bristol, England: Accelerated Development.

Phillips, N.and Straussner, S. (eds) (1997) *Children in the Urban Environment: Linking Social Policy and Clinical Practice*, Springfield, Ill.: Charles C. Thomas.

Prilleltensky, I., Peirson, L., Gould, J. and Nelson, G. (1997) 'Planning mental health services for children and youth: part I, a value-based approach', *Education and Programme Planning* 20 (2): 163–72.

Richman, N. (1993) 'Children in situations of political violence', *Journal of Child Psychology and Psychiatry and Allied Disciplines* 34 (8): 1286–302.

Rogers, C. (1966) 'A theory of therapy as developed in the client-centred framework', in Art, A., Jr. (ed.), *Counselling and Psychotherapy*, Palo Alto: Science and Behaviour Books.

Rose, S. (1998) *Group Therapy with Troubled Youth: A Cognitive-Behavioural Interactive Approach*, Thousand Oaks: Sage.

Rosella, J. and Albrecht, S. (1993) 'Toward an understanding of the health status of Black adolescents: an application of the stress-coping framework', *Issues in Comprehensive Pediatric Nursing* 16 (4): 193–205.

Seidman, E. and Rappaport, J. (1986) *Redefining Social Problems*, New York: Plenum.

Shelton, C. (1995) *Pastoral Counselling with Adolescents and Youths*, New York: Crossroad.

Suarez-Balcazar, Y., Balcazar, F. and Fawcett, S. (1992) 'Problem identification in social intervention research', in Bryant, F., Edwards, J., Tindale, R., Posavac, E., Heath, L., Henderson, E. and Suarez-Balcazar, Y. (eds), *Applied Social Psychology*, New York: Plenum.

Tan, S. (1994) 'Lay counselling: a Christian approach', *Journal of Psychology and Christianity* 13 (3): 264–9.

Watzlawick, P., Weakland, J. and Finch, R. (1973) *Change*, Palo Alto, Calif.

Wolfe, D., Wekerle, C., Gough, R. and Reitzel, J. (1996) *The Youth Relationships Manual: A Group Approach with Adolescents for the Prevention of Abuse of Women and the Promotion of Healthy Relationships*, Thousand Oaks, Calif.: Sage.

Part II

The multinational study

'There is no one I can turn to with my problem. I have given up trying.'

Part II, which comprises just one chapter, Chapter 3, presents the multinational findings of our study: a composite portrait of youth coming from twelve national backgrounds: American, Brazilian, Canadian, Chinese, English, Filipino, Greek, Indian, Israeli, Japanese, Venezuelan and Ethiopian (Ethiopian Jewish immigrants and mainstream Jewish-Israeli youth were both surveyed in Israel); and two socio-economic backgrounds. It also includes results taken from surveys conducted in two time periods, 1989 and 1997; describes the answers of our subjects to our research questions; provides suggestions as to their meaning and importance; and creates a backdrop from which one can interpret the national and special population studies that follow in later chapters.

Highlights of findings only are reported. The reader may refer to Appendicies III and IV for full statistical details of all findings.

3 The multinational study

Reports from Brazilian, Canadian, Chinese, English, Filipino, Greek, Indian, Ethiopian-immigrant-Israeli, mainstream Jewish-Israeli, Japanese, American and Venezuelan young people

Janice Gibson-Cline, University of Pittsburgh, and the Youth and Coping *Research Team*

(Brazil: Elizabete Pereira; Canada: Louise Martinson, Brenda Shaw and Bill Borgen; China: Qi Chen, Fengchun Miao and Xin Lu; England: Kevin Feaviour and David Acres; Greece: Maria Dikaiou and Mika Haritos-Fatouras; India: Lina Kashyap; Israel: Benjamin Shafrir, Rachel Erhard (Ethiopian immigrants in Israel); Japan: Keiko Honda and Ishu Ishiyama; the Philippines: Gundalina Velazco; the USA: Lisa Maccarelli, Janice Gibson-Cline, Carol E. Baker and David Botwin; Venezuela: Maria Felce DiPaula)

INTRODUCTION

Chapter 3 provides a composite picture of the concerns, coping strategies and help-seeking of male and female youth from advantaged, non-advantaged and poverty populations in eleven countries, using responses collected in our 1997 and 1989 surveys. Chinese subjects surveyed in 1989 and Russian subjects surveyed in 1997 and 1989 have not been included in this composite because data was not described by the authors in terms of subjects socio-economic status and therefore could not be directly compared to responses of other subjects defined in terms of this variable. The specific questions we asked were:

1 What did our 1997 male and female subjects from advantaged, non-advantaged and poverty populations tell us about the concerns that caused them stress, how they coped and the people they sought to help them and how did the responses of the two genders compare with one another?

2 For those subject groups whose responses were collected in both 1997 and in 1989, how did 1997 answers compare with those from 1989?
3 What do the responses of our subjects suggest, if anything, regarding intervention strategies effective for helping young people in the nations studied?

Hopes, dreams and worries – with cultural variations

'I believe in simple living and high thinking, and I hope for a better world for everyone.'

Salim is an 18-year-old non-advantaged male, the son of a cloth merchant and the eldest of a large, religious Moslem family in Mumbai. This is Salim's first year of college. He is studying business and hopes to become 'a business tycoon'.

Salim says that the reason he wants to make money is not himself, but his fellow human beings. He wants to please God, worries about discord in the world and wishes for harmony between different religions groups. *'I want everyone in the world to do the utmost to make the most of the gift of life, both for themselves and for God.'*

'I hope to be a cellist in a symphony orchestra, just like my father.'

Twenty-year-old Debra is a third-year university student majoring in music. She is American. Her recently widowed mother teaches elementary school.

Debra began studying the violin at 5 years old and switched to cello when she was 15. She worries whether she will be able to reach this goal and, if so, whether the life of a professional musician will permit her to build a satisfying personal life at the same time. Will she and her fiancé, a flautist, be able to find jobs together or will they have to live in different cities at the start? They both want children. Will they be able to raise a family?
'It was easier in my mother's day when women selected careers that let them follow their husbands. We want to work together and dream of having a family too. But will it be possible for us?'

METHODOLOGY

In this chapter, we compare the reports of 4,781 subjects by both gender and socio-economic group (advantaged, non-advantaged and poverty, as described in Chapter 1). Most of the advantaged and non-advantaged subjects of the 1997 study were students, distinguished not only by the SES characteristics described in Chapter 1, but also by the fact that advantaged youth most frequently studied in universities and non-advantaged studied more often in colleges or technical schools. By contrast, most poverty subjects tended either to work at low-paid and part-time occupations or to be searching for work. (Poverty subjects from England (1997) sometimes attended higher education classes while working part-time; subjects from Venezuela (1997) were attending night classes in programmes established by the government illiteracy project. Some Filipino subjects (1989) begged on the streets when they could not find employment.)

For those youth in countries and SES groups where we conducted surveys in both 1997 and 1989, we compare findings also by year of survey. All studies included in this composite are described in later chapters with the exception of the Philippines study. The nationality and special populations chapters (Chapters 4–16) that follow provide detailed descriptions of each population group.

Table 3.1 describes the subjects in our *Youth and Coping* study. This includes both those that make up our composite picture and those subjects not classified by SES and not included in this chapter but that are discussed in sections II and III.

To present our composite picture, we utilized mean composite percentages of subjects' responses that fell into classes and categories within those classes of problems, coping strategies, choices of helper, desired helper qualities and modes of helping. (See Chapter 1 for our procedure.) The data used to create these percentages were based on SES and gender descriptions provided in the national and special youth populations described in Chapters 4–16 which were corrected for variations in sample size among national, SES and gender groups. (Because there are a greater number of subjects and subject samples in higher SES groups and in 1997 than in lower SES groups and in 1989, readers are cautioned that the reliability of results decreases with SES and year of study from 1997 to 1989.)

Table 3.1 Populations included in the Multinational Study by year of survey and SES background of subjects

1997 (3,193 subjects)	
Advantaged (n=1846)	Brazil, Canada, China, England, Greece, India, Israel, Japan, the Philippines, the USA, Venezuela
Non-advantaged (n=983)	Brazil, China, England, Greece, India, Venezuela Ethiopian immigrants in Israel
Poverty (n=163)	Brazil, England
Non-classified (n=201)	Russia
1989 (1,963 subjects)	
Advantaged (n=949)	Brazil, Greece, Israel, Japan, the Philippines, the USA Venezuela
Non-advantaged (n=400)	Brazil, England
Poverty (n=200)	the Philippines
Non-classified (n=414)	China, Russia

HIGHLIGHTS OF OUR FINDINGS

The Multinational Study is described in this chapter in terms of highlights of our findings only. For full statistical results see Appendix IV.

Concerns

At a macro level, schooling issues were of greatest concern to advantaged subjects and males; self-identity was of greatest concern to non-advantaged subjects; family issues worried poverty subjects and females more than any other concern. We examine these findings individually next.

Schooling

Socio-economic status appeared to be a factor related to reported schooling concerns, with the percentage of these concerns decreasing from advantaged to non-advantaged status in both the 1997 and 1989 surveys and with males tending to report schooling concerns more frequently than females. (See Appendix IV.) In general, for both advantaged and non-advantaged subjects, worries about schooling increased quantitatively from 1989 (from 20–32 per cent in 1989 to 29–39 per cent in 1997). Males reported far more schooling concerns than females.

Because most advantaged and non-advantaged subjects in our 1997 survey were students, we might have expected their schooling worries – in particular, academic achievement and time pressures – and related them to their student status. However, while schooling was also the primary concern of these SES groups in 1989, the majority of non-advantaged subjects had left school for the work force and were employed at occupations that did not require higher education. While the concerns of these non-advantaged subjects (who had been low achievers when they were in school) tended to be related to time pressures and academic achievement, their focus was quite different from that of their more advantaged peers: rather than worrying about whether they could get high grades, this group worried about whether they could be successful enough to learn when they now had additional work and financial pressures that they did not have before.

> 'My problem is that I can't understand what the teachers are telling me to do.' (Brazilian)
>
> 'I worry about not understanding completely and failing.' (English)
>
> 'I must study continuously for hours in order to understand even the basics and I feel pressured from the (enormous) load of material I am supposed to understand.' (Ethiopian in Israel)

For our 1997 poverty subjects, schooling worries were reported less frequently than by more advantaged subjects (only 17 per cent of reported concerns compared with 29–39 per cent of the reports of their more advantaged peers). This was true even though a large proportion of the 1997 poverty population were Venezuelan night-class students who were trying to improve their educational backgrounds so as to be more eligible for employment.

One reason that they may not have reported more concerns is that their economic social realities included severe immediate concerns that probably prevented them not only from looking to their futures, but from changing their positions in the social structure. As Yunex (1982) and Nidelhoff (1984) suggested, impoverished populations are aware that there is little possibility for them to change their social reality, no matter what they do. According to Gomes (1997), this situation is exacerbated by impoverished family culture in which parents with lower levels of education themselves and with little personal experience of the value of education on long-term goals place less value on education for their children. (This issue is discussed in some detail in Chapter 16.)

The fact that major concerns of our impoverished subjects by and large reflected day-to-day unmet and immediate needs as opposed to long-term concerns gives some credence to these arguments. In order of the rankings of the responses of poverty subjects from most to least frequently reported concerns were:

1 family issues (28 per cent of reported problems) related primarily with ways to help family members meet their needs or to deal with other family problems
2 interpersonal concerns (25 per cent of reported problems) related to the immediate issues regarding gaining of employment
3 self-identity (20 per cent)
4 schooling (17 per cent).

When poverty youth discussed schooling worries, they often spoke of needing more education to get jobs and obtain money to meet immediate family needs (although they also worried they would not be able to succeed at this task).

The frequency of reported schooling problems increased for our poverty subjects from 7 per cent in 1989 to 17 per cent in 1997, probably due to the opportunities provided our Brazilian poverty subjects to obtain remedial education and their subsequent involvement in schooling.

Identity and self-concept

The second major concern of both advantaged and non-advantaged subjects was 'personal identity and self-concept'. This was often reflected in worries about 'becoming adult' (attaining social maturity and adult status; dealing with choices regarding future careers, gender roles and educational choices; becoming financially independent), as expected of this age group:

> 'I wanted to go to law school, but I'm not sure anymore that this is an advantageous choice if I am to become the person I want to be in the future.' (Greek)
>
> 'I feel pressure to find a career, happiness, pay for school, do well in school. I want to have all of these things. What will happen if I cannot become what I want to be?' (American)

Concerns regarding self-identity appeared least frequently in the results of poverty subjects. This was true in both years of the study and was probably due to other more immediate and more serious problems that impinged on the lives of these subjects.

Family

For impoverished youth, the most frequently reported concerns in both 1989 and 1997 were related to their families. These worries regarded not only their parental families, but also the new families that many of our subjects were in the process of planning or had already created. Females from most cultures worried more about family issues than their male counterparts. The specific issues about which they worried were often related to their cultural backgrounds. From India, a country in which arranged marriages are still common:

> 'I worry about my future marriage. I am looking forward to it, but am anxious about the kind of spouse and marital family I will be given and all the adjustments I will have to make.'

From Brazil, in which members of large, closely knit families are responsible for one another:

> 'My parents are already old and tired. I would like to help them to stop working and take care of them.'

From England, where there is a high rate of family dysfunction and divorce:

> 'I hate going to my Dad's. I have not gotten along with him since he and my Mum broke up.'

Employment

Concerns about family choices often were intertwined with other issues that worried our subjects, most frequently, employment or future employment.[1]

This was true, not only for males but for young females from countries in which women now have more freedom than in past generations to choose their own adult lifestyles:

> 'While I'm not so worried about finding employment, I am not sure about how my plan for marriage and having babies will fit in. To be sure to attain my future (professional) goals, I need to face these issues right now.' (a young Japanese female)

Unemployment was a more frequent concern among our poverty populations than employment issues, although poverty subjects reported far more worries related to obtaining work than more advantaged subjects. In 1997, 24 per cent of their reported problems dealt primarily with the category 'work' as compared with non-advantaged (8 per cent) and advantaged subjects (3 per cent).

Schooling, family, self-identity and employment problems of the impoverished were often intertwined:

> 'I worry about the lack of opportunities for youth. I am without a work option. I must learn to read if I want to ever get a job that will feed my family. But I have so little time for lessons. It is so hard just to live.'
>
> 'It's hard for me to meet my own essential expenses when I must take care of a small child.'
>
> 'I have done well in my studies and know that I could do well at a job. But how can I convince an employer to hire me at a good job if I look so shabby? And I have no money to buy clothes!'

Gender played a role in determining worries. As reported earlier, while schooling issues were prominent in male reports, females discussed school problems less than half as frequently (in 1997, 8 per cent of responses as compared to 22 per cent of male concerns). By contrast, females reported almost twice as many family concerns (welfare of family members, divorce/separation, domestic violence, sexual abuse involving family member) as did males. (The sole concern reported sufficiently often by males to appear in Appendix III as a family category was 'family honour.') While males and females both reported a relatively high percentage of problems related to self-identity, particularly to 'becoming adult' and 'self-confidence' (27 per cent for both genders), males worried about 'behavioural issues' and 'self-expectations', while females reported a variety of other concerns, including as self-abuse and physical appearance. These findings, shown in Appendix III categories-within-classes, are similar to what was found both in the previous study by our research team on adolescence (Gibson-Cline *et al.* 1996) as well as in other earlier research literature (Gilligan *et al.* 1990, 1988).

It is incredible that the youth in both our 1997 and 1989 studies, just as their younger 13–15-year-old peers in 1989 (Gibson-Cline *et al.* 1996), failed to report major problems affecting this age group. One such example is AIDS. At the end of 1999, a United Nations global study found that 2.6 million people world-wide were expected to die of AIDS within the year (Perlman 1999: A15). Although some impoverished 1997 subjects couched worries about AIDS and drugs as humanitarian (societal) concerns, these worries were not couched as personal concerns sufficiently frequently to list them among those represented by at least 5 per cent of reported problems in the populations of our study. The author of 'Impoverished youth' (Chapter 16), Elizabete Pereira, suggests that this might be due to a reticence to discuss these issues in the first person on the part of subjects who deemed it unsafe as a 'topic for open discussion'. The poverty subjects who stated, 'I worry about AIDS that kills million of young people. Many poor youth don't have resources even to treat themselves' and 'Drugs available to youth lead me to despair' did not report these worries in the first person. There are other possible explanations, for example, that youth are actually engaging in unsafe sex or are using drugs, but simply do not consider this an important problem or that they are not worried because they are not involved in any unsafe activities. Discussion of this extremely important issue appears further on in this chapter and in Chapter 17.

In summarizing the worries that were reported, several interesting differences between SES groups and genders as regards reported concerns, stand out from the others. Figures 3.1 and 3.2 show through bar graphs, first, that advantaged and non-advantaged SES groups report a lower percentage of family concerns and a higher percentage of schooling concerns than poverty groups and second, that this difference holds across the two years of our study. Figure 3.3 suggests, further, that 1997 females tend to differ from males as regards family and school concerns in much the same way that poverty subjects differ from their advantaged and non-advantaged peers, with males, like more advantaged subjects, reporting fewer family concerns and more school concerns than females.[2]

These results conform with those reported in our 1989 study of 13–15-year-olds in thirteen countries in which we used the same survey instrument (Gibson-Cline *et al.* 1996: 31–2):

> That family problems increase with decreasing SES and that females report a higher percentage of problems related to family issues than males within each SES group, with poor females reporting the highest percentage of family problems of any group in our study is an indication of the important role of our environment. In this case it probably represents family stress and disruption due to economic problems that are often compounded by cultural values that specify the feminine helping role in these matters.
>
> That males report more school problems than females may be due to

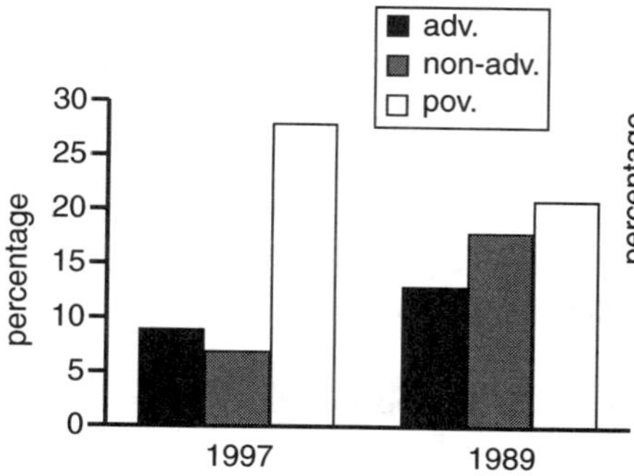

Figure 3.1 Percentage of reported family concerns in 1997 and 1989 by SES grouping

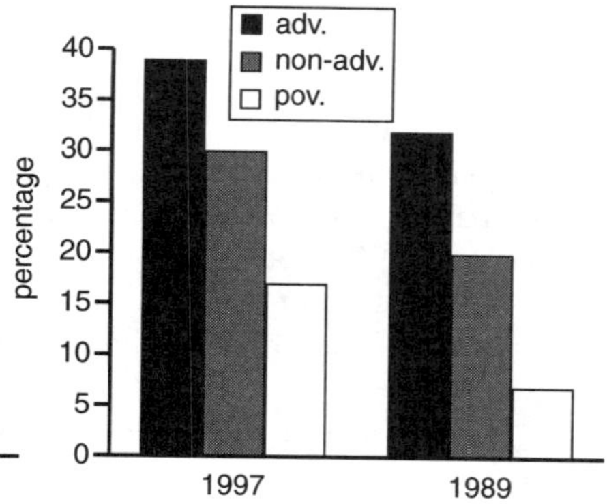

Figure 3.2 Percentage of reported schooling concerns in 1997 and 1989 by SES grouping

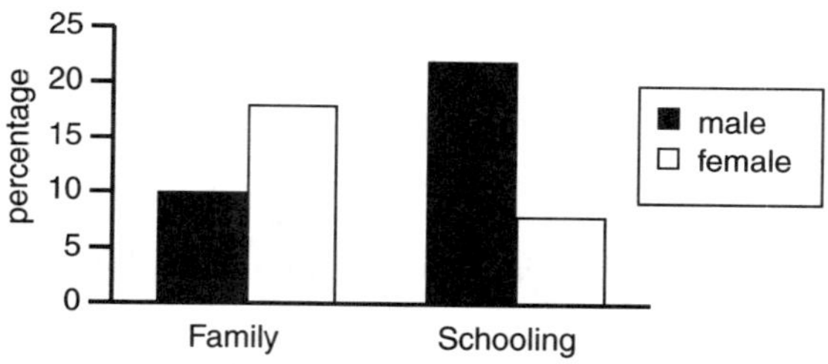

Figure 3.3 Percentages of responses of males and females regarding family and school concerns 1997

> males actually having more problems, females worrying less about them or a combination of both. We cannot tell from this research. At the same time, we are aware that, although academic achievement is still more valued for males than females in most countries of our study, cultural values nevertheless continue to reinforce behavior in males that conflicts with school learning. By contrast, the more passive feminine behavior valued for females is more compatible with the types of learning that take place in school.

Although we cannot prove definitively why these differences occur in more certain terms today than we could in 1996, the fact that they resulted in both 1989 from both adolescent and youth and again in 1997 from youth reports, suggests that the differences are real. It also reinforces the belief that, although the cultural roles of women vary in the countries of our study, females – just as impoverished persons – tend to have some different problems than their male peers that might require different types of assistance to reach the goals important to them. We will discuss this in further detail in Chapter 17.

Coping strategies: their relationship to SES, year of study and gender

All SES groups and both genders reported individual problem-solving (attempting to solve problems by themselves, usually by planning or trying harder) far more frequently than any other reported strategy (48–65 per cent of 1997 and 54–74 per cent of 1989 coping reports). Planning (includes assessment and analysis of situation to plan action) was indicated as a category in approximately 23 per cent of reports:

> 'To make sure I get everything done, I created (a chart) to space my time and now everything has a time when I do it.' (Canadian)
>
> 'I meet with everyone I know who can help me, put all the information together, and when I think I know enough, I decide on a plan of action.' (Venezuelan)

Trying harder (without planning any specific action), another coping category, was indicated in approximately 20 per cent of reports:

> 'I just study harder.' (English)
>
> 'I will try anything to solve the problem.' (Ethiopian in Israel)

Many sought assistance, with females seeking help somewhat more than males. This was suggested by the research literature regarding gender differences in help-seeking and was probably due to cultural training of males to be independent and females to work with others as reported by Basow (1992) and Nadler, Maler and Friedman (1984.)

> 'I go to my best friend and ask for help. She understands me and gives me advice.' (American)

It should not assumed that all of these strategies led to reduction of the problems reported by our subjects, however. According to systems theory interpretation of coping (Watzlowick *et al.* 1973), and as we will discuss in Chapter 17, coping by 'trying harder' is often simply a repetition of a strategy that did not work in the past and that leads to a scenario in which the solution becomes the renewed cause of the problem. In addition, while attempting to solve their problems themselves, both our 1997 subjects talked frequently of being 'mentally preoccupied' or being 'anxious without a definite plan for solution'. They also reported 'disengaging' (escaping/avoiding, distancing themselves physically or mentally from the problems) or 'resigning' themselves (giving up or doing nothing).

Disengagement:

> 'I'm very afraid of taking exams. So what do I do to solve my problem? I go off and listen to music.' (American)
>
> 'I just stop thinking about it [my problem], go off with my mates and relax.' (English)

Resignation:

> 'I don't know what vocation to choose and how my future should go. Sometimes I believe that the fates have arranged it for me and I don't think about it any more. . . . I simply talk myself into believing that there's nothing I can do except wait for the future.' (Chinese)
>
> 'I just stop doing anything at all because I don't know what to do.' (Venezuelan)
>
> 'I try my best not to give in to fear and despair because I know that everything will crumble if I go. Unfortunately, it is difficult. I do not always succeed and then I just give up and stop trying.' (Brazilian)

We found it alarming that, when percentages of responses in each original class were combined to create a new class, 'resignation and disengagement' became the second most frequently reported coping strategy in all groups of our study. This was true in both 1989 and 1997!

Figure 3.4 combines resignation and disengagement to create what might be described as a 'non-goal-oriented' coping approach. It shows, first, that not only are advantaged subjects using more coping responses ineffective in reducing their stated problems than their less advantaged peers, but second, that use of these strategies increased among all SES groups from 1989 to 1997. It also shows that poverty subjects chose this 'new class' of coping less frequently than their advantaged peers. This was true in both years of our study. We discuss the implications of this important finding on pp. 52–4.

Concerning possible gender differences and given our results regarding SES and coping, it should not be surprising that, first, the most commonly used coping strategy of both males and females was individual problem-solving and that males utilized these individual approaches more frequently than females, and second, resignation and disengagement together are the second most frequently used approach of both genders.

Finally, while females seek assistance from others and use other interpersonal methods of coping more than their male peers, males tend more to accept responsibility for solving their problems (acknowledging their role in the problem without actually planning a solution). (See Appendix III, categories of coping.)

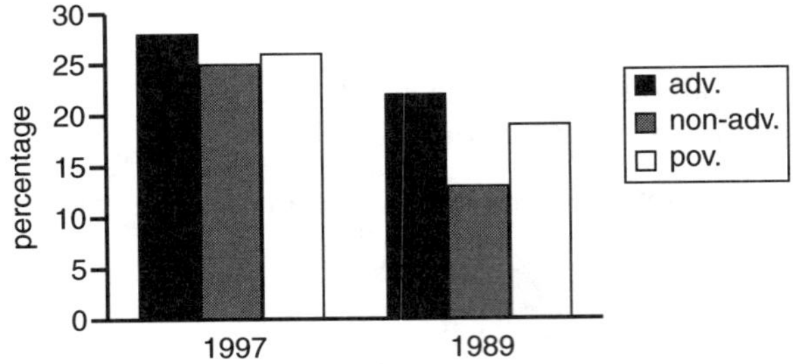

Figure 3.4 Percentage of responses indicating coping by resignation or disengagement

Helpers: their relationship to SES, year of study and gender

> I seek help from my classmates because we understand each other. I hope that they will assure me that I can actualize my potential. (advantaged subject, Chinese)

Most of the young people in our study, regardless of SES or gender, went to people from outside their families when they needed help. Advantaged subjects in both our 1989 and 1997 studies went to other people almost three times more frequently than to family members.

To whom, specifically, did our subjects go? Personal friends were the first choice for all groups in both years of our study. Advantaged youth went to professional helpers more frequently than other SES groups. Mainstream Jewish-Israelis made the most use of counselling help (shown in 14 per cent of 1989 and 8–10 per cent of 1997 responses). Non-advantaged Ethiopian immigrants to Israel also made use of professional counselling help (reflected in 10 per cent of their responses). Reports of English advantaged and non-advantaged subjects, approximately 25 per cent of whom were in counselling or other special services, provided somewhat fewer responses indicating that subjects would seek help from a counsellor. Possible reasons for the success of Israel's counselling approaches in terms of client usage are discussed in Chapter 17. Other countries in which subjects indicated some use of professional counselling help in at least 5 per cent of their responses were Canada, England, Venezuela and the USA.[3] (See Appendix III.)

Other sources of professional help noted in more than five per cent of responses, primarily among poverty populations, included employers, political leaders and instructors.

Desired helping qualities and modes of helping

What did our subjects desire in their helpers? In both 1997 and 1989, the two paramount qualities reported by our advantaged and non-advantaged subjects were 'personal qualities' (being a good listener, being trustworthy and being honest) and 'knowledge' (having experience or being sufficiently similar to subjects to make it possible to understand their concerns. 'Personal attributes' were reported more frequently in 1997 (represented in 42 per cent of advantaged and 43 per cent of non-advantaged responses as compared with 38 per cent of 1989 reports). 'Knowledge', however, was reported less frequently (from 50 per cent of 1989 reports to 32–33 per cent of 1997 reports).

When asked what they most wanted helpers to do, the choice paramount to all subject groups was to 'counsel' them, that is, direct, advise and share information and 'attend' to them, that is, comfort or give reassurance. These findings are not surprising in light of research literature regarding helping which suggests that, unless problems are seriously incapacitating to individuals, the functions sought are information, problem-definition and instrumental assistance. The fact that, while desire to be counselled decreased from 1989 to 1997, desire to be attended to increased in the same period of time (see Appendix IV), however, suggests that the level of subject distress is increasing (Wills 1983: 113). This is an important consideration for help-providers. We will discuss this issue further in Chapter 17.

SUMMARY AND CONCLUSIONS

Our composite picture of the coping strategies and choices of helpers suggests, at a macro level, many similarities regardless of socio-economic status or gender that match in many ways what we found in our previous study of adolescents (Gibson-Cline *et al.* 1996). The most frequently reported problems of our youth subjects were related to 'schooling' and 'identity and self-concept', a finding that is predictable from a developmental point of view and consistent with the view that argues that youth is a stage in which young people have given up rebellion and are preparing to take on the tasks of adulthood. Our subjects did not report concerns related to problems we know that do exist, including AIDS, drug use and unwanted pregnancy. The primary coping strategy was 'individual-problem-solving' followed by 'resignation and disengagement'; the primary helper was a personal friend.

At a micro level, both our 1997 and 1989 multinational findings demonstrated that our subjects' concerns varied in some important respects. A number of reported problems vary quantitatively with SES as well as with gender. When we consider schooling problems, we find that males – and advantaged subjects – have the highest percentage of problems, and that females – and poverty subjects – have the highest percentage of family problems. When our authors compared the written responses contained in their nationality studies with those from other countries, they found qualitative variation in subjects' responses as well. For example, while the young Indian woman in Mumbai (Chapter 9) and her American counterpart in

Pittsburgh, USA (Chapter 13) both worried about their impending marriages, the *foci* of their concerns (parental choice of a husband for the Indian woman and combining marriage and a career for the latter) were quite different.

A finding that concerns us greatly is the lack of reported problems regarding existing and very serious problems affecting youth today: AIDS and drug and alcohol abuse. It may be that most youth are uncomfortable describing these problems in the format of an open-ended questionnaire, even if they are very much concerned. Maccarelli's (1994) comparison of open-ended questionnaire formats and checklists demonstrated that problems of a personal nature are far more likely to be elicited by checklists in which problems than are of concern are checked off rather than described in subjects' own words, as required in our study. However, the lack of reported concerns regarding AIDS and drugs may also be due to another finding that concerns us regarding coping by 'resignation' and 'disengagement' and is described in the next paragraphs.

Our young subjects tended to cope in ways that did not necessarily solve their reported problems. For our advantaged and non-advantaged subjects, approximately 20 per cent of 1997 coping reports and 16 per cent of 1989 reports described coping by 'trying harder', which systems theory suggests may actually lead in some cases to increasing of the problem (see p. 24). By contrast, less than five per cent of poverty reports suggested 'trying harder'. At the same time, advantaged and non-advantaged subjects also tended either to resign themselves to their fates and give up, or disengage themselves physically or psychologically from the situation. Descriptions of the coping of our subjects differ from those of earlier studies of coping (Pearlin and Schooler 1978, Hallahan and Moos 1987, Billings and Moos 1981) that suggested that impoverished populations tend to cope more 'passively' than more advantaged groups. (Again, less than 5 per cent of poverty reports were devoted to 'resignation' or 'disengagement'. If we assume that 'resignation' and 'disengagement' are passive in the sense that they do nothing to solve the stated problems of our subjects, it was the advantaged population rather than the impoverished group that appeared to cope most passively. If, on the other hand, we consider this behaviour to be 'maladaptive', it is alarming that it has increased from 1989 to 1997 for all SES groups. There is, however, another interpretation.)

While 'resignation' and 'disengagement' can be considered 'non-goal-oriented' if we assume that our subjects' goal was to solve the problem they reported, it may also be that our subjects had decided correctly that it would not be productive for them to use all their energies to try solving a problem that was impossible for them to solve, no matter how they tried. The authors of Chapter 8, Maria Dikaiou and Mika Haritos-Fatouras, attempt to explain the resignation and disengagement of their Greek subjects, by pointing out that, from the social systems perspective, coping is a process rather than an outcome. In this sense, 'coping' refers to all efforts expended to manage a stressor (see Lazarus and Folkman 1984). In the case of their Greek subjects, Dikaiou and Haritos-Fatouras examined their written responses and noted that resignation and disengagement were usually reported in cases in which subjects were facing larger social problems which they, personally, did not have the ability to surmount. In this case, the authors suggested that resignation and disengagement were productive in the sense that they reduced stress. It cannot be considered productive, however, to resign oneself to problems such as AIDS and drug use, whether or not it reduces stress and the possibility that our subjects might be using these coping strategies for that purpose is alarming!

Examination by our researchers of other of their subjects' written responses in other countries of the study suggests that young people tend to resign themselves to their fate or disengage themselves physically or psychologically from the situation when they feel it impossible to solve their problems. In this sense, we feel that, for some problems and some situations, it may appear to be a more positive decision for some subjects to give up trying and get on with their lives rather than to continue using all their resources to avail. This interpretation, however suggests three alarming possibilities:

1 The subjects who most frequently report that they resign themselves or disengage from the situation are advantaged. This group usually has goals that would have been attainable had they used different coping strategies! While this suggests that these subjects could be helped by counselling assistance that teaches them how to direct their actions, very few advantaged subjects sought professionals equipped to help them.
2 Impoverished youth deal with urgent and immediate problems which often are related to larger societal problems beyond their control. For them to solve these problems a different response is required than for advantaged subjects. The author of the poverty chapter (Chapter 16), Elizabete Pereira, suggests counselling designed to help poverty youth help themselves by working to change their situations. Unfortunately, like their advantaged peers, few poverty subjects sought any help from professional counsellors.
3 Youth of all socio-economic backgrounds, who we know to have strong reason to worry about AIDS and drugs, are using ineffective coping strategies to deal with a very serious problem and are not seeking professional help to deal with them.

What do these possibilities suggest for the counselling process? Our findings regarding coping by resignation or disengagement strongly suggest the importance of helping young people 'empower' themselves to respond more effectively to their problems, as suggested by the authors of Chapter 7, Kevin Feaviour and David Acres. (See pp. 28–30.)

It is also clear that there is need to create counselling processes that deal with differing needs of subjects. This need becomes greater when we realize that the most frequent individual to whom youth of all SES groups and both genders now go for help is a close friend, usually a same-aged peer from the same background as our subjects and with resources for problem-solving similar to their own. Today, family members, to whom most youth turned to in previous generations, no longer appear to their children as useful sources of help whether they need information, advice, support or comfort.

One population included amongst the non-advantaged groups in this chapter is the Ethiopian immigrant population described in Chapter 15, 'Immigrant youth'. With increasing migrations across the world's surface, special attention will be needed to help new immigrant populations. These populations, like our Ethiopian immigrants, face, in addition to concerns similar to other non-advantaged and poverty groups, some very specific worries related to feelings of discrimination, need to adapt quickly to new cultures in the face of loss of their own cultural support systems and enormous practical concerns such as immediate need for education and mastery of a new language. As author Rachel Erhard pointed out, immigrant concerns require adaptation of some counselling approaches to deal simultaneously with enormous adjustment problems and practical issues. Counsellors need to be prepared to supply far more social-emotional support at each step of the adjustment process. (See pp. 28–31.)

The implications of these findings and those of the nationality and special populations in our study are the basis for Chapter 17, 'Conclusions and implications for theory and practice'.

Notes

1 The categories of employment and unemployment are listed in the class, 'interpersonal issues', which includes immediate concerns associated with working and interacting with others on a day-to-day basis.
2 Gender results were not determined for 1989 data for all groups because of some low sample sizes.
3 Because of small sizes of some of our subject groups and to keep our reliability as high as possible, we did not record responses that represented less than 5 percent of responses.

References

Basow, A. (1992) *Gender: Stereotypes and Roles* (3rd edn) Pacific Grove, Calif.: Brooks/Coles.

Billings A. and Moos H. (1981) 'The role of coping responses and social resources in alternating the stress of life events', *Journal of Behavioural Medicine* 4: 139–57.

Gibson-Cline, J. *et al.* (1996) 'The multinational study', in *Adolescence from Crisis to Coping*, London: Routledge 27–42.

Gilligan, C., Lyons, C. and Hammer, T. (eds) (1990) *Making Connections: The Relational Worlds of Adolescent Girls at Emma Willard School*, Cambridge, Mass.: Harvard University Press.

Gilligan, C., Ward, J. and Taylor, J. (eds) (1988). *Mapping the Moral Domain*, Cambridge, Mass.: Harvard University Press.

Gomes, J. (1997) 'Impoverished urban youth: their school and employment concerns', *Revista Brasileiro de Educação* 52 (4): 53–61, in Portuguese.

Hallahan C. and Moos R. (1987) 'Personal and contextual determinants of coping strategies', *Journal of Personality and Social Psychology* 52: 946–55.

Keniston, K. (1972) 'Youth: a "new" stage of life', *American Scholar*: 109–27.

Lazarus, R. and Folkman, S. (1984) 'Coping and adaptation', in Gentry, W. (ed.), *Handbook of Behavioral Medicine*, New York: Guilford, 44–68.

Maccarelli, L. (1994) *Problems Reported by Adolescents: A Comparison of Data Collection Methods*, unpublished Master's thesis, University of Pittsburgh.

Nadler, A., Maler, S. and Friedman, A. (1984) 'Effects of helper's sex, subjects' androgyny, and self-evaluation on males' and females' willingness to seek and receive help', *Sex Roles* 10: 327–39.

Nidelhoff, M. (1984) *A School for the People,* São Paulo: Brasiliense, in Portuguese.

Pearlin L. and Schooler C. (1978) 'The structure of coping', *Journal of Health and Social Behavior* 19: 221.

Perlman, D. (24 November 1999) 'AIDS toll higher than higher than ever', *San Francisco Chronicle* A1, A15.

Watzlawick, P., Weakland, J. and Finch, R. (1973) *Change*, Palo Alto, Calif.: Change.

Wills, T. (1983) 'Social comparison in coping and help-seeking', in DePaulo, B., Nadler, A. and Fisher, J., *New Directions in Helping, Vol. II: Help-Seeking*, New York: Academic Press: 109–41.

Yunex, J. (1982) *The Poor, the Young and the Market-Place*, Rio de Janeiro: Zahar, in Portuguese.

Part III

National studies of advantaged and non-advantaged youth

> 'I have a 'split-level' dream: Being a good actress and having my own family at the same time.'

Part III takes us to Brazil, Canada, China, England, Greece, India, Israel, Japan, Russia, Continental USA, and Venezuela to examine advantaged and non-advantaged youth and their coping in the separate nations of our study.

The authors of Chapters 4–14 relate highlights of their findings to social, political, educational and economic conditions particular to their homelands, compare them to the composite picture given in Chapter 3 and discuss implications for developing helping strategies in their own countries. Readers may refer to Appendix III Tables A and B for full statistical details of all findings.

4 Brazil

University and college students in Campinas

Elisabete Monteiro de Aguiar Pereira, State University of Campinas

INTRODUCTION

Brazil, the fifth largest country in the world, occupies half of South America. Most of its inhabitants live in its eastern, mostly tropical, section. Although the 1996 census listed its population as 158.6 million, the population growth rate has been declining in recent years and is projected to create a population drop by the year 2000. Brazil is a very young country,

'What animates me most . . . is the possibility of being an effective, financially and professionally independent woman. Unfortunately there are very few opportunities for success!'

Paula, an education student at the State University of Campinas; father: agricultural engineer; mother: history teacher.

'In ten years, I think that I will be working at a research institute where I can have control of my time. I don't know if I will be married or not. I see myself working a lot and studying. I think of having the chance to choose what gives me pleasure. I want to do something significant, but I would not like my work to suffocate me. I want to have a life balanced between work and pleasure. What animates me most when I think about the future is the possibility of being an effective, financially and professionally independent woman. Everything will depend on what I can accomplish through my work.

What worries me most is that, unfortunately, there are very few opportunities for success! I am always thinking which are the best ways to proceed. I think I must invest a lot in myself and become the best person I can. I must also invest in my relationships with friends.

The person whom I would seek to help me would be my mother. She knows how to talk to me and is the person who knows me best. She is educated and wise . . . I talk with her about job perspectives. She understands our economic situation because she reads a lot. I want her to continue talking and motivating me.'

with more than half its population 29 years of age or younger and an average age of only 23 years (UNESCO Statistical Yearbook for Latin America and the Caribbean 1998). At the same time, it is expected to contain the world's fifth largest contingent of people over 60 years old in twenty-five years time (Barros and Mendonca 1996).

Brazilians face many problems in their country. Although economic analyses point to Brazil's growth and production, inflation has been seriously eroding incomes for many years, with the poor affected most strongly. Although inflation decreased in the 1990s, other economic problems remain. The 1990s will probably be remembered for governmental retreat from social issues, increase of privatisation, disarray in the labour market and an increase of 3.3 million people in the unemployment ranks (Toledo 1997). By 1999, unemployment had already reached approximately 7 per cent of males and 8 per cent of females in the working population over 15 years of age (IBGE 1999). For the past five years, it has been accompanied by increased social instability and urban violence. This has led to calls for fair land distribution, improved education, better housing and health services, higher wages and more and better employment opportunities. On a more positive note, a government economic stabilisation programme begun in 1994 is beginning to reduce the situation sufficiently that the country can begin preparing for the global economic and information technology demands. In the 1990s, these new issues occupied the agendas of all economical, political, social and educational endeavours.

Brazil's educational system also has problems. Fifteen per cent of Brazilians are non-literate, a high figure compared to the world average (IBGE 1998). Because of local inefficiencies and insufficient allocation of funds for basic education in many parts of the country, school 'dropping out' and poor performance in primary schools are high. Not surprisingly, most of those who remain non-literate are the poor. To begin remedying this problem, the present government has given basic education top priority. Since 1997, states and municipalities have been required to allocate 15 per cent of their annual revenue for basic education. Annual spending on basic education is expected to rise from US$1.2 billion per year to some US$8.8 billion (CBMM 1998: 128).

Brazilian family life

The Brazilian family plays a far more important role in the lives of its members than does the family in virtually any Western country. The most important family relationship is between mothers and children, with mothers taking on responsibility for all family matters and fathers usually somewhat distant. Brazilian youth usually remain home until they marry, at which time the new married couples live close to their relatives. Before and after marriage, immediate and extended family members maintain responsiblity for helping when needed.

Brazilian youth

Regardless of close family ties, Brazilian youth have a history of upsetting the older generation. In the 1950s, older adult concern was focused on the contentious music, art and life style of this age group; a decade later it moved to the political activism of university students (Ianni 1968). Since the 1970s, youth have become the visible image of Brazil's crises (Forrachi 1972) with the focus turning to their activities leading to drug use, crime, violence, social exploration, AIDS, etc. At the same time, Brazilian higher education institutions, together with other political, government and non-government institutions began recognizing youth as victims rather than as perpetrators of societal ills, finally changing the focus to needed specialized social services. Today youth are viewed as a national group needing help!

At the same time that some Brazilians perceive youth as persons in need of assistance, however, other groups are exploiting them. The media, recognizing the potential use of youth as consumers in the Brazilian marketplace, have enticed this age group via TV, magazines and even newspapers designed specifically for them. Today, advertisements daily feature cultural and musical programmes, fashion, lifestyle, leisure time and sports, all designed to reach the pocketbooks of a beautified Brazilian youth. This new approach, coupled with worries about Brazilian drug use, crime, violence and social exploration, has left the Brazilian public with a confusing and contradictory portrait of youth, which we intend to clarify in our study.

The importance of our study

Few studies focus on youth's perceptions of their problematic situations or how they live. In the Brazilian literature, very little work is related to youths' views of their experiences in attempting to resolve their problems. Although this study was created by academic researchers, it has the objective of organising knowledge useful to all involved people – parents, educators, doctors, psychologists, sociologists, etc. Its value is in leaving the perception of 'youth as a social problem' rather than considering this age group as what they are: capable of proposing action, formulating solutions, sustaining dialogues with other social actors and contributing to the solution of social problems. The greatest importance of our work lies in its attempts to recover human problems from the actor's perspective.

OUR STUDY AND ITS METHODOLOGY

The Brazil study asked advantaged and non-advantaged youth the problems that concern them, the coping strategies they use and the types of helpers they seek, comparing their answers by SES group and gender within this study and by SES group and gender with their counterparts in the multi-national study.

Subjects

Subjects in the 1997 survey included 247 young peoples aged 18–20 years, including seventy-one males and fifty-five females from 'advantaged' SES levels and sixty-one males and sixty-three females from 'non-advantaged' backgrounds. The 1989 survey included an additional fifty-three advantaged subjects. Because of the small size of this sample, male and female responses were analysed as one group to compare with their 1997 counterparts.

Socio-economic status was determined by the Hutchinson Professional Categories Inventory which classifies seven levels of professions in relation to their social prestige and the financial condition of the family measured by the amount of minimum wages that compose the family income (Hutchinson 1960). Subjects surveyed in both 1997 and 1989 also met the requirements for advantaged and non-advantaged SES status as defined in Chapter 1 and used in all countries of the Multinational Study.

Advantaged subjects surveyed in 1997 were enrolled in day classes in engineering, biological sciences or economics at the State University of Campinas–UNICAMP with the majority having no outside employment and 22 per cent exercising some professional activity as trainees in their professional areas. Both parents possessed higher education and worked in professions as lawyers, system analysts, doctors, engineers, managers and university teachers. Family income was more than thirty times above the Brazilian minimum wage. Parental characteristics were described in Professional Categories I and II of the Hutchinson Inventory, with Professional Category I corresponding to professions of the highest social prestige, such as high political and administrative positions, proprietors of great companies and bankers; and Professional Category II to professionals, holders of positions of management or direction and proprietors of medium-size companies.

Non-advantaged subjects were enrolled in evening classes in education or mathematics at UNICAMP or in management or economics at the Catholic University of Campinas–PUCCAMP. Of these young adults, 50 per cent were employed outside of school as clerks, administrative assistants, primary teachers, salespersons or waiters. Their parents had obtained secondary educations and worked as mechanics, public functionaries, bank employees or metallurgists; mothers (30 per cent were housewives) often worked as dressmakers, public employees or hairdressers. Characteristics of these parents were described in Professional Categories III and IV as proprietors of small companies, in lower positions of supervision or inspection, merchants, sales persons and with family incomes which were below thirty minimum wages.

A third socio-economic group of surveyed Brazilian young people from impoverished backgrounds as defined in Chapter 1, are described in Chapter 16.

Procedure

Surveys were conducted in Campinas, a city in the south-east state of São Paolo known for its industrial, commercial and cultural activities and for its inhabitants having come together from many parts of the country. The open-ended survey questionnaire was translated into Portuguese and administered in university classrooms by the standardized procedure described in Chapter 1 with the exception that an additional question regarding paid professional activity of the subjects was added.

Procedures used to administer the survey and code the results also matched those of the multinational study and are described in Chapter 1. Appendix II details the reliability of the coding of data. The subjects appeared interested in the survey and motivated to answer the questions.

HIGHLIGHTS OF FINDINGS

The following section outlines highlights of the findings of the Brazil study. Appendix III Tables A and B provide full details of statistical results.

Concerns

Analysis of the Brazilian data showed far more similarities to that of subject samples from other countries than it did differences. What is described below applies primarily to the specific Brazilian context.

Interpersonal interactions and schooling

The concerns of Brazilian young people, regardless of SES or gender, were described most frequently as issues related to interpersonal interactions, schooling and material desires. This matched the three most common concerns of Brazilian youth surveyed in 1989. In addition, a high percentage of additional worries among non-advantaged males concerning identity and altruism caused schooling to fall to fifth place.

Interpersonal interaction concerns (with advantaged and females reporting the highest percentage of responses) ranging from 18–32 per cent of reported problems) were usually related to employment outside of school and tied to the search for current jobs as well as entry into the professional marketplace (as in having successful interviews). Some typical worries were:

> 'lack of available jobs. The labour market isn't large enough to accommodate all the workers who graduate from university.'
>
> 'the kind of employment I will be able to obtain in the future [after finishing school], if I will be successful professionally, intellectually, financially and personally.'

Schooling concerns ranged from 10 per cent to 34 per cent of reported concerns, with advantaged subjects reporting a higher percentage of problems than non-advantaged (17 per cent as opposed to 34 per cent), as shown in the multinational SES trend. The highest percentage (34 per cent) was reported by advantaged males. Many school-related concerns, often worded in terms of anxieties about achievement, were directly tied to employment worries, as suggested earlier by Mercuri (1994) in a study of Brazilian university students.

> 'I am afraid of not doing well in college, graduating and not being able to find a job.'

Reports of material desires (ranging from 12 per cent of reported concerns of advantaged males and females and 21 per cent of their non-advantaged peers) usually specified money needs, and again, often were tied to payment of tuition or other expenses related to education.

> 'I want to buy things (I need) . . . and I can't.'
>
> 'The loss of my job would create a financial crisis for me.'

These results point to a complex relationship between employment, finances and schooling in the lives of Brazilian youth. Yunex (1982) and Nidelhoff (1984) pointed out that, although schooling is needed to provide non-advantaged people the tools to increase their social status and better their lives, adequate financial resources are also required. The fact that advantaged subjects were more worried about schooling than non-advantaged when both groups were composed of students gives credence to this argument. Gomes (1997) suggests that the difference is caused by family experiences and attitudes: students from advantaged families already had finances necessary to meet their goals and families who could teach them what to do, leaving them to concentrate on the school learning. Non-advantaged students, by contrast, not only needed financial support but learned from their parents how many obstacles stood in their way before they could begin to learn.

In the Brazil study, as in all of the national studies of our multinational research, educational level of parents decreases with SES from advantaged to non-advantaged (and, as shown in Chapter 16, to poverty). At the same time, the need to work in order to obtain financial resources increases, making work of more immediate importance. This might explain not only why non-advantaged subjects concentrated on finding financial resources through employment, but also why 1997 non-advantaged males worried so much about their personal identities and self-concepts as compared with subjects from other countries. (See Appendix III Table A2.)

Approximately half of our non-advantaged Brazilian subjects worked by day in order to attend school at night. Even though they recognize the importance of schooling, they see evidence all around them that schooling might not lead them to better lives:

> 'When a female graduates, she faces countless difficulties obtaining employment because there are so many professionals already available in the market place and new graduates have the least experience.'

By contrast, their advantaged peers have parents who are able to provide financial support and who demonstrate through their own experience that education provides the tools to better lifestyles. With fewer financial burdens, the greatest pressures often come from the teaching/learning process:

> 'Bad quality of teaching. The teachers know their subject areas, but they don't have the skill to develop them.'
>
> 'I (have trouble) understanding everything that is said by the teachers.'

Schooling represents more than the opportunity to qualify for better employment: it also provides social experience important for the development of self-identity. While our non-advantaged subjects worried about 'improving their lives' and 'acquiring financial stability', and had chosen to continue schooling as their method of reaching this goal, schooling represented far more for these subjects. As Marques suggested (1997: 67), 'improving life' and 'acquiring financial stability' means for the non-advantaged establishing positive identities by creating better ways of life than they had had growing up

Another explanation given by Abramo (1997) suggests that the difficult search by these youth to find better situations in life than their parents attained is related to a complex net of meanings built into the culture. Our non-advantaged males were concerned with their own expectations of self in attaining adult status, rather than defining themselves in terms of the attributions given them within their families. Unfortunately, according to our subjects, these pressures sometimes resulted in self-abuse (self-inflicted use of alcohol, drugs, etc.), leading to further identity worries.

Coping strategies

Our young subjects were unanimous in their desire to solve their problems by themselves (55–57 per cent of reported coping strategies of advantaged subjects and 55–61 per cent of non-advantaged), similar to their 1989 peers and also to the multinational subjects surveyed in 1997. The primary individual coping strategies were planning and trying harder.

Our 1997 subjects described disengaging themselves from the situation or resigning themselves to it. These two coping strategies together represent 20 per cent of reported responses for advantaged subjects and 20 per cent for non-advantaged subjects, making the two together second in frequency only to individual problem-solving. Similar findings were reported by our 1989 Brazilian sample and the 1997 multinational study as well. We might suppose this high percentage of responses indicates that Brazilian youth and their peers frequently act in counter-productive ways. Jeanter (1979) argued, however, that when individuals feel fragile in the face of their difficulties, they often try to assure their identity either through resigning themselves or ignoring their external adversities. In this case, paradoxically, while the purpose of their behaviour is to maintain their self-images, they may well be doing so to the detriment of creating positive change. We suspect that our subjects want to decide their destinies for themselves and, when they assume that adversities are superior to their forces, attempt to preserve their individuality by simply resigning themselves or disengaging from the entire situation.

Another possible explanation, according to Stirner (1974: 16), is that youth, unlike their younger adolescent peers, tend more to accept the world as it is, but, at the same time, act more frequently in their own interests. Adults, Stirner says, more often than adolescents make themselves the 'centre of the world', worrying less about the homeland, God, etc. and more about their own personal and material interests, putting themselves foremost. Marx (reported in Souza, 1993: 52) suggested further that it is during 'youth-hood' that young people develop consciences, through which they develop personal and global interests. The antagonistic postures represented by these two views of adult thinking seem to be described by many of our youth reports:

> 'My worries sometimes confuse me and keep me from deciding how to solve (my problem). But finally, I face (them) even if what I do is to postpone action eternally.'
>
> 'When I see youth my age stealing garbage because they are hungry – or drugging themselves so as not to feel the hunger, I despair. But I don't do anything, because I am afraid of violence.'
>
> 'I accept my condition now, but I hope in the future it will change.'

In the case of our Brazilian subjects, we think it possible that they are demonstrating the first steps of a long learning process concerning the role that democratic participation and collective struggles might play in creating change. We believe this is taking place at the same time that they become discouraged by the apparent inability of these approaches to create change in their country. This explanation justifies both their decisions to solve their problems themselves and, at the same time, resign themselves or disengage from the situation completely, or do nothing at all about them. In fact, although many subjects discussed participating with others to solve social ills, they doubted the ability to do so via Brazilian democratic institutions:

> 'The politicians always continue to be the same ones, only thinking about their own benefits and they forget about the workers.'

Although Brazil is known as a Catholic religious country, our subjects did not look to a 'superior being' to solve their problems.

Helpers and their characteristics

In a study of university students, Pachane (1998) found that students' personal growth was directly related to their personal relationships with friends and, to lesser extents, by their relationships with parents, other family members, teachers and counsellors. The responses of our 1997 and 1989 Brazilian subjects as well as their 1997 multinational peers supported this conclusion. The helpers sought by our subjects were, first and foremost, their friends. Because our subjects often lived far away from the universities they were attending at the time of our study, their closest friends, by and large, were their fellow students. Reasons given included personal attributes such as trustworthiness and loyalty, being good listeners, approachability; power to change problematic situations (not of importance to advantaged females); and concern. Knowledge, expressed as helpers' life experience and similarity of helpers' and subjects' problems, was important as well, as was concern, understanding and caring. All of these characteristics were important also in the 1989 Brazilian and 1997 multinational studies.

> 'I [call on] my friends because [we] know a lot about each other.'
>
> 'They have my confidence and they are always disposed to help me.'
>
> 'The [helpers I choose] are honest and [provide me with a] deep friendship.'

Parents were also often desired as helpers, second only to friends, with males and non-advantaged females preferring their same gender parent. The reasons usually given were their reinforcement of subjects' independence and self confidence, as well as the support they provided. Interestingly, males reported seeking parents for help more frequently than females, perhaps because many females relied on their fiancés. This choice also was true for our impoverished sample (see Appendix III Table A).

> 'My parents and my friends because they want to help and they give me comfort.'

What did our subjects want their helpers to do? First and foremost, subjects wanted helpers to counsel them, that is, to give advice or to help them learn how to solve their problems. They also wanted their helpers to be attentive, paying attention, comforting them, listening to what they had to say.

> '[I want] my friends and teachers to help me. They recognize what I can do and increase my self-esteem.'
>
> 'My friends' support makes me feel more capable of great accomplishments.'
>
> 'When I talk with [my] friends, they help me believe much more in what I am.'

Some subjects wanted helpers who were powerful. Those who made this choice had broad concerns that they could not resolve themselves and they wanted action to be taken to solve the problem:

> 'I would go to government [officials]. Only they have the power to change the actual Brazilian picture.'
>
> 'The people [I would go to] have money, prestige and power to do some thing.'

All of these responses are similar to those found in our 1989 survey and in the 1997 multinational study as well.

Our subjects did not choose counsellors as helpers. Since the universities they were attending did not provide counselling services, we cannot say how they might have responded if counsellors were available on campus.

CONCLUSIONS AND IMPLICATIONS FOR COUNSELLING

This study confirms others about the 'generation of the nineties' in which youth are considered indifferent to collective concerns and political commitments, individualist and great consumers. Abramo (1997) stated that this age group has no interest whatsoever in trying to change their culture for the better as did their predecessors in the 1960s. Today's youth, unlike those of the 1960s, however, see human and social problems in a more individualistic and pragmatic way.

The results of our surveys, conducted in 1989 and 1997, portray a strong link between individual and work. One of our subjects' major concerns was with their entry into the labour market and their concern in arranging employment now and for the future. For these young people, this meant preparing for desired employment through schooling. Our subjects thought of their work as a means of constructing positive self-identities, although they did not appear ready yet to define themselves in terms of conscience and social actions.

In Brazil, the primary difficulty for youth in beginning and maintaining independent lifestyles is lack of employment and placement in the labour market requiring youth to prolong living within their parental family homes. The fact that educational matters appear be a major source of worry for advantaged male subjects (in this research, these all are university students), indicates the importance of developing guidance counselling in institutions of higher education. We believe that it is the lack of counselling in higher education that leaves university students alone to solve their problems or sends them to friends who might not be sufficiently knowledgeable to help.

In relation to coping strategies, we find that most subjects try to solve them alone or go to with friends for help. Examination of both their personal problems and coping methods showed that they tended to respond most actively to problems related to financial and personal pressures, such as personal limits, conflicts and crises. By contrast, they tended to respond to societal issues such as the economic situation in Brazil with escape strategies or resignation. This may mean that they felt capable of fighting to solve their problems only if they were competent to do so and not when problems were realistically beyond their control.

Brazilian youth already face wide societal problems, however. We feel it is unfortunate that they so often view the solution to social problems as the purview of politicians and external to themselves. While our subjects appeared not to realize their own capabilities to act collectively in solving common problems, it is of a positive note that they revealed negative images and perspectives of politicians and of politics, and appeared morally and ethically to express revolt at corruption and the lack of attention to social matters by public men and public institutions.

The results of this study suggest the importance of counselling in Brazil. Young people need and search for the right persons to help them. They seek helpers who will listen to them, advise them and support the directions they take in specific situations as well as in the ways they build their self-images. It is our belief that, so long as financial and other societal ills continue to affect Brazilian life adversely, the appropriate role for youth should be to learn the causes of these problems and to help create positive change. It follows that the appropriate role of the counsellor is to help youth learn what to do in order to build strong personalities sufficient to deal with all important problems, not just those that affect their own immediate lives. It follows that, whatever the national, societal or socio-economic problems of youth, the most important role of the counsellor is to help them become better human beings. (See pp. 25–31 for suggested approaches to helping.)

Note

1 Thanks to Professor Isaura Roche Figueirdo Guimaraes for her contributions in collecting and coding the data for this study. Maria Angélica C. M. Miranda

contributed to the 1997 survey research as an assistant researcher with the financial support from PIBIC–CNPQ–UNICAMP.

References

Abramo, H. (1997) 'Considerations about the social theme of youth in Brazil', in *Brasil. Revista Brasileira de Educação*, ANPED 6: 25–36, in Portuguese.

Adamo, F. *et al.* (1987) *Youth: Work, Health and Education*, Rio de Janeiro: Forense Universitária, in Portuguese.

Barros, R. and Mendonça, R. (1996) *The Evolution of Welfare and Inequality in Brazil since 1960*, Washington, D.C.: World Bank.

CBMM (1998) *Guide to the Brazilian Economy*, Fundation Institute of Economic Research (FIPE), Sao Paulo: Government of Brazil, in Portuguese.

Chiesi, A. & Martinelli, A. (1997) 'Work as an option and opportunity', *Revista Brasileira de Educação*, ANPED 6: 110–25 in Portuguese.

Folgueiras, D.and Morelli, S. (1985) 'Assessing student problems', *Ciência e Cultura* 37, 7 SPBC in Portuguese.

Foraccchi, M. (1972) *Youth in Modern Society*, São Paulo: Pioneira, in Portuguese.

Gomes, J. (1997) 'Urban poor youth: their school and employment concerns', *Revista Brasileira de Educação* 52 (4): 53–61, in Portuguese.

Hutchinson, B. (1960) *Mobility and Work*.: Rio de Janeiro: MEC–CBPE, in Portuguese.

Ianni, O. (1968) *Radical Youth*, Rio de Janeiro: Zahar, in Portuguese.

IBGE (1998) *Brazilian Institute of Geography and Statistics Yearbook: 1998*, Brazilia: Government of Brazil.

IBGE (1999) *Brazilian Institute of Geography and Statistics Yearbook*, Brazilia: Government of Brazil.

Jeanter, M. (1979) 'Youth and school', in Abranches, S. (ed.), *Social Politics and the Fight against Poverty*, Rio de Janeiro: Zahar, in Portuguese.

Jeanet, T. (1986) *The Social Individual*, São Paulo: Vértice, in Portuguese.

Marques, M. (1997) 'Night school and youth', *Revista Brasileira de Educação*, Special Edition 6: 63–76, in Portuguese.

Martins, H. (1997) 'Youth in the market place', *Revista Brasileira de Educação*, Special Edition 6: 96–108, in Portuguese.

Mercuri, H. (1994) 'The conditions of study: the words of students and teachers', *Proposições* 5, 1, Campinas: F. E. Unicamp, in Portuguese.

Nidelhoff, M. (1984) *A School for the People*, São Paulo, Brasiliense, in Portuguese.

Olievera, C. and Mattoso, J. (1996) *Crisis and Work in Brazil: Contemporary Problem or a Return to the Past?* São Paulo: Scritta, in Portuguese.

Pachane, G. (1998) *Experiencing University Life*, Dissertação de Mestrado, F. E. Unicamp, in Portuguese.

Pais, J. (1993) *The Youth Culture*, Lisboa: Imprensa Nacional, in Portuguese.

Souza, J. (1993) *Individuality in a Critical Position*, Campinas: Editora da Unicamp, in Portuguese.

Stirner, M. (1974) *The False Principles of our Education System: A Criticism*, Paris: Aubier Montagne, in French.

Toledo, L. (1997) 'Short cuts: a history of youth and at-risk conduct', *Revista Brasileira de Educação* 5, set/out, 209–22, in Portuguese.

UNESCO Statistical Yearbook for Latin America and the Caribbean (1998) *Statistical Yearbook for Latin America and the Caribbean*, Santiago: UNESCO.

Yunex, J. (1982) *The Poor, the Young and the Market place*, Rio de Janeiro: Zahar, in Portuguese.

5 Canada

18-year-old youth in their last year of a Vancouver high school

Louise Martinson, Brenda J. Shaw and William A. Borgen, University of British Colombia

'It doesn't really matter . . .'

'It doesn't really matter to me what I'm doing or where I am. Just as long as I'm happy for what it is. I don't know that I can say right now whether I really want to do {anything} ten years from now. Ten years down the road, I could be interested in something completely different...I don't want to be dependent on anybody else but myself . . . I hate depending on my parents for money and I don't have a job right now. It's frustrating thinking how are you going to do this and how are you going to pay for that . . . to think a university education is supposed to be for everybody, but you're restricted so much by these huge tuitions and grade point averages . . . And you can't get a good job without having some kind of post-secondary school . . . I've got to get things done right away and smarten up . . . Take control in whatever I am going to be doing.' (a female student)

'Ten years from now? I guess I want to be in technology, manufacturing. I did work experience in it and {it was} interesting. I just liked the big machines and all the cool technology . . . That's the way it seems to be going. I like computers but I don't like to be on {them} eight, ten hours at a time. I know I don't want to be flipping burgers . . . I'd like to own a house . . . Fix {it} up and buy things for it. My own car in my own driveway . . .

What worries me? That I know I won't be able to buy a house. I'm not too worried about a job because I know it's out there somewhere and I know if I worked hard I could do it.' (a male student)

INTRODUCTION

Canada and its people

Canada, a growing nation of 30 million people, achieved nationhood only 130 years ago. Geographically the largest country in the world, she encompasses a variety of climatic zones from rain-forest to semi-desert, and regions from mountains to prairies to maritime shores. Her boundaries are defined by the Atlantic Ocean on the east, the Pacific Ocean on the west and the Arctic Ocean in the north. Canada's only two land borders are with the USA; the major border to the south runs the width of the country, while a smaller border to the northwest flanks the State of Alaska.

With a relatively small number of people spread over a large and varied landmass, Canada has always relied on having its diverse populations coexist in a way that has allowed them to survive as one nation. Historically, this began with the Aboriginal (First Nations) peoples, the English, and the French. Although early immigrants to Canada came predominantly from European countries, today a growing immigrant population from more that twenty-five different countries stream into Canada, with over one-half coming from Asia and Southeast Asia. These immigrant populations tend to settle in urban centres.

Over twenty years ago, Canada began a policy of multiculturalism which recognized the over 100 different ethnic and cultural groups within its borders. These groups were encouraged to maintain their cultural identity, form communities, and share their values with other Canadians. With this policy, Canada became a country where diversity is not only permitted but encouraged.

While many Canadians speak other languages, English and French are the official languages, reflecting the origins of Canada's European settlement history. With Canada's now diverse ethnicity, a diverse religious population also exists. Christian denominations of Catholicism and Protestantism still predominate, but they coexist with Eastern non-Christian religions, such as Buddhism, Hinduism, Islam and Judaism.

Canada is an industrialized nation with a relatively high standard of living. About 70 per cent of men and 55 per cent of women work, earning annual family incomes averaging $55,000, and over one-half of Canadians live in a home that they own. Unemployment rates for men and women are relatively high at 9 per cent, with 15–24 year olds having the highest unemployment (17 per cent). Literacy rates are also high, over 90 per cent across the country, with more than one-half of Canadians having some post-secondary education, ranging from trades and diplomas to university degrees. This is not surprising in a country where high technology has been incorporated into many industries and where an increasingly well-educated workforce is required. While over 80 per cent of post-secondary schooling costs are covered by government funding, tuition fees are not. These rose 9 per cent in 1997. Canada is a democratic country with a politically involved population. Consistently over two-thirds of eligible voters vote during elections (Statistics Canada 1996–7).

Counselling services

Counselling services are available to youth in the schools and community through a variety of avenues. For students in secondary schools, counsellors are available at ratios as low as 1:300 and as high as 1:690 students. School counsellors deal with personal issues and developmental and mental health concerns, as well as academic and career planning. They also provide consultative support for educational programmes and guidance curriculum in the school dealing with social issues, such as substance abuse, sexually transmitted diseases and pregnancy, and myriad other personal management concerns, and may teach in classrooms. In some schools, they initiate and oversee peer helper programmes. School counsellors act as liaisons with post secondary institutions to facilitate student transition and with community agency support personnel. Community counselling and social service resources are also available to students, either directly or through their school counsellor at no cost.

THE STUDY AND ITS METHODOLOGY

The Canadian study surveyed male and female high school students, using the methodology and survey instrument described in Chapter 1. This chapter outlines the responses of the Canadian subjects, and includes comparisons with other advantaged subjects in the Multinational Study (Chapter 3) and of Canadian males and females.

Subjects

Our sample consisted of eighty-nine male and 126 female students between 18 and 20 years old with the majority of the students just over 18. These students were enrolled in their senior year of high school in a suburb of Vancouver. The reader needs to be aware, when comparing this national study with the larger multinational study, that the Canadian subjects constitute the only student sample in our multinational study enrolled in high school rather than in college or university. Our subjects are considered 'advantaged' as defined in Chapter 1, by virtue of their economic and educational status.

The community in which the survey was conducted has a new immigrant population from India, Pakistan, China and Japan. About one-quarter of the students surveyed reflected these ethnic origins. More than one-half of the sample had at least one parent who was not born in Canada, while approximately 20 per cent lived in homes where English was not the spoken language.

Procedure

The procedure used for administering the questionnaire and coding the results matched those of other studies constituting the Multinational Study as described in Chapter 1, with one exception: Although English was spoken as a Second Language for some students, all had sufficient written

English to write their final provincial government examination in English. Methodological limitations in this, as other national studies, as well as descriptions of the procedure used for coding of data. Appendix II provides details of coding reliability for all studies.

HIGHLIGHTS OF FINDINGS

Results are reported in terms of highlights of findings only. Full statistical results appear in Appendix III, Table A.

Problems

The two most frequently cited concerns reported by both Canadian and multinational advantaged samples were related to schooling and personal identity. Schooling and and identity issues combined accounted for almost 55 per cent of the responses of Canadian youth and 64 per cent of the responses of the multinational group.[1] (See Appendix IV.)

Schooling, particularly fear of failure, appeared more worrisome to males, although both genders reported academic worries (31 per cent of male responses as compared to 22 per cent for females).

> 'I am worried about graduating. I ask my teachers what my chances are.'
>
> 'I worry that maybe my marks aren't good enough, that I'm not ready to leave high school.'

Females in contrast to males, appeared more worried about high achievement:

> 'I have to get good grades in school to get accepted to a good university and to receive scholarships.'
>
> 'I don't enjoy school, it's frustrating and it's a lot of hard work, but I feel I have to do well – get good grades.'

The fact that males reported many more problems about schooling than females matches the multinational trend shown in Chapter 3.

Time pressures were also important for Canadians, just as they were for their advantaged multinational peers:

> 'My problem is trying to juggle school, a part-time job and schoolwork. There just doesn't seem to be enough hours.'

Contrary to the youth included in the multinational group, Canadians reported few concerns about being unable to learn. This may reflect the Canadian system of schooling which includes less streaming according to academic achievement than other countries where academic achievement defines the programme and students may enter into at an early stage of high school. Although our subjects were still in high school when the study was conducted, most were already aware of their acceptance or non-acceptance into higher education programmes.

Identity issues appeared more worrisome for females but were also a concern for males (33 per cent of females responses as compared to 22 per cent for males):

> 'How will my life be in the future? Will I have money? Where will I live?'
>
> 'I worry about succeeding in life, what career I will obtain and if I will be happy with my life and family.'

Both Canadian and multinational youth worried about interpersonal relationships. Canadian males reported these concerns, often related to employment or friendship issues, somewhat more than did females (19 per cent as compared to 14 per cent). Males were somewhat more worried about employment than friendship; the reverse was true for females. These results are similar to those obtained in our Multinational Sample (Chapter 3) as well as to our previous multinational study of adolescents (see Gibson-Cline *et al.* 1996: 29).

Males:

> '[I worry about] work, not getting treated fairly and not getting along with certain people.'
>
> 'If I don't get a job I can't pay off my loan which my Dad is paying off now until I do get one.'

Females:

> 'I am left out of my circle of friends often. They don't include me in their activities, if I phone them, they aren't home.'
>
> 'I don't have any close friends and this makes me feel lonely and depressed.'

Family issues were also important (although reported less frequently than the previously listed concerns) for both the multinational and Canadian samples:

> 'My stepfather is very strict, everything I do is wrong and whenever he's at home I feel so depressed.'
>
> 'My family has been fighting more in the last few weeks. More than ever before. I guess I'm worried that our family is falling apart.'

Females in the advantaged Canadian sample reported family concerns twice as frequently as males (12 per cent as compared with 6 per cent), in agreement with the findings of our team's previous adolescence study (Gibson-Cline *et al.* 1996). This result may be reflecting the importance of the relational aspect of women's lives revealed in previous research (Gilligan *et al.* 1990; Gilligan *et al.* 1988).

While only 1 per cent of the responses of multinational advantaged young people reflected concerns about needing money to improve their standard of living, continue their education or to obtain luxuries, 8 per cent of the responses of our Canadian males and 7 per cent of the responses of our females expressed money problems, most frequently tied to payment of school tuition fees. This is not surprising in a society whose highly technological workplaces require highly educated youth and whose post-secondary education, although publicly funded, requires most students to pay tuition.

> '[I] need to find a job so I can have enough money for college and other activities I enjoy.'
>
> 'I have a difficult course load and am trying to earn scholarships to help pay my tuition.'

Within the current climate of relatively high unemployment, young people are aware that finding work may be difficult and that the competition for work demands more education.

Coping strategies

Canadian advantaged youth, like their counterparts in the Multinational Study, reported using individual problem-solving, primarily planning toward solutions to problems or trying harder, with males reporting trying harder more frequently than females (39 per cent as compared to 23 per cent of responses) and females reporting planning almost twice as frequently as males (21 per cent as compared to 13 per cent of responses).

Males:

> 'As long as you work hard, everything else will work out.'
>
> 'I worry about getting a good mark. To deal with this I study as hard as I can.'

Females:

> 'I study diligently for weeks before the exam in order to slowly absorb the material and make pressures less.'

'I space my time and everything has a time when I do it. I would try to do most of my homework at school, so I wouldn't have to worry about it.'

Females reported seeking support more than twice as frequently as males (13 per cent of female responses as compared to 6 per cent of male):

'I talk to my friends and let them know how I feel.'

'Nothing makes me feel better unless I talk to him about it.'

Females also reported dealing with the problem through discussion (7 per cent of responses):

'I try to talk to justify or explain my actions.'

'[I] confront him [the accuser] and try to calmly work out the misunderstanding.'

If these two interactive strategies (seeking support and discussion) are combined, the coping strategies females reported divide almost equally into 'trying harder', 'planning' and 'interaction' (about 20 per cent each). Males' responses showed a different pattern: 'trying harder' (40 per cent), 'planning' (13 per cent) and 'interaction' (6 per cent).

These results agree with research that has found that females have more interest in affiliation and more positive feelings about social interactions than males (Maccoby and Jacklin 1974, Pollak and Gilligan 1982) who are encouraged to be autonomous and independent (Basow 1992). It may also help explain why females have been found to be more successful at resolving interpersonal problem situations (Murphy and Ross 1987).

Canadian males and females reported equally often that they resigned themselves to their problem (considered the problem unsolvable and gave up):

'I wait and hope that everything will sort itself out because I don't know what else I can do.'

'[I] sit and think and feel depressed.'

Both also chose with equal frequency to disengage themselves from the problem, psychologically or by physical escaping:

'I don't let their concern overwhelm me. I tend to ignore them or put their concerns to the side.'

'I just stop thinking about it.'

When resignation and disengagement are combined, these non-goal oriented coping responses total about 23 per cent. This is second in frequency only to trying harder for males and almost equal to the three other main coping strategies of females. Although the use of non-goal oriented coping strategies may appear inappropriate, they may be more effective than problem-focused coping in a situation where subjects have no control over the problem or its outcome, as discussed in Chapter 3.

Helpers

Over 50 per cent of the reports of Canadian youth, like those of their advantaged multinational peers, indicated that their first choice of someone to help them deal with their problem was a person from outside their family. Thirty per cent of these reports specifically indicated a personal friend.

The second highest response for both Canadian young adults and their multinational counterparts was a family member (for Canadians 36 per cent). Canadian males and females indicated their mother most often as the preferred helper, as did the subjects in the adolescent study (1996). The Canadian response agrees with other Canadian research in which adolescents reported using their fathers less often than their mothers for support (Schonert-Reichl and Muller 1996), and other North American research that found adolescents perceived their fathers as giving poorer emotional response when they attempted to be near (Paterson *et al.* 1994), while mothers were described more than fathers as being available to help and supportive of their problems (Youniss and Smollar 1985).

Canadian young men and young women chose someone close to them as a helper in about 60 per cent of their responses, either a personal friend, a fiancé or fiancée, or a family member. They specified at about a 6 per cent response level that they would go to someone outside of this group whom they viewed to have the right qualities to be a good helper.

A little more than 6 per cent of the young women specified that they would seek out professional counsellors as helpers, something the young men rarely specified. In addition, 7 per cent of the young men's responses indicated that they would seek help from no one, while few young women had this response.

Males:

> 'I feel I cannot discuss this with anyone. I must try to solve it myself.'
>
> 'I don't really think that I would discuss it, because there's no one that I know who would understand.'

Research with adolescents, including the international study conducted earlier by our research team (Gibson-Cline *et al.* 1996) as well as other national studies in this book, notably Israel and Ethiopian refugees, has also found that females are more likely to seek help from professional helping resources than males (Dubow *et al.* 1990, Schonert-Reichl and Muller 1996). Other research has found that twice as many males as females are 'social isolates' who indicate that they would not seek help from a list of helping resources (Windle *et al.* 1991). Since our culture values autonomy and independence, especially in males, it is not surprising that females are more willing to seek and receive help than males (Nadler *et al.* 1984). Help-seeking behaviour in females may also be an extension of women's preference for interpersonal problem-solving (Basow 1992).

Helper qualities and modes of helping

Canadian subjects, like their counterparts in the multinational study, indicated most frequently that certain personal attributes were most desired in helpers. This was also true for all socio-economic groups in the multinational study. The personal attribute reported most desirable was 'being approachable' and 'being a good listener', in particular, someone who readily extends an opening for conversation and listens in earnest.

Both Canadian and multinational youth wanted their helpers to be knowledgeable in terms of having experiences similar to those of the subject, being similar in personal characteristics, or having personal knowledge of the subject and/or the problem:

> 'He has the same view I do.'
>
> '[I would talk] to my friends because they also experience the same problem.'

Canadian females, but few males, also described helpers' life experience and professional knowledge as important to their ability to help. This may provide an explanation of why it is that females seek out professional counsellors while young men generally do not:

> 'I would discuss this with my counsellor because she is the one who is knowledgeable in matters like this.'
>
> '[I would talk to the] school counsellor; they know everything about school and university.'

For our multinational subjects, life experience and professional knowledge were reported more often than being similar. This may indicate a higher regard for authority from young people in other countries than Canadian young people have, or perhaps a belief that problems need to be viewed from one's own perspective for solutions to be valid. This possibility has already been suggested in a North American study of Asian-American university students where Western-identified subjects who, although quicker to recognize and acknowledge the need for help, appeared to assign less credibility to a professional counsellor than Asian-identified subjects (Atkinson *et al.* 1990).

Canadian subjects shared another desired helper quality with the multinational subjects, in showing concern, in particular by being understanding of the meaning or motive of the person seeking help.

> 'She listens to my problems and understands them.'
>
> 'She understands me and is very emphatic.'

Canadian males also indicated that they want the helper to be supportive, in particular by being encouraging and communicating a belief in the person seeking help.

> ''She would say, of course you will do fine and convince me that I'll succeed.'
>
> 'Give me confidence and assure me that everything will work out.'

Canadian subjects, like their multinational counterparts, responded overwhelmingly that they wanted the helper to counsel (as shown in approximately 40 per cent of reports) and/or attend to them (as shown in another 40 per cent of reports).

In one-half of the responses, counselling meant receiving advice about how to deal with the problem:

> '[She] listens and gives me firm advice on the 'pros' and 'cons' of a situation.'
>
> 'The good friend would not meddle but give good advice on how to handle the problem.'

For some, this meant that they wanted to receive help in thinking through and solving the problem.

> 'He is awesome to talk to. He would help me figure things out.'
>
> '[I hope] that they would give me their truthful opinion and listen to me without interrupting or arguing.'

Being attended to usually meant being comforted and reassured that the problem would be solved, or for some, simply encouragement. Females also cited being really listened to as important, while the young men generally did not:

'She doesn't say anything. The important thing she does is listen.'

'He is willing to listen to me, to let me yell and scream, to let me get it all out and, of course, he's trustworthy and very caring.'

Few Canadian subjects, similar to their multinational counterparts, wanted the helper to exercise power by changing the situation, preventing the problem, or solving the problem for them, indicating, perhaps, that these young people want to deal directly with their own problems, not evade them or have someone else speak for them.

IMPLICATIONS FOR COUNSELLING 18–20-YEAR-OLD CANADIAN STUDENTS

How youth want to be treated

Our subjects stated clearly that their most important requirements for choosing helpers are that they be approachable and good listeners. Fortunately, counselling programmes in Canada teach precisely these skills. However, counsellors have many roles and corresponding duties within the school system in British Columbia, and in the rest of Canada, resulting in many demands on their time. While the reasons for this situation are complex, the result is that counsellors may not be available to the student when and if the student does approach. It would appear that the roles of counsellors need to be examined if we are to be of more help to students.

Most counsellors have excellent listening skills, however, their many required activities may impact their listening ability during a session, especially when they are aware of the limited time to complete many duties. While the issue of being available may be affected by the constraints of the job and require bureaucratic changes, efforts must be made at a personal level to be approachable and to ensure that when time can be made for the student, listening in earnest occurs.

Students have been clear that they require non-judgmental listening. When asked what they wanted of their helpers, many simply responded, 'Just listen'. In some cases, counsellors may be able to provide useful information but only after listening long enough to be certain of a true understanding of the meaning of the situation.

Students have also been clear that they want to solve their own problems. Therefore, rather than being directive, counsellors should give advice carefully, only when it is requested, and then only in the form of knowledge-based information, reflecting alternatives and possible consequences of different actions.

Our subjects have expressed in a variety of ways a desire for encouragement and support. One of the ways to help is for the counsellor to express a belief in the students' own ability to solve or get beyond the problem. If appropriate, normalizing the problem and its emotional impact can lower the threshold of distress and heighten the students' motivation to cope.

Problems worrying youth

Canadian subjects, like subjects in the other national studies, bear more similarities to their multinational counterparts in their survey responses than they do differences. Their frequent worries regarding school and identity appear to reflect the life stage in which young people ordinarily search for both career and adult identities (Erikson 1959, 1963, 1968) as well as environmental factors. Their coping methods and choices of helpers is also similar. This is true, regardless of the fact that the Canadian sample represents the only secondary school sample in the Multinational Study.

Our subjects expressed concerns about becoming adults. Leaving school, making plans for the future, and building adult identities all mark the transition from high school and are part of the developmental process. Helping students understand this transition, in particular the accompanying fluctuating emotions that occur when one moves from one known area of their life to an uncertain new area, would ease that transition.

While the inability to learn was not a concern for these students, having time to complete their homework, study for exams, and maintain a part-time job or partake in extracurricular activities was. In many cases, the concern with failure centred on getting through day-to-day time-related pressures. While some students indicated planning as a problem-solving strategy, many did not. Instruction in time-management and stress management may be helpful for these individuals.

Social pressures were clearly evident in students' lives, in particular, pressure to do well in school in order to be accepted in a programme of higher education or to find a good job. Our subjects were concerned about their future and whether they would have money to fulfil goals. At the same time, they felt pressure to avoid causing their parents problems. Many also were experiencing conflict or losses within their families as their parents fought or divorced. For these students, counselling programmes that help young people understand the complexity of relationships and the experience of loss would be relevant.

The number of Canadian and multinational youth who indicated that they were resigned to their problem or coped by disengaging from their problem rather than seeking help may be a concern. While young people may perceive that nothing can be done to change their situations, counsellors' more experienced and objective assessment might verify the truth or falsehood of that perception and provide support in either way. Although counselling services are readily available and used extensively by students in schools, it appears that there may be some discrepancy between student perceptions and actual services if students are not accessing what is available when they could. Counsellors may need to be more proactive in informing students about what services are available, ensuring that there is awareness of their role and the extent of their services. This is especially true in the case of students who feel unable to help themselves.

The role of counsellors

As counsellors and researchers in the counselling field, it was interesting, and perhaps disquieting, to have students in the school system report that they rarely seek out counsellors as helpers for their problems. In the cases where students indicated that they would seek out counsellors, they usually required information specific to school issues. Given the large number for whom school concerns were cited as a problem, the latter response is not surprising. For the former, two other help-seeking responses must be considered. Over one-half of the responses of our subjects indicated that they try to solve their problems themselves and over 50 per cent of the responses indicated that, when they did seek assistance they chose personal friends or family members, usually their mothers. If young peoples are able satisfactorily to resolve their problems through individual problem-solving, and if the choice of personal friend or family member is seen to be helpful for those who do choose to seek assistance, the number of young adults remaining who actually require a counsellor's assistance becomes small. Choosing family and friends first as desired helpers may be a natural and healthy choice indicating solid relationships, as is individual problem-solving for young adults on the verge of independence. The need for professional assistance in this situation occurs primarily in those unable to resolve their problems through these avenues.

It is the experience of one of the authors (LM) that, besides attending to students' scheduling and school-based issues, much counselling time is spent dealing with students' personal crises, relationship issues, and mental health issues. Perhaps these students are part of the small percentage of young adults who are unable to solve their problems alone or are unable to ask for help elsewhere. While this type of counselling will always be an integral part of the school counsellor's role, it is equally important for the counsellor to put into place developmental and preventative programmes that concentrate on the concerns of the majority of students. (See pp. 28–31.)

In the training of school counsellors emphasis needs to be placed on developmental knowledge so that counsellors view their role not just as remediation and crisis intervention but as serving as a resource for students and teachers supporting students through their normal developmental passages of life, in particular working through schooling and personal identity concerns. Since young people prefer problem-solving as a coping strategy and counsellors have the skills and language to facilitate effective problem-solving, counsellors need to take an active role with teachers and students by supporting guidance programmes that teach effective and personalised problem-solving strategies which allow students to act on their problems. In addition, many of the qualities that young people are seeking in a helper are the very qualities that counsellors have developed. Providing programmes which teach empathy and communication skills, including assertive coping, to both students and teachers not only enlarges the pool of helping resources for young people but also improves their ability to interact positively in future personal and business relationships.

It is clear that counselling cannot be restricted to individual sessions with single clients if it is to be a more widely accepted resource for a broader range of young people. To achieve this end, counsellors need to be able to work together with teachers to initiate developmental guidance programmes in schools, programmes which will increase the visibility, accessibility, and acceptability of counselling and counsellors. (See pp. 30–1.)

THOUGHTS CONCERNING RESEARCH

Studies such as this one are important because of the opportunity they provide students to inform us of what they perceive as their problems, so that we can adjust our programmes and actions to accommodate them. Educator's conceptions of youth may reflect society's concerns rather than young people's. For instance, issues of substance abuse and the effect of sexually transmitted diseases are often highlighted in the media as the major problems facing youth and young adults today. However, students in this survey reported school and identity issues as their major problems, with few responses related to sexually transmitted diseases or substance abuse (and those were about being pressured to drink or concerns about their friends drinking and driving). This is a finding also of both the multinational adolescent study conducted by our research team earlier (Gibson-Cline *et al.* 1996) and of most national studies in our larger multinational young adult sample.

Although this survey does not ask how young people view counsellors, it may be important to examine their image more closely. Counselling needs to be viewed as another available and acceptable coping strategy when concerns arise, just as is talking to a friend or a parent, rather than as a sign of pathology, if it is to be considered by all and not just a minority.

In conclusion, it should be remembered that this study is a snapshot of

215 Canadian young adults in one city in Canada in 1997. The vast size of Canada with its regional differences and multicultural aspects make generalizations to other Canadian young adults difficult. Indeed, such generalizations may not be possible within this diverse country and its ever changing ethnic composition. Further research is necessary to examine young adults, and possible gender differences, within different regions and of varying socio-economic status to better understand all Canadian young people.

Note

1 Timing of the survey (administered three weeks prior to final exams) may have influenced the schooling concerns.

References

Atkinson, D., Whiteley, S. and Gim, R. (1990) 'Asian-American acculturation and preferences for help providers', *Journal of College Student Development* 31: 155–61.

Basow, S. (1992) *Gender: Stereotypes and Roles* (3rd edn), Pacific Grove, Calif.: Brooks/Coles.

Dubow, E. Lovko, K., Jr. and Kausch, D. (1990) 'Demographic differences in adolescents' health concerns and perceptions of helping agents', *Journal of Clinical Child Psychology* 19: 44–45.

Erickson, E. (1959) 'Identity and the life cycle', *Psychological Issues* 1: 18–164.

Erickson, E. (1963) *Childhood and Society* (2nd edn), New York: Norton.

Erickson, E. (1968) *Identity: Youth and Crisis*, New York: Norton.

Gibson-Cline, J. *et al.* (1996) 'Results of a multinational investigation', in *Adolescence: From Crisis to Coping*, 27–42, London: Routledge.

Gilligan, C., Lyons, C. and Hanmer, T. (eds) (1990) *Making Connections: The Relational Worlds of Adolescent Girls at Emma Willard School,* Cambridge, Mass.: Harvard University Press.

Gilligan, C., Ward, J. and Taylor, J. (eds) (1988) *Mapping the Moral Domain*, Cambridge, Mass.: Harvard University Press.

Maccoby, E. and Jacklin, C. (1974) *The Psychology of Sex Differences*, Stanford, Calif.: Stanford University Press.

Murphy, L. and Ross, S. (1987) 'Gender differences in the problem-solving performances of adolescents', *Sex Roles* 16: 251–64.

Nadler, A., Maler, S. and Friedman, A. (1984) 'Effects of helper's sex, subjects' androgyny and self-evaluation on males' and females' willingness to seek and receive help', *Sex Roles* 10: 327–39.

Paterson, J. Field, J. and Pryor, J. (1994) 'Adolescents' perceptions of their attachment relationships with their mothers, fathers, and friends', *Journal of Youth and Adolescence* 23: 579–600.

Pollak, S. and Gilligan, C. (1982) 'Images of violence in Thematic Apperception Test stories', *Journal of Personality and Social Psychology* 42: 159–67.

Schonert-Reichl, R. and Muller, J. (1996) 'Correlates of help-seeking in adolescence', *Journal of Youth and Adolescence* 25: 707–33.

Statistics Canada (1996–7) Government of Canada @ www.statcan.ca

Windle, M., Miller-Tutzauer, C., Barnes, G. and Welte, J. (1991) 'Adolescent perceptions of help-seeking resources for substance abuse', *Child Development* 62: 179–89.

Youniss, J. and Smollar, J. (1985) *Adolescent Relations with Mothers, Fathers and Friends*, Chicago: University of Chicago Press.

6 China

College students during China's period of reform, 1989–97

Qi Chen and Fengchun Miao, Beijing Normal University

INTRODUCTION

This chapter examines the concerns and coping of young people during a period of important changes that have impacted on the lives of all Chinese people.

1989–97: ECONOMIC, SOCIAL AND POLITICAL REFORM IN CHINA

Economic reform

China had just begun a major economic reform in 1989, when our research team conducted its first study of Chinese youth. Since that time, great progress has been made toward changing to a socialist market economy. The

> ***'I worry about my future.'***
>
> She is 19 years old. Her father is chief secretary of his unit and her mother is a staff member in a company. Both her parents are middle school graduates.
>
> *'I don't know what vocation I should choose or how my future will go. Sometimes, I believe the fate has arranged these matters for me so I needn't worry too much. But other times I tell myself I need to take action to create a better future. When I worry like this, I make myself feel better by convincing myself that everything will be all right.*
>
> *The person I most want to discuss this problem with is my mother. She understands me better than anyone else and shares her experiences with me. She makes me believe that I can achieve everything I want if I work hard enough. She never laughs my worries off or calls them 'girls' weakness' and she never treats me casually.'*

country's gross national product has increased dramatically, amounting to a full 6,770 billion RMB in 1996.[1] Today, more than 80 per cent of all prices in China are regulated by market principles. China's capital, technology, property rights and futures markets have all developed rapidly (Zhao 1998).

In general terms, these changes have led to improvement of the living standard of Chinese people and reduction of discrepancies between living standards of the various occupational groups. Major changes rarely occur without some problems, however. While the new market economy is advantageous to most of the population, not everyone has always benefited equally. While most rural people no longer live in extreme poverty, a new type of urban poor has been created. As shown in the government's Blue Book of Society (1997), profits from China's state-owned enterprises have been decreasing. By 1996, many were operating at deficits or had fallen into bankruptcy. The group known as the 'New Poor' was created when 4.69 million employees lost their jobs or salaries. By 1996, the unemployment rate reached 3 per cent. While this is not a high figure for Western countries, workers had never before faced unemployment under the socialist system. To make things worse for those affected, prices rose annually (1992–3: 16 per cent; 1993–4: 25 per cent; 1994–5: 17 per cent; 1995–6: 9 per cent).

Social and political reform

Before the 1980s, China's social structure consisted of only three strata: farmers, workers and literate professionals, with status and income for each determined by the government. Today, following China's reforms, there are many new occupational groups including owners of private enterprises, managers, soldiers, policemen, etc. as well as underemployed and unemployed. Zhu (1998) suggests that, while political differences between occupational groups have decreased, economic differences between them have increased.

In the past, the Chinese government assigned jobs to its people, and individuals did not have the right either to choose or change their employment or place of work without government approval. Today, Chinese people are free to seek employment wherever they wish and everyone must compete for positions.. Most importantly, there are economic and social differences in the various types of work, and Chinese must prepare well and 'prove their skills' to obtain the opportunity for the better jobs (Chen 1998).

Value changes

China's economic resurgence and general increase in standard of living appear also to have had a major effect on values. With people no longer doing their jobs in order to satisfy primary needs, they have developed a desire for secondary needs, such as self-actualization, knowing and understanding (Fu 1998). With the new market economy, people have begun to emphasize material goods rather than ancestors, rank or status. Some results include a weakening of family ties and decrease in influence of elders (Yang 1998).

Results include other changes in values as well. Given their new freedoms, some individuals pursued material profits blindly and began to value material goods more than other human beings (Shi 1998). Chen argued (1998) that some Chinese people are beginning to value the individual above the collective group, and placing the individual at the centre of a new moral order. Today, money is becoming a life goal and an index of social status and success. The new economy is creating other new social needs as wells: needs for occupations that bring higher income, need for income insurance, etc. It follows that more and more people are taking from society rather than devoting themselves to society. Traditionally, the popular belief about self–other relationships was 'only for others not for self at all'. Today, it is becoming, 'If you do not take care of yourself, you will stand condemned by God'.

The young people we surveyed in 1997 were facing all of these issues.

Chinese youth today

The youth we surveyed in 1997, like their 1989 peers, were students preparing in university for their adult occupations. Because of China's family planning policy begun in the 1970s, our subjects, like most same-aged Chinese youth, were 'only children' (without siblings in their families). Research regarding this population has suggested that their special status as 'only children' has influenced their development in a number of ways. When compared to peers with siblings, college students who are 'only children' tend to have more learning difficulties, feel more dissatisfaction about their lives, are more anxious about whether their ideas can ever be actualized, worry more about their future occupations; and feel more uneasy about their economic reliance on their parents (Li 1998). Most 'only children' had not reached college age at the time of the 1989 study. By 1997, however, the number had increased dramatically. We estimate that the percentage of college students who are 'only children' is well above 50 per cent.

COUNSELLING SERVICES OFFERED TODAY IN CHINA FOR COLLEGE STUDENTS

Today, there are counselling centres with trained counsellors for college students in most large Chinese universities, including the one in which our subjects were studying. In Beijing Normal University, as in many large universities, there are courses that prepare teachers and counsellors to assist young people deal with their personal and academic needs. Counselling programmes are new to China, however, and, although statistics are not yet available, it is clear that the number of counsellors is still low in comparison to need.

THE STUDY AND ITS METHODOLOGY

Research questions

This chapter asks how our 1997 advantaged and non-advantaged subjects compare as to their responses to the survey questions, whether their socio-economic status or gender appears related in any way to subject groups' responses; and how our 1997 young subjects compare with their 1997 multi-national peers. In order to better understand what effects the period of reform might have had on China's youth, it also compares the responses of our 1997 young respondents with their peers surveyed in 1989.

Subjects and their SES backgrounds

Chapter 6 describes the results of a survey conducted in 1997 of 320 Chinese young people between the ages of 18 and 20 years. Of these, 163 (sixty-one males and 102 females) were 'advantaged' and 157 (eighty-one males and seventy-six females) were 'non-advantaged'. All were residing in Beijing, after having passing the national unified entrance examination and then coming from many different areas of China to study at Beijing Normal University. Our subjects represented almost all nationalities in China.

The authors classified subjects as advantage or non-advantaged using the procedure described in Chapter 1 for all studies with one exception needed to meet China's specific characteristics as a socialist nation. Specifically, we replaced questions related to family economic level and housing arrangements on the questionnaire with the following: 'What economic status do you think your family holds in the area in which you reside?'

We compare the responses of our 1997 subjects in this chapter with those of a previous survey taken of 18–20 year-old Chinese students in Beijing and conducted prior to the onset of China's economic reform. Although the 1989 study included students from backgrounds similar to those of 1997, it was administered prior to China's economic reforms when the term 'socio-economic status' had no relevance in China. For this reason, the 1989 data is listed only by gender and not by SES. The 1989 survey included 239 youth (106 males and 133 females).

Procedure

The authors used the procedure standardized for all countries in the Multinational Study and described in Chapter 1, to prepare, administer and code subjects' responses. The questionnaires matched those of other countries with the exception noted above and asked the problems that caused subjects concern, the strategies they used to cope and the help-seeking methods they chose. Subjects were surveyed in classrooms by teachers and case histories. The authors coded survey results and conducted case histories. Appendix II describes the reliability of coding.

HIGHLIGHTS OF THE FINDINGS

This chapter reports highlights of our findings. Appendix III Tables A and B provide complete statistical findings for both classes and categories-within-classes of responses as described in Chapter 1.

THE 1997 SURVEY

'I want to decide myself what I do. I don't want anyone else to decide for me.'

He is 20 years old. His father is a cadre with a college degree. His mother is a staff member of a company and a graduate of elementary school.

'I want to accomplish something having to do with what I am studying now in college, because I really find it very interesting. I hope that I will never have to live in a narrow space or be unable to take care of myself. The future will be wonderful for me if I can succeed in this. I worry sometimes that my goal is too high for me to reach or that something else will keep me from reaching it. I am studying hard and help other people as much as I can. I plan {to} keep working step by step to get there. My possibilities? I think I have about a 60 per cent chance of succeeding.

The first people I look to for help me are friends who are older than I am. I only rarely ask my teachers to help me. My older friends have a lot of life experience, especially when it comes to college life, and they have had problems similar to mine. I want them to discuss my worries with me, and listen when I pour out my troubles to them. It is extremely important to me that I can trust them to listen to everything and not ever let anyone else know what I have said in private.'

There were far more similarities between our subject groups than differences.

Concerns

Personal identity and self-concept (perception of self) and schooling ranked among the top two problem areas cited by our Chinese subjects, similar to the multinational findings. For Chinese advantaged subjects, identity was a concern in 32–34 per cent of responses, and schooling worries appeared in 22–24 per cent of responses. For non-advantaged subjects, identity issues appeared in 26–35 per cent of responses and schooling in 23–24 per cent of responses. Concern regarding identity was focused primarily on self-confidence and becoming adult:

> 'What can I do in the future? What kind of job am I competent for? I hope I can find a [good] job. I am terribly worried that I won't be able to fulfil my potential.'

Schooling worries dealt mainly with academic achievement (success or failure):

> 'I know that how well I do in school now is related to whether my future career is successful or not. But my grades are a complete mess, and I have no other talents. I feel very pressured!'

Altruism (concern regarding society and humanity) appeared more frequently in 1997 Chinese responses than in multinational responses the same year. This concern was reported far more frequently by Chinese subjects than any other subject group in the Multinational Study with the possible exception of Brazilian poverty subjects (see Appendix III). Altruism appeared in 19–20 per cent of advantaged reports and and in 14–23 per cent of nonadvantaged reports. Males produced the higher percentage in each SES group. The prominent altruistic worry was related to the new materialism that has followed China's reforms:

> 'What worries me most is that more and more people are plotting against each other for their own material gain.'

Coping strategies

Both advantaged and non-advantaged subjects reported trying to solve their problems by themselves more than by any other coping method, most frequently by trying harder or planning more. This was true in both our Chinese and the multinational studies. However, this coping method was reported far more frequently by Chinese subjects. For advantaged subjects, solving their problems alone appeared in 65–71 per cent of responses; for non-advantaged, it appeared in 68–73 per cent of responses.
Trying harder:

> 'I will try harder and study more.'

Planning:

> 'I will study hard and, at the same time, do some part-time job so I can learn how to conduct myself and handle my affairs. I will work toward my my goals step by step.'

> 'I will first work to lay down a firm foundation [in my subject matter] while I'm in college, to insure that I will be accepted to graduate study.'

Resignation (surrender to the conclusion that one's problem is not solvable) and disengagement (avoidance or distancing oneself from one's problems) were the second and third ranked coping strategies of both Chinese and multinational subjects. However, Chinese subjects reported these strategies slightly less frequently than did multinational subjects. Chinese advantaged reports of resignation appeared in only 8–11 per cent of responses; non-advantaged in only 9–10 per cent. In similar fashion, advantaged reports included disengagement in 8–15 per cent of reports and non-advantaged in only 8–9 per cent.

Desired helpers, helper qualities and modes of helping

Both SES groups reported seeking helpers from outside the family much more often than family members, with 61–73 per cent of responses designating a helper outside the family and 10–25 per cent designating a family member. Chinese subject groups all reported seeking helpers from outside their families more than their multinational peers, and reported less frequently seeking out family members. When turning to help outside the family, favorite choices were personal friends or schoolmates. Only a few male subjects went to teachers for help, and very few even considered professional counsellors.

Our subjects wanted helpers with personal qualities such as honesty and trustworthiness, loyalty and willingness to help. After that, they wanted them to be knowledgeable (having had experience related to the concern or being similar to the subject in some way related to the problem) and concerned (understanding or caring). Subjects also wanted to be counselled (helped to solve their problem by having someone share useful information, advise them as to what to do or give them attention, encouragement or reassurance. (Appendix III Table A provides statistical details of all findings.)

> 'When I have problems, I seek help from my classmates because we are the same age and facing the same problems. We have sympathy for each other.'

PROBLEMS AND COPING OF CHINESE YOUTH BEFORE AND DURING CHINA'S PERIOD OF REFORM: A COMPARISON OF THE 1989 AND 1997 SURVEY FINDINGS

Problems

Subjects surveyed in 1989, prior to China's reform period, were similar to our 1997 subjects in having self-identity and schooling as their primary concerns. Altruism, however, appears far more frequently in the 1997 reports, with worries concerning materialism. Materialism did not appear as a concern in 1989.

Coping strategies

Reports of individual problem-solving occur in a higher percentage of responses in 1997 than in 1989, especially for male subjects. Reported resignation, however, appeared in 14–19 per cent of 1989 reports and was somewhat lower in 1997.

Desired helpers, helper qualities and help-seeking methods

While in both the 1997 and 1989 surveys, most reports suggested searching for help outside the family, responses to the 1997 survey showed a somewhat higher percentage of such reports than did the 1989 survey in which 55–62 per cent of responses indicated the seeking of outside help. In similar fashion, the 1997 survey showed a higher percentage of responses indicating the choice of family members as helpers than in 1989 when 21–33 per cent of responses suggested family members.

While personal qualities ranked first as desired helper qualities and included higher percentages of reports in 1997 than in 1989, being knowledgeable ranked first and included higher percentages of responses in 1989.

Finally, while the first two choices of subjects in 1989 and 1997 as to what they wanted their helpers to do were to attend to them and counsel them, 1997 subjects reported far more frequently than their 1989 peers they wanted to be attended to. (See Appendix III Tables A and B.)

CONCLUSIONS AND IMPLICATIONS

Development of the self versus development of society and humanity

This study found that Chinese youth are similar to their multi-national peers in their concerns regarding identity and schooling, which is not surprising when societal expectations the world over pressure young people to plan for their futures. Their worry about altruistic issues is different. The increase in this concern since 1989 is due to the pursuit of material profits that followed China's new reform policy and which made some conscientious young people worry about the long-term effects on the morality of our society.

Our Chinese subjects expressed a strong desire to act independently in

'I don't want to be involved in intrigues, plotting against others to get what I want.'

She is 20 years old. Her parents are farmers with elementary school educations.

'In the future, I want to be a staff member in a company. I want to write papers about what I studied at University at the same time. I am working. I don't want to be spending my time plotting against other people or in having poor relationships. When I think that I will be able to leave my hometown and actually accomplish something important in the future, I feel very excited. At the same time, I worry about whether I will be able to actualize my full potential.

I think I have learned a lot and have done a good job of adapting myself to college life. I believe I have a 70–80 per cent chance of getting everything I want.

I always go to my classmates when I have learning problems, because we understand each other.

I hope they'll assure me that I am on the right track. I definitely don't want them to decide for me what I should do or ignore my problems.'

solving their problems, a necessary activity for their personal development within a market economy. Today in China, independence and hard work is rewarded and individuals must be able to compete aggressively for positions in the workforce. While their independent approach to coping is important in a free market economy, however, it creates potential moral problems. In the new system, there will always be some individuals who try their best to succeed but are trampled by the crowd and never reach their goals. While only a few of our subjects coped by giving up and resigning themselves to disappointments, they, like China's new 'urban poor', may become a problem for China unless youth can begin to struggle for societal goals with the same energy devoted to individual goals.

The choice of our subjects to seek help from outside their families points to a major and recent change from traditional family values in China and is related to the new independence of youth. While seeking some independence from parents has always been typical, Chinese young people traditionally were not eager to walk away from their families to the extent that they are today. Unfortunately, it is not clear that the persons to whom they go for help when they do not go to their families are able to provide the support that is needed to better our society.

It is important that our subjects wanted helpers to attend to them, comfort them and support them. It is interesting that most of our subjects, unlike those of the 1989 study, were 'only children' who, researchers tell us, received far more attention in their early years than did their parents (or their peers of 1989). Our subjects' choices of desired help suggest a loneliness in a new aggressive world.

Implications for providing active and adaptive counselling

The double concerns reported by our subjects concerning their development of self (self-identity) and the development of society (altruism) provide a clue to assist educators and counsellors to guide young people. We agree with the report of the Seminar of the Central CCP College on Current Issues of Concern to Chinese Cadres (1998) that, while much attention has been given to bettering the material life of the Chinese people, too little has been given to bettering their spiritual lives. We therefore propose a system that provides two-pronged support: first, help with personal concerns and second, teaching of the moral values required to build a strong society. We believe that both are necessary if Chinese youth are to become the builders of new moral order.

Providing support to individuals

Young people today need relevant counselling support as well as helpers to help them deal with their concerns. While most of our subjects wanted to be 'counselled', however, almost none chose professional counsellors. Unfortunately, although counselling services have begun to appear on college campuses, including the university attended by our subjects, counsellors who perform counselling duties often don't make themselves easily accessible. Few students today are even aware that this type of service exists. We believe that counselling services need to be extended by whatever means possible so as to become more available to Chinese youth.

According to western theories of counselling, understanding clients and their problems, attending to them, and being confidential concerning communications (trustworthy) is often far more effective than providing information on how to solve their problems based on professional counselling knowledge or acting as 'cool' experts. Cunningham (1993) found that Western college students tend to seek help from friends and classmates, often reporting that teachers show little concerns when students are facing difficulty and that friends usually are more concerned and available to help. This concurs with the findings of our study and the Multinational Study as well. We believe that professional counsellors are needed in China today to help resolve learning problems as well as other student needs. Since young people prefer friends and peers as helpers, we also suggest that professional counsellors and educators should develop personal skills that permit them to act as friends of this age group rather than as distant superiors. (See pp. 26–30.)

Finally, we suggest using trained peer helpers as part of the counselling service. Because most youth living together in student communities in which ages, experience and problems are similar, peers can understand each other easily and, if trained in ways to be most helpful, could become useful helpers. We suggest that educators and counsellors should teach peers to be good listeners, share information with their friends and encourage or direct their friends when they confront problems. It is also necessary to counsel the group they are in to create support systems for them. In fact, this approach has been popular in China in recent years. And because China still lacks sufficient professional counsellors, it is a most realistic approach for China to adopt at this time. (See pp. 30–1.)

Teaching moral values

> ***'I have not enough money on the one hand, and I can't spend money economically on the other.'***
>
> He is 20 years old. His parents are both farmers. His father is an elementary school graduate and his mother is illiterate.
>
> *'I worry a lot about not having money. I often use up all the money I soon after getting it, and I just don't seem to know how to save it. I never seem to have enough. This makes me very unhappy. Sometimes I daydream about all the different ways I could get my hands on money . But I think about it myself. I don't ever tell anyone even though I know that if someone would only comfort me, I would feel better.'*

Even with all the help we can give young people to develop strong personal strength, youth alone cannot solve large social problems such as the materialism that faces them today in China. Most of our subjects who worried about these issues felt helpless to solve them. The authors suggest, therefore, that educators in China should take responsibility to help students develop appropriate habits and necessary skills to enable them both to express their concerns and to seek help from others.

Note

The data reported for 1989 was collected in Beijing and coded by X. Lu.

1 Ren ming bin, Chinese currency

References

Blue Book of Society (1997) Beijing: Government of the People's Republic of China.

Chen, A. (1998) 'Changes of today's idea of employment and its value', *Social Science* 1 (209): 43–4, in Chinese.

Chen, W. (1998) 'Thoughts concerning the moral culture development of Chinese society', *Science, Economy, Society* 16 (70): 43–5, in Chinese.

Cunningham, M (1993) 'Evolutionary tensions and the future of social psychology', *Contempory Social Psychology* 17 (3): 68–73.

Fu, H. (1998) 'A test of differences in the social orientation of modern Chinese',

Journal of Social Psychology 1 (33): 25–30, in Chinese.

Hu, H. (1998) 'A survey on the psychological diathesis of university students', *Journal of Social Psychology* 1 (33): 20–4, in Chinese.

Li, Z. (1998) 'A comparison of the adaptation to school life of only-child and non-only-child college students', *Youth Studies* 4 (235): 31–6 in Chinese.

Lin, G. (1998) 'On vertical interpersonal relationships', *Journal of Social Psychology* 1 (33): 20–4, in Chinese.

Seminar of the Central CCP College on Current Issues of Concern to Chinese Cadres (1998) 'The general trend and prospect of China', *Developmental Strategies of Chinese Society* 1 (35): 15–7, in Chinese.

Shi, X. (1998) 'A social psychological description of the Chinese people during the 1990s', *Society*, CCCP: China Renda Social Sciences Information Center 4: 147–57, in Chinese.

Tang, J. (1998) 'A framework of the system to ensure the minimum standard of living of urban residents in China', *Social Science in China* 1 (109): 117–28, in Chinese.

Yang, L. (1998) 'Cultural exploration of marketing economy', *Journal of Humanities* 2 (112): 43–6, in Chinese.

Zhao, D. (1998) 'New development and new characteristics of China's economy', *Reference Materials for Social Science Studies* 10: 570, in Chinese.

Zhu, G. (1998) 'From status to contract: features and nature of social stratification in contemporary China', *Contemporary World and Socialism* 1: 35–7, in Chinese.

7 England

Youth from the south and south-west of Britain

Kevin Feaviour and David Acres,
College of St Mark and St John

'When I think of the future, I think about independence – doing what I want, when I want, being happy.'

Wendy, 19 years old; father: maintenance fitter-engineer; mother: unemployed.

'Ten years from now, I want to be a youth worker . . . I want to help kids who are homeless, kids who are on drugs. I hope that in ten years, there will be fewer problems, but, unfortunately, I can't really see that happening. I doubt that I'll be married yet, since preparing for my career will take a lot of work and time.

What is important to me {personally} is independence: doing what I want, when I want, being happy and having security. I need to work now at reaching my career goals and also at organizing my personal life. I am {preparing for my career} now by working toward my national qualifications. And I am also working on the relationship I am in, deciding if we can build on it and what the future would hold if we eventually decide to marry. Someday I also hope to have other adventures, travel out of the country and see how everyone else lives. There is so much to think about: trying to guess all the things that might happen {in my life} and looking at them realistically. Being dreamy and waiting for everything to fall into place by itself won't get me anywhere.

My biggest worry about the future? Uncertainty about what is going to happen . . . Will I really be able to cope on my own?

When I worry, I always go to my Mum for help. I can tell her anything. Both my parents listen without judging me, and then suggest different ways to solve my problems, instead of telling me what to do. I always want to think about it and make my own decision as to what to do.'

INTRODUCTION

This chapter presents the concerns and coping of English 18–20-year-olds growing up today in social, economic and political conditions radically different from those of their forebears, and facing new problems that threaten their ability to take on the tasks of full adulthood as their parents did. Two of the most serious are economic and employment problems and changes in family structure and lifestyle.

Economics, employment and education

Economic and employment problems for young people in Britain today are caused by a series of related factors. First, young people must stay in school longer to develop skills needed by modern technology; second, as a result of new technologies, there has been a major decrease in lower-skilled jobs; and third, England has recently reduced state welfare support for unemployed youth (Coleman 1997). At the time of our surveys, many young people were working only at low-paid, part-time jobs which they needed in order to pay for educations that would make them employable in the new professions. By the mid-1990s, less educated and most vulnerable youth were already beginning to be excluded from society and threatening to create a new 'underclass' in Britain. While fortunate young people had supportive family networks and constructive paths to education and employment futures, for a growing minority the process of transition to adulthood was blurred and programmes designed to help only worsened the opportunities. By the late 1990s, education controlled future employment and defined the 'haves' and 'have-nots' of this generation of young people (Roberts 1995, Macdonald 1997, Williamson 1993).

Lifestyles

Independence is a major developmental task in Britain as in most Western countries, and failure to create independent professional lives or to move from parental homes is often viewed as failure to achieve adult status. Because of economic circumstances, lack of job opportunities and increasing costs of continuing education, however, many young people are unable to develop professional lives or must remain at home. Many who leave must return, further blurring their sense of a transition to adulthood (Coles 1995).

Another family problem affecting youth is the increase in family breakdown, divorce and subsequent creation of new stepfamilies in both parental and new young families. The number of unwanted pregnancies and children born outside marriage has increased, with the largest increase among parents under the age of 20. Amongst the problems resulting from this situation are dysfunctional family relationships, poor parent–child communication and increased depression among youth (Coleman 1997).

Drugs and alcohol addiction are also problems of youth, often related to dysfunctional family life. HIV infection, a scourge in countries throughout the world, increased in England by 30 per cent between 1996 and 1999. For the first time in England, AIDS was reported as spreading rapidly among both men and women with the 1999 infection rate for heterosexuals almost equal to that of homosexual men. According to British Health Laboratory Service statistics, the percentage of new cases rose from 39 to 47 per cent of new cases among heterosexuals (Rumbelow December 1999).

Counselling young people in Britain

The term, 'counselling', has usually been used in Britain to describe activities that form personal and academic support through preventative, developmental and crisis intervention activities. Present-day counselling for youth in England developed largely from the work of three services: child guidance provided by medical services, educational guidance by local education authorities, and school vocational guidance or career services by the voluntary sector through youth counselling and advisory services. Institutions of higher education have taken on the responsibility for training counsellors.

School counselling first emerged during the 1960s to improve the quality of schools as caring institutions. It was offered as a mental health service in the 1970s by educational psychologists and other linked specialist services. In the 1980s, it was integrated into school curricula as part of the work of some teachers. Today, a minority of schools employ specialist counsellors and a majority have 'pastoral' tutoring staff who often have other roles as well. Many further – and higher – education institutions offer specialist counsellors. For British youth outside of the formal educational system, counselling is at least theoretically available through health and social services.

During the period in which school counselling was developing and in response to growing support needs of young people, England began to create additional services to provide support to 14–24-year-olds (Feaviour 1994). These were often community-based organizations designed with young people in mind, provided by the voluntary sector and operated largely by volunteers and a few paid staff. Today, charitable organizations funded through grants play an important role in providing services, particularly with reference to mental health (Feaviour 1992, Tyler 1978, Department of Education and Science 1989, Kurtz *et al.* 1994, Malek 1997). They offer a range of services from financial and accommodation advice through befriending and counselling for young people facing bereavement, self-harm and abuse to the more acute psychiatric illnesses, liaising with other specialists as needed. Some of the subjects of our study were using the services identified earlier.

Today, many community-based organizations designed to help young people are provided by the voluntary sector and operated largely by volunteers and few paid staff. These, together with charitable organizations funded through grants, fall between informal and formal networks of support and play major roles in providing services, particularly with reference to mental health. (Feaviour 1992, Tyler 1978, DES 1989, Kurtz *et al.* 1994, Malek 1997). One such organization is the Youth Information, Advice and Counselling Service (YIAC). YIAC works in partnership with government services. in many areas of England to deliver informal, confidential, independent, young person centred, voluntary, multi-intervention and community-based care (Feaviour 1992, 1998). This and other agencies now offer young people a range of support from advice about financial matters to befriending and counselling for abuse matters. As such, they provide a bridge between informal help provided by friends and family members and more formal support provided by professional and statutory services (Feaviour 1994).

Some of the subjects of our study were participating in programmes conducted by the YIAC at the time of our survey.

THE STUDY AND ITS METHODOLOGY

Our subjects included thirty-three advantaged and sixty-one non-advantaged youth. Advantaged subjects consisted of thirteen males and twenty-one females; non-advantaged subjects consisted of twenty-two males and thirty-nine females. Subjects were 18–20 year-olds studying at a university college or a further education college or clients using YIAC centres in the south and south-west of England. Many were students who were financially and socially dependent on their families. Others were employed at least part-time.

The English advantaged and non-advantaged samples were unique in the Multinational Study in that, while their SES descriptions largely match those of their counterparts in the Multinational Study as described in Chapter 1, six advantaged and seventeen non-advantaged subjects – almost a quarter of our sample – were receiving counselling or other helping services at the time of the survey.

An additional sample of impoverished English 18–20-year-olds are described as part of Chapter 16. Because of the small sample size both of the English subjects described in this chapter and those described in Chapter 16, we present them as 'pilot samples' included for the purpose of stimulating larger scale research with the caution that the sample size precludes definitive conclusions.

Method

Questionnaires were administered to small groups of youth by the researchers at colleges or YIAC drop-in centres. The administration of the survey instrument and the coding of subject responses into classes and categories-of-classes utilized the standardized procedures developed by our research team for that purpose and described in Chapter 1. Reliability of coding is described in Appendix II.

HIGHLIGHTS OF FINDINGS

The results of Chapter 7 conform to those of the Multinational Study in most respects. The few major differences that appear are discussed below. This chapter describes highlights of most frequently reported concerns and coping strategies. Detailed statistical descriptions of all reported results are listed in Appendix III, Table A, in terms both of classes and categories-within-classes.[1]

Problems

Schooling and identity

The two concerns most frequently cited by our subjects, schooling and identity, accounted for 36–48 per cent of reported responses of all subjects. (One exception was the advantaged male group which reported the lowest percentage of identity worries (7 per cent of responses) of all the advantaged national groups of the Multinational Study. We will discuss this finding later in the chapter.)

Schooling problems were frequently tied to time pressures due to work commitments:

> 'I always leave revision until too late and try to do it all in the last minute. I find it hard because my job makes me busy.'
>
> 'Exams and work! – I am at college all week and work on weekends – I never have time to do homework.'
>
> 'I have a job in the evenings; I often get behind in my (college) work and then get unmotivated and get further behind.'

Fear of academic failure appeared to worry our non-advantaged subjects more than advantaged, just as in the Multinational Study:

> 'I feel highly stressed, moody, irritable. I become unfriendly on days of exams. I feel that I can't cope and – tell myself I can't do it.'

Identity worries included, among other issues, becoming adult (choosing a career, education, becoming financially independent); physical appearance (particularly weight problems); and self-abuse (eating disorders and self-inflicted injuries).

Becoming adult:

> 'I feel insecure about my future life from financial and emotional points of view.'
>
> 'What will my future contain? Will I live a long time? Will I be happy? I don't want to be alone!'
>
> 'The way my life is going! I am concerned that I am doing badly in life and that my future prospects won't be good. I have taken a wrong course in life!'

Physical appearance:

> 'I want to be slim: I have never been really fat, but have always had a fat stomach and bum, my family is always saying how horrible it looks.'
>
> '[My problem is] food. I have had problems with anorexia and bulimia for eight years.'
>
> '[I hate] my appearance: I am quite big and worry that everyone notices.'

Self-abuse:

> 'I binge and make myself sick . . . I [used to be anorexic] – and I am frightened of this returning.'

Family issues and material desires

Family issues and material desires each represented a total of approximately 12–17 per cent of reported worries of all subjects. English advantaged males gave a higher percentage of reported problems than any of their multinational counterparts. A large range of issues were identified. Family problems represented 22 per cent of reports of advantaged females.

Family:

> 'My brother is ill and sometimes I am frightened he might die.'
>
> 'My parents interfere with my social life (wanting to know) where have I been and what have I done.'
>
> 'My parents have unrealistic expectations (of me). . . . They want me to conform to what they consider to be normal and expectable behaviour.'
>
> 'I had a friend who is four years older than me and we got on really

well . . . I was not allowed to see her because [my parents said] she was too old.'

Material desires focused on money our non-advantaged subjects felt they needed for necessities and our advantaged subjects felt they needed in order to satisfy other desires.

Advantaged:

> 'I need more money to keep up-to-date in fashion.'

Non-advantaged:

> 'I am on income support while I am at college and am always worrying about money. There is always a bill to pay. I get no help from the college for books.'

The continuing spread of AIDS

> 'My boyfriend and should be tested for AIDS. But he won't go and I'm afraid to go alone.'

Noticeably missing in our subjects' reports, at least in terms of meeting the requirement of 5 per cent or more of responses falling into the appropriate categories-within-classes as mandated by our methodology,[1] were problems such as AIDS, drug addiction, alcoholism and the like, which, we know, faces this age group throughout the world today. While some problems may have decreased slightly in the past few years, AIDS has continued as a scourge throughout the world and is still rising in England (Rumbelow 1999). Reports such as the one above were given by only a few of our subjects. Why should this be when the disease is so deadly and so much information concerning prevention is being provided in Britain? The authors suggest two explanations. In the first place, it might be that English youth are terribly frightened of AIDS, but choose to disengage themselves from their fear by pretending that the possibility does not exist. A second possibility is that an extremely dangerous complacency has set in among youth, possibly because of mistaken beliefs that AIDS can be cured by new drug therapies or that heterosexual young people believe that only gay youth are at risk.

Coping strategies

Our young adult populations followed the multinational coping trends.

Individual problem-solving

From 32–47 per cent of responses of advantaged and non-advantaged subjects showed our respondents trying to solve their problems themselves. They chose most frequently to do by 'trying harder' (attempting to solve the problem without demonstrating how this can be accomplished) or 'planning' (analysing how to plan action).

Trying harder:

> 'I work hard to do better in my lessons.'

Planning:

> 'I make a list of every piece of work that has to be done and try to do some. Then I talk to the lecturers and tell them that I have been tired from working in the evenings. Then I sort out new deadlines with them.'

It should be noted, as discussed in Chapters 3 and 17, that 'trying harder' by itself does not necessarily lead to reduction of the reported problem, but may recreate ineffective strategies, thus increasing the problem.

Resignation and disengagement

Resigning oneself to one's fate and disengaging from the problem also featured strongly. We considered both of these strategies as 'non-goal-oriented coping' in the sense that they did not lead to reduction of our subjects' reported problems, although they might have served to reduce stress. When we combined the two coping strategies into one as was done in the Multinational Study (Chapter 3), we found that our male subjects appeared to use this approach approximately twice as frequently as our female subjects. For our advantaged males, this was the primary coping strategy, (representing 60 per cent of male responses) and for both females and non-advantaged males, it ranked second only to individual problem-solving, just as in the Multinational Study. (The only exception was the advantaged female group who tended to cope more frequently by interacting with others; seeking companionship or asserting themselves actively in relationships with others.

Disengagement:

> 'I eat, drink, go out and have a laugh with friends.'
>
> 'I wear the outfit I feel good in and go clubbing.'

Resignation:

> 'I just stop trying! What's the use anyway?'

Some subjects reported that they resigned themselves to their situations even when they recognized that doing nothing not only failed to help them reach their stated goals but even led them to more difficulties:

> 'I had a serious problem dealing with my parents' divorce. I was ashamed and didn't share it with anyone for almost a year. When I finally did share it, I was so uncomfortable that I broke down and cried in front of my friend. I decided not to try talking to anyone about it again.'

Most subjects made no attempt to explain why they chose to resign themselves or disengage, but their choice of words suggests that they had no faith that help would ever come.

> 'I keep quiet. She'll never change [no matter what I do].'
>
> 'I don't do anything: there is no point in trying.'
>
> 'AIDS? I just don't think about it. It really couldn't happen to me.'

Interpersonal strategies and seeking support

Interpersonal coping was reported more frequently by advantaged than non-advantaged subjects and by females more than males. Interpersonal coping featured as the most frequently discussed strategy of advantaged females, represented in 36 per cent of their reported strategies. Seeking support was also reported more by females than males (from 14 per cent for non-advantaged male to 18 per cent for advantaged females).

Helpers and helper qualities

In 65–67 per cent of reports, English subject groups all chose helpers from outside their families, going particularly to friends or fiancés/ fiancées and also to professional or paraprofessional helpers such as counsellors, social workers and youth support workers. Of preferred family members, mothers featured most highly.

The three qualities they sought most frequently in their helpers were personal qualities (being a good listener, trustworthy), followed by concern (being understanding, attentive, empathetic) and knowledge (being similar to the subject in experiences or worries). Listening was often linked with other elements, suggesting a complex mix of qualities that also included understanding and respect.

Listening:

> 'He listened to me and let me release my emotions.'
>
> 'He has ability to listen and make me feel better about things: I can talk to him honestly.'
>
> 'My friend listens to me and she lets me say anything I want and she doesn't say anything until I've finished. I trust her totally and I feel as though she understands me.'
>
> 'He's a good listener and supportive. It is a mixture of qualities that allow me to speak to him.'
>
> 'She listens and is not judgmental or critical or negative.'
>
> 'They listen and offer good practical advice.'

Understanding:

> 'They understand how important it is for me to be independent, but realize that I love my work and it's something I must do.'
>
> 'She is a good listener and she understands where I am coming from. She always gets me to look at the bright side of things.'
>
> 'He seems to understand how I feel and tries to reassure me.'

Being trustworthy:

> 'I need to [be able to] trust him.'

Knowledgeable:

> 'She is very intelligent and looks at things from a realistic perspective.'
>
> 'He is old and wise! He is very reassuring and understanding and realistic.'
>
> 'She has been through the same things as me.'
>
> 'My sister . . . went through the same thing.'

It is important that, although approximately 25 per cent of our subjects were receiving counselling or other services at the time of the surveys, less than 10 per cent of responses suggested that subjects would seek counsellors in order to obtain help.

The qualities our respondents desired in their chosen helpers appeared to be related to the ways they wanted helpers to intervene: pay attention to them (listen, comfort/reassure, understand, encourage); give them counsel (help them solve their problems by giving advice, opinions or information) or direct them. Each of these intervention approaches require the skills and qualities of listening and being understanding.

Being attentive:

> 'I want a helper who gives support and shows understanding without trying to intimidate me or say, 'I know what you are going through'.'
>
> 'I want a helper who makes me a cup of tea and reassures me that what I do [wrong] doesn't matter.'
>
> 'Sit down with me and talk it through, give me advice and reassure me.'
>
> 'Just make me feel wanted.'
>
> 'Convince me there is nothing wrong with me.'
>
> 'Be there for me.'
>
> 'Reassure me and make me feel loved.'

Giving advice, opinions or information:

> 'My helper lets me solve the problem myself but provides her help.'
>
> 'I want her to tell me not to get so worked up and that I have the ability to do well. She should help me revise [my work].'
>
> 'Sit down with me and talk it through; give me advice.'

Many subjects, particularly males, also wanted their helpers to 'give them something':

> 'I want her to get me a better place.'

DISCUSSION

Problems

Our English study found that our advantaged and non-advantaged subjects worried generally about problems similar to those of their multinational peers. Primary reported problems included schooling, identity, material concerns, relationships and family issues. Schooling was the main focus for most subjects, and was related often to the seeking of immediate and future employment. The fact that some respondents felt a 'need' for luxury items such as cars or stereos to be important concerns, while others worried about genuine hardship and the struggle to maintain a living points to the growing divide described by researchers between the more and less advantaged in Britain (Williamson 1993). Some young adults have access to resources and money as well as parental support, and can obtain higher education. Other more vulnerable youth, some of whom may have financial but not psychological support, can experience a very different transition process that may result in exclusion from traditional routes to adulthood (Roberts 1995; Williamson 1993; Macdonald 1997; Bates and Riseborough 1993).

Like the counterparts in the Multinational Study, our English subjects were noticeable in the absence of their reporting of issues such as AIDS and other problems known to be extremely serious. Yet, with HIV and AIDS having increased in England during the past three years and the new infection rate for heterosexuals being almost equal to that of homosexual men (Rumbelow 1999), this issue still went largely unreported by our subjects. According to Rumbelow, a study of 16–18-year-olds by the British Health Education Authority showed in December 1999 that most of those surveyed said that the best source of information was the TV soap 'Eastenders' and also that they were unlikely themselves to use a condom during sex. This obviously poses serious problems.

Coping strategies

Most reported coping strategies showed that our subjects attempt to solve their problems by themselves, as did their multinational peers. As regards English subjects in particular, the authors suggest that the choice of individual coping strategies is consistent with British views that people should keep a 'stiff upper lip' and accept responsibility for their own actions, even when coping with social ills such as national unemployment and emphasis on personal responsibility within society.

Our subjects also provided a distressingly high percentage of reports of disengagement and resignation. With British youth facing what they perceive as a multitude of insurmountable problems and the particularly British attitude toward dealing with such problems, we do not consider this surprising. Unfortunately, disengagement and resignation are often associated with apathy, non-involvment, depression and, unfortunately, quiet despair, none of which leads to productive problem-solving.

Helpers

By and large, our subjects sought people outside their families as helpers, with a high percentage of responses suggesting professional counsellors, instructors or social workers when compared with subjects from other countries. Subjects were clear in what they wanted of these helpers: for many, this was comfort and reassurance, although this took different forms for different people. Others desired practical advice. Subjects seemed more concerned that they find psychological support than specific knowledge, that is, they appeared more concerned with their helpers' approaches than the content of what they offered. This emphasis on relationship characteristics rather than definition of the helper–helpee relationship (such as counsellor–client) suggests that being understood might have been even more important than solving the problem, and seems to be strong indication of youth's extreme need to be heard in the face of their difficulties.

IMPLICATIONS FOR COUNSELLING YOUNG PEOPLE

Coping strategies and helper selection

Caught in the process of transition from adolescence to adulthood, our subjects appeared trapped by their situations with many perceiving correctly their powerlessness to create change. As the research literature on help-seeking would suggest (Wills 1983), we believe that it was severe distress regarding powerlessness that led our subjects to seek psychological support rather than practical advice regarding change. (See pp.20–3.)

As pointed out earlier in this chapter, approximately 25 per cent of our subjects were receiving some type of counselling or other service at the time of the survey, although less than 10 per cent of responses indicated that they would seek out a counsellor to help them. What does this tell us about our counselling? Unfortunately, interventions currently featured by British agencies emphasize 'content' strategies designed to 'make things happen' rather than 'make clients feel good'. We suggest that, to increase the positive effects of counselling for severely stressed clients, practitioners need to stop viewing this age group as a homogeneous whole, recognize the entirety of their different situations and develop a larger repertoire of intervention techniques that take into consideration social as well as individual issues. In this regard, it is important to understand the social context of young adult's lives, including the increasing gap between racial and ethnic groups as well as between SES groups. To view the picture in its entirety, agencies offering community services will need to bring into the counselling process professionals in other areas relevant to these situations. National and international agencies will also need to develop new policies to provide youth opportunities for genuine engagements and active participation. (See pp. 30–1.)

As regards specific approaches, we believe that although our subjects suggested that what they wanted was listening and understanding, this is necessary but insufficient to deal with many of the external problems they are facing. Counselling needs to work toward teaching members of this age-group to empower themselves and take control of their lives. Practitioners will need to make informed decisions about how to go about getting to grips together with young people on this issue. For practitioners, this will mean reconsidering our roles in supporting, influencing and developing lives of young people as well as our relationships with others with whom we are working, including professionals from other agencies, and the law. In this regard, we must decide what should be our appropriate roles as professional helpers of youth, given society's demands for social control of young people. Are we part of the societal management system or are we separate? The issue of where we fit should be reviewed as part of training.

We suggest the following counselling approaches as part of the knowledge base of all helping professionals:

- A thorough understanding of the place of the relationship in developing a feeling of empowerment in young people. The qualities that Rogers (1966) advocated in the person-centred approach – active listening that emphasizes empathy, unconditional positive regard and genuineness – are central to this position. We believe that this is particularly important in serious issues such as AIDS in which utilizing appropriate and effective strategies can make the difference between life and death. Rumbelow (1999) suggests that there has been concern in England that insufficient monies are being made available for prevention programmes, in part because of the large expenditures required to make the new drug therapies available. While we agree that one part of the solution is improved prevention services, we believe that these will continue to be less-than-optimally-effective so long as they don't take into consideration the coping strategies being used by youth faced with this problem as well as the type of help they seek. (See pp. 23–5.)
- Group-based strategies to a) encourage the development of a sense of collective or community, b) reduce non-goal-oriented coping strategies such as disengagement and resignation and c) encourage the development of action planning skills in problem-solving. (See pp. 28–30.)
- 'Informal counselling' approaches offered through community-based programmes that utilize informal and easily accessible networks of support and 'ordinary' helpers to create the type of 'ordinary' relationships that clients frequently seek in their friends. We suggest teaching agencies how to provide services in homes, schools and communities, using trained specialists as consultants to informal helpers.
- Multi-intervention approaches designed for different types of clients and situations and which provide support in many forms, for example, dissemination of information, advice, counselling and, at the same time, befriending. Young people do not present problems in categories requiring a specific intervention but often have material physical concerns alongside emotional and psychological issues. Counselling in these case is seen as crucial and necessary but not sufficient intervention.

Note

1 See p. 13 for details regarding reporting of findings in into categories-within-classes.

References

Bates, I. and Riseborough, G. (eds) (1993) *Youth and Inequality*, Buckingham: Open University Press.

Coleman, J. (1997) *Key Data on Adolescence*, Brighton: Trust for the Study of Adolescence.

Coleman, J. and Adamson, W. (eds) (1992) *Youth and Policy in the 1990s*, London: Routledge.

Coles, B. (1995) *Youth and Social Policy: Youth Citizenship and Young Careers*, London: UCL Press.

Cooper, C. (1996) 'Psychological counselling with young people', in Woolfe, R. and Dryden, W. (eds), *Handbook of Counselling Psychology*, London: Sage

Department of Education and Science (1989) *Youth Counselling Services*, London: HMSO.

Feaviour, K. (1992) *The Attitudes of Clients and Providers of Youth Counselling and Advisory Agencies Toward the Dimensions of Confidentiality, Informality, Specificity to Youth and Independence*, unpublished M.Sc. thesis, University of Surrey.

Feaviour, K. (1994) *Who's Really Listening?* Leicester: Youth Access.

Kurtz, Z., Thornes, R. and Wolkind, S. (1994) *Services for the Mental Health of Children and Young People in England: A National Review*, South-West Thames: Regional Health Authority.

Macdonald, R. (ed.) (1997) *Youth, the Underclass and Social Exclusion*, London: Routledge.

Malek, M (1997) *Nurturing Healthy Minds*, London: National Children's Bureau.

Roberts, K. (1995) *Youth and Employment in Modern Britain*, Oxford: Oxford University Press.

Rogers, C. (1966) 'A theory of therapy as developed in the client-centred framework', in Art, A., Jr. (ed.), *Counselling and Psychotherapy*, Palo Alto: Science and Behaviour Books.

Rumbelow, H. (1 December 1999) 'Gay men cease to be most at risk for HIV', London: *The Times* B2.

Tyler, M. (1978) *Advisory and Counselling Services for Young People*, London: HMSO.

Williamson, H. (1993) 'Youth policy in the United Kingdom and the marginalisation of young people', *Youth and Policy* 40: 33–48.

Wills, T. (1983) 'Social comparison in coping and help-seeking', in DePaulo, B., Nadler, A. and Fisher, J. (eds), *New Directions in Helping, Vol. II, Help-seeking*, New York: Academic Press: 107–41.

8 Greece

University and technical institute students in Thessaloniki

Maria Dikaiou and Mika Haritos-Fatouras,
University of Thessaloniki

INTRODUCTION

> Why should you be as noble as a sparkle of light?
> Wouldn't you have been better as a thunder in the sea?
> I could only then have said that I was not looking for you.
> M. Dikaiou (1999)

Changes in culture and tradition

The research reported in this chapter took place at a time when considerable attention was being focused on the role and potential of youth in responding to social and economic conditions. Today, as in 1989 and 1997, Greek families and youth are experiencing unprecedented social change and must cope daily with a variety of new problems. Urbanization and accompanying internal migration have frequently been identified as making daily life more complex and impersonal. Traditional values are being questioned and even traditional conceptualizations of family have changed in the last fifteen years. Nuclear forms of families have steadily replaced the older, extended definition of families, leading to confusion and loss of confidence among youth (Dikaiou *et al.* 1996). Feminist and other social movements have challenged prevailing assumptions about the family by raising questions about gender relations, equity in family relationships and the viability of a monolithic family form.

Entry into the European Community

The ideal of progress that emerged when Greece joined the European Community proclaimed that economic, political, social and cultural integration would make life progressively better. However, as Greek families and youth have striven for continuing improvement in their lives, they have experienced a decrease in economic and socio-cultural well-being in recent years. A changing economy – resulting mainly from ongoing transformation processes in Central and Eastern Europe – has introduced uncertainty into the lives of many people; job security and career advancement are less certain even to those who have received formal education that had guaranteed employment in the past. Today, despite the popularity of contemporary measures designed to guarantee equal opportunities for men and women, a rise in educational standards for everyone and a rise in employment opportunities, there is considerable divergence of views concerning their meaning and value to society (Arnot 1997).

For some, equality is seen in ideological terms. For others it is seen as a useful tool with which to study the rising effects of unemployment among young adults today (Lagree 1995). At the time of writing, 30 per cent of Greek young people were unemployed. This figure included both genders and secondary school as well as graduates of higher education. Traditionally defined occupations for young men and women were no longer available (Deliyannis-Kouimtzi and Ziogou 1995).

Greece's new residents

The situation was aggravated by the presence of refugees and asylum seekers who had entered Greece both with and without legal permits. The number of migrants residing in the country today has increased from 5,000 in 1989 to over 1,500,000. This influx of migrants is perhaps the greatest change which has taken place in Greek society in several decades. While Greece is usually perceived as ethnically, culturally and religiously homogeneous, the arrival of refugees from Albania, the former Soviet Union and the Middle East has created a new mosaic of inter-ethnic and inter-cultural orientations. New conflicts, prejudices and racist attitudes towards new comers have now come to characterize inter-group youth relations (Dikaiou 1996). Much discussion in Greece regarding this social problem has focused on the way local youth construct their notions of the 'other' and how, in this context, newcomers are often blamed by local youth for the increase in unemployment and in anti-social behaviour.

The continuously increasing numbers of minority youth working and/or living on the streets adds another dimension to already-tense inter-group relations, with the local Greeks emphasizing their 'Greekness' as a protective factor in fighting unemployment. From this perspective, it might be said that Greek youth are developing a new sense of identity ominous to the migrants. Although in reality, newcomers to the country are not in a position to compete with locals in any sector of life, the fact that they are perceived as future antagonists creates a 'self-fulfilling prophesy' that they are dangerous.

Given all of these factors, it is clear that young Greek people today are faced with a social reality in which traditional ideas and values about employment, education, family and socio-political life are creating pressures over and above the difficulties presented by external socio-economic changes alone. As one specialist noted:

> Nobody is yet in a position to predict the direction in which these changes will take us. But one thing is certain: they will deeply influence people's lives, particularly those of today's children and young people.
> (Chisholm 1995: 1)

Some sociologists have suggested that one effect on youth of stress caused by societal change is increased drug and alcohol use. No systematic analysis has been conducted to assess a possible association between recent social and demographic changes in Greek society and trends in drug abuse. However, some trends in youth population composition and drug use appear to be related. For example , there was a dramatic increase in the abuse of all types of drugs during the last ten years among youth aged 12–17 years at a time when new waves of immigrants and refugees began arriving in Greece. While these parallel changes do not necessarily imply a cause-effect phenomenon, they may imply that instability in socio-cultural environments imposes increases any existing stresses upon young people. The manner in which youth deal with this reality is explored in the present study.

Higher education in Greece

Higher education is highly valued by the Greek culture. The percentage of young people of both genders who pursue university studies is 85–95 per cent of the university-aged population of Greeks.

This figure is extremely high when compared with university level participation rates in countries of Western Europe (Lampiri-Dimaki 1974; Petmetzidou-Tsoulouvi 1987). At the same time, female students at Greek universities represent the majority enrolled in the Faculties of Arts (75–80 per cent), while they still comprise only 10–15 per cent of those in the Faculties of Sciences (Vretakou 1990). This stereotypic educational division is reflected in the present study with 70 per cent of the women in advantaged and non-advantaged groups in both time periods of the survey studying Arts.

THE STUDY AND ITS METHODOLOGY

Subjects

The Greek study was conducted in 1989 and 1997, two time periods separated by eight years. The research participants were young men and women of advantaged and non-advantaged SES as defined in Chapter 1. All were in the process of completing their first or second year of studies either in arts and sciences at the University of Thessaloniki or at one of the several technical institutes in Thessaloniki. Although not representative of all youth across the entire country of Greece, our respondents portray the mainstream majority culture in the sense that, first, they represent the prevailing cultural norms concerning family expectations about their offspring's entering to higher education; and second, they are not members of any other cultural group including those of return migrants and refugees of Greek origin who have returned to Greece in recent years. Subject populations consisted of 799 young people, 400 surveyed in 1989 and 399 in 1997 as shown in Table 8.1.

Instruments and data collection

Development and administration of the survey questionnaire used the standardized procedures listed for all countries and described in Chapter 1. For the Greek study, the questionnaire was distributed to students in classrooms by four post-graduate students of psychology with experience in applied research settings. Minor revisions were made to the following questions as follows:

- For each of the three questions regarding problems, respondents were asked to rate on a five-point scale the importance of each of the problems reported.
- While answering the questions subjects were encouraged to express their views freely and if possible, personal experiences related to specific situations of problems, coping and help-seeking matters.

Coding of responses

Coding of responses was completed for the 1989 data by the first author and by the 1997 data by the first author (Maria Dikaiou) with the assistance of four research assistants, using the coding scale standardized for that purpose and following the standardized directions provided in Chapter 1. The following procedure was used to determine the reliability of coding by 1997 research assistants: following review by the first author of the coding scale with the assistants, each of the four assistants then coded the same ten Greek questionnaires. Disagreements were discussed and the same procedure was then repeated for an additional ten questionnaires to determine agreement between the four assistants and between the first author and each of the assistants. The coding scale itself is replicated in Appendix I. Reliability of the 1989 coding by the first author and the 1997 data by the first author and coding assistants is listed in Appendix II.

Table 8.1 Greek populations surveyed in 1997 and 1989

	1989		*1997*	
Gender	*adv.*	*non-adv.*	*adv.*	*non-adv.*
Male	100	100	99	100
Female	100	100	100	100

HIGHLIGHTS OF FINDINGS

This chapter reports highlights of the findings of the two Greek surveys conducted in 1989 and 1997. For reasons detailed in Chapter 1, we focus on similarities and differences between subject groups. In the Greek study, this includes gender and SES groups as well as year of the survey. To explain the social significance of our young subjects' reports, their underlying beliefs, ideas and socio-economic or gender practices as they relate specifically to Greek perceptions of present and future realities, we have gone directly to our subjects' own words. Detailed statistical findings provided in Appendix III answer questions of interest to the reader.

In this section, we compare Greek responses collected in 1997 with Greek reports collected in 1989 prior to the current mass immigrations. We also compare findings from 1989 and 1997 surveys by gender and SES. Finally, we compare the Greek findings with those of the Multinational Study.

Problems

The problem reported more frequently than any other by both male and female subjects, regardless of SES or year of survey, was related to personal identity and self-concept with the *foci* on becoming adult and on future careers. These represented more frequent worries of subjects in 1997 (ranging from 24–37 per cent of reported responses) than in 1989 (22–26 per cent of responses) with the highest percentage of responses reported in 1997 by advantaged females.

> 'It is good to feel in control of your life but it only happens when you can practice the profession you are trained for. . . . Our prospects for something like this to happen are minimal.'
>
> 'I worry about my future career. . . . What I want and what I will be forced to do professionally don't match. Unemployment scares me.'
>
> 'I am afraid the government policy to appoint expatriate teachers in schools is far from logical . . . Leaving aside the fact that we [Greek graduates of Greek universities] are properly educated, this policy restricts our prospects for employment [as future teachers].'
>
> 'The way things go everyone, not only Albanians, will be considered suspect in the future. . . . I am afraid the only sector in which one will be able to find a job in the future will be on the police force or at the migration office.'
>
> 'It is true they [immigrants, refugees] get the jobs . . . but only as workers. . . . If the government gives those who have degrees in medicine permission to work as doctors, then we will have a real problem. Authorities will employ them since they cost less.'

When asked to rate problems by importance (see p. 117), ratings showed that subjects considered this to be their most important worry, with non-advantaged subjects considering it more important than advantaged.

Interpersonal problems were second both in frequency of reporting and, in 1997, in rated importance. Concerns about future careers were evident here with a prevailing theme of making and keeping friendships in an antagonistic society:

> 'Making profit sometimes comes before friends. Will I be able to resist pressures?'
>
> 'I don't know whether I can trust my friends to help me . . . people look after their interests first and friendship comes second.'
>
> 'I would hate to lose my friends, but things happen and people lose touch.'

Looking further, worries related to family matters appeared far more frequently in the reports of females than males in both years of the survey. While frustration at what was perceived to be inappropriate strictness of parents was reported frequently in 1989, this issue gave way in 1997 to thoughts of the type of family roles females wanted to play in the future:

> 'I would like to share most of the responsibilities with my companion and not divide tasks according to whether one is the man or the woman. This might be a way for us both to have children and still each keep our teaching career.'
>
> 'I do want to get married and have children, but I am afraid that I will have to compromise a lot and sacrifice many aspects of my career.'

Males, by contrast, were more concerned with 'making money'.

> 'First I need to make enough money to support myself and build an independent life. . . . Other things come second.'

Whenever males expressed views about family, their worries tended to be related to employment and finance.

> 'Will I be able to find a job so I can become financially independent and able to create a family of my own?'

Males worried more than females about material possessions and 'money-making'. Despite the fact that both advantaged and non-advantaged males emphasized acquisitions and money-making, their perceptions of what they 'needed' as well as the time perspective from which they viewed them differed according to their SES backgrounds. That is, advantaged males tended to aim for more expansive goals that might require greater time to reach, while non-advantaged males often worried about – and reported reaching for – 'smaller' and more immediate goals.

From an advantaged male subject:

> 'I want to make enough money to acquire a high position with influence and power. This is the only way to survive.'

From a non-advantaged male:

> 'I always have less money than I need. I can't go where I would like. I can't eat at restaurants [with my fiancé].'

Finally, males generally mentioned schooling concerns such as academic failure and time pressures more than did females, (with the exception of the 1989 non-advantaged sample). In addition, both males and females tended to worry about schooling issues more in 1989 than in 1997, regardless of SES backgrounds.

Coping strategies

Advantaged and non-advantaged Greek subjects of both genders and in both years of the survey coped most frequently by trying to solve their problems themselves, as did their multinational peers. They tried to do so most frequently by planning (analysing the situation and using their assessments to plan action) and 'trying harder' (endeavouring to improve themselves by increasing or decreasing specific behaviours) , also in similar fashion to their multinational peers.

Besides individual-problem-solving, two types of coping strategies, resignation (surrendering to the belief that the problem cannot be solved) and disengagement (disengaging oneself from the situation be escaping or distancing oneself from the problem), were reported with frequency. These two strategies together, both representing non-goal-oriented behaviour, were reported in 23–28 per cent of responses in 1997 and from 21–24 per cent of responses in 1989. They were often used in relationship to concerns regarding attaining success in future careers or finding jobs.

> 'It is out of my control. There is nothing I can do to change the situation.'
>
> 'I don't face it at present. I'm still studying and haven't entered the labour market yet.'

Resignation and disengagement strategies were also used when subjects were reporting their personal feelings about their lack of ability to control the situations in which they lived or about their general despair concerning social values and ideals in Greek society:

> 'When everybody thinks of nothing else but success and money, and when trustworthiness is generally absent from almost every aspect of social life, what can you do? Just distance yourself!'

Those subjects who worried about every-day jobs not being given to Greek nationals often resigned themselves to their situations:

> 'Because they pay Albanians and refugees from Eastern countries less than Greeks, they give them the every-day jobs. There is nothing you can do about it.'

Desired helpers, desired qualities and modes of helping

Our 1997 study showed that Greek subjects, like their multinational counterparts, tended to choose helpers from outside the family, particularly personal friends. Forty-three per cent of advantaged Greek reports and 44 per cent of non-advantaged reports, however, designated a family member first as a desired helper as contrasted with 49 per cent (advantaged) and 50 per cent (non-advantaged reports designating a helper from outside the family.[1] In 1989, advantaged subjects also gave a higher percentage of reports indicating a preference for a family member. Greek preferences were indicated, however, by a lower percentage of responses specifying outside helpers and a higher percentage listing family helpers than in the multinational sample (see Appendices III and IV).

It is important to note that subjects did not always seek the same helper for all their concerns, but made their choices in some instances at least on the basis of their specific problems:

> 'For everyday things like money, clothing and renting a place to live, I turn to my parents; Since they pay all my bills for me, they play a big part in my decision-making.'
>
> 'It depends on the kind of help that I need. I would ask my parents for financial help, but if I wanted to feel better or if I needed moral support, I would ask my boyfriend or another friend. They are the people around me whom I trust. They care about me and are willing to help.'

Choosing to accept help from a family member or someone from outside one's family had to do with other factors, as well). Some of our subjects chose friends as helpers because they found their parents lacking:

> 'I don't go to my parents because I can't communicate with them easily.'

> 'I don't go to my parents because they want to control my life.'

Availability also appeared to be an important issue. One 1997 subject noted:

> 'I seek help from a friend living near me and not from my parents because I am living a long distance from home as a student.'

When our subjects listed what they sought in helpers, all groups, regardless of gender, SES or year of study, suggested helpers who were mature, trustworthy and loyal; caring, understanding, supportive and generous; who could provide useful knowledge because of similarities with the subject in terms of past or present experience.[2] What they wanted their helpers to do also remained the same across time, SES and gender groups: first and foremost, our subjects wanted their helpers to 'counsel' them, that is, to give them advice, to direct them or to help them solve their problem (evidenced in 50 per cent of 1997 responses and 54 per cent of 1989 responses). Next, they wanted their helpers to 'attend' to them, that is, give them encouragement, comfort them and agree with them (shown in 28 per cent of responses in 1997 and 32 per cent of 1989 responses).

COMMENTARY ON OUR FINDINGS

Problems, coping and help-seeking

Self-reported problems, coping strategies and help-seeking methods of advantaged and non-advantaged Greek males and females seem to be much more similar to each other in 1997 and 1989 than different. Our subjects reported problems expected of their age-groups in modern societies in which education is important in deciding futures. Their concerns also reflected realistic interpretations of existing and very real present-day societal problems. There were some gender differences reflective of societal demands, with females still taking on more responsibility for care of families and males responsibility for financial support of families. Deliyanni-Kouimtzi and Ziogou (1995) described this gender distinction in interests, suggesting that, among Greeks, it is related to intense contradictions inherent in Greek society. On one hand, women are directed to traditional roles and typical female professions, and on the other, there is a tendency on the part of parents, educators and society in general to consider university studies as absolutely necessary for both sexes, so long as those studies do not prevent women from their primary mission of caring for the family. Today, family is no longer seen as an autonomous sphere of life as it once was; but is instead more dependent on socio-economic factors.

The fact that there were no apparent differences between SES, gender groups and survey years as regards the major coping strategies reported (individual-problem-solving, resignation and disengagement) underlines the importance of examining the meaning of these strategies in developing appropriate intervention strategies. While resignation and disengagement were appropriately described as non-goal-oriented when we assume that the subject's goal is to solve a particular reported problem (see Chapter 3), we must not assume that these behaviours are necessarily 'maladaptive'. Although coping is sometimes equated with adaptational outcomes, from a social system perspective it is considered a process rather than an outcome and refers to all efforts expended to manage a stressor regardless of the effect (Lazarus and Folkman 1984). In the case of our Greek subjects, we examined their written responses and noted that resignation and disengagement were usually reported in cases in which subjects were facing larger social problems which they personally, did not have ability to surmount. We suggest, therefore, that they are goal-oriented in the sense that they reduced stress.

Finally, it is important that, although our 1997 subjects – like their multinational peers – tended to choose helpers from outside their families, they did so with less frequency than subjects of the Multinational Study. It is also important that they tended to go to their families for help more frequently than outsiders in 1989. These findings suggest that, while Greek families still provide support desired by young people, this support is eroding. The Greek family has always been known for its closeness and support of family members (see, for example, Vassiliou and Vassiliou 1982). The romantic images of life in the family presented in early descriptions, however, has limited value today in the context of the considerable social and economic change Greek society has experienced in recent years. Greek youth today have greater choices of where to live, higher levels of geographical mobility, private styles of living and more dispersed kinship networks. As Doumani (1989) suggested, the greater the freedoms provided to Greek youth, the greater the erosion of the significance of family in their lives. While there is evidence from this as well as from our earlier study of adolescent coping (Dikaiou *et al.* 1996) that families are still important, our findings suggest a decline in their importance in the eight years between our two surveys in which economic and social problems in society have been increasing.

Gender and year of study

We were surprised at the fact that there were few gender differences in our findings. That does not mean that they do not exist, however. As Ridgeway (1997) pointed out, within a social system perspective, whatever the attributions made about male and female coping behaviours, they must be regarded in terms of the interactional settings of the subjects. The status, the power and the attitudes of the other gender have strong effects on behaviour and certainly on reported behaviour, and it is possible that that the fact that our study was conducted in classroom settings in which males and females sat together may have affected our results.

Among the gender differences noted, the fact that males mentioned schooling issues more than did female is similar to the findings of a previous study by the research team investigating adolescent concerns and coping (Gibson-Cline 1996) as well as the 1997 Multinational Study. The fact that both males and females reported a higher percentage of concerns regarding their schooling in 1989 than in 1997 suggests that Greek university students today may not be assigning the great value to education they did in the past because it no longer provides a guarantee of employment.

Another issue worth discussing is related to gender variations across time. Gender role perceptions have certainly undergone significant changes over the last years. Young women although interested in creating a family of their own, are no longer adopting traditional cultural role divisions. This is true for both our 1989 and 1997 results. While young women share similar concerns with males about their interpersonal sphere of life and their self-identity, for example, examination of their words suggest that they also question many things related to their future family roles. (See p. 119 for quote.)

Males on the other hand, besides emphasizing material needs and money in 1997, described emotional problems; fears or worries about being alone or not having other people to talk to. This was not found in 1989 responses, suggesting that this might reflect a trend related to changing societal circumstances.

Finally, a word on how the nature of our study design might have affected the Greek results. As discussed in Chapter 1, young people might display normative coping behaviours when they feel that the situation demands it, and not in situations in which they are not expected to do so. This is to say that societal expectations and views held by those in power as to what youth should or shouldn't be doing, are, among other factors, likely to have influenced our results. This may have had some effect on all results, but there is some particular cause to think it affected the Greek results. At the time this research was conducted, there was a national dissatisfaction with media portrayals which consistently failed to capture the complexity of the behaviour of young people in Greek society. In particular, the presentation of young people was, and still is, often defined in relation to apathy, mediocrity, conservative values and lack of socio-political concerns. It is entirely possible that our young Greek subjects responded in ways they thought they should be feeling or acting based on what the media told them they did.

In summary, we believe that Greek young people today are caught in a contradictory situation: on the one hand, they want to become independent from their parents as soon as possible to build their own identities; on the other hand, they are forced to stay for longer in their parents' home since long educational paths, unfavourable labour-market conditions and high costs of living are making them economically dependent upon their parents. Almost all our respondents whose families reside in the same city as the university, lived with and were supported by their parents at the time of our surveys. Among those living on their own, those in danger of becoming unemployed were forced to rely upon the family as a support structure.

IMPLICATIONS FOR RESEARCH AND INTERVENTION

The Greek study examined perceived problems, coping strategies and help-seeking of young people. We found in our results many cases in which these variables appeared to be interrelated. We suggest that the next step should be thorough examination of the potential relationships between social and economic changes, family relationships and perceived problems and coping strategies from the perspectives of youth as well as the examination of the effects on youth of social and economic change.

While it is commonly assumed that contemporary European societies are in a phase of accelerated change (Chisholm 1995), the processes involved are usually described in theoretical terms such as similarities and differences in chances and risks taken by the various European national groups. The psychological and social policy issues remain poorly understood and lead to rhetoric describing equality of opportunity or common interests in national or European level but that mask inequalities, conflicting interests and lack of common understanding.

If we are to work for the betterment of society, research and policy-making go hand-in-hand. To develop effective policy principles and intervention procedures for young people, we must begin by learning what the specific realities under which young people live actually are. Such recognition requires taking young people's anxieties seriously, which in turn demands a commitment to an open, humanitarian society. We have seen in our study questioning of the social system by some young people who perceive the social system as creating a power struggle rather than a system of friendship and peer relationships. Whatever efforts are made to provide young people with good quality of information, advice and resources to meet their needs, these will be unproductive as long as young people remain mere observers of the policies made for them. Thus, interventions could begin by engaging youngsters in creating interventions. (See Chapter 2, pp. 28–31.)

POSTSCRIPT

The second author (Mika Haritos-Fatouras), together with colleagues from other European universities, visited Havana University in 1998 for one month.[3] During that time they studied and evaluated community-based programmes in the area. The method of intervention proposed in this chapter was influenced by one of these community-based programmes that has operated in a district of Havana under auspices of the University Centre for Orientation and Psychological Help and which had been reported in 1997 to have a high-risk youth population with a significant rise in aggressive and violent behaviour.

The overall aim of this programme was to 'increase the potential of the community'. Specific goals included:

- involving youth in projects in which they collaborated together with the adults of their community
- bridging the generation gap
- creating a balance between available resources and community needs.

To accomplish these goals, cross-aged community discussion groups organized by the working team of the Centre were carried out in open forums. The following themes were aimed at discerning a common community identity:

- a historical community memory
- common values of solidarity, collectivism and social welfare.

The programme lasted approximately one year, during which time aggressive behaviour on the part of youth dropped significantly. The end product was the creation of common projects which the groups had decided upon. These were operated by old and young community members according to their abilities (a library, a coffee house and so on). The projects were still going strong after a one-year follow-up.

While we do not propose that this kind of community intervention should be copied as it stands because intervention is culture bound, we do suggest that communities can play important roles in working with youth.[4] We believe that community help, if used to best advantage, can provide important help today, when rapid urbanization is causing disruption of social networks, as in Greece. Youth needs helpers, and the helping process should not be limited to merely having an expert – or friends – listen to their clients (or friends) and make pronouncements as to what should be done. Moreover, young people should not be cut off from the older people of their communities, thereby widening the age gap. Young people can learn how useful older people can be in many situations, as, for example, in mixed-age discussion groups designed to solve problems of common interest. Furthermore, groups should not be isolated from others behind closed doors in their discussing. Experts should facilitate conversation, help individuals learn to communicate with one another and express their attitudes, frustrations, desires and problems. The group should examine together social constructions which maintain the generation gap and determine what they lose in terms of available helping assets by talking and thinking this way. It is unfortunate that Greek counsellors rarely use this approach.

Communication groups can be carried out in the open, in front of other members of the community who can watch and listen, and then discuss among themselves, in their own families and social surroundings what is being discussed. In this way, the effect of group discussions can be spread and generalized. Common projects carried out together by old and young would help sustain gains over time and create a better future for the whole community. Overall, this approach should lead to increases in self-esteem of participants as well as in the collective image of the community, making people proud and happier living, working or studying.

When our young Greek subjects were in trouble, they frequently coped via resignation and disengagement. It should be noted that such coping strategies were most often reported when our respondents were facing large social problems. We think, therefore, that prevention programmes in which the entire community is involved could act as buffer zones protecting young people from such feelings and behaviour, while at the same time involving them and their community in a creative and rewarding life.[5]

Notes

1 'Averages' reported are means of males and female percentages reported in Appendix III.
2 These qualities are listed in Appendix III under categories of the classes 'personal helper attributes', 'concern', 'knowledge'.
3 This visit was financed by the 'Alpha' European Union Programmeme, a three-year project providing exchange of teaching staff and post-graduate students between Latin American and European universities.
4 The term 'community', as we use it here, is not be limited to a neighbourhood, village or even a town. We consider a community to be simply a group of individuals with common interests, such as a school community (students, parents and teachers) or a sports community, etc.
5 For a description of another type of community programme in a western country see pp. 101–2.

References

Arnot, M. (1997) 'Gendered citizenry: new feminist perspectives on education and citizenship', *British Research Journal* 23: 3.

Arnot, M., Araujo, H., Deliyanni, K., Ziogou, R. and Ivinson, G. (1998) 'Changing femininity, changing concepts of citizenship: social representations of public and private spheres in a European context', *European Journal of Women's Studies*.

Chisholm, L. (1995) 'Problems and challenges in developing European youth policies', in Chisholm, L., Buchner, P., Kruger, H. and du Bois-Reymond, M. (eds), *Growing up in Europe: Contemporary Horizons in Childhood and Youth Studies*, New York: Walter de Gruyter, 283–5.

Delligianni, K. and Ziogou, S. (1993) *Education and Gender*, Vanias: Thessaloniki, Greece, in Greek.

Deliyannis-Kouimtzi, K. and Ziogou, R. (1995) 'Gendered youth transitions in northern Greece: between tradition and modernity through education', in

Chisholm, L., Buchner, Kruger, H. and du Bois-Reymond, M. (eds), *Growing up in Europe: Contemporary Horizons in Childhood and Youth Studies*, New York: Walter de Gruyter: 209–20.

Dikaiou, M. (May 1996) *National or Minority Identity? Adolescents' Problems and Coping Strategies*, paper presented at the Sixth Panhellenic Conference on Psychological Research, Patra, Greece.

Dikaiou, M. (October 1996) *Forms of Social Exclusion of Children*, paper presented at the Comparative Research Programme on Poverty, Crete, Greece.

Dikaiou, M., Haritos-Fatouras, M. and Kiosseoglou, G. (1996) 'The Greek study', in Gibson-Cline, J. (ed.), *Adolescence: From Crisis to Coping*, London: Routledge, 87–102.

Dikaiou, M. and Kiosseoglou, G. (1994) 'Identified problems and coping strategies: Gypsy minority versus non-minority adolescents', *International Migration* 3: 473–95.

Doumani, M. (1989) *The Greek Mother*, Athens: Kedros, in Greek.

Gibson-Cline, J. (ed.) (1996) *Adolescence: From Crisis to Coping*, London: Routledge.

Lachman, S. (1993) 'Statistically significant differences or probable non-chance difference?' *American Psychologist* 48: 1093–4.

Lagree, J. (1995) 'Young people and employment in the European Community: convergence or divergence?' in Chisholm, L., Buchner, P., Kruger, H. and du Bois-Reymond, M. (eds), *Growing up in Europe: Contemporary Horizons in Childhood and Youth Studies*, New York: Walter de Gruyter: 61–72.

Lampiri-Dimaki, I. (1974) *Towards a Greek Sociology of Education*, Athens: National Centre for Social Research, in Greek.

Lazarus, R. and Folkman, S. (1984) 'Coping and adaptation', in W. Gentry (ed.), *Handbook of Behavioural Medicine*, New York: Guilford Press: 44–68.

Petmetzidou-Tsoulouvi, M.(1987) *Social Class and the Mechanisms of Social Reproduction*, Athens: Exantas, in Greek.

Ridgeway, C. (1997) 'Interaction and the conservation of gender inequality', *American Sociological Review* 62 (2): 218–35.

Vassiliou, G. and Vassiliou, V. (1982) 'Promoting psychosocial functioning and preventing malfunctioning', Athens: *Pedetican* 2 (1–2): 90–8, in Greek.

Vretakou, V. (1990) *School Vocational Guidance in Greece*, Athens: Papazisi.

9 India

University and technical institute students in Mumbai

Lina Kashyap, Tata Institute of Social Sciences

INTRODUCTION: THE INDIAN CONTEXT

> If there is one group above all others who should be our concern, it must be youth. They are the inheritors of our future. In all things, the torch must pass to the next generation.
>
> (Indira Gandhi 1984)

In 1985, the United Nations International Year of Youth, the government of India began what became its present major focus on the welfare of young people. What once was the national Ministry of Education with youth

'I want to invent something unique, to break a world record, to become famous.'

Prakash: tall, well-dressed, communicative, advantaged male, 20 years old, eldest son with two siblings. Father holds a Master's degree in business management and currently works in Dubai; mother is a housewife and a college graduate.

'My ambition is to become an aeronautics engineer. I want to invent something unique, to break a world record, to become famous. I'm fortunate to be able to prepare {for my career} in a good school. I work hard and get high grades. After graduation, I want to get a job to ease my father's {financial} burden. But I plan to study business management on a part-time basis at the same time.

Right now, my major concern is my younger brother. He is taking his studies lightly, has started smoking and is talking about dropping out of school to start a business. I am trying to motivate him to study.

Ten years from now? I will have a family of my own, live independently, somewhere close to my parents. I will have a good wife by my side (whom I will treat as an equal), and at least three children. I will have a luxurious house, a car at my door, several servants. I will be working on making a new type of car or airplane.'

services attached became the Department of Youth Affairs and Sports, which now serves under the Ministry of Human Resource Development to initiate national youth programmes. In 1988, Parliament passed its first National Youth Policy which recognized that Indian young people need opportunities to develop their personalities and functional capabilities if they are to become useful and productive adult citizens, and the government began the task of determining what needed to be done. It was a complex task, requiring understanding of social and socio-cultural realities of people living in a multi-cultural, multi-ethnic, multi-lingual and multi-religious society which is, at the same time, traditional, heterogeneous and diverse as well as stratified on the basis of caste and socio-economic class.

To complicate matters, India's emergence into the modern technological world has affected the economic, social and cultural fabric of all components of its society, including its youth. Today, Indian young people are expected to integrate into the social order into which they were born and, at the same time, serve as part of the force that will transform that order to meet the country's present-day needs. They form a heterogeneous population with statuses, problems and aspirations that vary with their demographic and socio-economic characteristics.

This introduction highlights Indian young people today. The chapter that follows describes one particular group of Indian youth: urban student youth in Mumbai (formerly Bombay), an island megalopolis, sea port, air traffic hub and centre of commerce, finance, technology and production. Mumbayites are immigrants and descendants of immigrants who came from all parts of the country. A city of many tongues, religions, life-styles, modes of dress and cuisine which co-exist separately in close proximity, Mumbai has many institutions of higher education and attracts student youth across the country.

Demographic characteristics of Indian youth

According to the most recent statistics available in India (Census of India 1991), approximately one-third of India's population – 154 million individuals – are between 15 and 24 years, and two-thirds are below 30 years. Male and female youth between the ages of 15 and 24 years constitute approximately 80 million and 74 million respectively, with a sex ratio of 924 females per 1,000 males. Well over 85 per cent of all births occur to females from 15–29 years of age, due in large part to a high rate of deaths during childbirth, low nutritional standards and lack of adequate medical facilities.

Indian young people account for 20 per cent of urban and 18 per cent of rural populations (Census of India: 1991), with a growing decline in youth populations in rural and increase in urban areas. The majority of 18–20-year-olds (the age of subjects of our study) are not in school and only a privileged few, mostly from urban areas, complete higher education. Unemployment is high and most of those employed work at unskilled jobs. The majority of rural youth are non-or barely-literate and work as day-labourers. These youth face the extreme poverty, lack of educational and vocational training facilities, exploitation from upper socio-economic groups, and unemployed and under-employment. The age of 'youth' as thought of in Western countries, is brief, if present at all.

Marriage and family life

Marriage in India is appropriately considered as a patriarchal alliance between two families rather than a uniting of two individuals. Arranged marriage is the pattern in both rural and urban areas. Even when young people are asked their choices, family approval is essential for the marriage to take place.

Early marriages are common, both because virginity is still prized in females and because unmarried daughters are considered economic burdens and social liabilities. Approximately 59 per cent of young women and 23 per cent of young men between 15 and 24 years old are married. The mean age at marriage of females is 19.3 years in rural areas and 21.5 years in urban, although this varies dramatically by state (International Institute of Population Studies 1995).

Dowries are still provided paid by parents of brides, often with the cost increasing with the age of the bride. Ironically, families that have not made great sacrifices for young daughters often make them in order to create large dowries so as to attract families with financially well-off, well-educated sons (Lakshminarayana 1985; Mishra 1993). Most couples begin married life in the home of the groom's parents. Today, two-thirds of Indian births take place while the couple is still living in that home.

Socialization of males and females

In India, male and female children are socialized differently from early ages. The young daughter's socialization is designed to equip her for the demands of her adult roles as wife and daughter-in-law. On attaining puberty, she is faced with her parents' anxiety about finding a marriage partner and her own uncertainty about the type of marital home she will enter. In a family system that remains patriarchal, patrilineal and patrilocal, young women have a subordinate status first in their parental and later in their marital families. Heavy demands on them are made in both homes in terms of house work and socially appropriate behaviour. However, as more young women obtain higher education, enter the occupational world and gain some economic independence, especially in urban areas, these females are beginning to question patriarchal norms and are becoming less willing to accept subservient roles. Such is the case of the female subjects of this study.

Sons, on the other hand, are looked upon as economic assets and are expected to fulfil parental aspirations. In contrast to their sisters, they are usually indulged from an early age and more frequently grow up carefree and psychologically secure. They achieve autonomy and maturity only when they begin to cope with the outside world. Married sons have a higher status in the family than their unmarried brothers, and are usually consulted in major family decisions. Unmarried sons and educated but unemployed sons have inferior status.

'What kind of spouse will I have? How would my family react if my marriage were to fail?'

Sarita, 20 years old, is the middle child of five daughters and one son in a lower middle class non-advantaged Gujarati family (a traditional Indian family from the State of Gujarat whose norms and rituals have passed with little change from one generation to another in spite of cultural changes taking place around them). The family's primary source of income is the rent from a dye-making factory owned by her late father. Sarita was educated in a 'gujarati' medium school and had difficulty with English language college studies. She dropped out of college after one year and works as a clerk in a travel agency. Ten years hence, she hopes to be happily married with two-to-three children. She longs to become a mother and the centre of her husband's universe.

Sarita's present worries are about her marriage. While looking forward to being a wife, she is anxious about the kind of spouse and marital family she will have and all the adjustments she will have to make. She is worried about how she would cope if her marriage failed and what her family's reaction would be. Recently, she read an article in a magazine that women have their own individuality and identity. This has made her realize that life and times around her are changing and she is at present quite frightened about the growing awakening of her own individuality and desires. She does not know whom she can talk with about her turmoil.

Indian youth, regardless of gender, are socialized to believe that it is their sacred duty to look after their parents, and most youth honour their believed duty.

Romance and sexuality

Mishra (1993) pointed to sexuality as an important cause of student anxiety. These authors observed that students are increasingly exposed to themes of sex and romantic love through the media, but, due to strict norms regarding sex segregation, they have very little socially approved opportunities even to mix with the opposite sex. Moreover, there is nothing in their upbringing or education that teaches them how to behave in situations where they find themselves interacting. Ambivalent attitudes among privileged youth concerning parent-arranged marriages aggravates the situation.

Education, employment and student unrest

In Mumbai, most colleges offering bachelor degrees in arts, science, commerce and home science are affiliated with the University of Bombay. There are also a few women's colleges affiliated to the SNDT (Shrimati Nathibai Damodar Thakersey) Women's University.

Indian educational policy is aimed at improving quality at all levels, and making education accessible to all castes in urban, rural and tribal areas as well as to persons with disabilities. Schools and colleges opened in most areas of the country after independence. Unfortunately, education has not yet been made available to many youth from urban slums, rural and tribal areas and some lower castes, and many from these groups, if they go to school at all, drop out before secondary level. Those privileged to pursue higher education usually come from urban middle or high socio-economic backgrounds. Government policy now provides assistance to a small percentage of young people from low socio-economic and tribal backgrounds and lower castes to pursue higher education. However, as first generation entrants, many find it difficult to continue for want of economic and, for some, cultural family support. While low income families must sacrifice in order for their children to obtain higher education, some, usually uneducated, parents do not fully understand the value of formal education in daily life. Some expect their sons to join them in whatever unskilled, semiskilled or skilled trade they are pursuing. Some parents of daughters fear that they will not be able to find suitable husbands for their daughters if they are 'over-educated'. In similar fashion, some young women who wish to pursue higher education are viewed with suspicion and have their moral character doubted by their caste community.

One young woman described her experiences as follows:

> 'Whenever I leave for college in the morning or come home from college in the evening, I hear loud comments made about me, my dress and what I must be doing all day away from home instead of helping my mother in the house.'

Most Indian families, however, view education as important to profitable adult life, with rural families wanting to educate their sons so that they will be able to obtain employment in fields other than farming (Parasuraman 1985) and urban advantaged parents wanting both sons and daughters to be educated: sons to find employment that will make them upwardly mobile and daughters to obtain urban educated husbands. Most Indian college students pursue their studies full-time. They are not employed in any part-time or seasonal jobs and except in rare cases, have not had any paid work experience of any kind, but are dependent on their families for support. For this and other reasons discussed earlier, families have a great say in the education and career choices of their children.

Most college students are less anxious about choosing occupations than about finding employment. In 1990, according to the National Convention on Youth, India had 16 million unemployed educated youth (Pathak 1995). Today the figure may be higher. One cause is India's deteriorating economic situation. Unemployment among educated Indian youth, however, has often been attributed to India's archaic higher education system and a curriculum that does not teach skills needed by employers and instead reinforces rote-learning so that students may learn to quote various points of view without understanding what they mean (Damle 1995).

In recent years, feelings of anxiety, purposelessness and frustration among students have been associated with rises in drug addiction, suicide and so on. Student agitation against government policies that they accuse of reducing their educational and occupational opportunities has taken place on many campuses, leading to government action against student militants in Punjab and the north-eastern as well as other states. In India, every major political party has a youth wing in metropolitan cities which consists mostly of college students. These become more active just before national or regional elections. Student activism against government policies is usually based on specific issues and is sporadic and fragmented. Interestingly, none of the subjects of this study discussed student activism as a problem or solution to a problem.

Student guidance services

Most Indian universities today have a department of student welfare to provide student guidance and counselling. However this department normally works with limited staff who play multiple roles. Most universities provide aptitude testing, vocational guidance and career information and some offer special courses on individual development and communication skills. Although some institutions use counsellors for student counselling and guidance, others utilize multi-disciplinary teams of college teachers. Thus, while some guidance is provided throughout the country, most services are neither adequate to meet student needs nor uniformly available (Hans 1994).

SUBJECTS AND METHODOLOGY

Subjects

The 18–20-year old-young people in this study are all undergraduate college students studying for arts, sciences or commerce degree in Mumbai. They include 136 'advantaged' subjects (thirty-nine males and ninety-seven females) and 102 'non-advantaged' subjects (thirty-five males and sixty-seven females) with SES statuses defined according to the descriptions given in Chapter 1 for all countries of the Multinational Study. Although both 'advantaged' and 'non-advantaged' subjects were privileged in the sense that they could attend higher education in India, they are distinguishable in the following way:

- Advantaged subjects came from educated families where 96 per cent of fathers and 67 per cent of mothers were university graduates.
- Non-advantaged subjects came from families in which 9 per cent of fathers and 28 per cent of mothers were non-literate. No parents had college degrees, although a majority of fathers and more than half of mothers had completed high school. The majority of non-advantaged youth were first generation entrants into higher education. It is probable that many of the families of these students had made considerable sacrifices to enable them to pursue their educations.

It should be noted that only a small percentage of youth in India are able to pursue their education beyond the matriculation or secondary school level. While for most of the subjects, Mumbai was their home and they lived with their parents, for quite a few, it was a place they had come to from other parts of India to pursue higher education. These students lived in college hostels or in paying guest accommodation or with relatives.

Setting of the surveys

The Indian sample was drawn from three colleges: a prestigious college in south Mumbai; a middle-class suburban college and a women's college. Students were reading for science, arts or commerce degrees. All colleges had adequate extra-curricular activities and active student unions.

Data collection and coding

The Indian Study, as other national studies included in the Multinational Study, asked subjects to describe the problems that caused them concern, the strategies they used to solve their problems and the types of help they sought in problem-solving (see Chapter 1 for details). Collection of students' responses to the survey and coding of subjects' responses also followed standardized procedure used in all countries and described in Chapter 1. For this study, data collection and coding was done by the author with the assistance of a psychologist and a social worker. Though the medium of instruction in all Indian institutions of higher education is English, some non-advantaged subjects were not totally fluent in English. The questionnaire was therefore translated into Marathi (the regional language of the state to which Mumbai belongs) for these students.

HIGHLIGHTS OF OUR FINDINGS

The responses of our Indian subjects are described below in terms of subjects' gender and SES background and compared with the same groups in our 1997 Multinational Study. Findings are reported in this chapter in terms of highlights only. Full statistical findings are available in Appendix III.

Problems

Regardless of gender and SES backgrounds of our subjects, their primary concerns were related first to identity/self-concept (33–39 per cent of responses) and second to schooling (17–24 per cent of responses). Schooling and identity/self-concept were also the two primary concerns reported in the Multinational Study.

For Indian male subjects, identity issues (representing 33–38 per cent of their responses) were most often related to 'becoming adult' and were frequently tied to choices regarding their future careers:

> 'I don't know what career I should choose. Should I go in for computer engineering or for business management? Which one will get me a good paying job? I wish I could discuss this with someone.'
>
> 'My parents expect me to find a job as soon as I graduate, but I would like to study further and come up in life.'

'Identity and becoming adult' was also a concern of female subjects of both SES backgrounds (representing 37–39 per cent of their responses). But while female identity worries were sometimes related to future careers, they also dealt with lack of self-confidence. This was related in some cases to taking stands regarding their gender roles.

> 'My parents don't even consider my wishes about my career and life goals.'
>
> 'My parents want me to get married as soon as I graduate, but I want a career. I want to stand on my own feet before I marry. How can I convince them?'

It was also related to interacting with others in general and being accepted socially by peers.

> 'I'm a very shy person and not able to take initiative in interacting, especially with the opposite sex.'

For non-advantaged males and females, lack of self-confidence also stemmed from embarrassment and awkwardness caused by attempting to imitate the life styles of more advantaged peers.

> 'I can't speak English well, so I hesitate to mix with my classmates. They might laugh at my English.'

Among the schooling worries of both genders (expressed in 17–24 per cent of responses), 'inability to learn' was reported most frequently. Non-advantaged subjects expressed this concern more than advantaged subjects (7 per cent of advantaged reports contrasted with 11 per cent (male) and 13 per cent (female) of non-advantaged reports).

> 'I need to get at least 95 per cent in my examination this year to be admitted to a good medical school. I don't know if I can do it.'

There were many complaints about problems in the Indian educational system:

> 'I don't find relevance in what they teach us.'
>
> 'Subjects are taught mechanically and there is no effort to relate them to real life.'
>
> 'At the end of the year, teachers hurry to finish by throwing everything together without taking time to explain. It becomes terrible confusing.'

The reports of some students from non-advantaged backgrounds suggested that they faced particular difficulties in coping with their studies because of lack of support from their uneducated families. Both men and women suggested that their families believe that they are wasting their time and should be working to supplement the family income.

> 'My parents have refused to finance my education any further because they believe I have sufficient education to work for my father in his business. I don't want to be my father's assistant! I want to become a professional person. So I must earn first class grades. That way, I can be eligible for a scholarship.'

Family related problems were reported more frequently by females than males, just as in the Multinational Study.

It is interesting to note that advantaged males reported worries about material desires for tangible items more frequently than their non-advantaged counterparts (11 per cent of advantaged contrasted with 1 per cent of non-advantaged male reports). This need for material possessions appeared in the responses of some other subject groups in the multinational study and may be a response among our Indian subjects to both the stiff competition in school and increasing consumerism in their society, leading them to work only toward what they feel are personally rewarding and prestigious lives.

> 'I believe that only those who are successful in life and who have well-paid jobs, apartments and cars are respected by their families and enjoy high status in their communities.'

By contrast, non-advantaged males reported a higher percentage of altruistic concerns than their advantaged peers (8 per cent as compared to 5 per cent for advantaged male). Indian responses suggested desire to serve others and dealt with public and social issues such as preservation of the environment, communal riots, violence against women, substance abuse, etc. It is interesting that this type of concern was reported more frequently among non-advantaged than advantaged subjects in the Multinational Study, as well, and that males tended to report this concern more frequently than females. This issue is discussed in Chapter 3.

> 'I want to do something about the misery and suffering of the deprived sections of the society.'

> 'I want to work towards making our population literate, then only will our country move ahead.'

Coping strategies

Most Indian subjects tried most frequently, just as their multinational peers, to solve their problems by themselves by trying harder (20–28 per cent of responses) or planning ways to solve their problems (11–17 per cent of responses). This was true regardless of SES or gender.

The next most frequently mentioned strategy reported by all subject groups, as in the Multinational Study, was resignation (surrender to the conclusion that the problem cannot be resolved). When the percentage of reports describing disengagement (avoiding or distancing oneself from the problem) are added together to describe a coping response that is not oriented toward solving the stated problem, this new class of coping accounts for between 20 and 25 per cent of all coping reports.

Male subjects tended more than females to seek others to help them solve their problems. While female subjects also sought other people, they preferred to seek them for their company

Helpers, their desired qualities and modes of helping

The young adult years are of a stage in their life when it is expected that friendships become more stable and strong. Thus it is not surprising that Indian youth, like their multinational peers, turned more frequently to their personal friends for help than they did anyone else. This does not mean that they did not turn to their families. To the contrary, while 49–51 per cent of Indian reports suggested that they went for help outside their families, another 38–41 per cent suggested going for help to a family member, most frequently the subject's mother. This is a high percentage, given the fact that approximately 30 per cent of subjects came to Mumbai, the site of our survey, leaving their families behind. For these subjects, if help was to be obtained, it had to come from outside the family.

Some kept their problems to themselves and none mentioned instructors as helpers.

> 'I have no one to tell my troubles to.'
>
> 'My problems cannot be solved, so I have not spoken to anybody about them.'

When our subjects did seek help, what influenced their choices? Personal qualities such as being understanding and good listeners were important. It is significant that all subject groups wanted helpers to counsel them by giving them advice worthy of being followed upon request and that advantaged subjects wanted, in addition, to be given 'authoritative directions' telling them what to do.

For advantaged subjects, having knowledge either from past or present experiences similar to the subject or experience with the subject's concern was also important. Non-advantaged subjects preferred helpers to counsel them by giving advice and being willing to help, thus providing some tangible support.

All subject groups (with the exception of advantaged males) wanted advice and clear directions as to what they should do, much like their multinational peers.

IMPLICATIONS OF OUR FINDINGS FOR COUNSELLING

Though this study is based on a small sample of student youth from only one city in India, the problems mentioned by our subjects are quite similar to those reported in other Indian studies (Gore 1977; Lakshminaryana 1985; Mishra 1993) and suggest what youth counsellors in India will need to do in the coming years. While our Indian subjects are concerned about developmentally related issues such as self-identity and preparation for adulthood, their concerns are culturally-related as well. Female subjects worry very specifically about difficulties inherent in their roles as Indian women while men worried about how to fulfil their male roles as future heads of families. Our subjects coped by trying to solve their problems themselves, and resigning themselves to their fates when they felt they could not succeed. They looked for helpers who would counsel them, actively listen to them and support them in their endeavours as well as help prepare them for their adult roles. To meet their expectations and reach out to the vast number of student youth in the country, Indian counsellors will have to expand their scope of work and use a variety of intervention approaches.

Should we be concerned about the high percentage of subjects resigning themselves to their fate? The fact is that most problems that evoked this coping strategy stemmed from large societal problems linked to India's current socio-politico-economic realities over which they have no control. Indian youth today are faced with severe competition and scarce resources, and the current employment situation does not give much hope for change. It is understandable that subjects felt powerless against the tight grip of family pressures and totally frustrated with the inefficient and irrelevant educational system. It is also understandable that, finding themselves suspended between traditional/conservative and modern perspectives and values, they suspend judgment and action. In fact, this may be the most productive response they can make without help. Unfortunately, the current situation provides little help and, on college campuses, students perceive, perhaps correctly, that teachers are indifferent to their needs and don't want to or can't help them (Mishra 1993). This is clearly the counsellor's needed role.

Following from the commentary of our subjects, counsellors need to ensure, first, that youth are provided with the opportunity to express positive qualities such as idealism, volunteerism, dynamism, pioneering spirit, willingness to make sacrifices, receptivity to new ideas, courage and potential for creativity and growth. The responses of our subjects indicate that they would benefit from person-centred guidance and counselling in matters related to human relations, self-development and anxiety about their future role as adults.

Considering the disadvantages that Indian female youth face, there is a need for feminist youth programmes in which counsellors work specifically with young women to help them explore their femininity and gender stereotyping, and to find avenues for utilizing their potentials to create positive change and equality of opportunity.

In order to reach out to large numbers of youth, especially those who may hesitate independently to approach adults with their concerns, Hans (1994) suggested that counsellors need to offer developmental activities in the form of life skill programmes which teach students how to function as useful members of their families, peer groups, colleges and society. These programmes could include sessions related to personality development, communication and negotiation skills, value clarification, problem solving skills, decision making skills, vocational guidance, family life education and health information on stress, addiction, HIV/AIDS, nutrition etc. should be participatory in nature and fully involve the students in the learning-sharing process. As it would be impossible in the near future to prepare a sufficient number of trained counsellors for the thousands of colleges in India, the contemporary youth counsellor will need to play the role of master trainers and prepare college teachers to offer these life skills programmes.

The altruistic expressions of student youth need to be encouraged through comprehensive National Service Schemes, as participation in such schemes would not only enable them to understand and respond to social issues but also provides personal benefits in terms of acquiring self confidence, developing better interpersonal communication skills and becoming a part of social group. At present this scheme is an extra-curricular activity and is voluntary in nature. The author agrees with Hans (1996), that there is a need for youth activists and counsellors to lobby with the government for institutionalizing this scheme so that it becomes a co-curricular activity in every college in the country. (See pp. 26–31.)

To succeed in helping young people to change the situations in which they are finding themselves, youth counsellors will need to go beyond providing traditional services to youth. They will have to lobby alongside youth to convince the government to revamp the system of higher education, increase its quality and make it relevant to today's world. Given the reaction of the government to past student activism, this may place counsellors in difficult positions. If they are to promote needed change, however, they will need to learn to tread thin lines, just as counsellors in many other countries of the Multinational Study whose clients face similar problems.

Finally, there is currently a paucity of trained counsellors in India and few of them are actually involved in working with youth. Since this situation is not likely to improve in the near future, it will be necessary to prepare volunteer and teachers as well as youth themselves to use a variety of strategies if we are to reach out to this important population. It is time for India to review its National Youth Policy and prepare an action plan involving participation of youth.

Note

The author wishes to thank Shireen Desai and Bhavna Kapadia for their assistance in data collection and coding.

References

Census of India (1991) *Final Population Totals*, New Delhi: Government of India.

Damle, Y. (1966) *College Youth in Poona: A Study of Elite in the Making*, Poona: Poona University.

Damle, Y. (1995) 'The role of youth in a transitional society', *Anubhav.* 7: 24–9.20.

Gandhi, I. (Novenber 1984) *Youth Bulletin*: 1.

Gore, M. (1977) *Indian Youth: The Process of Socialization*, New Delhi: Vishwa Yuvak Kendra, 301.431–G56I 44144.

Hans, G. (1994) 'Life style education for student youth: need and strategy', *Indian Journal of Social Work* 55 (1): 25–40.

Hans, G. (1996) 'Future perspectives on the youth policy and programmemes', *Indian Journal of Social Work* 57 (3): 461–73.

International Institute of Population Studies (1995) *National Family Health Survey*, Mumbai: IIPS

Lakshminaryana, H. (1985) *College Youth: Challenge and Response*, Delhi: Mittal.

Mishra, V. (1993) *Youth Culture: A Comparative Study in the Indian Context*, New Delhi: Inter-Indias.

Parashuraman, S. (1985) 'Youth: An Indian perspective', *Anubhav.* 7: 14–23.

Pathak, B. (1995) 'The need for a youth policy', in Mohammad, N. and Matin, A. (eds), *Indian Youth: Problems and Prospects*, New Delhi: Ashish.

10 Israel

Mainstream Jewish youth

Benjamin Shafrir, Takam Kibbutz Movement Child and Family Guidance Clinic

INTRODUCTION

This chapter describes the problems and coping of a sample of mainstream Jewish-Israeli youth. It does not include Arab or other minority youth living in Israel, not because of the author's disregard for these populations, but because of his professional involvement with Jewish subjects and their availability to him.

The country of Israel today is comprised of approximately 5,759,000 permanent residents, of which approximately 4,600,000 are Jews, 900,000 Arabs and 200,000 other minorities. Jewish adolescents and youth number approximately 508,000 of which 391,000 are 15–19 years of age (Israeli Statistical Abstract 1997). Jewish-Israeli mainstream society consists of third

'What worries me most? The next three years of army service . . .
Whether there will be peace or war . . .
First of all I want to be in one piece after my army service.'

Modi, a 20-year-old male Jewish-Israeli soldier. Father: vice-president of a bank; mother: musicologist, M.A. in Fine Arts.

'What do I want to be ten years from now? You want me to be a prophet? . . . OK! First of all I want to be in one piece after my army service. After that, I want to travel .for a year. Then I want to start at the university, probably computer science. After I graduate, I will marry, have one child and work as a computer analyst attached to the medical field.

I don't want to be absorbed in routine, have a boring existence, like paying the mortgage, meeting ends, adjusting to my bosses' whims.

What worries me the most? The near future: the next three years of army service and the question of whether there will be peace or war.

What do I need to meet my goals? Determination, will power and optimism. The possibilities? Here again you want me to be a prophet. I believe I have a good chance to succeed because I have a good supportive family who believe in me.'

or fourth generation families with European or established Sephardic backgrounds who have resided most of their lives in major metropolitan areas or kibbutzim. With 18-year-old males drafted for three years into the military services and 18-year-old females drafted for twenty months, most of the mainstream advantaged youths of our study were in the military service at the time of our surveys.

Historical background

No study of Jewish-Israeli society can ignore the compound influence of 'struggle and survival', particularly within the context of youth. Hitler's attempts during Second World War to impose a 'Final Solution for the Jewish People' led in its aftermath to the affirmation of Zionist yearning to return to the land of Jewish birth and existence. Approximately 400,000 Second World War displaced Jews embarked upon Israel's shores during the end of the 1940s and the beginning of the 1950s.

Following the adoption of the United Nations Partition Resolution of 1947 which declared that the territory of the British Mandate be divided between the Jewish and Palestinian peoples, the modern State of Israel, founded on the memories and ashes of the Holocaust, had no time for mourning. The Arab world did not accept the arrival of Jews on what they considered Arab soil and viewed Israel's declaration of independence and freedom as 'Al Naqba' ('Disaster'). Once more, the Jews found their existence imperiled physically and existentially by the fires of war. In the ensuing War of Independence, Israel paid dearly in human sacrifice to ensure its new and very vulnerable borders. This 'Struggle for Survival' became the modus vivendi, deeply ingrained in Jewish-Israeli young people.

With both male and female Jews drafted into military service at 18 and males continuing to serve in an active reserve system until the age of 50, military service is considered a 'Certificate of Entry' into adult Jewish society. This can be seen in the preoccupation of young people in defining their military status and social standing in the military organization with emphasis going well beyond the borders of conventional armies' services. It can also be seen in the admiration and respect of mainstream Jewish society for those who serve well, with the highest esteem reserved for those who participate in the most elite units.

The State of Israel has always encouraged immigration. With its open-gate policy allowing automatic citizenship to all Jews who come to live on its shores, vast numbers have arrived from all over the world to create a truly pluralistic society. Today Israel has a Jewish population more than three-times its size at its inception. The appearance of each new Jewish ethnic group expresses Israel's ability to absorb cultures while, at the same time, sharing a common Jewish unity. While successful in this respect, however, the process has not always been easy. Oriental Jews, who arrived in massive waves from the Near East and North Africa during the vast migration of Second World War refugees, provide a good example. These immigrants faced considerable adjustment insecurities on arrival, with many struggling for cultural identity and social acceptance which created, in turn, a deep sense of social, cultural and economic crisis for many Jewish mainstream Israelis. Later, when Oriental Jews began to relocate themselves physically to the country's urban centres in search of greater educational and economic equality, their Ashkenazi cousins felt that their own leadership positions were being threatened. The result has been a deep and far-reaching schism in Jewish Israel's physical and psychological being.

The migration of vast numbers of Ethiopian Jews to Israel in the last decade is a continuation of the long movement of Oriental Jews to Israel and of adjustments on the part of migrants and mainstream Jewish society. Ethiopian Jews began arriving in large numbers in 1989 following what had been a five year halt in immigration when diplomatic relations were established between Israel and Ethiopia, and are expected to have a significant impact on the future generations. A sample of this population was surveyed in our *Youth and Coping* study and is the subject of Chapter 15.

Another example of how Israel's migration policy is affecting the country is provided by the more than 600,000 Jews who arrived in Israel from the Soviet Bloc in the last decade. As Russian-Jewish immigrants, like their Oriental brethren, begin striving towards the 'Centre' through their activities and political organization, one of Israel's great immigrations is destined to change the face and direction of Israel.

Other segments of Israeli-Jewish society also contribute to Israel's pluralism: and often to political differences as well. Among these are the extremely religious who segregate themselves from secular life. The self-imposed alienation of this approximately 8 per cent of the Jewish population is most frequently noted in their refusal to do military service, leading many secular Jews to criticize their refusal to share the country's common burden of defence and security.

Jewish populations are not the only peoples creating the country's pluralism, of course. Israel today includes approximately 900,000 Arabs as well as other non-Jewish ethnic groups. A small percentage of the overall non-Jewish population (Druze and Circassian) have made strong efforts to assimilate by enlisting in Israel's armed forces. These communities clearly see their participation in Israel's struggle for survival as the key to greater assimilation and equality of opportunity in socio-economic life. By contrast, Israel's Arabs, excluding Bedouin community, do not serve in the Israeli army. While they are Israeli citizens, they live in their own separate townships and communities. There are noted expectations of limited Arab–Jewish integration in the cities of Haifa, Acre and Jaffa, but, by and large the Arab citizens of Israel preserve their own unique heritage. Unfortunately caught in the middle of the Palestinian and Israeli conflict, they are often accused by both of sides of double loyalty and find it difficult to define their self-identity.

Political conflict

In 1997, Israel and the Arab world are still in conflict as they were at the time of the 1947 UN partition as to who should have the rights to Israeli soil which contains holy places for the Arabs and is viewed by the Jews as their promised land.

While the 1967 War gave Israel a sense of renewed self-esteem and even a brief illusion of invincibility, a surprise 1973 attack by Egypt and Syria during the Jewish High Holy Day of Yom Kippur proved once again to the Israelis their vulnerability. Even though the nation emerged militarily victorious, it paid dearly in human losses. Israeli society divided over the questions of peace, with the Left believing in the doctrine of 'Peace for Land' and the Right viewing concessions as total capitulation to an implacable enemy and calling for the retention and reinforcement of all land in Israel from 1967. In 1979, the first peace agreement was signed between President Anwar Sadat of Egypt and Prime Minister Menachem Begin of Israel.

The outbreak of the Palestinian 'Intefada' (Uprising) in 1987 created shock waves and further divisions in Israeli-Jewish society. The Right demanded that Israel meet the warring Palestinians head-on in the conflict, while the Left called for an end to the bloodshed through negotiation and peace. Under the dual leadership of Yitzhak Rabin and Shimon Peres, the historic Oslo Agreements were signed between Israel and the Palestinian leadership headed by Yasser Arafat. The USA played a pivotal role in the realization of this important step towards peace. The historic agreement led to the partial return of territory and Palestinian self-rule in these lands, and it appeared that peace might really be on the way. Unfortunately, it was not to be.

Soon after the beginning of dialogue between Israelis and Palestinians and the signing of the 1995 peace treaty between Israel and Jordan, Prime Minister of Israel Yitzhak Rabin was assassinated by an extremist right wing Jew. This deplorable act provided new evidence that Jewish-Arab hostility is mirrored in the division between the secular left and the extremist minority factions of the national religious right. This is the political world in which Israeli youth live today.

Socio-economic conflict

Israel, like other free economic trading nations, is blessed and plagued by a free-market system which, while it provides opportunities, also creates socio-economic gaps among its citizenry. The 1997 Israeli Statistical Abstract declared only 3 per cent of the country's population as sub-poverty level. However, the cost of living is so high that many citizens who receive salaries at the minimal wage were just barely making ends meet. Jewish-Israeli society models itself according to Western demands, which in turn creates conditions that are both highly accommodating and highly adverse in their impact on the simple citizen. Young Jewish men and women from all social and ethnic groups today are inundated with Western cultural norms and values through the media. They are active and enthusiastic consumers of Western culture, including McDonald's and disco, Microsoft and Seinfeld and all their dazzling and dizzying side effects: at costs frequently beyond the means of Israeli youth.

Education and family life

Israel has a compulsory education law which promises education to all citizens aged 5 through to 16. In cases of special education recipients, these benefits are extended to the age of 21. This law enables at least ten years of education. Most Jewish adolescents study in college preparatory programmes or in technical schools. Israeli Statistical Abstracts (1997) revealed an increase in technical school enrollment over previous years. Today, 39 per cent of Jewish high school graduates receive a Bagrut certificate which is a prerequisite to learning at the university level. Technical education in Israel is on a very high level when compared to other western countries. The demands at these schools are correspondingly high and create a certain degree of pressure on their students. At the same time, college preparatory courses have become more liberalized and flexible in accordance with American educational principles of pluralism and integration. Teaching techniques are diverse and parental involvement in the classroom is clearly on the rise, all of which are serving to create a new character to Israeli schools. Despite the great variations in the types of students learning today in Israeli schools, there is a growing trend toward viewing tracking as less and less desirable and making classrooms more and more heterogeneous. Children with diverse backgrounds as well as learning abilities are learning together.

The Jewish-Israeli nuclear family is important to its members. Young people, at least until the age of 18, participate in family life. The country, as other Western nations, has experienced an increase in divorce, which in turn has led to greater relocation and an increase in single parent families. However, while the 6 per cent divorce rate in the 1960s increased to 10 per cent in the 1990s (Israeli Statistical Abstracts 1997), this is still lower than most other Western nations.

In the past the majority of Jewish youth was active in youth movements. Recent years have witnessed a decline in youth movement activity, however, and now only 35 per cent of Israeli-Jewish youth report being in such movements. Other preferred frameworks of social interaction include enrichment programme in art, music and sports.

Changes on the kibbutz

Kibbutzim, a type of rural community unique in the State of Israel that provides a different socialization process, were described in detail in the study of Israelis in our previous study, *Adolescence: From Crisis to Coping* (Shafrir 1996). The kibbutz's original premise remained until recently at the centre of its philosophical being: individuals give to and receive from the community according to their special intellectual and physical abilities, all within the framework of an elevated regard for the value of productive manual labor. The realization of this ideology lies in a precarious balance between the struggle of the individual's need for self-fulfillment and communal need for social cohesiveness, equality and conformity.

While kibbutzim have always absorbed new immigrants, their selection of new members requires first and foremost that individuals accept and adapt to a very precise set of social and cultural norms. The result has been that, until recently, kibbutz society was in general far more homogeneous demographically than cities or villages in Israel. For nearly the past two decades, however, the kibbutzim in Israel have been undergoing a crisis in reassessing their role and future in Israeli society. This crisis was initially sparked by poor economic investments by kibbutzim in the Israeli stock market. However the economic setback soon generated a comprehensive and painful reassessment of all aspects of communal living. People began to take note of the fact that what had once been considered sacred ideological, psychological and social tenets of kibbutz life were no longer being taken for granted, and this unique movement found itself locked in an agonizing 'search for self'. The Palgi Sarid Survey (1995) revealed that 65 per cent of all kibbutzniks would choose alternative life styles, were they not confined to the practical constraints and effects of relocation. Members expressed uncertainty as to whether the kibbutz as a way of life can continue to survive considering the growing doubts and debts of its high standard of collective living. Economic uncertainty led to a disintegration of social cohesiveness as the guiding principles of social equality and co-operation began to be seriously questioned by kibbutzniks. The philosophical foundation of kibbutz ideology wherein 'each and every member gives according to his ability and receives according to his need' began to be viewed by more and more kibbutzniks as idealization of human nature with no basis in current socio-economic realities. Those with ability wanted more, while those without ability refused to accept less. Interpersonal tensions and resentment began to threaten the ongoing existence of a once enviable institution.

Parallel to these unsettling internal crises from within the kibbutz was an ideological shift in other aspects of Israeli life. Israel, today, is no longer that intimate and small community of families it was when, in its early years of founding and consolidation, volunteerism, pioneering spirit and full reciprocity in social relations were its given norms of human conduct. The gradual adoption of and adaptation to western norms of individual assertion, competition and personal betterment at the cost of collective well-being marks Israel's joining of the family of nations. At the same time, it marks a sad and painful departure from a once intimate and collectively caring ideology in both kibbutzim and mainstream Israeli life.

Martin Buber (1958) once referred to the kibbutz as 'the bold Jewish undertaking of the twentieth century – a utopian socialism that finally works'. There is, however, a 'grounding' of all celestial utopias onto the earth-bed of realities and survival. When such a convergence takes place, it does not mean that the utopia must necessarily dissipate into the air; it merely means that the kibbutz, as utopia, must concede a bit of loftiness and remain true to its guiding spirit. The kibbutz will change, but hopefully it will not disappear from the Israeli landscape.

THE STUDY AND ITS METHODOLOGY

Subjects

Subjects of the mainstream Jewish-Israeli study included 294 advantaged young people, of which there were 147 males and 147 females, the majority of whom were serving in the Israeli armed forces at the time of the survey. Of this number, 143 young people were surveyed in 1989 and 151 subjects of the same SES background were surveyed in 1997. Approximately 28 per cent of the subjects in both the 1989 and 1997 survey came from kibbutz communities, while 72 per cent came from urban areas and their suburbs.

Procedure

The procedure employed by the Jewish-Israeli study matches by and large that of the larger Multinational Study (see Chapter 1). The questionnaire standardized for use in all countries of the Multinational Study was translated into Hebrew for use in Israel. All data were collected and coded exclusively by the author. (Appendix II lists reliability of coding.) Since subjects by and large were not attending school, surveys were usually administered in meetings that included two-to-three persons each, and, in some few cases, with small groups not larger than eight participants.

HIGHLIGHTS OF FINDINGS

The Jewish-Israeli study findings are reported in terms of comparisons of the reports of youth in 1997 with, first, the reports of young people in the 1997 Multinational Study, and second, the 1989 responses of youth given to the same questionnaire. In addition, findings are stated in terms of comparisons of male and female reports. The 1989 and 1997 studies were conducted at two different periods of time in which major political events were taking place in Israel: notably those reported on p. 145, which include the assassination of Prime Minister Rabin, the election of Prime Minister Netanyahu and his right wing government and the consequent polarization of socio-political alignments. All of these events may have affected subjects' thinking and orientation. Highlights of findings and their explanations are given in this chapter. Full statistical results of the 1989 and 1997 Israeli studies appear in Appendix III Tables A and B.

Problems

Comparison of the 1997 Jewish-Israeli data with that of the multinational data from the same year reveals little difference concerning two of the three most frequently reported problems in the Multinational Study. 'Identity and self-concept' and 'family issues' were reported in approximately equal percentages and were all among the top three problems listed for both genders (with the one exception that males in the Multinational Study did not include family issues among their top three concerns). Among the reports given by our subjects classed as 'identity and self-concept' was the category 'becoming an adult'. A problem unique to our Israeli population that is identified with becoming an adult is developing appropriate 'self expectation'.

A major difference that did appear between the Jewish-Israeli subjects and those of the Multinational Study was that the Jewish-Israelis reported far fewer schooling concerns than did their multinational peers. Indeed, 'schooling issues' appear low on the list of Israeli youth concerns, regardless of gender. This finding should not come as a surprise, however, considering the facts that, first, 18–20-year-old Jewish-Israelis face very different realities from those of their counterparts in other societies; and second, most subjects were serving in the military service rather than attending school.

By contrast, the Jewish-Israeli study clearly reveals that, while the problem of war was reported in the Multinational Study in less than 1 per cent of subjects, Jewish-Israeli subjects, particularly males, reported worries concerning war more frequently: in 4–11 per cent of their responses. This was true even though there was actually a decrease in terrorist activities in Israel between the 1989 and 1997 surveys. It was interesting, also, that the 1997 Jewish-Israeli female subjects, who reported war-related worries in only 4 per cent of their responses (still more than their multinational counterparts), mentioned 'courtship-dating' concerns in almost 19 per cent of their reports. This gender difference might be due to differences in time required in military service: While Jewish-Israeli females complete their army service at age 20 and then are free both to resume their schooling and to socialize with older males, their same-aged male counterparts continue another sixteen months in military service. This explanation is given credence by the fact that, although both male and female Jewish-Israelis reported few school problems, female reports were almost twice that of males (approximately 5 per cent for females versus 3 per cent for males).

The fact that 20-year-old female subjects may attend school while 20-year-old males remain in military service also may explain why this study does not confirm the Multinational Study trend that shows females to report fewer schooling problems than males. It does confirm, however, the trend that shows females to worry about family issues more than do males. The absence of mainstream non-advantaged subjects precludes confirming or denying multinational SES trends.

Although the Jewish-Israeli youth subjects did not demonstrate an increased fear of war in 1997 as compared to 1989, their altruistic concerns (representing from 2–8 per cent of their responses) clearly reflected an agonizing search for soul as they examined the issue of war and peace:

> 'I feel a terrible sense of injustice and despair, as if Rabin's assassin, by killing the Prime Minister killed the chance for peace as well' (male army recruit)
>
> 'I was lighting a candle at the city square at a memorial for Rabin . . . in the same place where he was shot . . .when suddenly I looked up and saw thousands of young people just like me with candles in their hands, and I thought how sad it was – that only pain and sorrow could unite a nation. (female university student)'

The relatively high ranking of 'sexuality' as a problem for female subjects in both years of the survey, (approximately 2–8 per cent in 1997) when compared with other national studies of our multinational research project (less than 1 per cent) might be explained by the fact that education programmes on family life begin in the first grade with basics of biology (reproduction, etc.) By the seventh grade, the focus is on the functioning of the family. Other possible explanations include an openness or freedom to discuss such issues in Jewish-Israeli secular society which resembles that in other Western countries and, finally, a possible 'show-offness' or reactive demonstration by female subjects who find themselves addressing topics which a generation earlier in Israel would have been clearly off limits to open discussion.

Coping strategies

The preferred coping strategy in both the 1989 and 1997 surveys was 'individual problem-solving', followed by 'interpersonal coping' (reported approximately twice as frequently as in the Multinational Study) and 'seeking or giving assistance'. Both indicate a tendency to assume responsibility for actions. That this trend was noticeable not only among young mainstream Israelis but also among the adolescent Israelis described in our previous work (Shafrir 1996) suggests that such coping strategies develop early.

While the Multinational Study showed a high percentage (approximately 28 per cent) of reports falling into the classes of 'resignation' and 'dis-engagement', two coping strategies that indicate that no attempt is being made to solve the problem, the 1989 mainstream Jewish-Israeli survey showed roughly 10 per cent and the 1997 survey 10 per cent of reports indicating these two strategies. While these percentages are lower than those of the Multinational Study, however, they nevertheless indicate cause for concern: passivity and feelings of helplessness raise question of adult life adjustments, particularly when subject concerns are overshadowed by disappointment and disillusionment. This is particularly significant, moreover, when expressed by a group of advantaged youth, and even more so when there appears to be an increase in the appearance of such coping strategies over time. Resignation and disengagement may be appropriate responses in situations that cannot be expected to change regardless of subjects' behaviour, although believing that change is not possible decreases the possibility that it will occur. An underlying force in Jewish-Israeli day life is reflected in the idiomatic expression 'Ein brerah' (No [other] choice). This expression, which is part of everyday speech among Jewish-Israelis, reflects in a nutshell the 'philosophy of existing day to day in a country that must uniquely deal with the extraordinary question of continued existence as a daily concern of de-facto life on the edge. If the youth of our society today choose to be passive, to feel helpless or to avoid what faces them, we of the 'older' generation must ask ourselves what we must do to change the situation.

Desired helpers

The results of the 1997 *Youth and Coping* Jewish-Israeli Study bear similarity to those of its predecessor, the 1989 Jewish-Israeli study of adolescence (Shafrir 1996) not only in that the role of the counsellor as 'desired helper', is prominent, but also in that a higher percentage of Israeli responses indicated seeking help than of responses of subjects from any other country; this was true in both 1989 and 1997. The tendency of our Jewish-Israeli subjects to prefer 'professional helpers' may reflect the fact that Israeli counsellors are highly successful in their work with their clients. Just as counsellors are available to help high school students in Israel, mental health officers serve as counsellors of soldiers. Another fact attesting to the success of Jewish-Israeli counsellors is that the only other major group in the Multinational Study in which a high percentage of subjects' responses indicated counsellors or teacher/counsellors as helpers were the non-advantaged Jewish-Ethiopian immigrants to Israel. (See Appendix III, categories of helpers, for both 1997 and 1989.)

Helper qualities

The 1989 and 1997 Israeli studies reveal no differences in the qualities desired of helpers. In both years of our survey, the quality most esteemed for helpers by our subjects was 'experience'.

'What do I want for my future? Not to worry every time my future husband has to go to reserve military service like my mother does now. I don't want to live in fear!'

Advah, a 20-year-old Israeli female soldier. Father: a school principal, B.Ed. in Education; mother: nurse, B.A. Nursing.

'Where do I want to be ten years from now? That is about the time I will have finished my studies as a paediatrician and after my internship at Children's Hospital.

What do I want for my future? Not to worry every time my future husband has to go into military reserve like my mother does now . . . I don't want to live in fear!

Right now I look forward to finishing my army service in three months and am excited about being accepted at Tel-Aviv Medical School. I worry about the well being of my boyfriend who is an officer in the regular army service. {Here again, I'm worrying just like my mother!}

To get what I want, I need to be strong, to decide and stick to my decisions. The possibilities? You mean my chances? I would say at least 90 per cent!

Why? Because since childhood, I have dreamed about it! I made my plans carefully . . . and my family supported me.'

IMPLICATIONS FOR COUNSELLING IN ISRAEL

The success of Jewish-Israeli counsellors in being sought as helpers is unique in the Multinational Study (see p. 151) and suggests the value of examining assumptions underlying Israeli counselling:

1 As compared to Jewish-Israeli adolescents, young people dealing with adult military problems perceive the professional counsellor more as an available crisis interventionist than an agent of change. The effective counsellor must convey experience and empathy.

2 'I know what you're feeling, because, I, too, was there. And now I'm here with you'. 'Ivory tower' intellectualism and escapism offer little relief to the 'reality of being' in Israel. 'Being' and 'being together' are far more effective, accessible, and credible approaches to counselling.

3 In terms of effectiveness, the Israeli counsellor should accept the fact that there exists among Jewish-Israelis, a 'youth culture' which needs to be respected and understood if professional counselling is to be effective in providing the all essential HOPE to those young people standing on the uncertain threshold of their adult lives.

4 Youth rebellion, if it exists, should be directed into constructive and dynamic vehicles for change in legal political, social, and environmental organization and involvement which provides a necessary outlet for idealism tempered by the reality of the system of which they must become functioning adults.

5 Counselling should include 'creative problem solving' strategies for this vulnerable stage of personal development, particularly as they relate to problems that are not easily solved.
6 Counsellors should become actively engaged in co-operative efforts to learn from each other. The intercultural exchange of ideas and methodologies should become a principal objective.
7 Mass media has technologically reduced the world into a global village. People of the twenty-first century have unprecedented visual, audio and literary access to each other. We read, see, and hear each other's cultures with surprising familiarity. Utilized correctly mass media can provide bridges to communication and resolution of human problems. Actively seeking 'common denominators' and co-operative solutions should become a new focal point for 'intercultural counselling'. See Chapter 2 for a discussion of theories related to these implications.

References

Almog, O. (1997) *The Sabra: A Profile*, Tel-Aviv: Am Oved.

Buber, M. (1958) *Paths in Utopia*, Boston: Beacon Press, trans. from Hebrew.

Cohen, E. (1976) 'The structural transformation of the kibbutz', in Zollschan, G. and Hirsh, W. (eds), *Social Change*, New York: Wiley: 703–42.

Diamond, S. (Summer 1975) 'Personality dynamics in an Israeli collective: a psycho-historical analysis of two generations', *History of Childhood Quarterly:* 100–4.

Eisenstadt, S. (1983) 'Some observations on historical changes in the structure of the kibbutzim', in Krausz, E. (ed.), *The Sociology of the Kibbutz*, New Brunswick: Transaction: 149–53.

Habermas, J. (1989) *Structural Transformation of the Public Sphere*, Cambridge, Mass.: MIT Press.

Melman, Y. (1996) *The New Israelis*, Tel-Aviv: Am Oved.

Israeli Statistical Abstracts (1997) Jerusalem: Central Bureau of Statistics of the Government of Israel.

Palgi-Sarid Survey (1995), Haifa: Haifa University Institute for Research of the Kibbutz.

Shafrir, B. (1996) 'The Israel study', in Gibson-Cline, J. (ed.), *Adolescence: from Crisis to Coping*, London: Routledge: 119–36.

Shapira, A. (1997) *New Jews, Old Jews*, Tel-Aviv: Am Oved.

Spiro, M. (1963) *Kibbutz Venture in Utopia*, New York: Shocken.

11 Japan

University and business school students in Tokyo

Keiko Honda, Tamagawa University

INTRODUCTION

The island of Japan has a mono-cultural population of 125,570,000. In 1997, the year of our survey, there were 38,467,000 young people below the age of 24 living within its boundaries. As in many countries, the average age of marriage in Japan has been increasing. In the year of our survey, 1997, it was 28 for males and 26 for females. Unfortunately, the divorce rate is also increasing. In that same year, there were 795,080 marriages and 206,955 divorces. Approximately one third of Japan's population was comprised of youth, children and babies (Japanese Government Executive Bureau for Youth Problems 1997:101–8).

Juvenile delinquency rates have been increasing both at school and at home for crimes such as speeding in cars, stealing, committing sex-related crimes and using illegal drugs. Of juvenile criminals arrested, 65 per cent

'I would like to work in the central office of a large international business company.'

Toshi, a 20-year-old student in his second year of university. Toshi lives with his parents, grandparents, elder brother and younger sister in a suburb of Tokyo.

'In ten years, I would like to work in the central office of one of the international business companies. I hope that I will already have married and, with my {future} wife's agreement, we will have one child.

While I am not so afraid of employment, I am not sure about my plan for marriage and having babies. In order to attain my goal, I need to face what I am dealing with and what I am right now. Dreaming only about future, I would surely be in trouble.

I talk with my friends whenever I have some problems. I have talked with them many times and I can trust them. I want them to listen to me. There is nothing {they can say} that would make me uncomfortable. They never do what I don't want them to.'

were 14–16 years old at their first arrest. Since 1980, school violence, refusal to go to school and bullying have also increased dramatically. Following a number of child suicides following bullying in school, this aberrant behaviour is now recognized as a major social problem. It is reported in approximately 34 per cent of public primary schools, 58 per cent of junior highs and 40 per cent of high schools (1997). In recent years, it has also been recognized among college students (Narusawa 1998).

Education

Japanese society places high value on academic background and much pressure is placed on young people to succeed in school. With 97 per cent of junior high school graduates continuing to high school and 45 per cent of high school graduates entering institutions of higher education or professional schools, education continues as an important part of the lives of 18–20-year-olds (Japanese Government Executive Bureau for Youth Problems 1997).

Japanese life

The role of respect and honour

Japanese have a strong cultural need to define interpersonal relationships in respectful and honourable ways. This is reflected in all interactions with family members as well as with people outside the family, with particular respect given to seniors and those in positions of authority. Japanese youth honour those they respect by refraining from refer to their seniors or their teachers by their names alone. Instead, they honour them by adding titles that rather than referring to them by their names only, instead refer to what these people do or what their relationship is to the speaker. Examples:

Question: Who are you?
Answer: I am Manager of Sakura Bank.

Question: Who are you?
Answer: I am a student at Tokyo University.

Question: Who are those people?
Answer: They are Auntie Kawaii and Elder Brother Yusuke.

Question: Who is she?
Answer: She is the daughter of Teacher Yamamoto.

Amae

A key factor in understanding the Japanese personality, *amae* is a strong cultural need of parents and children to take on the same values, love one another and feel 'sameness' with them. When one can *amaeru* to another person, that is, fully trust, rely and depend on that person, one feels happy and safe. *Amae* prevents breaking of trust or harming the other person. When it occurs between two people, they may feel as if they are sharing one body (Doi 1971, 1995).

Family styles

The Japanese family, like families throughout the world, has been greatly changed by modern life. New family lifestyles, including new roles afforded women in the workplace, have changed the traditional role of the Japanese family and lessened its role as a support system. Oda (1997) describes three types of modern Japanese family situations that contribute to problems:

1. Although many middle-class families provide comfortable accommodation, relationships among busy family members have become increasingly superficial until often there is little meaningful communication within the household. In this situation. Yuzawa reports (1995) that this lack of communication between parents and children is related to an increase in youth independence that often leads to disengagement from the family, school and social activities;
2. In many Japanese homes, fathers work long hours daily away from home and, because of their lack of presence, gradually lose their authoritative status within the family;
3. Some mothers who remain at home devote excessive time to child-rearing, permitting themselves no other interests or activities. As a result, these mothers often have difficulty permitting their children freedom and avoiding intruding on their children's privacy.

This is not to say that all Japanese families are in difficulty, of course. While there are some Japanese homes in which these and other problems exist, there are others in which children grow up happy and secure, do well in school and grow up to be happy and well-adjusted adults. An indication of the general problem showed itself, however, in the results of a recent international survey of youth reported by the Japanese Government Executive Bureau for Youth Problems (1997: 22–9). In this survey, the responses of Japanese youth to a checklist of survey items were compared with responses of youth from Brazil, France, Germany, Korea, the Philippines, Russia, Sweden, Thailand, UK and USA. To the question, 'When do you feel satisfaction in your life?,' choices included 'being with friends', 'engaging in sports or other interests', 'working', 'being with your family', 'being alone', 'studying' and 'working for the betterment of society'. With from 24 to 85 per cent of subjects in the national studies included in the survey providing positive responses to 'being with your family', Japanese youth provided the lowest percentage (24 per cent), a fact indicative of growing problems in the Japanese family.

Responses of Japanese students to life stresses

The Japanese traditional cultural response to stress is to turn inward rather than to appear in any way disrespectful or dishonourable. A wide variety of alternative problematic behaviours among Japanese young people have been related to various stressors, however. Bulimia and anorexia, for example, have increased dramatically in recent years, especially among females in the past decade, with some severe cases resulting in death. These diet-related disorders as well as general apathy has been associated by Japanese researchers with the self-denial by students of relaxation for years prior to high school graduation while they work for the high grades required for acceptance to university (Narusawa 1998). Resultant lack of opportunity to interact socially during this time leads in many cases to students entering university without appropriate age-related social skills (report of the Special Committee of the Japanese Association of Student Counseling 1997).

As regards possible effects of stress within families, lack of communication between parents and children has been related to an increase in youth independence, subsequent disengagement from the family, school and social activities (Yuzawa 1995). These behaviours – new to middle class youth – have been related to the increase in juvenile delinquency discussed earlier among youth from middle class families since 1985 (Okonogi 1993, Oda 1997).

In some Japanese families in which '*amae*' with its traditional Japanese emotional relationships still bind children tightly to their parents, young people respond either by trying to break free or, conversely, trying to strengthen already tight ties. Resulting anxiety is demonstrated in a variety of ways. Kawai (1980, 1999) pointed to cases of young girls who apparently developed bulimia as a way of acting out their desires to break away from unwanted attention, for example, noting that, when Japanese mothers devote themselves excessively to child-rearing, the closeness and interdependence between mother and child often causes difficulties.

The status of school counselling in Japan

College counselling services have been provided in Japan since 1952. According to the Special Committee of the Japanese Association of Student Counseling (1997), 53 per cent of universities and colleges and 29 per cent of junior colleges now have counselling services. Most counsellors, however, are employed part-time, resulting in an average of 0.9 counsellors per school or 2.5 counsellors to 10,000 students, with smaller colleges using the services more frequently than larger universities.

In contrast with university counselling services, counselling provided for primary through to high school students was begun only recently when several junior high school students who had been bullied by classmates committed suicide. In 1995, the Japanese Ministry of Education began an experimental counselling programme for younger students utilizing clinical psychologists as school counsellors. In 1995, counselling services opened one day a week in experimental programmes in 154 of Japan's 41,469 public schools. The number of schools being supplied with services has increased annually since then. In 1998, more than 1,500 public schools had counselling services. By this time, many cities had established special budgets to hire additional school counsellors. With need for counselling continuing to increase throughout the country, plans are underway to establish counsellor education training programmes in graduate schools and national licensing of counsellors.

THE STUDY AND ITS METHODOLOGY

This study was conducted in universities and business schools in the capital city of Tokyo, a metropolis including more than 3 million youth. It asks what advantaged Japanese male and female youth consider to be their concerns, coping strategies and choices of helpers. Subjects were studying full-time at universities and business schools in the area. Among the four schools from which they were chosen, only one provided counselling services. These were attended by only an approximate 7 per cent of the student body at least once a year and 20 per cent of students during their student life.

Results of this 1997 survey are compared with both the 1997 Multinational Study as well as with a less extensive 1989 survey of Japanese university students which used the same survey instrument.

Subjects

In 1997 subjects included 282 advantaged 18–20 year old university and business school students, of which 101 were males and 181 females. Socioeconomic status (SES) was determined by the same criteria as all other national and special populations studies of the 1997 Multinational Study. (Details are provided in Chapter 1.) Subjects all were born in Japan and had never been out of the country for more than a brief trip. Since they were selected on the basis of their positions as students rather than as clients in any type of therapy, there was no reason to assume serious emotional problems.

In 1989 subjects were fifty-nine male and female university students from the same city. Because of the small size of the 1989 sample, gender distinctions are not reported for this group and only striking similarities and differences in the findings of the two surveys are discussed. Readers are cautioned that the small sample size precludes more than conjectures in making interpretations.

Procedure

Our survey instrument was standardized for use in the Multinational Study and translated into Japanese using the procedures described in Chapter 1. Surveys were conducted in 1997 in classrooms and subjects' responses were coded, using the same standardized procedures as all other countries of the larger study . The 1989 Japanese sample of Japanese students was collected and coded by the same procedures. Reliability of coding is listed in Appendix II.

HIGHLIGHTS OF FINDINGS

Highlights of results are reported below. The reader is directed to Appendix III Tables A and B and Appendix IV for full statistical details of all findings.

Concerns

The four most frequently reported concerns given by Japanese males and females in both 1989 and 1997 were related to first, personal identity, second, interpersonal issues and third and fourth, schooling and courtship, appearing in this ranked order for the 1997 sample and with only a few slight variations in 1989.

Personal identity and self-concept issues, the first ranked concern of all Japanese subject groups, accounted for 23–31 per cent of 1997 responses and 61 per cent of 1989 responses. While most 1997 identity concerns were related to 'becoming adult' (attaining physical and social maturity), most 1989 identity concerns were associated with physical appearance (mainly a female worry) or personal health (primarily a male concern). Following are examples from the 1997 responses describing the entrance to adulthood:

Male:

> 'I know it is important to be physically healthy if I am to attain my goals, but it is difficult to eat regularly and keep a healthy life when I am a student.'

Female:

> 'Even though they say ability and character are important, a female's appearance has a great deal of influence on whether she gets a good job.'

The second most frequently reported concern in both 1997 and 1989 dealt with interpersonal relationships, particularly employment or friendship, and accounted for more female than male worries.

Employment:

> 'My hourly payment is too low, considering how much work I am doing [for the company].'

Friendship:

> 'I am not good at developing [personal] relationships with other people.'
>
> 'Our friendship is superficial. Neither of us seems to say what the other really thinks or feels.'

Third and fourth ranked worries in 1997 dealt with courtship (12–17 per cent of responses) and schooling (12–13 per cent of responses).

Courtship:

> 'After graduation my girlfriend and I will live far away from each other. I wonder whether we will be able to continue our relationship.'
>
> 'My boyfriend loves me more than I [love him]. He calls me often and if I don't answer, he gets upset.'

Schooling:

> 'I know that my grades will influence my entire future: where I get a job; where I continue my education. . . . I want to study abroad.'
>
> 'I received low grades last semester and again this semester. My academic advisor called me to his office and I am afraid my parents will find out.'
>
> 'I took supper at about 10 p.m. after I returned from my part-time job. I sat up studying until a.m., then jumped up to get ready to go to school. I have no time to eat in the morning and I hate to cook at night when I am so tired.'

Our subjects reported far more concerns regarding interpersonal relationships than they did schooling, which was ranked first or second as a source of worry in most other countries. In addition, they reported family worries very rarely (3–5 per cent of 1997 responses in 1997 and 4 per cent of 1989 responses). This was true despite the fact that Japanese youth described in the government survey described on p. 156 did not consider being with their families as a source of satisfaction to them (Japanese Government Executive Bureau for Youth Problems 1997: 22). There were only a few countries in our Multinational Study where the percentage of responses designating family issues as problematic were lower.

Coping strategies

Our Japanese subjects attempted generally to solve their problems by themselves, as did their multinational peers. The percentage of reports suggesting individual coping appears to have decreased between 1989 and 1997, however (from 96 per cent of 1989 responses to from 56–62 per cent of 1997 responses). They did so primarily by 'planning' (analysing the problem and describing a problem-solving strategy) or 'trying harder' (increasing a behaviour without specifying a specific strategy). 'Planning' decreased from 44–46 per cent of reports from 1989 to 26 per cent in1997.

Planning:

> 'I easily catch colds, so I take medicine every day to make myself a little stronger.'
>
> 'I have trouble getting up early, so I set more alarm clocks.'
>
> 'I am concerned about the oil spills that are ruining our seashore, so I have arranged to go [with an environmental team] to help clean up the beach.'

Trying harder:

> 'It takes me a lot of time to memorize the answers in my driving course, so I try again and again.'
>
> 'I am not sure whether I will be able to graduate. I have to try much harder.'

The second most frequently reported strategy was 'seeking assistance'. In this case, the percentage of 1997 responses was seven times that of 1989. While this included both genders, males tended to seek specific help in solving their problems. Females, by contrast, wanted comfort. In other words, males looked to results and females to a more pleasant process.

Male:

> 'I was being bullied. At first, I didn't want to ask anyone for help. But now [I'm not afraid] and have decided to ask someone to help.'
>
> 'I didn't want to ask my father for help with my job problem because I didn't want him to force me to do anything I don't want to do. But when I finally told him, he [did what I wanted and] used his wide human resource network to help me.'

Female:

> 'I want to talk with some members of my club about my problems and have them listen to me, but it is difficult to develop close relationships with senior club members.'

While an extremely low percentage (2 per cent) of the 1989 responses suggested resignation (giving up) making no attempt to solve the problem) or disengagement (trying behaviourally to escape or avoid the situation), our 1997 data showed that these two coping strategies together included 17–19 per cent of male responses. If we combine the 1997 percentages of responses indicating the two strategies to represent 'non-goal-oriented coping', as in the Multinational Study (see Chapter 3), they are ranked second in frequency of coping strategy reports.[1]

Resignation:

> 'My friends stay away from me and I can't do anything about it, [so I don't try.]'
>
> 'There are a lot of serious environmental problems, such as dioxin pollution that worry me, but I accept them because there's nothing I can do that would make any difference.'

Disengagement:

> 'I know I should do something to change the situation, but instead I go to sleep in the daytime, go out and get something to eat, or spend my time meaninglessly changing the TV channels.'
>
> 'When I don't want to talk with anybody, I unplug the phone and stay by myself doing what I want.'

Helpers and desired helper qualities

The Japanese subjects in both our 1997 and 1989 samples desired helpers from outside their families, especially personal friends, just as their multinational peers. The percentage of responses indicating going to family for help decreased from 1989 (36 per cent) to 1997 (21–22 per cent of responses). 1997 results showed, in addition, a relatively high per cent of responses (18–23 per cent) suggesting that subjects did not go to any person for help. Perusal of subjects' written responses on the survey questionnaire suggested that this was not because they thought they could handle the problem themselves, but rather that they did not know of anyone who could help them.

When our 1997 subjects did seek helpers, both males and females sought individuals who were 'knowledgeable.' (27–35 per cent of 1997 reports as contrasted to 60 per cent of 1989 responses). Examples of 1997 responses:

Knowledgeable (experience in issues related to the problem):

> 'My friend and club member has much more experience than I on this issue [how to be a good leader].'

Knowledgeable (experience in issues similar to subject):

> 'I go to my friends because they have problems similar to mine.'

Knowledgeable (professional content area):

> 'I go to my advisor, because he is a professional and knows that topic well.'

Both males and females also looked for 'powerful' helpers. (This increased from 4 per cent of responses in 1989 to 14–20 per cent in 1997.) Examples:

Powerful (can exercise authority to solve a problem):

> 'I go to my professor because he is the person who decides my grade.'

Personal attributes, such as 'trust', 'ability to listen' and 'supportive' were discussed in 19 per cent of male and 23 per cent of female reports in 1997, as in the reports of their multinational peers.

'I want to work for a middle-sized company.'

Naho, a 21-year-old university student. Both of Naho's parents attended schools of higher education. Today, Naho's mother does volunteer work and is chairperson of a volunteer circle whose aim it is to increase international understanding.

'In ten years, I want to be working for a middle-sized company. I am thinking of changing my life and getting married. But I never want to quit my job because of my marriage. And I never want to be in an ambivalent situation in which my career development conflicts with my marriage relationship.

What I am afraid of most is that when I marry, I will have to quit my job even if we don't have a baby. That would mean boring days at home. Most of my worrying is that I think I have to decide whether to get married or to continue my career. I have no interest in just being somewhere and being bored.

When I have problems, I like to talk with my friends. They tell me objectively what they really think. Their advice helps me, but just the process of talking with them make me calm down and organize my thoughts.'

Although counsellors are expected to be experienced and knowledgeable, they were not selected as desired helpers by our subjects, most probably because so few are available to this age group. In terms of what our subjects wanted their helpers to do, they clearly wanted them to attend to their needs (listen to them, pay them attention) and counsel them (give them advice, help them solve their problem), much like the subjects of the Multinational Study.

Attend to (listen):

> 'I want my helper to just listen to me and be there for me.'

Counsel (give advice):

> 'I want my friends who are in their senior year [and have gone through this themselves] to give me advice on how to find employment.'

DISCUSSION OF FINDINGS AND IMPLICATIONS FOR COUNSELLING IN JAPAN

Concerns and coping

> 'I am not sure who I really am and what I really want to do from now on.' (Male student, 1997)

Our Japanese subjects were deeply concerned in defining their identities and determining their employment options, much like their peers of the same age from around the world. Also like their multinational peers, they tended to describe their coping strategies first by analysing their problems and describing a problem-solving strategy.

Family and *amae*

It was extremely interesting that Japanese youth did not report many family worries, particularly so in light of the recent Japanese government survey of youth that showed that young Japanese people did not consider being with their families as a source of satisfaction to them (see p. 156–60). We believe that Japanese youth still expect their families to be available, knowledgeable and helpful in problem-solving and that older relatives continue to serve today as authority figures, as they did in the past, with parents rearing their children by giving them lessons, lecturing them when they make mistakes or making themselves available when they seek support. However, the importance to youth of traditional family roles and vertical relationships in which authority is exercised from the top appears to be weakening.

Our subjects not only sought help from outside more frequently than from within their families just as their counterparts from other countries, but also sought any type of help far less frequently than their SES counterparts in those countries.[2] These findings together suggest that our Japanese subjects had ambivalent expectations of their families. We suppose that, while they want to depend on their families, at the same time they also want to distance themselves from them as part of the process of becoming adult.

The term *amae* has as its closest English translation, 'passive objective love'. While *amae* still occurs among Japanese family members, many researchers (Okonogi 1993; Yuzawa 1995) have suggested that it is decreasing in modern Japan.

Schooling

Although Japanese researchers have noted that Japanese students are under high pressure to succeed, our student subjects seemed not to think of academic pressures when responding to our questionnaire, although they did report concerns regarding time pressures. It may be that they had already learned before entering university what they needed to do in order to succeed, and now were only worried about having sufficient time to do it. None of our subjects worried that they were unable to learn.

Counselling and gender

Our study showed males and females to be more similar than different in most of their concerns, coping strategies and desired helping relationships. One gender difference worth noting, however, is that Japanese female subjects, unlike males, were deeply worried about their physical appearance in determining their self-identities. They are influenced by the social image of the 'ideal woman' who is thin, smart, intelligent, and active. At the same time they are still expected to be accepting, supportive and passive by males. With dieting remaining popular and college women developing eating disorders, especially bulimia, still increasing (the Special Committee of the Japanese Association of Student Counseling 1997), counsellors need to focus on their conflicts and help them develop strong self-identities.

Males were more concerned with their personal health and sought support of others in solving their problems less than our females. These differences were perhaps due to their finding it more difficult than their female peers in controlling their daily lives while they were growing up. This may be related to the traditional Japanese mother-son relationship in which sons grow up being cared for most of their daily lives by their mothers and are not taught how to care for themselves. Still, when burdened by over-protective mothers, they seek independence.

One question not asked in this study was how males and females compared in their hopes and aspirations. In thinking of the subjects in this study, it is interesting to guess what might have been found had our subjects been asked this question. Our case studies provided on pp. 154 and 163–4 might give some indications. While Toshi, the 20-year-old male subject, aspired to 'work in the central office of a large international business company', his counterpart, 21-year-old Naho, dreamed of working for 'a middle-sized company'. And while both young people were planning their careers in seemingly modern fashion, Toshi hoped that he and his future wife would have one child (with her agreement, of course) and Naho was not at all certain about her plan for marriage. Her biggest fear was having quit her job because of her marriage, 'even if we don't have a baby'. These commentaries, together with many of the concerns voiced by our subjects in the survey responses suggest that changes in gender roles that have accompanied the modernization of Japan and with it, changes in family style, might not be affecting the two genders with equal ease. This would be a fascinating topic for further investigation.

NEW DIRECTIONS FOR COUNSELLING SERVICES IN JAPAN

In Japan today, most college counselling services provide clinical psychologists who offer one-on-one counselling of clients in closed rooms, providing an image of psychiatric hospitals serving severely disturbed students. This is extremely important to a minority of Japanese youth with severe emotional problems. Both the concerns of our subjects and the types of helpers they seek suggest, however, that what is needed in Japan today for the majority of youth are services more closely tied to their daily lives. In order for those who require counselling services to access them, we suggest outreach programmes such as psychological education which can be provided to groups in classrooms. This could include programmes such as assertiveness training, project adventures in the field, group dynamics, understanding of self and others, how to seek help and stress management. In recent years, such programmes have been utilized successfully in elementary, junior and senior high schools (Honda 1997, 1999a, 1999b; Ninomiya *et al.* 1997).

Another suggestion relevant to counselling in Japan is to make positive use of *amae* in problem-solving and helping relationships. Japanese research suggests that Japanese children and adolescents utilize *amae* in coping while growing up. Subjects in our study, nearing the stage of adulthood, face the problem of balancing *amae* with desires for independence. Japanese counsellors should be sensitive to their discomfort. One way to help this age group actualize in positive ways the need for independence and transfer this to daily life is to make use of *amae* in their counselling relationships. Youth who are able to establish *amae* relationships with their counsellors during the counselling process can be helped to gain trust needed to deal with this problem. (See p. 28.)

Another method of helping youth to build successful interpersonal relationships can be found in family education. In Japan today, cultural centres, public educational centres and even geriatric hospitals are beginning to make use of family seminars that teach how to strengthen family relationships. The author provides seminars on this topic. (See p. 31.)

Notes

The sample of Japanese youth surveyed in 1989 and referred to in this study was collected by Ishu Ishiyama, Professor of Counselling Psychology, University of British Columbia.

1 'Non-goal-oriented' in this case refers to coping strategies that are not designed to reduce subjects' stated problems, although they may reduce stress caused by the problems.
2 One exception is the advantaged Chinese male sample.

References

Doi, T. (1971) *Structure of Amae*, Tokyo: Kobunsha, in Japanese.

—— (1995) *Psychoanalysis and Psychopathology*, 2nd edn, Tokyo: Gakushoin, in Japanese.

Honda, K. (1997) 'A case study of assertion training for university students', *Annual Report of the International Christian University Counseling Center*, Tokyo: International Christian University 9: 31–3.

—— (1999a) 'Helping school counsellor training through the Teachers' College consultation model', *Japanese Journal of Counselling Science* 32: 55–65.

—— (1999b) 'The effects of psychological education workshops for university students', *Annual Report of the International Christian University Counseling Center* 11, Tokyo: Christian University.

Japanese Government Executive Bureau for Youth Problems (1997) *Annual Survey of Japanese Youth*, Tokyo: Okurasho Insatsu Kyoku, in Japanese.

Kawai, H. (1980) *Concerns Regarding Family Relationships*, Tokyo: Kuodan kha Gendai Shinso, in Japanese.

Kawai, H (1999) *Rearing Children Heart-by-Heart*, Yokyo: Asahi Press, in Japanese.

Narusawa, M. (ed) (1998) *Support for Mental Development-Case Studies of College Counseling*, Tokyo: Honnomori Shuppann Enjo.

Ninomiya, T., Nakayama, M. and Morozumi, T. (1997) *Introducing Adventure Education to Schools: A Program for Mental Education*, Tokyo: Gakuji Shuppan, in Japanese.

Oda, S. (1997) *Juvenile Delinquency and Bullying*, Tokyo: Frevel, in Japanese.

Okonogi, K.(1993) *A Generation of Families without True Interaction*, Tokyo: Shueisha Bunko, in Japanese.

Special Committee of the Japanese Association of Student Counseling (1997) 'A report on the survey of student counseling institutions', *Student Counseling Journal* 19 (1): 81–112.

Tomabechi, N. (1997) 'A report on the use of counselling centres in one year', *Annual Report of the International Christian University Counseling Center*, Tokyo: International Christian University, in Japanese.

Yuzawa, Y. (1995) *A Graphic Explanation of Present Problems Surrounding Families*, Tokyo: NHK Books, in Japanese.

12 Russia

University students in Moscow before and after *perestroika*

Nina F. Talyzina, Gueorgui Emelianov and Anna Adaskina, Moscow State University

Editor's prologue

This study was conducted in Moscow by Professor Talyzina and her colleagues in 1989 and 1997, two years separated by major political events that changed Russia and the other former USSR republics irrevocably and that dramatically altered all phases of life in those countries. The first surveys were conducted in 1989, the year during which Eastern Europe threw off Soviet rule and less than two years before the Russians shattered the old Communist order in their own republic.

In the years prior to 1989, Soviet Russian children were taught to be proud of their country, one of the largest (one-sixth of the world's land mass) and most powerful nations in the world. Before Eastern Europe's precipitous withdrawal from Soviet rule, the USSR was comprised of more than 100 nationalities whose core and centre of government was Moscow. Children hold high priority in the Russian culture, and while most Russians lived under spartan conditions, Russian families expected that their children would have better lives than previous generations. By the mid-1980s, however, increasing shortages of food and other goods were critically eroding the already low quality of day-to-day life. In the late 1980s, when *glasnost* brought the Russian people information about how people lived in other countries as well as how much government corruption and inequities in the distribution of goods affected their own lives in the USSR, hopes of bettering the life of the next generation under that system were destroyed. When the first data for this study was being collected in 1989, the setting was ripe for what has since been called the 'second Russian revolution' (Smith 1990). By the time of the second survey, this revolution had been largely completed: and the Russian people were faced with new types of problems.

This study is of the reported problems and coping strategies of a unique group of Russian young people affected by the changes in their country: university students aged 18–20 years of age. It does not purport to describe the problems and coping of any of the many other groups of Russian young people living in that country who are not in school, such as farmers or workers. In 1989, students were still thought of as the hope of Russia's future, and held esteemed positions in their society. By 1997, the chaotic disintegration of the USSR and subsequent rebirth of Russia as a country in its own right had forced education to the bottom of governmental priorities. Since then, student lives have become more difficult. Because of financial exigencies in educational institutions, stipends designed to cover basic needs of students have been withdrawn, curtailed or delayed. Some institutions have found it necessary to shut their doors. Those students who have managed to graduate have found it difficult to find employment that will provide income necessary to meet needs.

Conducting regular business in Russian universities is also difficult. Preparation of manuscripts for publication outside of Russia when not everyone has access yet to e-mail and other forms of communication are peripatetic. While Professor Talyzina and her research team conducted interviews using the standardized procedure planned for all countries and sent in their manuscript in timely fashion for inclusion in *Youth and Coping*, they were unable to respond to my queries. The result is a chapter whose content and methodology differ slightly from those of our other national studies. It is presented here together with an explanation of methodological differences as a unique example of the concerns and coping of youth during a revolutionary period of their country's history.

Janice Gibson-Cline

INTRODUCTION

Russian higher education: 1997

As scholar-educators working at Moscow State University in 1997, the authors can say that the serious crisis within the Russian system of higher education is over today. Our institutes, closed at the beginning of *Perestroika*, are once again open. Competition for acceptance into universities is high, as in Soviet times. In addition, new programmes have opened and new institutes and universities have been created in every city of Russia. Most importantly, the humanities and social sciences, such as psychology and sociology, as well as economics and law, have been given new importance and have become a popular part of the curricula. We can say that Russian education is 'humanizing' its education system. This is shown in conferences of scholars, introduction of new specialty studies as well as in opening of new departments. If the materialistic Marxist-Leninist philosophy was a basis of education in the Soviet Union before *Perestroika*, we can say now that psychology – and the study of the human person – has taken its place. Psychology has become a compulsory cross-discipline subject in all Russian universities. We have returned to what was described in the famous saying, 'Man is the measure of all things'.

This is not to say that there are no serious problems. Our state universities, as other institutions, lack money to run easily or smoothly. Faculty salaries and student stipends are often delayed because of lack of

Moscow 1989: ***'My dream is to be an interpreter . . . I want to travel . . . I want to talk with people from different place and hear new ideas.'***

Olga, an 18-year-old female language student at Moscow State University:

'My dream is to be an interpreter. This would let me have an interesting life.. I want to travel . . . I want to talk with people from different places and hear new ideas. I want to see what the rest of the world {outside the USSR} is like. I have been working hard toward this goal and have already learned two foreign languages.

What don't I want to happen? I don't want to be lonely and have no friends or not to be able to learn new things. My problem now is that I have difficulty communicating my thoughts to other people. I have tried to find out what I am doing wrong. When I am most unhappy, I try to analyse the situation so I can decide what to do. My friends are very important to me. Sometimes I discuss my problems with them. Sometimes I just distract myself.

When I need help, I go to my mother and father, or else to my best girlfriend. They listen to what I say, help me analyse the situation and help me decide what to do. I don't want anyone to thrust their ideas at me and try to make me do what they think is right.'

Moscow 1997: ***'I remained a student for many, many years because I wanted an intellectual life . . . but now I worry whether I'll have enough money.'***

Sergei, a 22-year-old male graduate student in the Department of Psychology at the Russian Centre of Humanistic Education:

'I remained a student for many, many years because I wanted an intellectual life. I love to travel and have worked in many different places: I was once a waiter in a restaurant and I was also a salesperson in a video shop. I have spent time working with one of our new Russian political parties to help elect a candidate to office. Right now, I am employed in the office of one of the international companies that opened in Moscow. In my free time, I listen to music; I like non-traditional cinematography; I like to write letters to my friends. I like my life, but I am afraid I waste too much time.

What do I want to be doing in ten years? Whatever I am doing, I want an intellectual life. I don't want to work in a psychiatric clinic or to be a waiter.

I think that all you need to reach your goal is to know what you want and then put all your force into reaching it. I think I will succeed {at finding an intellectual life}, but now I worry whether I'll have enough money. I also worry about finding a place to live. . . . I am very afraid of another war.'

government funding. Most importantly, being a faculty member at a state-operated university no longer carries the prestige it did before 1989. As in the West, people often choose to work in businesses rather than at state universities because they can earn more in business. To solve these problems, our institutes and universities are beginning to operate more and more frequently on commercial bases, taking into consideration the cost of operating programmes in deciding what will – and will not – be offered. We expect that all of Russian higher education eventually will be privatized. As we write, those students wanting to acquire second degrees in higher education are already being required to pay tuition. The quality of education is considered to be better in those departments now operating on a commercial basis than in state departments of universities operating on the 'old' system. This is because these new departments have additional money to attract the best faculties and the greatest number of possibilities to use modern educational tools.

SUBJECTS AND METHODOLOGY

Subjects

The 201 Russian participants surveyed in Moscow in 1997 included fifty-seven males and 144 females between ages of 18 and 22 years. They were Moscow State and Moscow City University students enrolled in education and psychology and Moscow State Technical Institute students enrolled in electrical machine-building and tool-construction. All subjects were residing in Moscow at the time of the survey. Their parents were reported to be literate with the majority (67 per cent) having had higher education.

The 175 Russian participants (111 males and sixty-four females) surveyed in 1989 were same-aged Moscow State University students, also living in Moscow. Again, the majority of parents had higher education.

No SES distinction has been attributed to either subject group. In 1989, advanced education of parents and parental professions might have qualified subjects to be considered 'advantaged' in Western countries but not in Russia under the Soviet regime. In 1997, with Russia's tenuous economic situation and with less prestige given to higher education than during the Soviet era, SES distinctions are still blurred. For this reason, the Russian subjects have been listed in Appendix III as 'non-classified' and were not included with any of the three SES groups in Chapter 3, the Multinational Study. (See Chapter 1 for details.)

Procedure

In both years of the Russian study, procedures for translating survey questions into Russian and administering the surveys in students' classrooms followed the standardized procedures described in Chapter 1 for all national studies. Coding of responses was done by the authors utilizing the standardized procedures with the following exception: in order to describe the 1997 descriptions of problems as accurately as possible and to give attention to problems new to Russian students, the authors added a number of 'new' classes by 'folding' into the list what are for other national studies 'categories-within-classes of problems'. 'New' classes are listed in Table 12.1. To permit readers to compare the Russian findings with those of other national studies, Appendix III Table A 'refolds' these 'new' classes back into categories-within-classes. (Details appear in Chapter 1.) (Appendix III Table B includes 1989 data.)

HIGHLIGHTS OF FINDINGS

Findings of the Russian Study are reported in terms of highlights only, as in the other national studies. These are presented as percentages of responses that fall in each class and category-within-classes of problems, coping strategies and help-seeking. Comparisons are made between survey findings in 1989 and 1997 and between male and female responses during those years. Appendix III contains full statistical results of the study.

Table 12.1 Reported problems of male and female Russian subjects 1989 and 1997

	1989		*1997*	
Problems	*M*	*F*	*M*	*F*
Poverty	0	1.2	3.6	2.4
War	3.1	0	0	0
(Army)	x	x	2.1	3.1
Catastrophy	0.3	0	0	0
Material desires	10.5	9.8	14.9	8.5
Family	4.1	6.1	3.6	8.2
(Dwelling)	x	x	1.4	4.4
Schooling	20	15.9	19.2	17.5
(Time deficit)	x	x	3.6	4.4
Identity	12.5	13.4	11.3	11.4
(Health)	x	x	5.4	6.6
Sexuality	1.4	1.4	6.3	6.3
Courtship	3.8	7.9	0	0
Interpersonal	12.4	8.5	12.1	12.9
(Employment)	x	x	3.3	4.3
Emotions	3.1	3.0	0	0
Self-fulfilment	3.4	2.4	0	0
Altruism	22.3	29.1	7.1	10
(Living conditions)	x	x	3.7	0
No problems	3.31	1.5	2.4	0

Problems

Table 12.1 lists the percentage of responses falling into each class of reported problems by gender and year of survey. 'New' classes of problems are noted in parentheses..

Table 12.1 shows that our 1997 subjects worried principally about their schooling and what was required for them to continue in school. This included meeting their material needs, finding housing, finding and keeping employment and finding time to complete all these outside required tasks as well as to study and achieve in school. All of these concerns accounted together for from less than 50 per cent of all reported problems in 1997, as contrasted with 1989, when fewer problems were reported.

Academic achievement has always required a great deal of studying. While this was true in Soviet Russia, students were esteemed and the government provided services to make life easier. It has become increasingly difficult since 1989, however, for Russian students to concentrate on achieving. This has been due, in large part, to the facts that government stipends are frequently delayed and insufficient to cover living needs when they do come. Students must now find time and ways to earn sufficient money to pay their living expenses, leaving little time for their academic work. While our 1989 subjects were particularly concerned with their achievement, our 1997 subjects had a myriad of other immediate worries before they could even begin studying.

It is important that, in 1989, the highest percentage of worries were related to altruism (concerns regarding humanity and society) rather than to schooling. Concerns related to Russia's economic, political, ecological and social problems accounted for approximately one-in-four responses in 1989, but less than half this amount in 1997. The fact that our 1997 subjects worried about living conditions in Russia testifies to the serious nature of the economic problems that Russia now faces. [Editor's note: Although these worries were voiced as altruistic concerns, we believe that they reflect serious problems in the personal lives of these students in much the same way that the altruistic concerns of poverty subjects in the Multinational Study as described by author Elizabete Pereira in Chapter 16 also described highly personal worries.]

In contrast to the multinational findings, in which identity and self-concept were reported most frequently, concerns regarding identity ranked only second for Russian subjects, with worries about personal growth (health) first noted in 1997. Similarly, concerns regarding sexuality were few, although they increased between 1989 and 1997. This concern about sexuality may have been related to the facts that some of the subjects were married and that these concerns have, for Russian students, usually been associated primarily with lack of private space as well as intensity of workload. Males have tended to worry more about sexuality than females.

Finally, while family problems might have increased slightly from 1989 to 1997, intergenerational disputes within the family also increased. Females reported a higher percentage of family problems than males in both years of this study as well as in our previous investigation of Russian 13–15 year olds (Talyzina and Gabay 1996). In Russia, this phenomenon is probably related to the fact that Russian parents are still strict. They may also be meeting demands from their daughters for increased freedom more harshly than they do for their sons' demands.

Coping strategies

'Individual problem-solving' (attempting to solve problems by oneself) was the top-ranked coping strategy of all our Russian subject groups, regardless of year of survey. Female responses (49 per cent of reports in 1989 and 48 per cent in 1997) indicated more individual problem-solving than did male reports (47 per cent of responses in 1989 and 45 per cent in 1997). Slightly fewer reports of individual problem-solving were given in 1997 than 1989. Resignation (surrendering to the conclusion that there is no way to solve the problem) ranked second in 1989 (25 per cent of male and 26 per cent of female responses), while disengagement (avoiding or distancing oneself from the problem) ranks second in 1997 (19 per cent of male and 17 per cent of female responses). Both of these 'non-goal-oriented' types of coping suggest that subjects felt that they were not in control of solutions to their problems.[1] That these strategies decreased from 1989 to 1997 suggests to us that, regardless of the new and very serious problems facing Russian students since *Perestroika*, our subjects are more hopeful that they will ultimately succeed.

It was fascinating to us that, in reviewing the statements given on our survey questionnaires, we found females to be far more communicative than males, attempting to call for help and more often trying specifically to manage their stresses and feelings of emotions. The case study of Olga, presented earlier in this chapter, for example, shows that she took time to analyse her situation when attempting to solve her problems. Our male subjects, by contrast, appeared more passive, giving more details of their worries, with fewer and often more vague solutions, as shown in the case study of Sergei (p. 170).

Helpers and desired helper qualities

When our 1997 female subjects needed help, the majority of responses (53 per cent) indicated a family member first. The opposite was true for males, with a minority of responses (36 per cent) indicating that they sought a family member. In 1989, the majority of male and female responses indicated going for help outside their families (see Appendix III Table B). These findings indicate both that, one, females sought help from families more than males, and two, our 1997 subjects went more frequently to their families for help than did our 1989 subjects. We interpret the first as demonstration of the closeness of Russian young females to their families and the relative independence of males and the second as a demonstration that today, Russian youth with university educated parents tend to depend closely on their families when dealing with the new problems that they face and about which their parents, who had to live under relatively more spartan conditions when they themselves were children, might have had more experience.

In spite of their reliance on their families, however, the single person chosen most frequently as a helper by both males and females was a 'personal friend', just as in the 1997 Multinational Study. Female more than male responses indicated going to their mothers; a higher percentage of male responses indicated seeking 'officials' and fathers; and a higher percentage of female responses suggested seeking a psychologist. Males and females were divided as to the qualities they desired in helpers, as well. While males sought 'knowledge' most frequently, females sought 'concern' and 'understanding'.

Most interestingly, although a relatively small proportion of our subjects chose psychologists or other types of professional helpers, they clearly wanted to be counselled, that is, to be given advice and to be helped in solving their problems.

IMPLICATIONS OF OUR FINDINGS

Our subjects were more clear in describing their problems than in solving them. However, the majority of students knew what they had to do and the type of helper they needed. It is important that, in 1997, some subjects named a psychologist as the best person to go to in dealing with their personal problems. While the percentage of responses indicating this choice was low (2 per cent of male and 6 per cent of female responses), no such responses appeared in our 1989 data. We feel that this indicates a growing awareness by our young people of new and needed types of help for dealing with crisis situations as well as long-term problems. The Russian government has recognized this need, and, since 1989, has been developing and making available to youth special help programmes, including telephone crisis centres that provide confidential service, counselling programmes and psychotherapy. (See p. 31.)

Despite their immediate financial problems, most problems of Russian students are similar to those of their counterparts in the Multinational Study. In the case of the Russian study, most concerns are related to Russia's current economic and political situation in Russia. Fortunately, our society is more democratic now than it was before *Perestroika* and provides students more freedom to choose solutions to these problems as well as to choose their way of life.

Notes

Data gathered in 1989 and coding of this data were done by Tatiana Gabay of Moscow State University, under the guidance of Professor Talyzina. Statistical analysis of 1997 data was performed by I. Mescheriakov, also of Moscow State University.

1 We consider 'non-goal-oriented' strategies in this situation to be strategies that are not designed to reduce our subjects' reported problems, although they might serve to reduce stress.

References

Smith, H. (1990) *The New Russians,* New York: Avon.

Talyzina, N. and Gabay, T. (1996) 'The Russia Study', in Gibson-Cline, J. (ed.), *Adolescence: From Crisis to Coping*, London: Routledge.

13 Continental USA

University students in Pittsburgh, Pennsylvania

Lisa Maccarelli and Janice Gibson-Cline,
University of Pittsburgh

INTRODUCTION

The Continental United States, its citizens and its problems

The USA is a multicultural nation embodying more than 100 ethnic groups and racial backgrounds. The majority of US citizens are white; major minority groups are African-Americans and Hispanics (representing approximately 12 per cent and 9 per cent, respectively, of the population) and Asian-Americans (approximately 3 per cent). The US satisfies the dreams of many citizens for a high standard of living. In 1993, 79 per cent of the population had completed high school and 21 per cent had graduated from college; life expectancy was approximately 72 years for males and 79 years for females (US Bureau of the Census 1993). The median family income (1996) was $42,300 (US Department of Commerce 1998).

Life has not been ideal for all Americans, however. With the US divorce rate on the increase for several decades, by the mid-1990s, approximately 50 per cent of American marriages were ending in divorce with no sign of abatement. The year 1996–7 saw 4.4 divorces per 1,000 population. More than 14 per cent of Americans and a far higher percentage of minorities were living on incomes below poverty level. (White median family income $44,756 versus $26,522 for African-Americans.) Many of these families came from single-parent homes. Violent crime was affecting ordinary citizens more than ever before in the country's history with 1,682,280 violent crimes out of a total of 13,473,600 crimes that year (World Almanac 1998). Seventy-four million Americans were functionally illiterate (see Brough 1990; Grant *et al.* 1991, Lawrence 1994, National Commission on Children 1991,National Institute on Drug Abuse 1988, US Bureau of the Census 1993).

The problems of the US – as of all countries – are reflected in its youth: at the time of our earlier study, more than 20 per cent of youth under the age of 20 were admitting to drug or alcohol abuse; increasing numbers were perpetrators or victims of crimes ranging from theft to violence; more than 30 per cent were reporting depressive symptoms and in the mid-1990s,

'I want to help African-American children . . .
I want to look back someday and be able to say that I made a difference.'

William, a 19-year-old African-American university student planning to major in psychology and then go on to graduate study in either psychology or social work; oldest of three siblings; parents are high school teachers with Masters degrees in education.

'My parents don't want me to want me to major in psychology. They think I should go with computer science. My Dad says that I would be good at that because I have always taken to computers easily and because you can really go far in the field now. Look at all those young millionaires . . . I guess that this is really the time to do it – if that's what you want. The field is really expanding quickly and there's no telling where it will go.

The problem is, I don't want to be a computer scientist. I like fooling around with computers, but for the fun of it. And I agree it would be nice to be rich. But I really want to help African-Americans. There are so many problems today that they need helping with. I 've enjoyed my psychology courses so far and I've gotten good grades. Maybe I'll want to stay with that in graduate school . . . Maybe work in an agency that helps needy people – or something like that. Last summer I worked with Habitat and worked with a team of people to build a house for poor people who wouldn't have been able to afford one otherwise. Thinking that I helped make it possible for a boy like me to have a chance to grow up in that house gave me a real thrill. That's where I met my girlfriend. She feels the way I do and she's going to major in psychology. {I met her in one of my classes.}

What do I think I'll really be doing in ten years? I'll have made all my professional decisions by then. Maybe I'll be married. If I am, I'm sure we won't have children yet; we'll still be establishing our careers. But we'll be thinking about it. Probably I'll follow my heart – and be working as a psychologist or a social worker. But who knows? My Dad is a really good "convincer" and he hasn't stopped trying yet. I don't mind his trying – and I promised to keep an open mind. So long as he doesn't try to force me to do anything, I'll listen. I want to make up my own mind.'

approximately one in ten were attempting suicide; 25 per cent of those who were sexually active had contracted a sexually transmitted disease before leaving high school; this age group accounted for 15 per cent of pregnancies and 7.5 per cent of births, many of which were producing new single-parent families. (See Carnegie Council on Adolescent Development 1989, Garland and Ziegler 1993, Petersen *et al.* 1993, Sullivan and Englin 1986, US Bureau of the Census 1993.) Today, although these figures are somewhat lower, youth are still considered endangered species. And, as William argued (p. 177), they need help.

Pittsburgh, Pennsylvania, the site of our study

The US Study was conducted in the east coast city of Pittsburgh, Pa. and its environs. Its population of approximately 2.4 million in 1993 remained the same during the years of our study (US Bureau of the Census 1993, Pennsylvania Abstract 1998). It has for some time included a higher percentage of white and a lower percentage of minority residents than the nation as a whole, with its minority population comprised primarily of African-Americans (Slater and Hall 1992). City residents also include, at any given time, university students from a wide variety of countries.

Social and economic problems of the city mirror those of other US urban centres. In the early 1980s, Pittsburgh lost jobs through the closing or cutting of production in its steel mills. Unemployment and underemployment rose, especially among African-Americans and youth (Bangs 1989). Since then, new businesses have entered the area, ameliorating this situation, although it has not been able to provide the employment advantages for semi-skilled or high skilled workers that it did before the closing of the mills.

Counselling services available to our subjects

The University of Pittsburgh provides its students with a wide range of services in addition to its regular academic studies and extra curricular activities. The University Counseling Center offers counselling services from crisis intervention to preventive programmes; the University Medical Health System provides psychiatric assistance; the Learning Skills Center offers remedial programmes in reading, math and study skills. In addition, there is a financial aid programme to help economically needy students.

THE STUDY: RESEARCH QUESTIONS, SUBJECTS AND METHODOLOGY

Research questions

1. What did our 1997 male and female subjects report regarding the concerns that caused them stress, the methods they used to cope and the people they sought to help them? How did the 1997 responses compare with those from 1989?
2. What do the responses of our subjects suggest, if anything, regarding intervention strategies effective for helping them?

Subjects

The subjects of our study included 195 youth (seventy males and 125 females) surveyed in 1997 and ninety-four youth (forty-two males and fifty-two females) surveyed in 1989.[1] All subjects came from advantaged backgrounds, as defined in Chapter 1, and were enrolled at the time of the surveys as students at the University of Pittsburgh in the undergraduate programmes of the Schools of Arts and Sciences and Education. The University of Pittsburgh is a private institution, although it draws a small proportion of its funding from the State of Pennsylvania. More than half its students come from Pennsylvania, with the remainder from other states in the USA as well as many other countries. The students whose responses were used in this chapter all were born and grew up in the USA.

Methodology

Students in the 1997 study were distributed the questionnaires in their classrooms by the first author who explained the study and answered all questions before students began answering the questions. In the 1989 study, the same procedure was used, with the exception that questionnaires were distributed by a faculty member of the Department of Psychology in Education who was familiar with the study.

Coding of responses was done in 1997 by the second author, who translated subjects' responses to questionnaire items into classes and categories-within-classes, using the standardized method designed by the research team for that purpose. Coding was done in 1989 by members of the 1989 research team who developed the taxonomy of classes and categories-within-classes used for all countries in the study. (See Chapter 1 for details of the development of the questionnaire, the standardized method used for its administration and the method used for measuring coding reliability; see Appendix II for the determined reliability scores obtained by all coders in the multinational project.)

HIGHLIGHTS OF OUR FINDINGS

The following section reports highlights of our findings only. For detailed information describing percentages of responses falling into classes and categories-of-classes of subjects' responses for this and other national and special population studies in our project, see Appendix III, Tables A and B.

Because of the small size of some of the sample groups reported here, particularly those of the 1989 survey, the reader is cautioned that reliability for these group findings may be lowered.

Problems

Schooling

Concerns regarding schooling amongst US subjects included worries about success or failure and time constraints. This was true regardless of gender or year of study, as in the Multinational Study. These concerns increased quantitatively from 1989 to 1997, also as in the Multinational Study (from 28–41 per cent for males and from 32–39 per cent for females).

> 'Sometimes I feel as though I'm failing when I'm not even close to doing that. But I can't stop myself.'
>
> 'I lack motivation to study.'

The US findings did not support the multinational trend that suggested that males had a greater percentage of concerns regarding school than females.

Identity and self-concept

The second major concern was related to 'personal identity and self-concept', again just as in the multinational findings. (In the US Study, it was represented in 26–28 per cent of reported responses of males' and 16–32 per cent of females' responses.) Both males and females worried about 'becoming adult': attaining physical and social maturity and adult status. Females also worried about their 'self-confidence' (ability to interact successfully with others and to be perceived positively).

Becoming adult:

> 'My problem is finding a job when I graduate. There are so many people today who graduate and don't find jobs. What will happen to me? What will I do?'
>
> 'I wonder if I'll ever meet the man who will become my husband and live a glamorous life. I daydream a lot about it . . . I want it very much!'
>
> 'I want to be on my own, but I live at home. I feel like a loser.'

Self-confidence:

> 'I want to be liked and fall in love, but I feel very unattractive and ugly. I am afraid no one will like me and I will always be alone.'

Interpersonal and socialization issues

A third-ranked concern of males in 1997 (7 per cent of responses) and 1989 (9 per cent of responses) was 'interpersonal and socialization issues', including worries about working, friendship, frustration over what others expect of them.

> 'If I don't do well in school, I won't ever get a good job or have a good home and family. But my parents expect me to visit every weekend and if I don't, they are hurt.'

Material desires

Money worries also ranked third for both males (7 per cent) and females (12 per cent) in 1997, producing higher percentages of responses than in 1989. Very often, many worries co-mingled with one another in described concerns:

> 'I work two jobs and go to school at the same time. It seems sometimes as if all I do is go to work and school. I don't seem to be getting on with my life – and I don't have time even to have friends. I haven't anything to show for what I am doing!'
>
> 'How will I ever save up enough to get married? I want to marry and be a responsible husband and parent, but I have a lot of trouble just paying off my credit card now. It's too easy to build up debt and then end up paying all your money to the bank and have nothing left over! I know that this isn't an 'adult' way to behave and I'm ashamed. But I don't seem to be able to stop.'

Family

For American advantaged subjects, family concerns appeared less frequently than these other reported worries. Perusal of written responses on questionnaires, however, suggests that when they did appear, they were often related to difficulties in family relationships rather than to worries about how to help family members, as discussed, for example, by Brazilian impoverished subjects:

> 'My parents are in the process of getting divorced. My father is trying to delay making any financial commitments to my mother and me. He's always arguing that he's the one in control and he can do whatever he wants. I hate it!' (American youth)

The US data confirms the findings of the Multinational Study that females report a higher percentage of family responses than do males. This was true in both years of the study, although the percentages of reported problems of both males (4 per cent in 1989 and 5 per cent in 1997) and females (7 per cent in 1989 and 11 per cent in 1997) was low.

Self-abuse and other 'personal' problems

Our American youth subjects reported extremely few concerns related to what we know to be real problems facing American youth today, such as drug or alcohol abuse, AIDS, unwanted pregnancies, etc., just as in the other countries of our study. It was suggested in the Chapter 1 list of limitations of our research (p. 15–16) that the format of our research instrument may have prohibited us from obtaining such sensitive and personal information from subjects and this might well have been the case with many of our subjects. Perusal of their responses by the second author showed that at least some subjects were not hesitant to talk about these topics (although these were insufficient in number to make up the 5 per cent necessary to be listed as a category-within-a-problem-class):[2]

> 'I'm worried that I might have AIDS. I want to get tested for it, but I'm afraid to go alone. I want my best friend to come with me and get tested, too.'
>
> 'I'm afraid of getting pregnant but I'm even more afraid of someone telling me I have to have an abortion. I don't want a baby, but I don't want that!'
>
> 'There's a lot of pressure to do drugs.'
>
> 'I drink too much socially.'

This issue is discussed in further detail in Chapter 17, 'Conclusions and implications for theory and practice'.

Coping

Individual problem-solving

Our American subjects, like subjects from every other country in our Multinational Study, did their best to solve their problems by themselves. The percentage of responses falling into this class of coping increased from 1989 (49–53 per cent) to 1997 (62–65 per cent of reported responses).

Just like the reports from other countries, however, the US data suggested that a fairly high percentage of these responses either were ineffective in reaching the desired goals of our subjects, or may not have even been directed toward doing so. Although our subjects reported 'trying harder' as their major individual coping strategy (shown in more than 40 per cent of reported strategies in 1997), it is not clear that 'trying harder' is at all effective in problem-solving. To the contrary, it may well be repeating responses used earlier that did not solve the problem and, in the process, making the problem even greater. (See discussion of this issue in Chapter 2.).

Resignation and disengagement

Two other common coping strategies display responses ineffective in reaching reported goals. When 'resignation' and 'disengagement' are combined as one strategy which is not designed to reduce a reported problem, we find that, in 1989, 25–26 per cent of reported strategies involved either resignation or disengagement, making this the second most frequent reported coping strategy. It has been suggested elsewhere in this book that resignation and disengagement may actually be productive in the sense that they reduce stress and that subjects who have chosen to respond this way may have decided rightly that it is not in their power to solve the problem. If this is true, however, then large percentages of our subjects feel that their situations are hopeless. While they may be right in some situations, in others they may be creating enormous problems for themselves.

While we believe it heartening that our 1997 findings showed a major decrease in resignation and disengagement (from 25–26 per cent of reported responses in 1989 down to 12–18 per cent in 1997), these coping responses still formed the second most frequent strategy in 1997. We would have liked to suggest that this change was due to our subjects having found more effective ways of solving their problems. However, it appears to be related to an increase in coping by 'trying harder' from 1989 (24–26 per cent of reported strategies) to 1997 (41–43 per cent of reported strategies). This strategy, as we discussed earlier, may – or may not – be effective in reducing the reported problems of our subjects.

> 'I want my parents to stop fighting more than I want anything else in my life! So what do I do when they are fighting? I stay away from the house and do things with my friends.'
>
> 'I have had unprotected sex with three different people a number of times, but I don't really think I could ever get AIDS.'

Helpers, desired helper qualities and modes of helping

Our American subjects, like their multinational peers, said that when they needed help, they went to people outside their families far more frequently than they did to family members. The first person they went to usually was a personal friend. When they went to their families, it was their mother they sought most frequently. Only rarely did they go to their instructors or professional counsellors for help, although our 1997 subjects reported going to their instructors for help and our 1989 females reported going to their counsellor.

Why did they choose the helpers they did? Our subjects in both years of our study looked for helpers who were knowledgeable (had experience and similarity to the subject), concerned (were understanding, supportive and caring) and had the personal attributes of being approachable, a good listener, understanding and caring. They wanted to be counselled (to be advised, to be directed, to have their helper share information with them and to help them solve their problem). They also wanted to be attended to (encouraged and comforted).

I want my helper to:

'agree with me and tell me everything will be OK.'

'help me motivate myself to study.'

'tell me that that I am not a bad person.'

'understand me and realize I'm not OK, even when I say I am.'

I don't want my helper to:

'tell me not to worry because I know (my problem) will become very serious if I don't do something about it.'

'tell me there is nothing I can do about it.'

These comments provide some directions for counselling in the USA, which we will discuss in the next section.

'What worries me most is my 'split-level' dream: being a good actress and having my own family at the same time'

Wendy, a 20-year-old university student. Parents: college educated. Father: marketing co-ordinator; mother: homeschool teacher of Wendy's younger sister and brother.

'In ten years, I'll probably be an actress, somewhat established in whatever field of acting I wind up going into. Hopefully I'll be famous {laughs}. Hopefully, I'll also be married by then, but I'm not sure whether we'll have kids yet. First I have to focus seriously on my career. I get so excited when I think about it, not just getting famous but how I'm learning to get better and better at acting. Getting to a point where I feel comfortable 'slipping into roles' which intimidate me now. And when I see someone else in a role and I think, 'I could do that!

What don't I want to be doing? Waitressing with six kids waiting at home in a really messy house and a miserable unemployed husband. I also don't want to sell out my dream for something more stable that wouldn't make me happy because I chickened out.

What worries me most is my 'split-level' dream: being a good actress and having my own family at the same time. I don't know how it's going to come about because I couldn't be married to someone with a stable job in one place who couldn't travel with me and yet I really would prefer not to marry someone with a career unstable as mine because we wouldn't be able to rely on each other. I don't see how that's going to work out. So I just don't think about it.

My possibilities for getting everything I want? I'm a dreamer and – I think – no! I know somehow I can.'

IMPLICATIONS OF OUR FINDINGS FOR AMERICAN COUNSELLING THEORY AND PRACTICE

Similarities between the reported problems and coping of our subjects support developmental theories that suggest some qualities shared across other countries of our Multinational Study, and, at the same time, developmental tasks imposed by the various countries and SES groups.

In this study, as in our previous study of American adolescents (Ondis *et al.* 1996), coping with problematic situations by resignation or disengagement ranked second only to attempting to solve the problem by oneself. Moreover, 'trying harder' – which may or may not have led to positive solutions – accounted for the majority of individual-problem-solving strategies. At first glance it appears difficult to make the leap between these types of 'ineffective coping' and strong feelings of helplessness amongst advantaged university students. However, we believe this to be the most parsimonious explanation of reports such as the following, given by one of our subjects:

> 'My father died of lung cancer and I always hear horror stories about the effects of smoking, but I just can't see that happening to me and, anyway, I'm a very weak person and just can't seem to stop. So I get very upset when anyone tells me I have to!'

We believe further that these feelings of helplessness might be due, in turn, to an inability of our subjects both to conceptualize the 'true' cause–effect relationships in their problematic situations and to use this information to create change. If this assumption is correct, it follows that counselling of advantaged youth, just as of downtrodden young people, should teach empowerment, participation and responsibility.

The fact that our subjects turn, first and foremost, to their peers for help in solving problems suggests that ongoing counselling groups and utilization of peer and other para-professionals trained in basic helping skills to lead them in supportive environments might be of benefit. In dealing with some extremely personal issues, such as unwanted pregnancies or AIDS, peers and para-professionals can often work more closely, provide more time and demonstrate knowledge of subjects' concerns gained by personal experience.

Preventive outreach that includes specific empowering strategies from study skills to use of condoms should be useful if utilized together with demonstrations of how to deal with personal feelings of powerlessness by conceptualizing solutions within the context of solving personal immediate needs so as not to help perpetuate individuals' feelings of failure and helplessness. A systems-based focus that encompasses intervention in 'real-life' situations within families, schools and society would create more meaningful outreach than a 'top-down' focus of presenting information from designated authorities. (See p. 31.)

All of these types of activities dictate expanded counselling roles in the US for the twenty-first century that require efforts that transcend liberal or conservative political agendas to utilize all indigenous support systems. By becoming change agents, ombudsmen and facilitators of available sources of support, counsellors must take on still another role as consultants to these support systems.

Finally, although the US is known as the wealthiest and most powerful nation in the world today, the US government, just as governments in developing countries, provides far fewer resources than needed to fund and staff needed counselling roles. One solution being tested in the US involves using public and private monies to create family and community centres, and to form volunteer programmes that create new support systems. Working with communities, as already proven successful in many other countries, to meet shared needs is another way that professional counsellors may exert influence to create change. Regardless of the political situation, we believe that the way counsellors choose to respond to this opportunity is of critical importance both to our nation and to the counselling profession. (See pp. 30–1.)

Notes

The 1989 survey of university students in Pittsburgh, Pennsylvania was conducted by David Botwin.

1 Because of the smaller sample size in 1989 and to increase reliability of reported results, data listed in Appendix III combines the two genders.
2 See Chapter 1 for a detailed description of the methodology used to create the classes and categories-within-classes used in Appendices III and IV.

References

Bangs, R. (1989) 'Recent regional economic and demographic trends', in Bangs, R. and Singh, V. (eds), *The State of the Region: Economic, Demographic and Social Trends in Southwestern Pennsylvania*, Pittsburgh, Pa.: University of Pittsburgh Center for Social and Urban Research: 1–17.

Brough, J. (1990) 'Changing conditions for adolescents: Reminiscences and realities', *Educational Horizons* 68: 79–81.

Carnegie Council on Adolescent Development (1989) *Preparing American Youth for the 21st century*, Washington, D.C.: Carnegie Council on Adolescent Development.

Garland, A. and Ziegler, E. (1993) 'Adolescent suicide prevention', *American Psychologist* 48–169–82.

Grant, B., Harford, T. *et al.*. (1991) 'Prevalence of DSM-III-R alcohol abuse and dependence: United States 1988', *Alcohol Health and Research World* 15: 91–6.

Lawrence, C. (14 May 1994) 'Home sweet home', *Daily Telegraph Weekend*, B1.

National Commission on Children (1991) *Beyond Rhetoric; A New American Agenda for Children and Families* (*Final Report of the National Commission on Children*), Washington, D.C.: Government Printing Office.

National Institute on Drug Abuse (1988) *National Household Survey on Drug Abuse*, Rockville, Md.: NIDA.

Ondis, G., Gibson-Cline, J. *et al.* (1996) 'Continental USA', in Gibson-Cline, J. (ed.),

Adolescence: From Crisis to Coping, London: Routledge 213–28.

Pennsylvania Abstract (1998) *A Statistical Fact Book*, Harrisburg, Pa.: Pennsylvania State Institute of State and Regional Affairs.

Petersen, A., Compas, B. *et al.* (1993) 'Depression in adolescence', *American Psychologist* 48: 155–68.

Slater, C. and Hall, E. (1992) *Country and City Extra (Annual Metro, City and County Data Book)*, Lanham, Mo.: Bernon Press.

Sullivan, W. and Englin, A. (1986) 'Adolescent depression: its prevalance in high school students', *Journal of School Psychology* 24: 103–9.

US Department of Commerce (1998) *Statistical Abstract of the United States: 1998*, Washington, D.C.

US Bureau of the Census (1993) *Statistical Abstract of the United States: 1993*, Washington, D.C.

World Almanac (1998) *World Almanac Book of Facts*, Primedia: World Almanac Books.

14 Venezuela

Advantaged and non-advantaged youth in Caracas

Maria Eugenia Felce-DiPaula,
National Experimental University,
Simon Rodriguez

Editor's prologue

Dr Maria Eugenia Felce DiPaula died in Caracas in June 1998 following a long illness. She was an active ten-year member of our research team and first author of the Venezuela study in our research team's earlier publication, *Adolescence: From Crisis to Coping*. Dr Felce DiPaula had surveyed the advantaged and non-advantaged youth described in this chapter prior to the onset of her illness. Deeply concerned with the project, she continued to work at home and was able to complete the coding of her data before illness stopped her. In her last conversation with me a few days prior to her death, she worried about not having completed her work. I promised then that it would appear in this publication. I keep that promise with this chapter, presenting her results together with my analysis of her data. I have done my best to report her findings correctly and have noted procedural questions that I could not answer. I hope my interpretations of her findings would have met with her approval and apologize for possible errors of omission or mis-understanding of data.

I thank the DiPaula family for reviewing an earlier introduction that Maria had prepared before her illness and providing interviews for the two case studies in this chapter. I also thank Lisa Maccarelli for providing some updated statistics for the introductory description of Venezuela.

Dr Maria Felce DiPaula received her Ph.D. at the University of Pittsburgh, and was Chief of Clinical Psychology at the Military Hospital of Ft. Tiuna and Associate Professor and Head of the Programme in Educational and Family Counselling at Simon Rodrigues University in Caracas at the time of her death. She was also wife to Dr Freddi DiPaula and mother to George and Daianna DiPaula. I am privileged to have had Dr. Maria Felce DiPaula as my doctoral student at the University of Pittsburgh and as my longterm colleague on this project. The members of our research team family – and I – miss her deeply.

Janice Gibson-Cline

'My major worry regarding life in Venezuela as well as my own chosen profession is the present economic instability.'

Twenty-year-old female student majoring in tourism management; parents both are employed in their own businesses.

'I am very glad that I decided to study tourism. It's a very exciting field, and promises to expand over the next decade. Right now, I'm particularly excited about the possibilities afforded by the increase in access to our country from new carriers. This really promises to increase tourism. My major worry regarding life in Venezuela as well as my own chosen profession is the present economic instability. It makes life hard for the people and, in terms of tourism, threatens to frighten people from other countries away. Ten years from now, however, this should be all resolved and I expect that I will have a happy life and will be enjoying a very successful career.

Right now, rather than worrying about it, I work as hard as I can to prepare myself through my course-work. I am optimistic. I know that if I am to be successful as a promoter of tourism, I will have to know a lot.

To whom do I go when I worry about things? My mother. She is really my best friend. My father left my family a long time ago and I don't see him anymore.'

INTRODUCTION

Country, culture and economic crisis

The small South American nation of Venezuela, with a population of 22,396,000 (Statistical Abstract of the United States 1997) has a climate that is a paradox to those who observe it. Facing the Caribbean Sea, its northern coastline enjoys a year-round climate with temperatures that average 70 degrees Fahrenheit. At the same time, its mountains suffer biting cold. Caracas, the site of our study, is situated on the northern coast.

Venezuela is rich in oil and other natural resources. At the same time, it suffers from a wide range of maladies ranging from severe poverty and malnutrition to violence and civil unrest. Children and youth comprise approximately half of Venezuela's population. It is this population that will determine the country's future.

Population

Venezuela's population is racially heterogeneous. Meztizos (a people whose ancestry includes white, Indian and Negro people) comprise 65 per cent of its habitants (Report of the Venezuelan Central Statistics and Information Office 1990). Another approximately 25 per cent considers itself white and consists primarily of descendants of early Spanish settlers. Other peoples include approximately 1,252,590 immigrants who came to Venezuela from Italy, Spain, France and Portugal as skilled worker during the country's 1950s economic expansion. Other small percentages include indigenous Indians (5 per cent) who inhabit south-west and north-east Venezuela and continue the poverty lifestyle that existed in the past and Negroes (5 per cent) whose ancestors were brought to Venezuela by the fifteenth century conquerors to do heavy manual labour together with Indians. Most Negroes still dwell in small towns on the east coast under marginal conditions, although many have moved to the cities (Report of the Venezuelan Ministry of the Family 1988). At least 90 per cent of Venezuelans are Roman Catholic; the official language is Spanish.

Historical background

As in other oil-rich nations, Venezuelan history – and its current problems – can be described in distinct phases: 'pre-oil', 'oil' and 'current economic transition'. Before its 'oil age', Venezuela was a poor, rural nation with a population that was three-quarters non-literate and that had a life expectancy of 34 years (Dehollain and Perez 1990). The discovery of oil in the twentieth century changed the country in irreparable ways. At first, it opened the door to a new and affluent way of life, and permitted the emergence of a new urban entrepreneurial middle class. Venezuelan oil appeared at this time to assure social, health and educational development for all.

Unfortunately, the government (democratic since 1958) was unable to contain the too-rapid national economic development that followed the new affluence. One result was the creation of increasingly noticeable inequalities in income distribution that presented problems both for the poor and new middle class. Within a short time it became clear that wealth was being increased only for members of a small, already wealthy Venezuelan upper class at the expense of the rest of Venezuelan society. The toll in the past several decades was great, and included monetary inflation, falling health, social and educational indicators, and increasing malnutrition across the country (Report of the Venezuelan Ministry of the Family 1988, Cartaya and d'Elia 1991).

While the nation actually increased its literacy rate from 25 per cent in the pre-oil period to more than 90 per cent in the early years after the discovery of oil, in the years that followed national literacy began a decline. As Venezuela entered the 1990s when our first subjects were being interviewed for this study, 25 per cent of her rural poor and 13 per cent of her urban poor were non-literate (Dehollain and Perez 1990), although this figure was reported to have decreased by the latter half of that decade, returning the national literacy rate to more than 90 per cent (UNESCO Statistical Yearbook 1998).

The economy today

While Venezuela remains rich in natural resources today, their inefficient use, coupled with years of governmental corruption and a gradually decreasing value of petroleum, created a national debt of crisis proportions. The government continues to operate emergency remedies that ranged in the past from devaluation of currency, free pricing and increased prices of services (light, telephone, and others) to privatization of corporations and decentralization of policy. Most, unfortunately, were unsuccessful. The government attempted to improve the abysmal conditions of the poor through projects aided by the World Bank, such as development of daycare facilities, programmes to decrease teenage pregnancy and to increase breast-feeding of infants and the like. All were sorely needed in the slums surrounding Caracas, but they were not able, by themselves, to stem the tide (Banco Mundial 1990, Delgado 1993). A dissatisfied middle class and an increasingly impoverished lower class began to threaten Venezuela with widespread civil unrest as well as government coups, both in the name of the need for a better life for Venezuelans.

At the point in time in which data for this chapter was being collected, living expenses were still rising while income for the masses was falling. Increasing numbers of rural poor were leaving the countryside in search of work. Approximately 40 per cent of Venezuelans – primarily families from rural areas – lived marginally in squatter camps in the mountains surrounding the country's urban centres (Report of the Venezuelan Ministry of the Family 1988, Report of the Venezuelan Central Statistics and Information Office 1990). These same camps still house a growing population of those now impoverished immigrants from other Latin American countries who began arriving twenty years ago in search of the 'oil dream'. Unfortunately, few found what they came for.

Dwellers in squatter camps in the mountains surrounding Caracas – usually Mestizos and Negroes – live today under squalid conditions in 'ranchos' (small houses, usually constructed inadequately with often no more than two rooms to house five or more people). While many camps are supplied electricity at no cost to the inhabitants, there is usually no indoor supply of water, which must be carried from long distances. Most squatters work as day labourers. The poor living conditions and economic difficulties of these people not only increase delinquency in these areas but make them dangerous for visitors and inhabitants alike.

The advantaged and non-advantaged subjects of our study were surveyed first in 1989, just prior to the onset of the major civil unrest that led to the fall of the government then in power. The subjects questioned in our 1997 study were surveyed after the new government had taken power although the problems that produced the social, political and cultural crisis had not been resolved.

Venezuelan education

Officially, eleven years of education are free of charge to all Venezuelans, with the first nine grades compulsory for all. With the opening of new private technical institutions and universities in the early-to-mid-1990's, the country had approximately fifty institutions of higher education for those who completed this schooling. In addition, the Open University increased access to higher education for many Venezuelans who previously would not have had opportunity for education.

Regardless of the free programmes formally in place, however, it is difficult for impoverished classes to obtain adequate education, so that very few reach higher education or even secondary education. For one thing, rapid growth of poverty populations in urban areas created severe shortages of schools, teachers and teaching materials (National Conference on the Rights of Children 1991). Public schools available to the poor provide few frills and extracurricular activities, most importantly, vocational guidance. In addition, impoverished youngsters often cannot attend classes for a variety of reasons, including malnutrition-related illnesses, the need to care for siblings or handle household chores while their mothers work and the need to give up schooling so as to enter the workforce at an early age (Dehollain and Perez 1990). Although Venezuelan law officially prohibits child labour and requires children to remain in school until the age of 18, almost 5 per cent of impoverished 10–14-years-olds and 70 per cent of 15–18-years-olds are in the workforce and not in school. For all of these reasons, only one in eight impoverished young children reached the third grade at the time of our first survey (National Conference on the Rights of Children 1991).

Both the 'advantaged' and 'non-advantaged' subjects of our study are considered 'privileged' in Venezuela because they are university students. This is true even though the socio-economic backgrounds of our 'non-advantaged' subjects is considered lower than average in their country.

Venezuelan family life

The Venezuelan family plays an important role in the lives of its members, with the most important family relationship often between mothers and children. Youth usually remain home until they marry. Throughout their lives, all generations of family members feel responsibility and maintain close ties.

Venezuelan family life, as all aspects of life, has been affected by the country's socio-economic crisis. In the past, fathers used to work outside the home and mothers were responsible for household chores as well as socialization and education of children. Today, in all segments of society, economic need places both parents in the workforce, creating new stresses in families and family relationships

A major and growing problem affecting Venezuelan families at the time of the 1989 survey (excluding Brazil's Indian jungle population) was divorce, officially affecting 40 per cent of families in 1988 (Leighton *et al.* 1988). Research concerning the effects of child-rearing patterns and marginality suggests that fathers' absence, lack of economic resources and changing social patterns that have reduced affection available to children make excellent predictors of crisis (Recagno 1982). The dangers that loomed heavily a decade ago for poverty families and portended serious difficulties for middle-class families reached their apex in the late 1990s in increased delinquency.

Increasing delinquency

Another indicator of the crises facing Venezuelans is the increase in crime and juvenile delinquency. Police reports show an increase in serious crimes committed by youth and children, with a rise from 60–79 per cent of infractions committed by juveniles in the year of the first survey, including not only robbery but homicides and drug related crimes (Rosenberg 1990). The problem was exacerbated by Venezuelan TV, which provided models of aggression and criminality with whom young people identified (Barrios 1989). TV programming now includes soap operas in which youth are often negatively characterized as gang members who use weapons and commit robbery or murders.

Counselling in Venezuela

Professional counselling was introduced in Venezuela approximately forty-five years ago. Since that time, the profession has increased its responsibilities to youth and to the educational process. The first National Counselling Programme was designed to assist public school students with educational, vocational, health and personal problems in order to enhance their development and facility their adjustment. Reforms made to educational laws in 1983 added that counselling should be provided for the welfare of students' families and community members as well as students. In 1991, the National Conference on the Rights of Children affirmed the need of guiding students not only in problems related to academic achievement but also to family, sexual issues and drugs. Preparation for counsellors to take on all of these tasks today requires post-graduate training that focuses on family, vocational and educational counselling as well as human development.

SUBJECTS AND METHODOLOGY

Research questions

1 What did our 1997 male and female subjects from advantaged and non-advantaged backgrounds report, regarding the concerns that caused them stress, how they coped and the people they sought to help them? How did the responses of the two genders compare with one another? How did the 1997 responses answers compare with those from 1989?
2 What do the responses of our subjects suggest, if anything, regarding intervention strategies effective for helping them?

Subjects

Subject populations consisted of 800 young people, 400 surveyed in 1989 and 400 in 1997 as described in Table 14.1. Subjects in both surveys were university students in Caracas and outlying districts. Non-advantaged students were enrolled in the Open University.[1]

Instruments and data collection

SES status was determined on the basis of characteristics defined for all countries of the Multinational Study, with advantaged subjects coming from families rated as above the mean and 'non-advantaged' below the mean in their countries as regards education and career expectations, type and location of residences, and employment and income. Advantaged subjects attended private schools before entering university, had opportunity to travel abroad for holidays and came from homes in which there was usually a maid to do the housework; non-advantaged rarely had these benefits.

Procedure

Data collection and coding The Multinational questionnaire was first translated into Spanish, using the standardized procedure developed for all studies and then administered in classrooms or other university facilities by faculty members.[2] Coding and testing for reliability of coding followed the standardized procedures for all countries. (See Chapter 1 for full details of procedures and Appendix II for reliability of coding.)

HIGHLIGHTS OF OUR FINDINGS

Findings are reported in terms of percentages of responses in various classes given by gender and SES group for reported concerns, coping strategies and chosen helpers and categories-within-classes discussed as appropriate. This chapter reports highlights of findings only. (For full details regarding findings, see Appendix III Tables A and B.)

Table 14.1 Venezuelan populations surveyed in 1997 and 1989

	1989		*1997*	
Gender	*adv.*	*non-adv.*	*adv.*	*non-adv.*
Male	100	100	100	100
Female	100	100	100	100

Problems

> 'We have to rid ourselves of corrupt politicians. The economic situation must change.'
>
> 'I try to study as hard as I can, but my grades are never good enough!'
>
> 'My mother thinks I have to do things the way she did forty years ago.'
>
> 'When I am at home, my father is always fighting with my 15-year-old brother.'

The single concern most frequently reported problem in both 1997 and 1989 for all groups except 1989 non-advantaged females was schooling, in particular, academic success or failure and, for non-advantaged males and females, inability to learn. Family concerns were paramount for 1989 non-advantaged females; both advantaged and non-advantaged females expressed particular concern about family quarrels.

Table 14.2 demonstrates that the Venezuelan findings are unlike those of the Multinational Study in that, as we go from advantaged to non-advantaged SES status, just as we go from male to female, although the percentage of family concerns increase, schooling concerns decreased for our 1989 but not our 1997 subjects.

Other frequently reported concerns were identity issues related to becoming adult, reported in 1997 by advantaged males (14 per cent of responses) and females (12 per cent; and, in 1989, material needs by non-advantaged males and females (12–15 per cent of responses respectively). Our 1997 advantaged male group also expressed concerns about interpersonal interactions (12 per cent of reported worries. It was interesting to note that 1989 advantaged females worried about altruism (12 per cent) while their 1997 peers worried about courtship (11 per cent of reports). It is significant that subjects did not discuss problems related to issues we know are serious in Venezuela, such as AIDS, drugs, unwanted youth pregnancy. (See Appendix III for details.)

We will discuss the implications of these findings later in the chapter.

Table 14.2 Percentages of responses indicating schooling and family concerns by advantaged and non-advantaged males and female 1997 and 1989

		Advantaged		*Non-advantaged*	
		M	*F*	*M*	*F*
1997	*School*	28	33	24	29
	Family	9	12	10	24
1989	*School*	37	32	25	21
	Family	7	11	15	29

Coping

All of our subject groups reported that, first and foremost, they coped by trying to solve their problems themselves, just as their multinational peers. One of the responses they used was 'trying harder'. As argued in Chapter 3, it is important to note that this coping strategy may or may not solve their reported problems and may, instead, lead to repetition of nonproductive coping. Another response reported frequently, and once again similar to the multinational findings (Chapter 3), is resigning to one's problems (and giving up) or disengaging from the situation, both designed to relieve stress but not to solve the reported problem. When these two strategies are combined, they form the second most frequently reported strategy for all groups (with the exception of 1989 non-advantaged males and females, for whom interpersonal coping was reported more frequently and nonadvantaged males who also sought help. (See Appendix III for full statistics.) This issue, also, will be discussed later in the chapter.

Helpers

The Venezuelan non-advantaged sample provided responses different from the Multinational Study as regards choice of a helper. While all subject groups chose a personal friend as the single most frequent choice of helper and mother as most frequent choice of family member, our non-advantaged male and female subjects selected a family member more frequently than anyone from outside their families in both 1989 and non-advantaged females made the same choice in 1997. (See Appendix III for details.) We believe that this finding attests to the extremely strong ties in Venezuelan families.

Desired helper qualities and modes of helping

Our subjects agreed on the attributes they would look for in a helper: first, personal attributes such as honesty, trustworthiness, loyalty, willingness to help; second, knowledge from experience, similarity to the subject's problems; and third, concern, which included understanding, caring, supporting and approachability. This was true regardless of SES, gender or year of study.

What did our subjects want helpers to do? Once again our subjects agreed both with each other and with their multinational peers. They wanted to be counselled – advised, directed, helped to solve their problem; and attended to – comforted, listened to, encouraged and reassured. (Data from which these conclusions were derived appear in Appendix III.)

CONCLUSIONS AND IMPLICATIONS

Advantaged and non-advantaged Venezuelan subjects responded to our Questionnaire in many ways similar to those of their multinational peers,

'What worries me most about the future is the economic crisis in Venezuela.'

Twenty-year-old male student majoring in business administration; parents both are college educated; father is a business man; mother is a secondary school teacher.

'In ten years, I want to have a successful profession in business. I want to have my own home and my own car. I worry most about having my own house – or even my own apartment – with prices going up every day and the terrible economic crisis in Venezuela.

Right now I am trying not to think about it and to study and work hard at my studies. If I don't do this now, I will never reach my goals no matter what happens to the economic situation.

Who do I go to when I need help? My parents. Because they care about me.'

although they did not confirm the relationships between schooling and family concerns, SES and gender. The fact that 1989 advantaged females worried about altruism while their 1997 peers were more concerned with courtship issues is interesting. This result may well have been due to the serious economic crisis through which Venezuela was going in 1989 and resulting soul-searching among young people at that time. The 1989 subjects were surveyed just prior to the civil unrest that ultimately led to the fall of the old government. The 1997 subjects were surveyed after the new government had taken power. Although the problems that had produced the social, political and cultural crisis had not been resolved, there was some reason for hope at that time and, for advantaged subjects, some time to give thought to their personal wants and desires. (Editor's note: Unfortunately, the original questionnaires containing the exact words of Dr Felce DiPaula's subjects were not available at the time this chapter was written. These might have permitted further explanation of this result.)

We worry greatly about the coping strategies used by our subjects. Although 'trying harder' might seem to be a good choice of responding to a given problem, it is important that the response that is being repeated is effective in solving that problem, otherwise it might serve only to increase an already bad situation.

'Disengagement' and 'resignation' also can be ineffective as coping strategies. While in many situations these approaches might reduce personal stress caused by insoluble problems, separating oneself from the problem or simply accepting the situation even reluctantly does not lead to its reduction. Our subjects' lack of reported concern about AIDS, drugs, unwanted pregnancy, etc. may be related to this type of ineffective coping. If the apparent lack of concern reflects our subjects' choice to ignore a problem about which they are aware, many solvable problems might never be reduced.

Systems and constructivist theories of coping suggest ways to utilize individuals' current coping repertoires to develop new and innovative ways of problem-solving. This approach helps to decrease non-productive coping. We believe it is a useful approach for Venezuelan youth who require new strategies to make the most of their future lives. (See p. 24–30.)

It is extremely interesting that so many Venezuelan subjects chose family members as desired helpers rather than outsiders. This finding is quite different from most other countries, including Brazil, the other Latin American country in our study boasting of close knit supportive families. While it probably resulted from the support offered by the Venezuelan family, it does not necessarily mean the family is the most effective source of help to resolve most of our subjects' problems, even though some are family-related. Our subjects' concerns regarding schooling had to do failing academic work; their identity concerns were related to gaining independence necessary to complete the transition between youth and full adulthood. In Venezuela, as in most countries today, this transition is completed when youth achieve independence. Today, society requires more education and greater skills to enter the workforce in a position that will provide a lifestyle commensurate to what is shown on the television. While families may have some of the attributes our subjects looked for – honesty, trustworthiness, loyalty, willingness to help and concern – professional help providers can supply knowledge necessary for problem-solving.

We suggest that an appropriate solution for helping Venezuelan youth who face complicated professional decisions is a two-pronged approach which provides on the one hand, professional helpers working to provide knowledge essential to adult professional decisions and the family-community service in which professionals work together with clients, community or family members to help organize family and peer help and to provide information.

Finally, it must be recognized that whatever approach is chosen, it must be cost effective or it will not take place at all. The author pointed out in her earlier study of Venezuelan youth (DiPaula and DiPaula 1996: 243) that:

> a useful and cost-effective approach to providing information to young people in developing countries is the group information workshop offered within schools and communities in which activities are planned by young people in co-ordination with teachers, counsellors and other relevant individuals. Since 1993, this approach has been used in Venezuela through national workshops on topics vital to youth, such as pregnancy, family living, improving health and so on.
>
> The key to effectiveness in workshops is using group commonalities such as age, SES and family type to bring the group together and to show how the various possible solutions to problems are relevant to particular groups. The approach works effectively, not only with [youth] but also with parents and responsible others such as managers of sports teams, directors of church music groups and so on. If conducted professionally

> with understanding of participants' needs, it can help participants to become sufficiently secure to discuss even their most personal problems with peers and personal friends and work out solutions. This includes even delicate issues such as those related to the very real and serious problems regarding sexuality, about which few of our subjects reported. Until [such issues] can be discussed openly, government programmes to combat the problems will have little chance of succeeding.

Notes

1 Editor's note: I assume this to be the case.
2 Editor's note: I am not certain where the non-advantaged students were surveyed.

References

Banco Mundial (1990) *Venezuelan Poverty Studies: From Generalized to Targeted Programs*, Caracas: Banco Mundial.

Barrios, L. (1989) *Family and Television in Venezuela: An Ethnographic Study*, unpublished Doctoral dissertation, Columbia University Teachers' College.

Cartaya, V. and D'Elia, Y (1991) *Poverty in Venezuela: Policies and Realities*, Caracas: Centro al Servicio de la Accion Popular, in Spanish.

Dehollain, P and Perez, S. (1990) *Malnourished Venezuela Towards the Year 2000*, Caracas: Alfadil Editions, in Spanish.

Delgado, C. (1993) 'Update', *Ambiente y Eologia* 2 (12) (June 30): 8, in Spanish.

DiPaula, M. and DiPaula, F. (1996) 'The Venezuela Study', in Gibson-Cline, J. (ed.), *Adolescence: From Crisis to Coping*, London: Routledge: 229–46.

Leighton, C., Bellorin, M. *et al.* (1988) *Infancy and Family*, Caracas: Family Programmes, in Spanish.

National Conference on the Rights of Children (1991) *The Children: The 1990s Compromise*, Caracas: Comision Presidencial por los Derechos del Nino, in Spanish.

Recogno, I. (1982) *Childrearing Patterns and Marginality*, Caracas: Publicaciones Universidad Central de Venezuela, in Spanish.

Report of the Venezuelan Central Statistics and Information Office (1990) Caracas: Venezuelan Central Statistics and Information Office.

Report of the Venezuelan Ministry of the Family (1988) Caracas: Venezuelan Ministry of the Family.

Rosenberg, C. (1990) *Juvenile Delinquency*, Caracas: El Universal, May 8, 2–18, in Spanish.

Statistical Abstract of the United States (October 1997) Washington, D.C.: US Government.

UNESCO Statistical Yearbook (1998): USA: UNESCO Publications.

United Nations Demographic Yearbook (1999). Issue No. 49, New York: United Nations Dept. of Economic and Social Affairs.

Part IV
Special youth populations

'The racism bothers me.'

'Rich people are able to obtain adequate schooling but the poor can't afford it.'

Chapters 15 and 16 describe samples of populations that are changing the face of countries across the world today: immigrant youth and poverty youth. Ethiopian immigrant youth in Israel share the religion of the mainstream culture in their new country. While they have their daily needs met, they arrived with few resources, many needs and dark skin.

The reports of poverty populations from Brazil, England and the Philippines demonstrate the effects of national and cultural customs on the problems of the impoverished and provide successful interventions.

15 Immigrant youth

Ethiopians in Israel

Rachael Erhard, Tel Aviv University

INTRODUCTION

The Declaration of Independence of the State Of Israel provides a guarantee that the nation 'shall be open to Jewish immigration and to the ingathering of the exiles'. This 'open gate' policy allows every Jew to immigrate to Israel and automatically to receive Israeli citizenship upon arrival. The Jewish settlement in the country in 1948, when the state was established, numbered about 650,000 persons. Today, thanks to the success of the immigration policy, over 5 million people live in Israel.

Today's Israeli society is truly pluralistic, built of various groups and micro-cultures that to one extent or another preserve self-identity and unique living patterns. The preservation of a shared framework can be attributed to the fact that all of these groups identify with the supreme norms and values of the society, and their loyalty surpasses narrow group interests. It can be said that the successive waves of immigration have shaped the development of Israeli society and, in fact, have preserved and expanded its social nucleus (Rahat 1983).

Together with these successes, however, the absorption of large masses of immigrants has led to problems. Geographic and institutional distribution

'The racism bothers me.'

Mashrat, age 19, entered Israel in 1990; father: counsellor at an absorption centre; mother: nurse.

'It's my dream to be a fashion designer. I hope I'll be one of the best . . . I don't want ever not to be in control of myself. What worries me most is how I will integrate into this country, with the racism. I don't have problems getting along with people. I'm open. But the racism worries me. Next to my army base, I see Ethiopians sitting alone instead of integrating. In schools, you see groups of Ethiopians, Russians and Israelis sitting separately. That bothers me.'

of immigrants is not perfect; there are concentrations with little contact with veteran residents. Whereas patterns of Israeli society, based on modern Western cultural foundations, were not foreign to immigrants from Europe and English-speaking countries, this was not true for newcomers from non-Western traditional, conservative parts of the world. For North Africa and Asian Jews, Western cultural patterns often remain foreign well past the absorption period (Smooha 1984; Schwarzhold and Amir 1984). As a result, immigrants frequently are shocked at the hostility with which they are received by the veteran population (Sharir 1995).

Although ideologically Israeli society is interested in the immigrants and in practice steps are taken to ease their absorption, this transition process is difficult. Many studies of the immigration have found that, although many immigrants ultimately benefit in terms of living accommodations and employment, the process of adjusting has negative effects on successive generations as regards mental health, academic behaviour and relationships with friends, family members and teachers, resulting in depression, anxiety and alienation. Until a way is found to assist the new immigrants to adjust to their new culture, this process is unlikely to change (Metrany-Gozlan 1993, Rahat 1983).

Ethiopian Jewry

Jews have lived in Ethiopia for hundreds of years. Ethiopia is situated in north-east Africa and throughout history has served as a bridge between Africa and Asia and a meeting place of different cultures and races. Its population of about 52 million people includes a variety of ethnic elements representing a mosaic of races, tribes and other groups.

Most of the Jewish community comes from isolated villages in northern Ethiopia cut off from the technological advances of the twentieth century and subsisted on primitive agriculture. They succeeded in avoiding assimilation through strong religious beliefs, strict adherence to religious customs and preventing mixed marriages and assimilation with their neighbours (Ben-Ezer 1992, Banai 1988). Externally, however, Ethiopian Jews are dark-skinned and resemble other residents of Ethiopia.

The family structure of Ethiopian Jewry is extended, with all members of the family sharing the same space. In Ethiopia, great importance was attributed to family size, since the larger the family, the better it could support its members and protect them in the difficult living conditions that prevailed. The family was ruled by an authoritative figure, usually a grandfather, father or the eldest brother, who decided what role would be held by each family member. The family head determined social status, vocation, marriage and place of residence. The father worked outside of the home and represented the family to the elders of the village. His wife was responsible for housework and agriculture close to the home. She was dependent on the man and he was responsible for providing what she needed. The woman's status was inferior to that of the man and if she did not fulfil her traditional roles, he was entitled to impose them on her (Budovsky *et al.* 1994, Banai 1988).

The education that most children received in Ethiopia was informal, based on experimenting and imitating adult behaviour. Children were taught obedience and respect for authority from generation to generation through conversations with adults and listening to stories. Boys went to the fields with their father and girls learned woman's work from their mothers at home. Officially, formal education began in Ethiopia after the Second World War, but most Ethiopian Jews did not send their children to schools for fear of assimilation and contact with Christians, and because the children represented the family's workforce (Budovsky *et al.* 1994, Banai 1988).

Spiritual leaders had wide-ranging authorities to solve problems and settle disputes so that only rarely did the community have to avail itself of the assistance of local authorities. Thus, insularism, strict adherence to religious custom, and punishment of transgressors together succeeded in preserving the Jewish identity among part of the community despite heavy pressures from outside to convert to Christianity (Banai 1988, Budovsky *et al.* 1994).

Although immigration to Israel of Ethiopian Jews began as early as 1948, immigration from Ethiopia was illegal until 1984 and had to be carried out in secret operations. By 1984, about 8,000 immigrants had arrived (Budovsky *et al.* 1994, Adler *et al.* 1997). During that year, civil strife and famine led to a mass exodus of Jews from their villages on foot to Sudan, leaving their relatives behind and hiding the fact of their 'Jewishness'. Thousands died during the trek to Sudan and during the stay in the camps there. At the end of 1984 the Government of Israel initiated evacuations of 6,300 immigrants from Ethiopia and, in 1985, an additional 500 Jews from Sudan (Budovsky *et al.* 1994, Adler *et al.* 1997).

The immigration halted after 1989, except for small groups. Later that year, however, when diplomatic relations were resumed between Ethiopia and Israel, the Ethiopian authorities approved emigration of 1,000 Jews per month, leading to an exodus of more than 20,000 people from their villages to the capital, Addis Ababa. The mass concentration of Jews in such a short time created unbearable conditions. In the aftermath, about 8,500 people succeeded in leaving for Israel from Addis Ababa (Budovsky *et al.* 1994).

The second wave of immigration began in 1991 during a revolt against the ruling Ethiopian government, when the Israeli government airlifted some 14,300 Ethiopian Jews to Israel in a dramatic period of thirty-six hours. The present government has continued assisting this immigration by allowing relatives who remained in Ethiopia to emigrate as part of unification of families (Budovsky *et al.* 1994).

The Jews of Ethiopia saw their return to Israel in utopian-idealistic terms both spiritually and materially. This ideology smoothed over the travails of the transition stage but could not prevent the dramatic 'culture shock' or reduce the high social and psychological prices that this transition exacted. The transition from Ethiopia to Israel caused the collapse of all primordial frameworks of affiliation, changing the village community structure and traditional family alignments. The new immigrants encountered a foreign and sometimes rejecting culture without the aid of familiar support systems.

ABSORPTION OF ETHIOPIAN JEWS IN ISRAEL

Housing

The Israeli plan for housing Ethiopian immigrants was to provide initial temporary accommodations that would permit extended families to remain together while they adjusted to their new country as well as to avoid large immigrant concentrations (Ben-Ezer 1992). While some immigrants eventually left these accommodations for permanent housing, others never did, even though the original centres were often located in non-advantaged neighbourhoods far from education and employment opportunities (Ezrahi and Rosiner 1993).

Employment

The dream of returning to Jerusalem was perceived by the Ethiopians not only in terms of its spiritual and material significance, but also as leaving behind a proletariat status (Ezrach and Rosiner 1993). Unfortunately, their early aspirations did not correspond to available employment and training opportunities. Even the minority of immigrants who arrived with vocational training found that it was not recognized in Israel (Ezrahi and Rosiner 1993).

The result today is that most men, when they do work, remain unskilled day workers with low pay, limited advancement opportunities and lack of job security. They often find it difficult to persist at tasks that are repetitive and boring, and their resulting work patterns often fail to meet standards of their host culture (meeting prescribed timetables, etc.). Because of their own cultural conceptions of themselves, most women do not see themselves as potential for employment (Ezrahi and Rosiner 1993).

Given the resulting large percentages of families with no adult workers and the small number of adults with meaningful training for employment in Israel, it should be no surprise that income rarely covers the basic needs of the large immigrant families (Benita *et al.* 1994).

Education

Upon arrival in Israel, elementary school-aged children were sent to religious schools on the assumption that a religious framework would be more compatible with their Ethiopian life style. Unfortunately, however, the locations of these schools were outside the residential areas of the immigrants, and the children were required to travel long distances if they wished to continue.

Most of the immigrant adolescents were sent to boarding schools, both because many of them arrived without parents and because a considerable part of the State Religious high school education system is concentrated in boarding schools (Ben-Ezer 1992). While life in the boarding schools accelerated acquisition of the external trappings of Israeli culture, it increased some adjustment problems. Although Israeli teachers did not form negative stereotypes of their students and teacher-student relations were characterized by mutual respect, teachers nevertheless lacked information about student backgrounds and had little contact with their families. Research shows that Ethiopian high school students tend to have some difficulties in reading comprehension, active motivation, analysing material, initiative, and speed of perception (Golan-Cook *et al.* 1987) as well as in integrating with Israeli-born children (Ezrahi and Rosiner 1993). By and large, however, they are integrating into Israeli society.

Immigrants who are young people of the age of our subjects when they arrived in Israel seem to have the most serious problems. Their previous education, by and large, did not provide entry to institutions either of vocational training or higher education. Many immigrants who applied to post high school institutions were rejected at the application stage. Others could not meet the academic requirements and later dropped out. Various projects have been initiated to resolve this problem:, including the special pre-academic preparatory programmes in which the subjects of our study are enrolled.

Social integration

The Ethiopians first learned on arrival to Israel that their being 'black' in a world of 'whites' could cause problems. Minuhin-Isaacson (1983); Nudelman (1993), Munitz (1985), Zipstein *et al.* (1980), Dotan (1985) and others have noted feelings of discrimination, social inferiority and difficulties related to self-acceptance on the part of these immigrants.

Understanding Hebrew is crucial for social integration, finding work and arranging personal affairs in Israel. Unfortunately, Ethiopian immigrants, by and large, demonstrate a low level of language ability even after many years in the country. Adults, particularly women, have more problems than their children. Most parents don't ever master Hebrew effectively and are less facile than their children, with the result that is often a role reversal in which children become the source of assistance and support for their parents (Shafat 1995, Smilansky and the NETA Staff 1988, Dotan 1985).

On the positive side, most immigrants acquire sufficient language to use basic services. Most can get along with Israeli currency, for example, and maintain their households themselves. While the immigrants tend to preserve the customs and tradition from Ethiopia, almost all feel that their children are Israeli. They report feeling relatively comfortable in their new country, and the problems that disturb them pertain to housing, money, employment, language, independence and health problems of a family member.

Ethiopians, like all immigrants to Israel, are required to do army service, the length depending on age of arrival. In order to prepare for successful absorption of this population within the army, the Israeli Defence Forces developed both a pre-army preparatory course for immigrants and training for the Israeli service people who work with them (Ben-Ezer 1992). The academic preparation programme in which our subjects were involved is designed in the same manner, in this case for assisting young immigrants to prepare for university education.

METHOD

Subjects

The Immigrant Study includes 142 non-advantaged subjects: seventy-eight male (55 per cent) and sixty-four (45 per cent) female young adults. All subjects were born in Ethiopia and immigrated to Israel during the mass emigration campaigns described above. Eighty-one subjects (67 per cent of the total) are 'veterans' who arrived in Israel in 1990 or before (since 1983), and 48 (34 per cent) are 'new comers' who came after 1991. Thirteen (9 per cent of those surveyed) did not respond.

The subjects who arrived in 1985 or earlier arrived on average at the age of 10 and went through the Israeli education system. Newer immigrants arrived during the past decade and are still undergoing the absorption process. All subjects attend pre-academic preparatory programmes intended to increase the representation of Ethiopian immigrants in institutions of higher education by intensive preparation over a one or two year period for matriculation examinations, a prerequisite for acceptance to institutions of higher education. In this sense, they are a very special group. Most older subjects had already fulfilled their army obligations.

Because the small size of this sample precludes definitive statistical statements, we present the responses of this important population as an initial source of information regarding immigrant problems and coping strategies, reminding the reader to take sample size into consideration in interpreting results.

Procedure

The questionnaire was translated into Hebrew. In order to ensure comprehension of the translated questionnaire, two pre-tests were conducted. The first was given to veteran Ethiopians who worked with new immigrants, and the second to students in the pre-academic preparatory programme.

Revisions were made in the wording to correct for any misunderstandings by the test subjects. The finalized questionnaires were administered in subjects' classrooms using the procedure for the multinational study described in Chapter 1, with the exception that the questionnaire was read aloud in its entirety and brief explanations were given for each question at the time of administration.

Coding of results was accomplished by the procedure described in Chapter 1. Coding reliability is described in detail in Appendix II.

HIGHLIGHTS OF THE FINDINGS

Highlights of the findings of this study appear below. (For full statistical results, see Appendix III Table A.)

Problems

Taking males and females together, approximately 22 per cent of the reported problems listed by both genders above and beyond all others fell into the class, 'interpersonal concerns' (related to working and interacting with others) with prejudice/discrimination the single most frequently category discussed (20 per cent of all male and 24 per cent of all female reports) in that class.

> 'People ridicule us. Not all [people] . . . but a lot say "You're not Jews; you're Blacks"'.
>
> 'Israeli society looks at us as a strange and different community. This bothers me at work and school – whenever I try to fit in.'

For males alone, material needs were the most frequently reported concern representing 24 per cent of reports: more than twice that of females, and described need for money to meet secondary needs such as studies and level of living.

> 'I am getting married soon and . . . I don't have the money to buy an apartment.'
>
> 'The problem that bothers me is . . . how can I build a future?'

Males also reported a high level of concerns (20 per cent of reports as compared to only 9 per cent among females) about their personal identities, primarily regarding becoming adult and choosing careers.

For females alone, schooling problems, primarily related to fear of academic failure appeared in 27 per cent of reports – more than twice that of males – and was paramount.

'It may be difficult [for me] to get into an institution of higher education.'

A most surprising finding is the low rate of responses indicating worries concerning the specific security situation prevailing in Israel, although many reports described altruistic concerns regarding humanity and society, such as the assassination of Prime Minister Rabin and concerns about peace (12–13 per cent of reports which were coded as answers belonging to the altruism domain). This might be a reflection of a high level of information about the prevailing situation, showing them not to be isolated or removed from the Israeli reality. Ethiopian immigrants gave a higher percentage of altruistic reports regarding the assassination and desire for peace than did either their mainstream Israeli peers or multinational in 1997.

Did the amount of time spent in Israel have any relation to the problems reported by our subjects? We compared between answers of 'veterans' and 'newcomers', looking at responses that fell into the most frequently mentioned classes of problems. We found that those who immigrated last expressed the most worry about problems in the interpersonal and socialization class (in which most of the references are connected with the problem of prejudice and discrimination (22 per cent) and the material desires class, which includes money problems (12–24 per cent). Subjects who arrived earlier, by contrast, tended to be more disturbed by problems connected to the personal identity and self-concept class, where most of the answers referred to the category of becoming an adult (19–20 per cent).

'If an Israeli guy born in Israel has to put up 50 per cent to succeed, I have to put up 100 per cent.'

Gadi, aged 22; Entered Israel in 1988; in Ethiopia, father was school principal; mother nurse.

'I want to study for a master's degree . . . {then} re-enlist for additional time and try to get accepted to a training course at the Foreign Ministry. The course is three years {and gives} all social benefits. {After you finish}, they make you an ambassador's assistant. Then, maybe, after time goes by . . . you can be an ambassador . . . {Now} I worry about my family. My parents are divorcing . . . My little brother . . . is not into studying . . . For me, I have to fit into society if I want to succeed . . . If an Israeli guy born in Israel has to put up 50 per cent to succeed, I have to put up 100 per cent, not to see myself as something different, but as equal. To deal with what is there.'

Coping strategies

As all other studies of our multinational research, the most prevalent coping strategy of male and female Ethiopian adolescents is individual-problem-solving (attempting to solve problems by oneself) appearing in 52 per cent of male and 44 per cent of female reports. Within this class of strategies, male reports tended to show more planning while female reports indicated 'trying harder' more frequently than male reports.

> 'I try to find work to solve the [money] problem but this doesn't always fit in with studies. If [nothing works] . . . the next thing I'll do is drop out of school and enlist in the army.' (Male)

> 'I must work hard and cope with my problem, and be equal to all my friends at the same level. I will try everything to solve the problem and also to feel better.' (Female)

Almost 25 per cent of male and female reports suggested seeking or giving assistance, with 21 per cent of both genders seeking support from others.

Almost three times the number of female reports as male suggested using interpersonal strategies (11 per cent and 4 per cent, respectively) with females, unlike their male peers, tending to say they seek company of others as a way of problem-solving.

Resignation and disengagement, two non-goal-directed coping strategies, appear in somewhat higher percentages of male than female reports (17 per cent and 14 per cent respectively), with males giving more reports of resignation (anger or depression, taking a fatalistic view or giving up) and females more of disengagement (escape-avoidance behaviour and psychological distancing from the problem). These are somewhat lower than in the multinational study, but higher than in the mainstream Israeli findings.

Is the type of coping strategy of our subjects related in any way to their reported problems? We examined the responses of our subjects denoting the most frequently reported classes of problems and found that the strategy used to deal most frequently with interpersonal/socialization issues (representing approximately 71 per cent of responses), schooling issues (approximately 64 per cent of responses) and material desires (61 per cent of responses) was individual problem solving (goal directed strategies). In problems related to altruism, by contrast, non-goal-directed strategies (resignation and disengagement) were the most prevalent (approximately 50 per cent of responses.)

Helpers

Persons chosen to be helpers

With approximately 70 per cent of reports stating that desired helpers came from outside the family, Ethiopian immigrants do not appear to be seeking help from relatives, like their multi-national peers. This was true despite the fact that Ethiopian families are extremely close-knit. Friends were most frequently chosen as helpers.

> 'The more you speak with friends, the easier it is to cope with the problem.'
>
> 'I would turn to someone who could solve my problems, not to just anyone. A helper should be an expert and able to hear the problem and be able to help.'
>
> 'I would go to the government and the person in the country responsible for the Ethiopian community.'

Twenty per cent of females and almost no males reported that they would turn for help to a teacher/instructor or a professional counsellor. This may be due to the fact that females' responses stem from their high percentage of schooling concerns as compared to their male peers.

Characteristics of desired helpers

The most common characteristic desired by males and females in helpers by our subjects is being knowledgeable (experienced):

> 'I would choose my brother who completed army service and understands what goes on in the army.'

Second is being knowledgeable (similar to subject in some way related to the problem):

> 'I would choose a person with the same problem as mine. It's easier to talk to such a person.'

A third characteristic is being powerful (having ability to exercise authority or amend a situation):

> 'I would choose someone . . . in a position to help.'

Other characteristics include being understanding/attentive/ empathetic:

> 'I can't talk to someone who doesn't understand me.'

An examination of qualities of helpers chosen from inside and outside our subjects' families showed that, while characteristics of helpers chosen from outside the family varied considerably, 50 per cent of those chosen from within the family were selected because they were considered knowledgeable. Since most Ethiopian immigrants were dealing with problems related to living in their new cultures, this should not be surprising.

Desired modes of helping

About two-thirds of the responses of both gender groups suggested that they preferred to be counselled and attended to.

> 'He can give me ideas of how to solve the problems.'
>
> 'I trust in her because she knows my problems.'

Many desired simply that helpers attended to them, and asked for comfort, reassurance and encouragement.

> 'He [my desired helper] . . . makes me smile.'
>
> 'Most [helpers] can't do anything except encourage me.'

About one fifth of subjects wanted their helper to exercise power:

> 'She will help me with money and other things.'

Males and females (8 per cent and 4 per cent respectively) reported wanting helpers to directly satisfy their needs (give them something), a finding related probably to the earlier finding that males are more troubled than females by material desires.

DISCUSSION

Can we relate the reports of our subjects primarily to their immigrant status, their non-advantaged SES or their cultural background? Or are they related to all of these factors?

The problems reported by our Ethiopian born subjects differed considerably from those of their mainstream Israeli counterparts. For Ethiopian immigrants, encountering prejudice and discrimination during interactions with mainstream Israelis in school and at the workplace, on the one hand, and facing economic problems on the other were of concern. By contrast, these issues did not appear important to the mainstream-Israeli sample, and, while it might seem logical to relate the economic worries of the Ethiopians to their non-advantaged SES status, their economic concerns as well as their worries about prejudice and discrimination were considerably higher than those of their multinational non-advantaged peers.

Our Ethiopian study results appear to have much in common with those of immigration studies that describe the difficulties encountered by mass migrations, particularly when immigrants are of ethnic, religious or racial backgrounds different from those of the host country (Benmayor and Skotnes 1994).

Since Israel differs from the usual immigrant country in that it was established for the express purpose of ingathering the Jews of the world to its borders and the absorption of immigrants is a value embossed on its standards, we might have assumed that results of this immigration would differ from those in other parts of the world. However, two factors unique to the Israeli situation compound the problem. First is the question discussed earlier, for some mainstream Israelis as to whether the Ethiopian community is a true part of the Jewish nation, particularly since the traditional village cultures from which they came were starkly different from that of Israel. Second, the recent wave of Ethiopian immigration overlapped the massive immigration of a half million Jews from the Soviet Union, with the two migrations together posing a heavy economic and social burden on Israeli society.

Finally, many of the economic concerns of males may be related to their cultural backgrounds: the Ethiopian gender role model requires males alone to be responsible for providing for the family, and many of the comments of male subjects provided earlier suggest that this value has been brought to their new country. Ethiopian ethnic gender roles may also explain why females report far more school problems than males: attending school is a new phenomenon for our immigrant females and they may feel doubly pressured: to succeed in difficult studies and also to prove themselves and justify their efforts.

Examining the coping strategies of our Ethiopian immigrants subjects provides more important information. Most of the coping strategies reported by our subjects were similar to those of the other studies included in this book (individual problem-solving, accepting assistance and interpersonal coping). Our subjects were also similar to other subjects in the other studies in choosing non-goal-oriented coping mechanisms such as resignation (7–14 per cent of reported coping strategies) and disengagement (2–7 per cent of coping strategies), the former anger, despair, giving up and doing nothing and the latter avoiding or distancing oneself from the problem. While fewer responses in this class came from the mainstream advantaged Israeli sample, the responses of the Ethiopian immigrants were closer in number to those of the multinational non-advantaged sample. Examination of the completed questionnaires suggested that the Ethiopian subjects reported feeling resigned or giving up more often when dealing with worries about war or discrimination than with concerns related to economic, academic and self-identity issues. This might indicate that, when dealing with discrimination, like war, our subjects feel helpless.

The fact that our Ethiopian-born subjects generally chose not to turn to their families for help (and reported choosing even fewer helpers from within their families than either multinational or mainstream Israeli samples) is an important change in thinking of young people for whom in Ethiopia the family was always perceived as a source of help. This change, due possibly to the loss of their families during the mass migrations and the arrival of these young people alone in Israel, portrays an immigrant group without benefit of their social systems for support.

In choosing helpers, Ethiopian subjects appear to be changing from what their cultural background alone would predict. Their turning for help to political leaders and other representatives of their host country rather than their families may indicate a breakdown of Ethiopian traditional values, which took place during their exodus. These immigrants, like many immigrant groups the world over experienced a change in their sources of social support, from intra-community factors to institutional agencies outside the community, and had become dependent on government officials and other representatives of their host countries for help in dealing with their urgent economic as well as other problems (Ezrahi and Rosiner 1993).

While many immigrant populations arrive in their host countries in need of economic help and adjust fairly rapidly to their new situations (Benmayor and Skotnes 1994), the Ethiopian immigrant population arrived in Israel in need both of economic and educational help, making initial adjustment more difficult. The fact that those who arrived most recently in Israel were more upset by problems of discrimination than were subjects who arrived earlier (see p. 210) suggests that recent immigrants might be more influenced by the dichotomy of feelings engendered by the clash between the messianic dream vision of Israel (of great significance to the Ethiopian Jewish community) and the very different Israeli reality. The fact that their 'veteran' peers did not appear so concerned suggests, however, that the adaptation process is a gradual one and that both veteran immigrants and mainstream Israelis do adapt to their lives together over time with positive results.

These results suggest that the immigrant status of our Ethiopian subjects, coupled with their non-advantaged SES and their cultural background together contribute to their concerns and coping strategies. Since perceptions of being discriminated against by immigrants in their early years in Israel slows the process of adjustment, people and agencies dealing with members of the community, such as educational counsellors or personnel in the Ministry of Absorption, would do well to be aware of the immigrants' strong feelings of discrimination and despair related to their status and to develop ways to prevent and to reduce these negative feelings.

IMPLICATIONS FOR COUNSELLING

1 Counselling of new immigrants (or refugees) should deal directly with feelings of deprivation and discrimination. When these feelings are shared by many of the members of the group, the counsellor might initiate (invite) counsellees to examine how they experience their social positions rather than waiting until they bring up the subject. Awareness, knowledge, and skills in multicultural counselling are crucial in this process.
2 As economic problems are so often on young adult immigrants' agenda,

counsellors should be prepared to help with practical problems. Instrumental issues are no less important than feelings.

3 Counsellors should be aware of gender differences in the traditional immigrant population. They must be taken in to consideration in the counselling process.

4 Since many Ethiopian immigrant young adults are 'family-less' and have not yet built their own new families, their situation leaves them particularly vulnerable. Thus, the emotional-social support element ought to be more prevalent in the counselling process. In addition, the counsellor intentionally should help the counsellee in gradually weaving a new social support net. (See pp. 30–1.)

References

Adler, H., Toker, D., Manor, Y., Foyerstein, R. and Feldman, M. (1997) 'Absorption of young immigrants from Ethiopia in Youth Aliya, 1985–1995', in Amir, E., Zehavi, A. and Parayi, R. (eds), *One Root – Many Branches: The Story of the Absorption of Young Immigrants from Ethiopia in Youth Aliya*, Jerusalem: Hebrew University of Jerusalem Magnes Press: 255–303.

Banai, N. (1988) *Absorbing the Ethiopians: The Hidden Challenge*, Jerusalem: United Appeal for Israel and the Jewish Agency Department of Immigration and Absorption.

Ben-Ezer, G. (1992) *'Yegan Nevraht': Migration and Absorption of Ethiopian Jews in Israel*, Jerusalem: Reuven Mas.

Benmayor, R. and Skotnes, A. (1994) *Migration and Identity*, Oxford: Oxford University Press.

Benita, E., Noam, G. and Levi, R. (1994) *Local Surveys of Ethiopian Immigrants: Findings from Afula, Natanya and Kiryat Gat: A Research Report*, Jerusalem: Joint Distribution Committee (JDC) and Brookdale Institute of Gerontology and Human Development.

Budovsky, D., David, Y., Akiva, B and Eran, Y. (1994) *Ethiopian Jews in the Transition between Cultures: The Family and Life Cycle*, Jerusalem: Beitachin Center for Information and Counseling about Family Matters.

Dotan, T. (1985) 'Jewish children from Ethiopia in Israel: some observations on their adaptation and education', *Journal of Intercultural Relations* 5: 301–28.

Ezrahi, Y., and Rosiner, A. (1993) *Absorbing the Immigrants of Operation Solomon: an Evaluative Study*, Jerusalem: Department of Jewish Immigration and Absorption Agency for Israel.

Golan-Cook, P., Horowitz, T. and Shfatia, L. (1987) *The Adjustment of Immigrant Pupils from Ethiopia to the School Framework*, Jerusalem: Henrietta Szold Institute for Research and Nurture in Education.

Metrany-Gozlan, M. (1993) *Ties with a Place: A Motive for Emigration and Gaps between the Environment of the Place of Origin and of Destination*, Haifa: The Technion: 8–33.

Minuhin-Isaacson, S. (1983) 'An anthropological description of the meeting of cultures of the Ethiopian Jews and the Israeli culture', *Studies in Education in Aliyat Hanoar*, 15–20.

Munitz, S. (1985) *Self-Perceptions of Skin Color: Evaluating Light and Dark Skin Color and the Colors 'White' and 'Black' among Ethiopian and Israeli Children in*

Kindergarten and First Grade, Ben Gurion University M.A. thesis, unpublished.

Nudelman, A. (1993) 'Understanding immigrant adolescents', *Practicing Anthology* 3: 1–2, 13–15.

Rahat, R. (1983) *Social Patterns in Israel: Trends towards Unity and Disintegration*, Tel Aviv: Open University: Unit 3: Immigration and Absorption.

Schwarzhold, J. and Amir, Y. (1984) 'Interethnic relations in Israel: a review', *Megamot {Trends}* 27 (2/3): 207–3, Jerusalem: Henrieta Szold Institute, National Institute for Research in the Behavioral Sciences.

Shafat, M. (1995) *Adolescent Ethiopian Immigrants in a Crisis of Identity*, Bar Ilan University, M.A. thesis, unpublished.

Sharir, M. (1995) *Predictors of Immigrant Absorption in Kibbutzim of the Northern Negev*, Tel Aviv University M.A. thesis, unpublished.

Smilansky, M. and the NETA Staff (1988) 'Adolescent-parent relations', vol. 3 of *The Challenge of Adolescence*, Tel Aviv: Ramot.

Smooha, S. (1984) 'Three perspectives in the sociology of ethnic relations in Israel', *Megamot {Trends}* 28: 169–206, Jerusalem: Henrietta Szold Institute for Research in the Behavioral Sciences.

Zipstein, D., Lichtmeyer, M. and Isenberg, C. (September 1980) 'Community and group work with Falash immigrants', *Youth Aliya Bulletin* 17–22.

16 Impoverished youth

Examples from Brazil, England and the Philippines

Elisabete Monteiro de Aguiar Pereira,
University of Campinas

INTRODUCTION

Much publicity has been given in recent years to the noticeable groups of homeless people in many countries who live their lives on the streets and who die early deaths from starvation, disease or drug addiction. This chapter does not deal with this destitute group, but describes another, less miserable but most important impoverished group: the economically poor who might have homes but lack the means to meet their basic needs regularly. Few in this group are like Boni, who has hope – or dreams – that he will improve his life.

'Hope or dream?'

Boni, a Brazilian education student and professional musician attending government sponsored night classes to prepare for college; father retired, mother housewife; parental education: primary school. *'In ten years, I want to have completed my doctoral thesis! I hope I will be teaching primary school students or that I will be on a Faculty of Education training teachers to help others. This is important work for my country! For my own inner self, I want also to keep up my work as a musician. I hope never to be unemployed. I will need money so I can continue my higher education if I am to reach my goal, and I don't want ever to be away from the music I love. Finally, I want to be married and have my wife and partner by my side.*

To accomplish all this, I must immediately plan and organize my time carefully. First I have to finish teachers' training and then begin studying for my Master's degree. It is a difficult route for someone of my background, but I will not give up. I am fortunate to have many people close to me who will help me: my friends who can advise me because they live in similar situations and know what I must go through if I am to meet my goals; my girlfriend because she is serene and understands me; my parents because they have great life experience. It is very important to me to have them listen and give their opinions to guide me.'

Impoverished peoples are vulnerable because of low levels of education that give the opportunity to obtain only low level occupations and low incomes. They live in low quality housing and neighbourhoods. They are continually hindered in their attempts to change their status in life by immediate financial need, lack of other resources and/or other personal problems. Observers of the poor have used many generalizations to describe reasons for these problems and for the high crime rate of this population, for example, that they come from disorganized families, have a high incidence of mental and physical disorders, feel alienated from the larger society and, to explain their low achievement in school, lower verbal abilities and a lowered 'need to achieve'.

In fact, however, many of our impoverished subjects had to abandon school for a variety of reasons related to their poverty, just when their countries were beginning to depend on modern technologies and businesses were beginning to require more schooling of their employees (Kawamura and Noronha 1993). Their fight to survive with dignity under these circumstances has been identified as a major factor related to what is known to be their high crime rate (Fonseca 1994, Gomes 1993).

Bogard (1991: 4–7) described poverty as the result of a cumulation of handicaps increased by a complicated interaction of social, cultural and economic processes that affect opportunities for employment, income, education, health, etc. We know that, while a few lucky ones may be able to beat the high odds against improving their lives, lack of needed skills will keep the majority in poverty unless changes are made in all these factors.

How do the increasing numbers of peoples that are afflicted with poverty view their problems? Are they aware of the social and economic complexities that placed them in their situation? 'The World of the Impoverished' describes the results of surveys of impoverished youth in Brazil, England and the Philippines, three populations in three different cultural settings. This study alone is insufficient to produce definitive conclusions, but it provides suggestions useful in formulating an outline of some of the things that help-providers need to know to help the impoverished with their problems. We present our results as 'pilot findings' for use in directing the next steps of needed and more conclusive research.

Family backgrounds

Family backgrounds of the impoverished in Brazil, England and the Philippines suggest that generalizations as to the nature of their family lives are meaningless. Our three impoverished subject groups differ in their family backgrounds in major ways, providing Brazilian and Filipino poor subjects with important support systems that are not provided their English counterparts.

The Brazilian family plays a far more important role in the lives of its impoverished (and more advantaged) members than does the family in virtually any Western country. The most important family relationship of the poor is between mothers and children, with mothers taking on full responsibility for all family matters and fathers usually somewhat distant. Brazilian youth usually remain home until they marry, at which time the new married couples live close to their relatives. The impoverished usually live in communities made up of extended family households, making them available to help one another. Before and after marriage, the many immediate and extended family members maintain responsiblity for helping. Impoverished youth learn their family responsibilities early. Throughout their lives, all generations of family members help each other, often making the difference between meeting basic needs and not. Poverty youth enter the work force earlier than their more advantaged peers, usually to assist their families (Guimaraes and Pereira 1996).

Filipino youth come from a society like Brazil, that has strong family ties, with immediate and extended families living close together and all family members sharing in the responsibility of caring for the family. Impoverished Filipino youth enter the work force at very early ages, taking on the lowest skill jobs, when these are available. Few support systems are available to them outside their families. Close friends are considered as family members, expected to come to one's aid and share in family suffering and happiness. Like Brazil, the Philippines is a religious Catholic country (Velazco 1996).

While families of English poor also play important roles in the lives of their children, however, problems within family settings, including dysfunctional family relationships, divorce, increases in stepfamilies and resulting single-parent-family problems serve to increase difficulties in adjustment rather than to provide positive support. Multiple family problems in this Western country have been related to psychological depression, causing a cycle that makes it even more difficult for this group of youth to remove themselves from poverty.

Schooling and employment

Quality of life for the poor is decreased in modern societies by many social and economic factors that together create a cycle that continues the poverty. This begins often before birth with less-than-adequate prenatal care. It continues after birth with poor living conditions and lack of schooling. The impoverished spend their time necessarily concerned with solving immediate problems to meet their basic needs. Many poor youth leave school to go to work at early ages simply to help their families survive while others leave because of various difficulties associated with attending classes and learning. Today, when modern technologies require more schooling than ever before to develop necessary skills for employment, opportunity to create better lifestyles is lost and the cycle of poverty continues.

Unfortunately, it appears true that poverty populations often place less value on formal schooling than more advantaged SES groups (Gouveia 1981, Gomes 1993, Sposito 1993). Gomes (1997) reported that the schooling history of parents is related to the education and professional routes of their children. Most impoverished parents have attained low levels of education and even when their children are able to go further academically than their parents, the younger generation rarely aspires to the higher occupational levels that their new knowledge prepares them for. One reason for their low levels of aspiration may be that the poor and their families have had little first-hand experience of being rewarded for this type of learning and it simply has not become part of their family culture. Another is that the delayed reward of schooling – creation of a better way of life – takes a long time, when it is important for the poor to satisfy immediate and more basic needs, as Skinner's (1968) theory of behaviorism and Maslow's (1954) hierarchy of needs would suggest. Either way, the poor are often trapped into what was described in the England study (Chapter 7) as a possible new underclass.

Given the schooling problems of the poor, it is not surprising that illiteracy affects this group disproportionately to other SES groups. To remedy the fact that 8 per cent of Brazilian poor are nonliterate and 12 per cent have only very basic educational skills (IBGE-PNDE 1996) the Brazilian government began literacy and basic education programmes in 1996 for impoverished Brazilian children. The original programmes have been extended experimentally to provide opportunity for poor youth to obtain secondary educations so that they can develop skills needed for entrance into higher education. The Brazilian youth in this study were attending this experimental programme.

By contrast, our Filipino subjects not only were not attending school, but most had dropped out well by before they reached adolescence to enter the work force. One of the many reasons that this group had dropped out of school is that the language of instruction in Filipino schools is English while the native language of the impoverished is Tagalag, making school learning far more difficult (Velazco 1996: 172).

While most youth in England have continued access to schools, there have been growing numbers of school exclusions based on inappropriate behaviour, and while our impoverished subjects had had opportunity to attend school, most had also left prior to completion of high school.

THE STUDY AND ITS METHODOLOGY

Subjects

Brazil: Subjects included fifty-nine males and seventy females 18–20 years of age who had left school prior to completing secondary education and were enrolled in one of the new public secondary school evening centres described above which were offered on the periphery of the city of Campinas. Their socio-economic status was determined by their presence in the centre as well as by the standardized socio-economic descriptors described in Chapter 1 and used in other studies of the Multinational Study. Most parents had completed no more than the first four grades of school and were employed at occupations requiring few skills. More than 70 per cent of parents worked as drivers, guards, bricklayers, machine operators, electricians' assistants, etc. Mothers, if they were employed, worked as kitchen help, maids etc. As in the Brazil Study (Chapter 4), these fell into the Hutchinson Inventory, professional categories V–VII (Hutchinson 1960). Brazilian subjects were surveyed in 1997.

England: subjects included fourteen males and twenty females 18–20 years of age in the south and southwest of England. Approximately 75 per cent of these were receiving support from voluntary sector agencies or other community-based counselling services designed particularly for youth that provided therapeutic, remedial and medical services, practical information and advice. These subjects usually were not attending school, were frequently estranged from their families and were, by and large, unemployed. Subjects matched the socio-economic descriptors of poverty described in Chapter 1. Many had been eligible to receive governmentally subsidized living assistance prior to the decrease in Britain's welfare roles (see Chapter 7). English subjects were surveyed in 1997.

The Philippines: subjects included 100 males and 100 females from areas surrounding Manila on the island of Luzon. Subjects matched the socio-economic descriptors of poverty described in Chapter 1 and had left school many years before being surveyed for this study. Those who had not found part-time low-level and low paid work were unemployed. Filipino subjects were surveyed in 1989.

Procedure

Poverty subjects were surveyed and responses were coded using the procedures described in Chapter 1 for other populations in our study. Appendix I describes the reliability of coding. In our 1997 study, Brazilian subjects were surveyed in their evening school classrooms and English surveys were administered at youth centres, a college and other places where youth congregated. In our 1989 study, Filipino youth, most of whom were nonliterate, were interviewed individually in the areas where they lived.

HIGHLIGHTS OF OUR FINDINGS

This chapter reports highlights of our findings only. Appendices III and IV provides full statistical results. We present these findings despite small numbers of subjects in some samples (particularly in the English sample) and the fact that two of our three subject samples were surveyed in 1997 and one (the Philippines) was surveyed in 1989, which precludes us from making a comparison between the two years of our study. We do so because of the importance of the impoverished to society today and the great need to understand as much as we can about them. We present our findings as pilot results in the hope that they will serve as impetus for further study, but remind readers that we can only make conjectures concerning similarities and/or differences between the two groups of subjects and between the two genders.

Problems

As regards reported problems, our impoverished subject reports differed greatly from those of their more advantaged peers.

Brazilian subjects Brazilian subjects worried in 1997 about interpersonal issues (represented by problems related to working with or interacting with others on daily bases and shown in 29 per cent of male and 21 per cent of female reports) more than any other single concern. Problems tended to be related especially to seeking entry into the workforce and maintaining jobs:

> 'I am very afraid of losing my job.'
>
> 'The lack of opportunities frightens me. I am without work options.'

Their second major worry concerned altruistic issues such as societal injustice. This was demonstrated in 15–16 per cent of Brazilian poverty responses as contrasted with 3 per cent of Brazilian advantaged and 4–15 per cent of Brazilian non-advantaged reports. Although most altruistic concerns appeared to be expressed at a societal level, they also described immediate problems that these young people face daily. The only other groups in the Multinational Study in which such concerns occurred more frequently were the Chinese advantaged and non-advantaged groups (see Appendix III).

> 'My worry? The unemployment that causes hunger, disease, violence, lack of compassion for neighbour, disputes – and greed.'
>
> 'It worries me to think about the world we will live in the future. Every day we see more new diseases, more children on the streets, more unemployment and violence.'
>
> 'I worry about the lack of schools for everybody. The rich are able to obtain adequate schooling but the poor can't afford it. This keeps increasing the difference between the rich and the poor.'

It is possible that some of these 'humanitarian' concerns might be thinly-veiled descriptions of personal problems deemed unsafe for open discussion. If so, this might explain why these same subjects almost never reported 'taboo' subjects such as drug usage or sexual activity in the first person.

> 'I worry about AIDS that kills million of young people [like me]. Many poor youth don't have resources even to treat themselves.'
>
> 'Drugs [available to] youth lead me to despair.'

As regards gender differences, for Brazilian females, family concerns accounted for another 16 per cent of female responses. (By contrast, only 9 per cent of male responses were related to family issues.) Written responses centred primarily on family welfare and usually indicated desires to help:

> 'My parents are already old and tired. I want to take care of them so they can stop working.'
>
> 'I don't like to see my mother sad. I want to make her happy.'
>
> 'My mother has diabetes. I try to keep her calm because when she's nervous her condition gets worse.'

While Brazilian females worried about their families, males worried about schooling, which ranked third in their listed concerns. That females had fewer worries than males regarding schooling (8 per cent of female and 14 per cent of male responses), might be related to their gender-specific family roles as defined traditionally in their culture. It is interesting that schooling ranked so low in a group provided government-sponsored special schooling.

English subjects English poverty youth, by contrast, worried first about family issues and provided more than twice the percentage of responses (24 per cent of male and 52 per cent of female reports, again indicating that females had more than twice the worries of males) regarding their concerns as their Brazilian peers. The issues they worried about were quite different, however: divorce, family strife and violence, inappropriate behaviour on the part of family members and sexual abuse. (They were also not uncomfortable in discussing these 'taboo' topics.)

> 'I hate going to my Dad's. I have not gotten along with him since my Mum and my Dad split up.'
>
> 'My problems started when my Mum and Dada split up and my Dad started hitting me.'
>
> 'My brother sexually abused me.'
>
> 'My brother is in trouble with the police. He was caught stealing cars and has to go to court.'

Second-ranked English worries concerned material desires (18 per cent of male and 11 per cent of female responses as compared with 10 per cent of the responses of Brazilian subjects).

> 'I don't have a nice place to live. I live in a bed-sit now and I need my own kitchen with a two-and-a-half-year-old and a new baby'.
>
> 'I have too little money and can't live comfortably on what I have.'

While these reported material desires might be actual descriptions of material need, it is not clear that most of our subjects understand, as Boni appeared to understand, the relationship that exists between obtaining schooling and employment.

For English subjects, another 18 per cent of responses indicated their emotional states. For English females, concerns about identity ranked third and showed in 11 per cent of responses. Interestingly, our English subjects did not report altruistic problems.

Filipino subjects Our 1989 Filipino subjects worried, first, about material desires (19 per cent of male and 25 per cent of female responses) and second, family problems (18 per cent of male and 24 per cent of female responses). 'Need for money to meet material needs' highlighted both male and female responses. This was followed in female responses by 'family welfare' (Appendix III).

Coping

Impoverished male and female subjects, regardless of nationality and similar to their multinational peers, were alike in their two most frequently reported coping strategies. First, both did their best to solve their problems themselves, with females reporting that they did so more frequently than males and Brazilians more frequently than English; and second, both resigned themselves to their situations or disengaged from them.

Brazilian subjects The most frequently reported individual coping strategy involved assessment of the situation and planning of action:

> 'As my problem is my mother's disease, I inform myself more regarding that disease and to see how I can help her.'
>
> 'I donated food for the people who are starving.'

Fewer subjects exhibited the desire to 'try harder' with no carefully thought out plan.

> 'I try to react positively because if I give myself to the fear and to despair, everything will finish crumbling.'

English subjects:

'I study harder and have a little hope.'

'I try to 'numb' it out of my mind and, hopefully, it will go away.'

Filipino subjects:

'I plan ways to get what I want.'

When resignation (surrender to the conclusion that the problem cannot be resolved) and disengagement (avoiding or distancing oneself from the problem) were combined to describe 'non-goal-oriented coping' as in the Multinational Study (Chapter 3), this 'new' strategy was the first-ranked strategy of English males and females (representing 53 per cent of all coping reports of males and 37 per cent of females') and of Brazilian males (35 per cent of coping reports). It was the second-ranked strategy for Brazilian females (representing 29 per cent of reports), Filipinos (20 per cent) and Filipinas (18 percent). These coping strategies were reported more frequently by our poverty subjects than by more advantaged peers from their own countries (see Appendix III Tables A and B).

Resignation:

'I don't try to do anything; I just cry.'

'I don't generally do anything; I just complain.'

'I don't do anything. I don't know what to do.'

Disengagement:

'I go out and drink with my mates.'

'I get stoned or wrecked in some way.'

'I try to think of other things.'

Helpers

The first choice of help of our impoverished subjects was people outside their families, just as in advantaged and non-advantaged groups of the multinational study. This accounted for 57 per cent of Brazilian male and 59 per cent of female responses; 74 per cent of English male and 81 per cent of female responses and 48 per cent of Filipino and Filipina responses. Among these non-family helpers were, friends, girlfriends and boyfriends first, followed by instructors, poll leaders, employers or counsellors.

Examination of subjects' written responses on the survey sheets suggested poverty youth sought people on the basis of, first, trust, loyalty, patience and concern. For Brazilian subjects, this was followed by knowledge based on similarity of experiences and power to solve their problems or to satisfy their material needs. Many subjects who described altruistic concerns looked to political leaders who represented for them power to modify the situation.

Family members represent the second source of help for our poor subjects. (This was shown in 27 per cent of Brazilian male and 25 per cent of Brazilian female reports; in 21 per cent of English male and 15 per cent of English female reports and 39 per cent of Filipino reports and 42 per cent of Filipina reports.) Written responses suggested that qualities sought from family members were loyalty, patience, honesty, reliability, generosity, affection and kindness, but not knowledge, similarity of experience or power. For poverty subjects, it appears that parents and other family members don't represent people who are sufficiently knowledgeable from their own experiences or sufficiently powerful to provide help.

Although Brazil and the Philippines are religious (Catholic) countries only 3 per cent of Brazilian female subjects and none of the male subjects indicated turning to religion as a coping strategy. At the same time, when females were asked to whom they went for help, 9 per cent of their responses indicated a 'supernatural being'.

> 'I look for help with Jesus. He is the only one who can solve our problems.'
>
> 'God is very important for me. He helps me in very precise ways.'

By contrast, 6 per cent of Filipino and and 14 per cent of Filipina responses indicated coping by seeking religious support, while only 3 per cent sought a religious helper. This difference between Brazilian and Filipino responses probably represent culturally different ways of expressing personal religiosities.

Our English subjects gave no indication whatsoever of religiosity in either their coping or their selection of a helper.

CONCLUSIONS

While our small sample sizes preclude definitive statements, our results suggest possible conclusions:

1 Our data confirm that impoverished youth in at least three countries are concerned with day-to-day worries related to their family situations, current employment and material needs. We suggest that concerns that

call for immediate responses make it difficult for them to consider future problems or worry about obtaining future goals.

2 Our data do not confirm that impoverishment is necessarily related to dysfunctional family backgrounds. To the contrary, while the reports of our English subjects suggested that dysfunction within many families were primary sources of their problems, our Brazilian and Filipino reports suggested both that they received social and emotional support from their closely knit families and that they worried about finding ways to help them.

3 Our findings support Gomes' (1997) report that the schooling history of parents is related to the education and professional routes of their children. While our Brazilian, English and Filipino advantaged and non-advantaged subjects had practical evidence that one can improve employment opportunities through education, this was at best only a supposition for our poverty subjects, a hope that their parents could not personally reinforce through evidence of their own experience. It is important that relatively few reports of our poverty subjects expressed a great deal of concern regarding schooling or discussed the relationship between obtaining further education and finding desired employment. Although this does not mean that they did not understand the relationship between education and employment opportunities, it might mean that they recognized so many obstacles to successful learning (lack of money, lack of time to study, difficulty of understanding the material, lack of knowledge, etc.) that they believed it was impossible for them actually to succeed.

4 Since there is world-wide evidence of a growing rate of drug usage, pregnancy and sexually related disease, especially AIDS, among youth, and certainly among impoverished youth, we were not surprised to see these problems discussed openly by our British subjects. The obvious silence on that subject by our Brazilian and Filipino subjects might support the belief that that drugs and sexuality are simply not part of their day-to-day concerns, and this is the reason why studies are finding that increasing numbers of young people are not protecting themselves from these dangers. However, the fact that our Brazilian subjects talked about this problem ('taboo' for discussion in their culture) as a societal rather than personal issue, suggests that they are, indeed, concerned. Unfortunately, examination of the coping strategies described by these subjects suggests that their pattern of behaviour involves resignation or disengagement from the problem rather than dealing actively with it. These results are consistent with studies of the reactions of young people to learning about AIDS (Abraham *et al.* 1991). While it may be in their best interests to ignore problems which they cannot control, this is definitely not true of this set of concerns.

5 With respect to coping strategies, it is alarming that poor youth are so frequently resigning themselves to most difficulties or disengaging from them, far more than their more advantaged peers. It certainly suggests

that they believe they cannot solve their problems. Here, educators and other professionals who work with youth need to help them learn how to develop positive and workable action plans.

IMPLICATIONS FOR COUNSELLING

Impoverished populations, like those surveyed in our study, are in dire need of help. While they actively seek help from friends and family, however, too frequently these people do not have adequate knowledge or resources to assist them in meaningful ways. Since impoverished youth are clear that they look for helpers who will pay them attention and respond to them in personal and comforting ways, helpers need to be able to be trained and to have time to do so. Studies have shown, in addition, that helpers must be able to convince youth not only of the severe dangers of problems such as those related to drugs and sexuality, but also of their personal vulnerability. This requires the personalization of risk appraisal and responsibility (Abraham *et al.* 1991). One feasible way to increase the numbers of help-providers so that they can provide more personal attention might be to utilize new types of helpers such as those provided now in England in their specialized youth programmes. We especially recommend utilization of trained same-aged peers in educating poverty youth about issues such as AIDS.

The answer for poverty youth, however, is not simply to provide more and better-trained counsellors. Our poverty youth appeared so overwhelmed with immediate crises that it seemed impossible that they had time or energy left even to worry about their futures. To change their lives in positive ways requires nothing less than helping them – and their families (since many of the worries of impoverished youth are about their families) – meet their basic needs. we propose that, so long as financial and other societal ills continue to affect this SES group adversely, the appropriate role of counsellors is to help them learn the causes of their problems so that they can begin to make positive changes themselves. In the case of our impoverished youth, just as of their more advantaged peers, if they are ever to be able to build a better world society, this must go beyond the problems that affect their immediate lives.

As regards the strong link between individual and work, while our subjects' major concerns dealt with finding employment now rather than preparing for desired future employment, it was not clear whether they understood the important relationship between education and future successes. This indicates need for community-based guidance and counselling services for children in the lower grade levels and their families as well as support services to assist younger students to remain in school. While the Brazilian government is to be applauded for providing schooling opportunities for impoverished Brazilian youth, we agree with Bourdieu

(1987) that, in order to help the impoverished achieve, the value of schooling must also be incorporated into family life so that it will be become part of the family cultural capital passed on to new generations. This must begin in all countries with creation of better opportunities for the labour force. Today, although our poverty subjects may recognize a link between schooling and better occupational opportunities, most know that, no matter what they do, they have only a very small chance to improve their opportunities in the labour market. To change this situation, they must learn not only that it is desireable but that it is also possible to succeed.

The question whether Boni, the subject of our case study on p. 218, succeeds in achieving his goals depends, of course, on how hard he tries. It also depends on the help he receives. If he depends solely on his parents and peers who have few resources for helping and his society does not insure that necessary help is provided, unfortunately he will fail. It is up to us to see that his dreams become reality. (See pp. 28–31.)

Note

Data in this chapter was collected and coded by E. Pereira and I. Giimaraes (Brazil), K. Feaviour and D. Acres (England) and G. Velazco (the Philippines).

References

Abraham, C., Sheeran, P., Abrams, D., Spears, R. and Marks, D. (1991) 'Young people learning about AIDS: a study of beliefs and information sources', *Health Education Research: Theory and Practice* 6 (1): 19–29

Bogard, G. (November 1991) *Education, Poverty and Insecurity: Rreport to the Council for Cultural Cooperation* DECS/AE 14, Strasburg: Council of Europe

Bourdieu, A. (1987) 'The excellence and the values of the French system', in Miceli, S. (ed.) *The Economy of Symbolic Change*, São Paulo: Perspective, in Portuguese.

Fonseca, C. (1994) 'Getting ready for the life reflections on school and adolescence in popular groups', *Em Aberto*, Brasilia, INEP (61) 144–55, in Portuguese.

Gomes, J. V. (1993) 'Family and school relationships: continuities and discontinuities', *Ideias, Sao Paulo* FDE (16): 84–92, in Portuguese.

Gomes, J. V. (1997) 'Impoverished urban youth: their school and employment concerns', *Revista Brasileira de Educação* 52 (4): 53–61, in Portuguese.

Gouveia, A. (July 1981) *Democratization of Teaching and Employment Opportunities*, São Paulo: Loyola, in Portuguese.

Guimaraes, I. and Pereira, E. (1996) 'The Brazil study', in Gibson-Cline, J. (ed.), *Adolescence: From Crisis to Coping*, London: Routledge: 59–72.

Hutchinson, B. (1960) *Mobility and Work*, Rio de Janeiro: MEC–CBPE, in Portuguese.

IBGE – PNAD (1996) *Brazilian Institute of Geography and Statistics Yearbook*, Brasilia: Government of Brazil.

Kawumura, L. and Noronha, O. (1993) *Qualifications for the Work Force: New Cultural Parameters*, Campinas: Ability of Education (mimeo), in Portuguese.

Lawton, A. (1985) 'Youth counselling', *British Journal of Guidance and Counselling* 13 (1) (January): 35–48.

Maslow, A. (1954) *Motivation and Personality*, New York: Harper.

Skinner, B. F. (1968) *The Technology of Teaching*, New York: Appleton Century Crafts.

Sposito, M. (1993) *The Fertile Illusion: The Battle for Education by the Popular Movements*, São Paulo: Hucitec, in Portuguese.

Velazco, G. (1996) 'The Philippines study', in Gibson-Cline, J. (ed.), *Adolescence from Crisis to Coping*, London: Routledge: 169–83.

Part V

Conclusions and implications for the helping professions

> If there is one group above all others who should be our concern, it must be youth. They are the inheritors of our future.
>
> Indira Gandhi (1984)

Chapter 17 assesses our multi-national findings as a basis from which helping professionals can develop successful interventions to assist the inheritors of our future to meet the demands of coming adulthood. It suggests new skills and practices that professionals will need to reach this goal in the new century.

17 Conclusions and implications for theory and practice

From reports of Brazilian, Canadian, Chinese, English, Filipino, Greek, Indian, Ethiopian-immigrant-Israeli, mainstream Jewish-Israeli, Japanese, Russian, American and Venezuelan youth

Janice Gibson-Cline with Louise Martinson, Brenda Shaw and the Youth and Coping *Research Team*

(Brazil: Elizabete Pereira; Canada: Louise Martinson, Brenda Shaw and Bill Borgen; China: Qi Chen, Fengchun Miao and Xin Lu; England: Kevin Feaviour and David Acres; Greece: Maria Dikaiou and Mika Haritos-Fatouras; India: Lina Kashyap; Israel: Benjamin Shafrir, Rachel Erhard (Ethiopian immigrants in Israel); Japan: Keiko Honda and Ishu Ishiyama; the Philippines: Gundalina Velazco; the USA: Lisa Maccarelli, Janice Gibson-Cline, Carol E. Baker and David Botwin; Venezuela: Maria Felce DiPaula)

INTRODUCTION

Modern epistemology asserts there is no one truth but only multiple discourses of truth. This position reflects an important change in thinking from the belief systems of our forebears and affects all our decision-making regarding issues varying from how we perceive the universe to how we conduct our personal lives. The modern civilization that faces us at the beginning of the twenty-first century has brought a multitude of changes to our economic, political, technological and social worlds, and together with these changes, a host of new requirements for successful management of our lives. The findings of the many studies in this book suggest that the most important of these may be the requirement to make – or be prepared to make – continual modifications of our behaviour, goals and life patterns to meet whatever changes are to come.

Youth, who remain the hope of our future today as they did in the past,

Hopes, dreams and worries: more cultural variations

'I worry about what my future will bring . . .'

Adam is from a kibbutz in Israel. His father is an electrical engineer and his mother is a nurse.
'When I have finished my military service, I want to travel awhile. Then I plan to study oceanography at a university in the USA. I worry, though, that no matter how hard I work, the future may not hold good things. Will there be constant danger of war? Will I be able to achieve my goals? While I believe in will power and determination, I know that the future will not necessarily be kind.'

'Should I come back home to live with my parents after I graduate from college or should I choose another place where I can more easily work at my profession?'

Fang is from China. Her parents are farmers. Her father completed middle school; her mother is illiterate.
'What worries me most is making choices about my future. I have difficulty deciding where I should work after I graduate from college. Will I make my parents unhappy if I don't live with them? When I worry too much about this, I try to detach myself and stop thinking. Sometimes I read novels or go rock-climbing to help myself relax.'

'I would like a scholarship so I can go back to school, but there are so many things I need to do first.'

Luis lives in Venezuela. His widowed mother is a cleaning lady. Luis is the eldest of six siblings.
'I want someday to have my own business as a car mechanic and live in a nice apartment building. I want to go to school to learn to do better at reading and arithmetic. {A man needs to keep financial books if he has his own business.} But before I can do that, I must keep working at what I do now – packing at a supermarket – so I can help my mother and bring enough money into the family for everyone to have enough to eat.'

'I worry about AIDS that kills million of young people.'

This anonymous impoverished Brazilian subject was in despair over the spectre of AIDS in her country, couching her concern as an altruistic (societal) rather than personal problem.
'Many poor youth don't have resources even to treat themselves.'

face this situation unprotected by the traditional support systems that we and our parents had to guide us. To make a successful transition to adulthood, they will require skills that we are just beginning to identify.

Our multinational portrait of youth: a brief summary

A review of our multinational and national studies (Chapter 3) show that the problems and coping of youth, although similar in many respects, also vary by SES grouping and gender as well as by culture and country. We assume (although we did not examine this variable in our research) that they also vary by locale: being 18–20 years old in a rural area, for example, is a very different experience from being the same age in a large city.

With the increase in level of education required for employment at the end of the twentieth century, our subjects were most frequently concerned with problems related to schooling and employment issues, self-identity or family issues. While advantaged, non-advantaged and male subjects reported problems related to schooling, employment and self-identity most frequently, these issues were superseded for our poverty group and females by immediate and family worries. Most subjects coped by attempting to solve their problems themselves.

It is extremely important that very few subjects reported worries concerning the increasing danger posed by AIDS. This same lack of reporting appeared in both our 1997 and 1989 results. It also appeared in our 1989 study of adolescence (Gibson-Cline 1996). It is particularly ominous in light of global estimates that 1999 would include 2.6 million new deaths by 31 December of that year, that another 5.6 million people would be newly infected with HIV in that same year, and that 33.6 million were living in with HIV/AIDS (Perlman 1999: A15). The lack of reported concern by our subjects may be due to a discomfort at reporting one's most personal concerns on a questionnaire, as suggested by the author of the poverty study, Elizabete Pereira, or as Louise Martinson and Brenda Shaw, co-authors of the Canadian study, suggest. It may also be that many youth do not consider these issues to be problems. The subject is not either engaging in unsafe sex or using drugs and therefore does not consider these issues problems. Another ominous possibility is that the subject or the subject's friends are engaging in unsafe sex or using drugs, but don't believe it to be a problem, just as many youth of the 1960s did not view experimenting with drugs as the serious problem that society-at-large considered it. Our subjects frequently chose strategies that were unlikely to help them reach their reported goals, such as 'resignation' and 'disengagement'. While these strategies may have reduced stress as suggested in the Greek chapter by authors Maria Dikaiou and Maria Haritas-Fatouras, they did little to reduce their reported problems. We suggest that they also did little to decrease the problems that went unreported, such as AIDS or drug and alcohol abuse. This is very dangerous, indeed!

When our subjects sought help, the single most frequent source they reported was a close friend, from whom they wanted comfort and support.[1]

Many reports suggested that they also wanted advice, although they only very rarely sought professional help for their problems. That our subjects rarely sought professional help is not surprising, given the research literature on 'help-seeking' of persons not in the process of undergoing therapy. However, the fact that they increased in their desire to obtain comfort and attention suggests, according to the literature, that problems for these subjects are increasing in their severity (see Wills 1983: 113).

Why would young people on the verge of making the transition to adulthood behave in ways that increase their vulnerability to serious problems? One reason might be that youth, today, regardless of nationality, socio-economic status or gender, are finding it far more difficult than their predecessors to achieve the independence required for full adult status, and as a result, often simply 'give up trying'. For our advantaged and non-advantaged subjects, whose problems were frequently related to increasingly difficult requirements for learning the technical skills needed for the new job markets, finding solutions was made more difficult by lack of information needed to determine the best course of action. For our impoverished and immigrant subjects, the same problems existed but immediate needs more frequently took all their attention, requiring them to 'give up trying' to meet less immediate goals. A final factor affecting all our subjects is the increasing speed at which social and economic conditions are changing throughout the world. It is far more difficult today to know what will be required tomorrow than it was yesterday and it will be even more difficult tomorrow.

To adjust satisfactorily to these issues young people – and older people as well – must begin by approaching the obvious: with life situations changing throughout the world; transitions from youth to adulthood different and more difficult than in past generations and a twenty-first century likely to increase the pace of change, youth and those who help them must increase their adaptability and flexibility to meet whatever comes.

Approaches to counselling

Chapter 1 began (p. 3) with a discussion of the importance to society of assisting youth to become worthwhile and productive adult citizens. Given the rapidly changing societies of the world today and the new challenges they generate, there is no one simple answer as to how we should accomplish this. We believe in the classical views regarding the importance of helping youth to deal with individual, personal and acute crises. We also believe that, just as problems and issues have changed for youth, so must our approaches to providing help. To validate the new needs of youth, we suggest the following additions to the classical approaches to helping discussed in Chapter 2.[2]

Eclectic, flexible and active approaches

While professional counselling was developed initially to aid clients of advantaged backgrounds who sought advice regarding education and career choices, our clientele have increased well beyond this group. Our new clientele come from a variety of backgrounds and have a variety of immediate and long-term needs. As we speak, new economic, political, technological and social issues are appearing that will create overnight new sets of problems for young people to face. To provide help today, counsellors must have flexibility and help their clients be flexible as well. They must also embrace the increasing diversities inherent in the belief systems and life styles of people in all nations and help their clients do the same so that they, too, will be able to change direction as needed. To meet new needs, helping professionals, like their clients, must be active, dynamic and capable of change. Their repertoire of approaches must be eclectic, flexible and, because many problems are interrelated, multi-modal. Finally, because young people often do not seek counsellors on their own volition, services will need to be locally situated with helpers joining young people in their worlds, not vice versa. The goal, above all, should be to enable youth to handle successfully any crisis they might face in the future.

Preventive approaches that emphasize coping

We suspect that many of our subjects' coping strategies might have increased, rather than decreased their problems. The common coping strategy, 'trying harder', is a good example. While it is true that 'trying harder' might lead in some instances to problem solution, it might also lead to repetition of the same responses that not only did not solve the problem in the first place, but actually increased it. Counselling can help young people by helping them understand the roots of their problems so that they can plan the most effective strategies to create change. Another example of coping strategies that do not lead to the reduction of problems is the large number of coping responses that indicated resignation, giving up or disengaging from the situation. While these strategies might reduce stress, as a number of our authors noted, they do not necessarily lead to solution of the problems listed by our subjects as causing them concern. In cases where these strategies are not appropriate, we suggest taking approaches from systems and constructivist theories (see Chapter 2) and teaching ways to cope more effectively by:

1. emphasizing the importance of fluidity – ability to respond to changes in the situation by changing coping strategies and
2. recognizing that when coping strategies are ineffective, learning how to develop new strategies that will be viable in the given situation.

This can begin with counsellors and clients determining the history of the needs and problems of clients (Seidman and Rappaport 1986) and using what they find to work toward empowering themselves so as to solve their problems. While this approach has been discussed by Freire (1983) and others in relation to the impoverished or down-trodden, our findings make it very clear that it is equally important for the advantaged populations.

Special responsibility as advocates of the poor

Counsellors in the twenty-first century are needed to provide more impoverished peoples greater amounts of help than ever before to meet immediate needs and to deal with immediate dangers. In times of crisis, these people will need resources to meet immediate needs. To build better lives, many will need access to education and to learn skills necessary for them to adapt to their new cultures. For these groups, interventions that are successful for the long term require different approaches than for more advantaged populations. Among the most effective approaches for impoverished youth are crisis intervention for immediate problems and systems and constructive approaches for long-term change. In both scenarios, many types of helping professionals will be needed, in addition to those who often care most: community members, friends, family members, peers. We suggest community-based assistance to help young people solve immediate problems. In addition, we suggest working with youth, families and government institutions to create understanding of the importance of education in bettering their lives and reaching the highest level of functioning possible.[3] To complete this scenario effectively, institutions must be prepared to provide the necessary educational possibilities. An additional role of the counsellor, therefore, should be as a mediator between clients and the institutions with power to make this happen. (See Chapter 2, pp. 8–31.)

Special responsibility for refugees, migrants and minorities

Historians expect the twenty-first century to bring continued small wars in which groups of people escape death and danger by fleeing their homes, crossing national borders and leaving behind them past lives, families, friends, professions, possessions and, often, language and culture. Refugees and migrants (peoples not forced to flee but who do so in order to better their lives) are increasing in numbers and impoverished minority immigrants are having a major impact on daily life and on institutions across the world. The expectation is that these migrations will continue throughout the twenty-first century and, in the process, increase the multi-national, multi-ethnic and multi-religious faces of the countries to which they come.

The needs of these people as they adjust to their new lives are often overwhelming, making information about these populations essential to planners as well as those dedicated to helping. The Ethiopian immigrant subjects of our study, for example, arrived in Israel without resources to meet their basic needs. Before they could begin caring for themselves, they required language training and basic education to prepare them for entry even into low-skilled work. Although they shared a common religion with those in their new country, their feelings of being discriminated against by their new communities because of their dark skin and different backgrounds increased the difficulties of their adjustment (see Chapter 15).

To help peoples such as the Ethiopians, long-term counselling is usually needed to make it possible to adjust satisfactorily to the enormous loss of what they had left behind. We suggest that counsellors need eclectic arsenals of counselling approaches that will permit them to vary their helping strategies with the needs of particular groups, and further, that these approaches be used by teams of helping professionals using their various skills together to solve this enormous problem.

Finally, arrival of needy populations, which created multicultural communities in what had previously been mono-cultural nations, has led frequently to negative reactions and civil unrest on the part of host countries, thus creating new problems for hosts as well as migrants. We expect that these problems will increase rather than decrease in the twenty-first century, and that counsellors can play important roles by working together with other professionals in community programmes to help host nationals to adjust to inevitable change.

Special responsibility for women

Our study demonstrated that women's problems bear a relationship to SES in that women most frequently reported problems relating to family, just as most of our impoverished subjects, in contrast to their male counterparts who most frequently reported schooling and employment problems, just as advantaged subjects. We believe that these gender characteristics are caused by cultural indoctrination that gives responsibility to women for child-rearing and care of families and to men for working.

With the twenty-first century poised to provide women more professional opportunities than ever before, many countries have already begun providing solutions for handling women's traditional role of child-rearing. However, although availability of help such as daycare is increasing in Western countries and Western women are 'free' to plan careers, most women who work outside of home still must struggle to handle work and family roles simultaneously. The young women of our study appeared to be aware of the compromises they need to make in their plans for the future, as exemplified by the comments (p. 163–4) of Naho, a 21-year-old Japanese university student:

> 'I never want to quit my job because of my marriage. And I never want to be in an ambivalent situation in which my career conflicts with my marriage . . . What I am most afraid of is that when I marry, I will have to quit my job even if we don't have a baby . . . [so] I will have to decide whether to get married or to continue my career.'

In non-Western countries where women have not yet been granted the freedoms given those from the West, females face different problems and have fewer resources to assist them. The author of Chapter 9, Lina Kashyap, suggests that the most efficient and least expensive way to help women in her country is to provide school programmes that explore important issues such as femininity and gender stereotyping, equality of opportunity and life skills such as decision-making.

How can counselling help women? We believe that, although problems and helping resources vary greatly by country, it is important for all modern women, regardless of their background, to understand their situations in the modern world and the possibilities open to them as well as the prices of acting on these possibilities. Counsellors who accept the responsibility, just like their female clients, need to envision new possibilities for adjusting to the modern and more complex ways of living that are coming. They must use whatever resources are available to contribute to a new vision of femininity that celebrates diversity, complexity, and co-operation.

Special responsibility for the down-trodden

The 'down-trodden' include youth of all backgrounds made more vulnerable than ever before because of the imminent threat of AIDS, drug and alcohol abuse, etc. destroying their lives. Assuming that our subjects did not report these problems because of their very personal natures and that their reported coping strategies, especially resignation or disengagement, cannot be successful in solving their extremely serious problems, counsellors have a major responsibility to find ways to help them transcend their discomfort in seeking help. Examination of the qualities youth now seek in problem-solving provides a clue. Because desired helpers offer comfort, reassurance and trust, it is especially important to provide counselling that includes these qualities in settings that feel safe. Youth today receive a great deal of information via the mass media and programmes that speak to large audiences. We suggest a better direction for counsellors is to provide help in a personal manner to small groups of youth with similar concerns with the goal of having peers work with peers and counsellors providing input in ways that are non-threatening as well as supportive. In some instances, individual counselling may be best.

Needed roles for helping professionals in the twenty-first century

Today, counsellors can be found working in numerous settings and at a variety of important tasks. The following sections describe the various roles they play. Although we have listed each as a separate entity, many overlap with one another, just as the problems of clients.

Conductors of traditional individual (one-on-one) and group counselling

These traditional counselling activities are usually designed at the individual level, to assist clients to deal with their needs and to provide emotional support to help them deal with personal crises; and, at the same time to assist clients to enlarge their repertoire of strategies and to replace ineffective ones and utilize other sources of help in their communities. At the group level, the focus is on helping groups or individuals within groups. Such groups of individuals may share a common experience or goal, such as being unemployed, facing war or difficult environmental conditions.

Members of multi-disciplinary helping teams that work together with para-professional and other professional staff

Members of inter-disciplinary teams today may include a wide variety of professionals such as health care personnel, counsellors, social workers, teachers, business people, community members, etc., depending on the situation with the purpose of assessing needs and helping to develop effective coping strategies. The fact that our subjects indicated that they most preferred friends as helpers and only rarely (perhaps as a last resort) sought help from professional help-providers reinforces the argument for including peers, family or community members as well as other non-professionals close to clients. These people can often provide the concern and understanding often sought by those in severe stress. Working as team members with counselling professionals and clients, they can provide major assistance in creating helpful coping strategies.

At the community level, the focus might be on youth populations that share a common problem that involves several parties and institutions. Examples include citizen groups, parent councils, or neighbourhood associations that may act together or as part of coalition. For instance, a local drug prevention organization may assist professionals in fighting drugs in the community (Holmila 1995; Harachi *et al.* 1996); violence (Osofsky 1997; Corvo, 1997) or homelessness (Shane 1996). Community interventions may also be designed to prevent general problems of non-advantaged or low status populations (usually high risk minorities) that do not have access to help organizations (Frank 1996). Overall, regardless of the type of intervention, the aim of helping is to mobilize individuals and all parties involved to act upon problems or disadvantages and to bring about change (fulfilment of needs). Helping in all these senses becomes multi-modal, and includes not only formal helpers but also any kind of group or agency that can contribute to the amelioration of problems, within a context of caring communities (Ianni 1996). (See, for example, the description of a Cuban community-based helping programme, pp. 125–7.)

Family centres have been developed in many countries of our study in which medical personnel are utilized to encourage behaviours that increase physical health and psychologists, counsellors and social workers help family members to reduce domestic quarrelling and increase communication. Programmes and team members vary with the situation. Other types of programmes include neighbourhood crime prevention monitored by police. In still others, centres supply support systems to new immigrant families, and so on. For any of these programmes to be successful, everyone on the team must be involved.

When paraprofessionals (non-professionals who work under the guidance of professionals) are team members, it is important that everyone, including clients, work together with each providing different skills to the situation at hand. This approach has been highly successful as well as cost-effective with self-help groups such as Alcoholics Anonymous. It is particularly useful when resources are limited, as, for example, in crisis management of refugee problems.

Participants in preventive outreach programmes

Preventive outreach is designed to assess client needs and help reduce problems before they result in acute distress. This type of outreach may include stress management programmes for youth who, like many of the subjects in our study, are attending school, working and, in some cases, caring for families.

Outreach programmes that deal with issues such as family life, femininity and decision-making skills, as suggested in the India study, can be very useful to men as well as to women. Programmes regarding gender and sexuality that include topics such as developing assertiveness and decreasing feelings of helplessness can be of particular assistance to women. Programmes regarding dealing with other personal issues such as AIDS or drug and alcohol abuse are important to both genders and all SES groups. Commonality of group increases feelings of security in discussing feelings relative to sensitive issues. Programmes planned and conducted by young people themselves in conjunction with teachers, counsellors or other relevant helping professionals. can be effective and cost-effective at the same time.

Participants in crisis intervention programmes

Since crises are usually situation-specific, the compositions of crisis management teams and the procedures used by team members necessarily varies according to the situation. Flexibility is extremely important. Theoretically, successful preventative outreach makes crisis management unnecessary. In practice, however, preventive outreach and crisis management often merge because of circumstances. For example, preventive programmes such as the Brazilian programme to provide remedial education to impoverished youth (Chapter 16) might be considered crisis management, given Brazil's existing crisis among its poverty population.

A crisis management programme used to help youth is the telephone 'hotline' available now in many countries, including Russia. Hotlines are usually staffed by teams of para-professional volunteers available to keep lines open twenty-four hours a day to answer calls for help of youth in acute distress, to assess need, to provide support and to bring in additional help in emergencies.

Helpers of the poor, migrants, refugees, minorities and females

Helping professionals might consider the roles of these helpers as 'transformers of societies', 'teachers of empowerment' or 'reducers of feelings of helplessness' who help clients assess their needs, interpret 'true' problems as opposed to symptoms and work together to develop coping strategies. While these roles might suggest need for political awareness to solve problems in some cases (see Chapter 2, pp. 24–5, 28–9), we believe that effective counselling must usually transcend politics, and that, while these roles may be used to assist peoples in economic need, they are also useful with other groups. While, for example, minority male youth are the focus of greatest concern in many countries today, females of non-minority status and all SES groups in our study also reported large numbers of worries regarding their self-confidence. It is important for these subjects to learn how to empower themselves.

Mediators between organizations and governmental and community agencies that provide help– and individuals and communities that need help

Because of the complexity of services available to provide various types of assistance to youth in many countries today, counsellors are needed to assist clients as well as services in determining needs and pairing clients with appropriate services. (In England, for example, charitable community-based organizations work in partnership with government services to deliver a range of services from financial and accommodation advice through counselling young people facing issues ranging from bereavement to acute psychiatric illnesses.) In some cases, as for example when a client has committed or is convicted of a crime, the counsellor may serve as ombudsmen in attempting to help place the client in a rehabilitation programme that best matches the needs of the particular situation. Success at this role requires of the counsellor sensitivity to a variety of institutions, awareness of effective approaches to communication and 'political tact'. It demonstrates to clients that professional helpers can assist effectively in reducing adversity.

Counsellor researchers who design and conduct studies to determine conditions under which effective intervention can take place

In this role, helping professionals function along the lines of the American Psychological Association scholar-practitioner model in which their practitioner activities permit them to ask questions important to the profession and their scholarly activities provide the skills needed to develop valid studies to supply the answers. They also use their expertise in evaluating theory and practice. This research provides a good example of what can be accomplished.

Abilities needed of twenty-first century counsellors

The roles listed above require specific abilities and awarenesses:

1 Ability to work actively with youth clients in a joint effort to understand the etiology of their needs, problems and coping strategies and to create new coping strategies capable of changing to meet new needs.
2 Ability to work with clients who need comfort and support as well as a trusting relationship in order to begin even to discuss personal and sensitive issues that affect their lives, and to provide them what they need.
3 Awareness of the etiologies of similarities and differences in the problems and coping strategies of youth, and their relationship to national, cultural, SES or other background factors; ability to use this information effectively in working with developing effective coping strategies. (This awareness is best learned from first-hand experience, according to Bronfenbrenner, who suggested (1979) the need in counsellor education for supervised field studies.)
4 Ability to utilize effectively traditional and modern counselling techniques and to select that which is most appropriate in a given situation.
5 Ability to work with clients who feel that they need to be advised by assessing client needs and using resulting information to offer forms of advice that maintain a delicate balance between being prescriptive and non-directive.
6 Awareness of the effects of institutions, communities and social processes of change as they affect client needs and problems, and ability to use needs assessments to access support systems.
7 Ability to assess outcomes of counselling, including continual evaluation of alternative approaches to providing help.

Figure 17.1 incorporates these abilities in a model that describes needed counsellor roles and strategies for the twenty-first century.

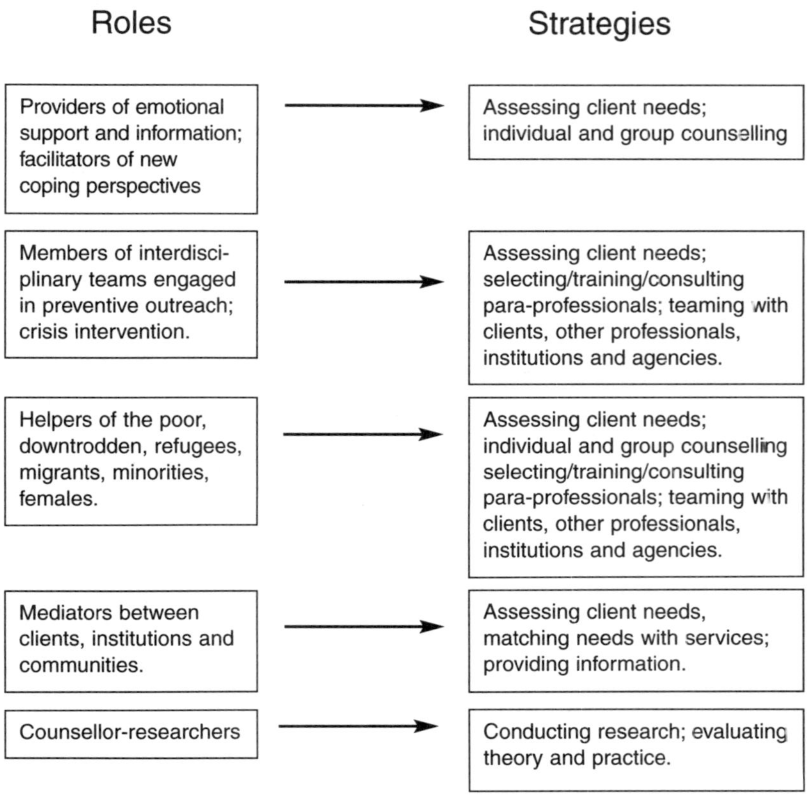

Figure 17.1 Counsellor roles and strategies for the twenty-first century

Counsellor education

How should counsellors be trained for their new roles? Figure 17.2 (p. 248) describes the knowledge base, skill training and hands-on experience that we believe would create skilled professionals. We do not suggest how this preparation should be given, the type of institution where it should take place or the length of time allotted to this preparation, as we are aware from the findings of Chapters 4–16 how much these vary from one country to another because of disparities in resources. Instead, we set it as a model that should be revised to meet the individual needs of specific locales.

Knowledge base

This should include a social-science foundation in developmental psychology with emphases in various national, cultural and ethnic groups

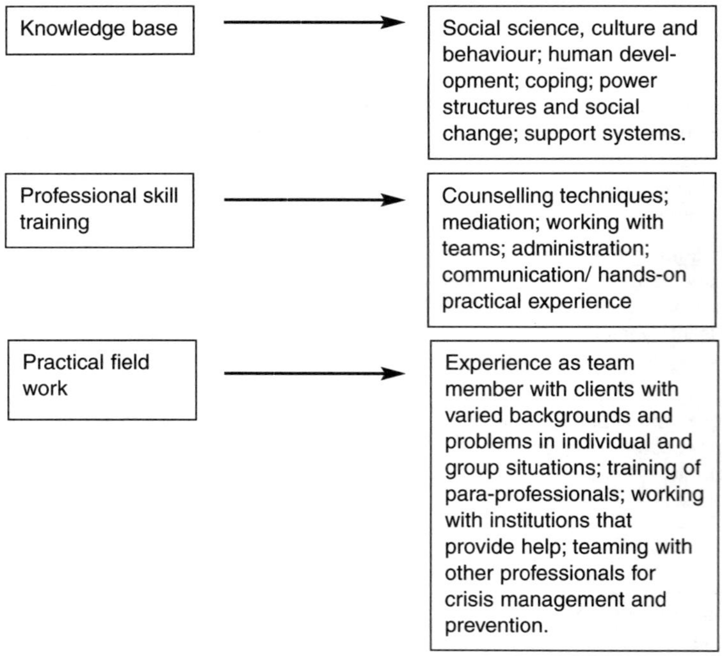

Figure 17.2 Knowledge base, skill training and 'hands-on' experience to create skilled professionals

as well as refugees, migrants, minorities and impoverished peoples, and of the effects of cultural, ethnic and socio-economic backgrounds on youth coping as well as personal experience in these settings; knowledge regarding how institutions and social processes of change and how these operate; and knowledge regarding existence of functions of support systems available and particular to a community.

Skill training

Skills should include various counselling techniques, counsellor approaches to working with teams, serving as mediators between institutions and clients. Practical experience offered concurrent to classroom skill training can provide hands-on experience of what is taught in the classroom.

Field work

Supervised hands-on practicum/field work should take place before, during and after skill training with supervision done by the training programme faculty. Assignments should be offered in an order that presents opportunity for supervised hands-on experience using skills taught in the classroom, for example, one, practice as volunteer in preventive programmes such as telephone hotlines; two, practice in some capacity (for as long a time period as possible) as part of a team of help-providers working together with clients who present varied problems; three, counselling of clients from a variety of backgrounds in individual and group situations; and four, working with governmental and business agencies and communities and teaming with other professionals for crisis management or preventive outreach.

A POSTCRIPT

We ended the first book of our team with the following statement (Gibson-Cline 1996: 278):

> As helping professionals across the world take over the new task of multinational and multicultural counselling, the importance of learning how backgrounds and situations affect perceptions of the world and how to cope [in that world], will increase dramatically.

Four years later, this task predominates all others in the personal, social and political arenas of a developing world culture in which advantaged peoples expect more gratification from their own lives at the same time that the impoverished and downtrodden hope for amelioration of very severe and immediate problems they must surmount in order to survive. We face formidable tasks that will not be reduced by resignation or disengagement.

It is time to begin!

Notes

1 We have described these in Chapters 3–14, and more distinctions can be found in the statistical data in Appendices III and IV.

2 The first three approaches listed here were discussed in our previous book (Gibson-Cline 1996: 269–71). In this book, we have added to each of these and, in addition, included three new approaches imperative in the 21st century.

3 See Chapters 9 and 16 for discussions of views of education in poor families and community-based services.

REFERENCES

Bronfenbrenner, U. (1979) *The Ecology of Human Development*, Cambridge, Mass.: Harvard University Press.

Corvo, K. (1997) 'Community-based youth violence prevention: a framework for planners and funders', *Youth-and-Society* 28 (3): 291–316.

Frank, I. (1996) *Building Self-Esteem in At-Risk Youth: Peer Group Programmes and Individual Success Stories*, Westport, Conn.: Praeger.

Freire, P. (1983) *Pedagogy for the Oppressed*, Rio de Janeiro: Ed. Paz e Terra, in Portuguese.

Gibson-Cline, J. (ed.) (1996) *Adolescence: From Crisis to Coping*, London: Routledge.

Harachi, T., Ayers, C., Hawkins, J. and Catalono, R. (1996) 'Empowering communities to prevent adolescent substance abuse: process evaluation results from a risk and protection-focused community mobilization effort', *Journal of Primary Prevention* 16 (3): 233–54.

Holmila, M. (1995) 'Community action on alcohol: experiences of the Lahti Project in Finland', *Health Promotion International* 10 (4): 283–91.

Hoskins, M. (1998) 'Constructivism and child and youth care practice: visions for the 21st century', *Journal of Child and Youth Care* 11 (4): 83–92.

Ianni, A. (1996) 'The caring community as a context for joining youth needs and program services', *Journal of Negro Education* 65 (1): 71–91.

Jaccard, J., Turrisi, R. and Wan, C. (1990) 'Implications of behavioral decision theory and social marketing for designing social action programs', in Edwards, J., Tindale, R., Heath, L. and Posavac, E. (eds), *Social Influence Processes and Prevention* 1: 103–42, New York: Plenum.

Mahoney, M. (1996) 'Connected knowing in constructive psychotherapy', in Goldberger, N., Tarule, J., Clinchy, B. and Belenky, M. (eds), *Knowledge Difference and Power*, New York: Basic Books: 126–47.

Osofsky, J. (1997) 'Community-based approaches to violence prevention', *Journal of Developmental-and-Behavioral Pediatrics* 18 (6): 405–7.

Perlman, D. (24 November 1999) 'Aids toll higher than ever', *San Francisco Chronicle*, A1 and A15.

Seidman, E. and Rappaport, J. (1986) *Redefining Social Problems*, New York: Plenum.

Shane, P. (1996) *What about America's Homeless Children? Hide and Seek*, Thousand Oaks: Sage.

Watzlawick, P., Weakland, J. and Finch, R. (1973) *Change*, Palo Alto, Calif.: Change.

Wills, T. (1983) 'Social comparisons in coping and help-seeking', in DePaula, B., Nadler, A. and Fisher, J. *New Directions in Helping, vol. II: Help-Seeking*, New York: Academic Press: 109–41.

Appendix I

Classes and categories-within-those-classes listed in taxonomy of problems, coping strategies, desired helpers, desired helper qualities and desired modes of helping

PROBLEMS

- Extreme poverty (inability to meet basic physical or psychological needs): Unmet basic physical needs; Unmet basic psychological needs; Other.
- War (impact of war on subject's life): Physical harm; Fear of war; Loss; Other.
- Catastrophe (impact on subject's life; other than war); Sudden disaster-causing event (apart from war); Fear of catastrophe; Other.
- Material desires (unsatisfied desires for other- than-basic needs): Money; Tangible items; Other.
- Family issues (families or relationships within families): Marriage; Divorce/separation/melded family; Intergenerational disagreement; Domestic quarreling; Domestic violence; Sexual abuse within the family; Psychological estrangement from family member(s); Lack of privacy; Parental strictness; Childrearing; Lack of love, feelings or responsibilities; Physical isolation from family; Family move; Self-abuse among family members; Welfare of family members; Misconduct; Other.
- Schooling (school, academic learning, social learning and socializing in school settings): Academic achievement; Academic failure; Time pressures; Inability to learn; Language barrier; Subject's misconduct; Teacher-related; Social success/failure; Extracurricular activities; School related abuse; Other.
- Personal identity and self-concept (human development or perceptions of self): Self-confidence; Growing up (assuming adult roles); Ageing (adulthood); Physical appearance; Behavioural issues (non-school related); Individuality versus conformity; Self expectations; Personal health; Physical disability; Self abuse; Other.
- Sexuality (sexual activity): Becoming sexually active; Sexual knowledge; Sexual inhibition; Sexual abuse (non-family and non-school); Sexual dissatisfaction (sexual dysfunction); Birth control; Pregnancy; Sexually transmitted diseases; Other.
- Courtship and dating (courtship, dating and selection of marriage

partner): Dating/marriage restrictions; Choice of marriage partner; Unrequited feelings; Not dating; Relationship pressures and fears; Separation; Other.

- Interpersonal problems and socialization (immediate concerns related to working and interacting with others on daily bases; non-family and non-school related); Employment; Friendship; Role conflict; Sharing of living space; Prejudice/discrimination; Time pressures; Other.
- Emotions and feelings (not described in association with specific life event): Loneliness; Generalized fear or anxiety; Grief; Serious depression; Boredom; Stress; Envy; Guilt; Anger; Other.
- Self-fulfilment (desire to understand life and play a meaningful role in it): Search for knowledge, understanding or wisdom; Struggle between good and evil; Creativity; Search for meaning/purpose in life; Having adequate time for religion and spirituality; Seeking a fundamentalist religious experience; Other.
- Altruism (concerns regarding humanity and society): War; Environment; Hunger in the world; Materialism; Poverty in the world; Justice and equality; Other.
- No problem/no response.

COPING STRATEGIES

- Seeking or giving assistance (asking for or giving direct help): Offer help to others; Seek support from others; Other.
- Interpersonal interactions (interacting with another person in order to solve a problem): Assertive coping; Hostile-aggressive; Seeks company of others as way of problem-solving; Other.
- Individual problem-solving (attempting to solve problem by oneself): Planning toward a solution; Trying harder; Reframing; Mental preoccupation; Accepting responsibility; Anxiety without definite plan for solution; Hope; Other.
- Stress management (adaptive attempts to reduce impact of a problem): Doing something of a comforting nature; Relaxation; Meditation; Other.
- Crying (sobbing or shedding tears):Crying; Other.
- Religious experience (seeking religious support): Prayer or religious ceremony/ritual; Seek support from clergy; Animism; Other.
- Resignation (surrender to a conclusion that problem cannot be solved): Anger or depression; Take a fatalist view; Giving up; Do nothing or make no attempt to find a solution; Other.
- Disengagement (avoiding or distancing oneself from the problem): Escape-avoidance (behaviour); Psychological distancing (thinking); Unrealistic response; Other.
- Anti-social responding (behaving in socially unacceptable ways): Steal; Cheat; Other.

DESIRED HELPERS

- Family (related through birth or marriage); Mother; Father; Grandmother; Grandfather; Brother; Sibling; Spouse; Child; Step-parent; Mother-in-law; Father-in-law; Aunt; Uncle; Niece; Nephew; Cousin; Other extended family members; Parents/family; Other.
- Non-family (not related through birth or marriage): Personal friend; Schoolmate/classmate; Friend of family; Acquaintance; Fiancé/fiancée/boyfriend/girlfriend; Teacher/instructor; Clergy person; Boss/employer; Political leader; Person possessing desired qualities necessary for help; Other
- Offender (person causing the problem): Person who is source of problem; Other.
- Supernatural (God or other (non-animal) deities): God; Other.
- Animate creatures/inanimate objects (animal, element or object): Animal, bird; Earth/sky/ocean; Natural element (rock, tree, etc.); Other.
- Non-specific response/nobody/no response.

DESIRED HELPER QUALITIES

- Powerful (has strength to solve problem): can exercise authority or change a situation; Can fulfil a material need; Other.
- Knowledgeable (has information that can provide help): Experienced; Similarity to subject; Content area knowledge; Intelligent/wise; Informative; Gives advice; Other.
- Available (physical proximity/accessibility to subject): Available; Distant; Other.
- Appealing personal attributees (includes personality description): Trustworthy; Loyal Honest; Approachable/good listener; Patient; Generous/willing to help; Sense of humour; Mature; Stable; Objective; Moral; Religious/spiritual; Other.
- Concern for others (personal characteristics that relate to ability to care): Understanding/attentive/empathetic; Caring/loving; Supportive; Other.
- Does not know/nothing/no response.

DESIRED HELPING MODES

- Direct satisfaction of a need: Give something; Other.
- Exercise power (solves problem for subject): Change the situation; Prevent problem or prevent subject from engaging in problem; Solve the problem for the subject; Other.
- Intercede with others: Mediate; Other.
- Counsel (provides counselling assistance): Direct; Advise; Refer; Share; Reveal self-knowledge; Admonish; Help subject to problem-solve; Other.

- Attend to (pays attention, inspires or comforts): Encourage; Care; Comfort/reassure; Understand/empathize/sympathize; Listen; Accept; Approve; Agree; Other.
- Evade (helps subject to escape or avoid): Help subject to escape or avoid; Other.
- Does not know/nothing/no response.

Appendix II

Percentage of agreement between responses of researcher-coders and 'master code' to sample responses from fifteen multinational subjects

Countries	*Categories*	*Classes*
Brazil	0.80	0.89
Canada	0.88	0.95
England	0.80	0.93
Greece 1989	0.77	0.93
Greece 1997[1]		
Agreement between coding assistants;	0.91	0.96
Agreement between primary coder and coding assistants	0.89	0.91
India	0.80	0.93
Israel	0.83	0.95
Japan	0.80	0.93
Philippines	0.89	0.97
Russia	0.70	0.89
United States (1989)[2]	0.85	0.96
United States (1997)	0.88	0.97
Venezuela	0.80	0.95
Special populations		
Ethiopian immigrants	0.87	0.95
Poverty populations		
Brazilian	0.80	0.89
English	0.80	0.93
Filipino	0.89	0.97

Notes

Unless otherwise noted, coding was done by researcher-authors.

1 The figures that follow show percentages of agreement found by comparing coded responses from Greek questionnaires of a) the first author (primary coder) and four coding assistants; and b) the separate coding assistants. See Chapter 8 for details.

2 Coding was done by 1989 research team members.

Appendix III

Statistical findings of the 1997 and 1989 national studies: advantaged, non-advantaged, poverty and non-classified SES groups

Table A describes 1997 findings, Table B 1989 findings. Classes and categories-within-classes refer to those in Appendix I. Categories are of those representing at least 5 per cent of coded responses (see p. 13).

Table A1 1997 percentages of responses to classes and categories of problems
ia) Advantaged subjects: classes of responses

National background	*Brazil*		*Canada*		*China*		*England*		*Greece*		*India*	
No. of Ss	71	55	89	126	61	102	13	20	100	99	39	97
Gender	*M*	*F*	*M*	*F*	*M*	*F*	*M*	*F*	*M*	*F*	*M*	*F*
Problems												
Poverty	0.0	0.0	0.4	0.3	0.0	0.0	0.0	0.0	0.0	0.0	0.0	0.4
War	0.0	0.0	0.0	0.0	0.0	0.0	0.0	0.0	0.4	0.0	0.0	0.0
Catastrophe	5.7	0.9	0.4	0.0	0.0	0.0	3.2	0.0	0.4	0.0	0.9	0.4
Material desire	12.3	11.9	8.2	6.6	2.7	3.3	16.1	16.0	7.5	4.3	10.7	4.0
Family	3.3	5.5	5.6	12.3	4.9	4.9	12.9	22.0	5.6	10.1	6.4	11.3
Schooling	34.4	19.3	31.3	21.9	22.4	23.9	25.8	20.0	9.4	9.7	18.8	21.2
Identity	6.6	12.8	22.3	33.3	34.4	31.5	6.5	22.0	32.7	37.2	33.0	37.4
Sexuality	1.6	0.9	3.4	2.2	0.5	0.3	6.5	2.0	0.0	0.4	0.9	0.4
Courtship	2.5	6.4	4.7	6.6	4.4	4.9	12.9	12.0	7.5	11.6	7.3	5.4
Interpersonal	24.5	32.1	18.9	14.2	6.0	6.9	12.9	6.0	14.3	13.0	12.5	10.8
Emotional	1.6	4.6	1.7	0.5	2.7	1.0	0.0	0.0	7.9	5.4	4.6	6.8
Self-fulfilment	1.6	1.8	0.0	0.3	2.2	4.3	3.2	0.0	1.1	1.1	0.0	0.0
Altruism	3.3	2.8	3.0	1.9	19.7	19.0	0.0	0.0	5.6	5.1	4.8	2.2
No problem	2.5	0.9	0.0	0.0	0.0	0.0	0.0	0.0	7.5	2.2	0.0	0.0

ib) Advantaged subjects: categories of responses

Brazil: Male: interpersonal problems and socialization 19 / schooling: academic achievement 13; academic failure 12; time pressures 9 / material desires: money 12 / catastrophe 6.
Female: interpersonal problems and socialization: employment 21 / material desires: money 12 / schooling: academic achievement 7; academic failure 6.

Canada: Male: schooling: academic failure 15; time pressures 5 / personal identity and self concept: growing up (assuming adult roles) 14 / interpersonal problems and socialization: employment 9; friendship 5 / material desires: money 7.
Female: personal identity and self concept: growing up (assuming adult roles) 21 / interpersonal problems and socialization: friendship 8 / material desires: money 7 / schooling: time pressures 7; academic failure 7; academic achievement 6.

China: Male: altruism: materialism 16 / personal identity: self confidence 15; growing up (assuming adult roles) 13 / schooling: academic failure 10 / interpersonal problems and socialization: friendship 6.
Female: altruism: materialism 17 / personal identity: growing up (assuming adult roles) 14;

Table A1 (continued)

National background	*Israel*		*Japan*		*Philippines*		*USA*		*Venezuela*	
No. of Ss	76	75	101	181	74	72	70	125	100	100
Gender	*M*	*F*	*M*	*F*	*M*	*F*	*M*	*F*	*M*	*F*
Problems										
Poverty	0.0	0.0	0.0	0.0	0.0	0.0	0.0	0.0	0.0	0.0
War	10.9	4.2	0.0	0.0	0.0	0.0	0.0	0.0	0.0	0.0
Catastrophe	6.3	3.2	2.8	2.1	0.0	0.0	0.0	0.9	3.6	8.7
Material desire	2.9	3.7	8.3	5.1	2.8	2.5	6.9	11.9	10.8	5.7
Family	12	19.5	2.8	4.9	11.3	14.8	5.1	11	9.0	11.7
Schooling	2.9	4.7	13.2	11.5	34.9	36.7	41.1	39.3	28.4	32.5
Identity	25.7	16.8	22.6	30.7	20.8	10.0	25.7	16.4	14.0	11.7
Sexuality	1.7	7.9	1.0	0.2	0.5	1.6	1.1	4.2	0.0	0.4
Courtship	7.4	18.9	11.8	17.2	15.1	11.4	8.0	8.6	10.8	10.6
Interpersonal	8.6	9.5	14.9	17.8	8.5	13.4	6.9	5.4	11.9	9.8
Emotional	9.1	7.4	6.3	5.5	4.2	2.9	3.4	2.1	2.5	3.8
Self-fulfilment	4.6	2.6	4.5	1.2	0.9	5.8	1.1	0.0	1.4	1.1
Altruism	8.0	1.6	11.1	3.3	0.9	0.8	0	0.3	5.4	1.1
No problem	0.0	0.0	0.7	0.6	0.0	0.0	0.6	0.0	2.2	3.0

self-confidence 10 / schooling: academic failure 13; academic achievement 6 / interpersonal problems and socialization: friendship 5.

England: Male: material desires: money 16 / schooling: time pressures 10 / courtship and dating 10 / family issues: other (honour) 7 / interpersonal problems and socialization: friendship 7.
Female: material desires: money 16; schooling: time pressures 8; personal identity and self concept: physical appearance; growing up (assuming adult roles) 6; self abuse 6 / interpersonal problems and socialization: friendship 6.

Greece: Male: personal and self concept: growing up (assuming adult roles) 18 / material desires: money 6 / no problem 8.
Female: personal identity and self concept: growing up (assuming adult roles) 16; physical appearance 6; self-expectations 6 / interpersonal problems and socialization: friendship 5.

India: Male: personal identity and self concept: growing up (assuming adult roles) 12; self-expectations 5 / schooling: inability to learn 7; subject's misconduct 7 / interpersonal problems and Socialization: friendship 6 / material desires 5.
Female: personal identity and self concept: self-confidence 18; growing up (assuming adult roles) 6 / schooling: inability to learn 7.

Israel: Male: personal identity and self concept: self-expectations 10 / war 7 / interpersonal problems and socialization: role conflict 6 / altruism 6 / catastrophe 5.
Female: courtship and dating 5.

Japan: Male: personal idenity and self concept: personal health 10; growing up (assuming adult roles) 7 / interpersonal problems and socialization: employment 8; friendship 6.
Female: personal identity and self concept: physical appearance 12; growing up (assuming adult roles) 6; personal health 5 / interpersonal problems and socialization: employment 10; friendship 20 / courtship and dating / no dating 9; relationship pressures and fears 7.

Philippines: Male: schooling: time pressures 14; academic failure 11 / courtship and dating 9 / personal identity and self concept: self-expectations 6; self-confidence 6 / interpersonal problems and socialization: friendship 5.
Female: schooling: time pressures 14; academic failure 12; academic achievement 6 / personal identity and self concept: friendship 11; self-confidence 6.

USA: Male: schooling: academic failure 14; academic achievement 9; time pressures 9; extracurricular activities 7 / personal identification and self concept: growing up (assuming adult roles) 7 / material needs: money 6.
Female: schooling: academic achievement 13; time pressures 12; academic failure 10 / material needs: money 12.

Venezuela: Male: schooling: academic failure 13; academic achievement 9; time pressures 7 / material needs: money 9.
Female: schooling: academic failure 18; academic achievement 7 / catastrophe.

Table A1 1997 percentages of responses to classes and categories of problems cont.
iia) Non-advantaged, poverty and non-classified subjects: classes of responses

	Non-advantaged									
National background	*Brazil*		*China*		*England*		*Ethiopia*		*Greece*	
No of Ss	61	63	81	76	22	39	78	64	100	100
Gender	*M*	*F*	*M*	*F*	*M*	*F*	*M*	*F*	*M*	*F*
Problems										
Poverty	0.0	3.3	0.0	0.0	0.0	0.0	2.0	1.3	0.0	0
War	0.0	1.1	0.0	0.0	0.0	0.0	1.0	1.3	0.0	0
Catastrophe	0.0	0.0	0.0	0.0	0.0	0.0	0.0	0.0	0.0	0
Material desire	20.0	21.1	7.0	4.9	17.3	13.7	23.5	11.5	15.6	11.2
Family	6.7	15.6	3.7	8.3	17.3	13.7	6.1	6.4	4.6	14
Schooling	10.0	16.7	24	22.8	21.2	27.4	11.0	26.9	9.5	7
Identity	20.0	6.7	25.6	34.8	25.0	21.1	20.4	9.0	24.8	23.6
Sexuality	1.7	1.1	0.4	0.0	1.9	7.4	0.0	0.0	0.3	1.4
Courtship	6.7	0.0	7.0	2.8	7.7	5.3	2.0	0.0	12.2	7.8
Interpersonal	18.3	28.9	3.3	7.0	7.7	6.2	20.4	24.4	15.6	18.9
Emotional	1.7	1.1	0.8	1.9	0.0	4.2	1.0	5.1	6.0	4.3
Self-fulfillment	0.0	0.0	5.0	3.5	1.9	1.1	0.0	1.3	0.4	1.1
Altruism	15.0	4.4	23.1	13.9	0.0	0.0	12.2	12.8	5.0	3.9
No problem	0.0	0.0	0.0	0.0	0.0	0.0	0.0	0.0	6.1	6.8

iib) Non-advantaged subjects: categories of responses

Brazil: Male: material desires: money 17 / interpersonal problems and socialization: employment 13 / personal identity and self concept: self-expectations 8; self-abuse 5 / altruism 8 / schooling: academic failure 7 / family issues: parental strictness 5.

Female: interpersonal problems and socialization 21: employment 6 / material desires: money 16 / schooling: academic achievement 7; academic failure 6.

China: Male: altruism: materialism 18 / personal identity and self concept: growing up (assuming adult roles) 12; self-confidence 10 / schooling: failure 11.

Female: personal identity and self concept: self-confidence 15; growing up (assuming adult roles) 14 / schooling: failure 12 / altruism: materialism 11.

England: Male: material desires: money 5 / schooling: time pressures 14; academic failure 6 / personal identity: growing up (assuming adult roles) 8; self-abuse 6 / interpersonal problems and socialization: employment 8.

Female: material desires: money 13 / schooling: time pressures 11; academic achievement 7; academic failure 5 / family issues 5.

Ethiopia: Male: material desires: money 24 / interpersonal problems and socialization: prejudice 20 / personal identification: growing up (assuming adult roles) 12; self-confidence 5 / schooling: academic failure 5.

Female: schooling: academic failure / interpersonal problems and socialization: prejudice 24/ material desires: money 12 / personal identity and self concept: growing up (assuming adult roles) 6.

Greece: Male: personal identity and self concept: growing up (assuming adult roles) 17 / material desires: money 15 / courtship and dating: not dating 6 / no problem 6.

Female: material desires: money 11 / personal identity and self-confidence: growing up (assuming adult roles) 9 / interpersonal problems and socialization: employment 5.

Table A1 (continued)

National background	Non-advantaged				Poverty				Non-classified	
	India		Venezuela		Brazil		England		Russia	
No of Ss	35	67	100	100	59	70	14	20	57	144
Gender	*M*	*F*	*M*	*F*	*M*	*F*	*M*	*F*	*M*	*F*
Problems										
Poverty	5.0	0.0	1.0	2.8	0.0	4.0	2.9	0.0	3.6	2.4
War	0.0	1.6	0.0	0.0	0.0	0.0	0.0	0.0	2.1	3.1
Catastrophe	2.0	0.0	8.3	3.4	0.0	0.6	0.0	0.0	0.0	0.0
Material desire	1.0	0.0	16.6	18.4	9.6	10.3	17.9	11.1	14.9	8.5
Family	4.0	6.8	10.2	24.8	8.7	16.4	23.5	51.9	5.0	12.6
Schooling	16.8	9.5	24.4	28.6	14.4	7.9	8.8	13.0	22.8	21.9
Identity	37.6	24.2	13.2	2.9	10.6	9.7	14.7	11.1	16.7	18
Sexuality	0.0	38.9	2.9	0.5	1.9	0.9	0.0	1.9	6.3	6.3
Courtship	10.9	0.0	2.0	4.9	3.8	5.5	0.0	7.4	0	0
Interpersonal	13.9	2.1	5.9	6.8	28.8	20.6	11.8	1.9	15.4	17.2
Emotional	1.0	10.0	0.5	1.7	6.7	2.4	17.6	1.9	0.0	0.0
Self-fulfillment	0.0	4.2	1.0	1.5	0.0	4.8	2.9	0.0	0.0	0.0
Altruism	7.9	0.0	6.8	1.0	15.4	16.2	0.0	0.0	10.8	10
No problem	0.0	2.6	7.3	2.8	0.0	0.8	0.0	0.0	2.4	0.0

India: Male: schooling: inability to learn 11; subject's misconduct 8; time pressures 5 / personal identity and self concept: self-confidence 11; growing up (assuming adult roles) 12 / courtship and dating: not dating 6 / altruism 5.

Female: personal identity and self concept: self-confidence 21; growing up (assuming adult roles) 12 / School: inability to learn 11.

Venezuela: Male: material desires: money 16 / catastrophe 8 / schooling: academic failure 7; time pressures 6; inability to learn 6 / altruism 5.

Female: material desires: money 18 / family issues 15; domestic quarreling 6 / schooling: time pressures 6.

iic) Poverty subjects: categories of responses

Brazil: Male: interpersonal problems and socialization: employment 19 / altruism 12 / material desires: money 10.

Female: interpersonal problems and socialization: employment 10 / material desires: money 2 / altruism 7.

England: Male: material desires: money 18 / family issues: divorce 9; welfare of family 6 / emotions and feelings: lonely 9 / schooling: academic failure 6 / personal identity and self concept: personal health 6.

Female: material desires: money 11 / family issues: divorce 7; domestic violence 7; welfare of family 7; sexual abuse within family 6; misconduct 6 / schooling: time pressures 10 / personal identity and self concept: physical appearance 6.

iid) Non-classified subjects: categories of responses

Russia: Male: family issues: intergenerational dispute 5 / altruism 5 / personal identity and self concept: other (personal growth) 11.

Female: material desires: money 13 / family issues: intergenerational dispute 9 / personal identity and self concept: other (personal growth) 9 / altruism 3.

Table A2 1997 percentages of responses to classes and categories of coping strategies
ia) Advantaged subjects: classes of responses

National background	*Brazil*		*Canada*		*China*		*England*		*Greece*		*India*	
No. of Ss	*71*	*55*	*89*	*126*	*61*	*102*	*13*	*20*	*100*	*99*	*39*	*97*
Gender	*M*	*F*	*M*	*F*	*M*	*F*	*M*	*F*	*M*	*F*	*M*	*F*
Coping strategies												
Seek/give aid	11.5	9.5	6.1	12.8	2.0	3.2	9.7	16.0	11.1	8.0	10.2	8.9
Interpersonal	5.3	7.6	6.6	10.0	1.3	4.4	16.1	36.0	3.3	6.1	6.5	14.1
Ind. prob.-solve	56.6	52.4	57.5	49.9	64.9	70.9	32.3	34.0	47.7	61.2	54.6	43.5
Stress managment	5.3	6.7	5.3	3.1	5.3	4.8	3.2	2.0	4.1	1.9	4.6	2.6
Crying	0.0	3.8	0.0	1.4	0.7	0.8	0.0	2.0	0.0	1.5	1.9	3.0
Religious exp.	0.0	0.0	0.4	0.3	0.0	0.0	0.0	0.0	1.2	0.4	1.9	2.6
Resignation	8.0	10.5	15.8	14.2	10.6	8.0	6.5	2.0	13.2	11.8	13	18.6
Disengagement	12.4	9.5	7.9	8.2	15.2	7.6	32.2	6.0	18.1	9.1	6.5	5.9
Anti-social	0.9	0.0	0.4	0.0	0.0	0.4	0.0	2.0	1.2	0.0	0.9	0.7
Do nothing	0.0	0.0	0.0	0.0	0.0	0.0	0.0	0.0	0.0	0.0	0.0	0.0

ib) Advantaged subjects: categories of coping responses

Brazil: Male: individual problem-solving: planning toward a solution 28; trying harder 25 / seeking or giving assistance: seek support from others 10 / disengagement: psychological distancing 9 / interpersonal interactions: seeks company of others as a way of problem-solving 9.
Female: individual problem-solving: planning toward a solution 32; trying harder 11 / seeking or giving assistance: seek support from others 8 / disengagement: psychological distancing 6.

Canada: Male: individual problem-solving: trying harder 39; planning toward a solution 13 / seeking or giving assistance: seek support from others 6.
Female: individual problem-solving: trying harder 23; planning toward a solution 21 / seeking or giving assistance: seek support from others 13 / interpersonal interactions: assertive coping 7, discussing the issue 7

China: Male: individual problem-solving: trying harder 38; planning 16 / disengagement: escape-avoidance behavior 10; psychological distancing 10.
Female: individual problem-solving: trying harder 42; planning 13.

England: Male: individual problem-solving: planning 19; trying harder 16; reframing 10 / disengagement: escape-avoidance behavior 31 / seeking or giving assistance: seek support from others 14 / interpersonal interactions: assertive coping 6.
Female: seeking or giving assisance: seek support from others 16 / interpersonal interactions: assertive coping 2; seeks company of others as a way of problem-solving 8; hostile-aggressive 5.

Greece: Male: individual problem-solving: planning toward a solution 6; trying harder 11 / seeking or giving assistance: seek support from others 11 / disengagement: psychological distancing 11; escape-avoidance behavior 7.
Female: individual problem-solving: planning toward a solution 32; trying harder 8; mental preoccupation 10 / interpersonal interactions: assertive coping 5 / seeking or giving assistance: seek support from others 8 / disengagement: psychological distancing 6.

India: Male: individual problem-solving: trying harder 24; planning toward a solution 17; accepting responsibility 6 / seeking or giving assistance: seek support from others 8.
Female: individual problem-solving: trying harder 20; planning toward a solution 11 / seeking or giving assistance: seek support from others 6.

Table A2 (continued)

National background	*Israel*		*Japan*		*Philippines*		*USA*		*Venezuela*	
No. of Ss	*76*	*75*	*101*	*181*	*74*	*72*	*70*	*125*	*100*	*100*
Gender	*M*	*F*	*M*	*F*	*M*	*F*	*M*	*F*	*M*	*F*
Coping strategies										
Seek/give aid	24.4	18.9	13.6	17.7	4.2	22.2	7.5	11.0	10.0	10.3
Interpersonal	21.6	23.7	2.2	5.6	9.9	7.2	6.4	4.2	14.9	15.4
Ind. prob.-solve	49.4	42.6	61.6	56.2	55.2	43.5	62.4	64.9	55.6	48.6
Stress managment	2.8	3.2	0.7	2.0	6.1	6.3	5.8	4.8	3.1	6.3
Crying	0.0	0.5	0.0	0.0	0.5	1.4	0.0	1.5	0.0	1.2
Religious exp.	0.0	0.0	2.9	1.4	6.6	8.2	0.0	1.2	0.0	0.8
Resignation	0.6	4.7	11.1	14	6.1	4.3	6.4	4.5	9.6	7.1
Disengagement	1.1	5.8	7.5	3.2	11.3	6.8	11.6	7.7	5.7	9.9
Anti-social	0.0	0.5	0.4	0.0	0.0	0.0	0.0	0.3	1.1	0.4
Do nothing	0.0	0.0	0.0	0.0	0.0	0.0	0.0	0.0	0.0	0.0

Israel: Male: seeking or giving assistance: seek support from others 20 / individual problem-solving: planning toward a solution 18; trying harder 13; accepting responsibility 8 / interpersonal interactions: assertive coping 15.

Female: individual problem-solving: planning toward a solution 17; trying harder 10; accepting responsibility 7 / seeking or giving assistance: offering help to others 6 / interpersonal interactions: assertive coping 13; hostile-aggressive 8.

Japan: Male: individual problem-solving: planning toward a solution 46; trying harder 12 / seeking or giving assistance: seeking support from others 12.

Female: individual problem-solving: planning toward a solution 44; trying harder 10 / seeking or giving assistance: seeking support from others 16.

Philippines: Male: individual problem-solving: trying harder 27; planning toward a solution 13; accepting responsibility 8 / interpersonal interactions: assertive coping 9 / disengagement: escape-avoidance behaviour 8 / religious experience: prayer 7.

Female: seeking or giving assistance: seek support from others 22 / individual problem-solving: trying harder 18; planning toward a solution 12; interpersonal interactions: assertive coping 5 / religious experience: prayer 5.

USA: Male: individual problem-solving: trying harder 43; planning toward a solution 13 / disengagement: escape-avoidance behavior 9 / seeking or giving assistance: offer help to others 8.

Female: individual problem-solving: trying harder 41; planning toward a solution 16 / seeking or giving assistance: offer help to others 10.

Venezuela: Male: individual problem-solving: trying harder 25; planning toward a solution 13; accepting responsibility 9; mental preoccupation 5 / interpersonal interaction: assertive coping 8; seeking company of others as way of problem-solving 5.

Female: individual problem-solving: trying harder 22; planning toward a solution 15; accepting responsibility l7 / interpersonal interactions: assertive coping 12; seeking or giving assistance: seeking support from others 7 / disengagement: escape-avoidance behaviour 6; stress management 17.

Table A2 1997 percentages of responses to classes and categories of coping strategies cont.
iia) Non-advantaged, poverty and non-classified subjects: classes of responses

	Non-advantaged									
National background	*Brazil*		*China*		*England*		*Ethiopia*		*Greece*	
No of Ss	60	61	81	76	22	39			100	100
Gender	*M*	*F*	*M*	*F*	*M*	*F*	*M*	*F*	*M*	*F*
Coping strategies										
Seek/give aid	18.3	0.0	3.0	3.5	13.7	19.4	24.2	22.2	6.1	10.9
Interpersonal	5.0	0.0	2.5	3.0	9.8	12.9	4.4	11.1	3.7	8.1
Ind. Prob.-solve	55.0	61.0	73.0	68.2	47.1	36.6	51.6	44.4	64.5	51.2
Stress managmnt	0.0	7.9	4.5	6.1	5.9	1.1	3.3	2.8	2.0	3.1
Crying	1.7	8.1	0.0	0.5	0.0	4.3	0.0	5.6	0.4	1.2
Religious exp.	0.0	3.5	0.0	0.5	0.0	0.0	0.0	0.0	0.0	0.0
Resignation	13.3	16.0	9.0	9.6	3.9	8.6	14.3	6.9	10.6	12.4
Disengagement	6.7	3.5	7.5	8.6	17.6	17.2	2.2	6.9	12.7	13.2
Anti-social	0.0	0.0	0.5	0.0	2.0	0.0	0.0	0.0	0.0	0.0
Do nothing	0.0	0.0	0.0	0.0	0.0	0.0	0.0	0.0	0.0	0.0

iib) Non-advantaged subjects: categories of coping responses

Brazil: Male: individual problem-solving: planning toward a solution 43; trying harder 7; accepting responibility 5 / seeking or giving assistance: offer help to others 18 / disengagement: psychological distancing 5.
Female: individual problem-solving: planning toward a solution 42; mental preoccupation 17; accepting responsibility 7 / stress management: meditation 8.

China: Male: individual problem-solving: trying harder 46; planning toward a solution 5.
Female: individual problem-solving: trying harder 36; planning toward a solution 17; anxiety without definite plan for a solution 6.

England: Male: individual problem-solving: planning toward a solution 22; trying harder 16; reframing 6 / seeking or giving assistance: seek support from others 14 / disengagement: escape-avoidance behavior 16 / interpersonal interactions: assertive coping 6.
Female: individual problem-solving: trying harder 19; planning toward a solution 12 / seeking or giving assistance: seek support from others 18 / interpersonal interactions: assertive coping 9.

Ethiopia: Male: individual problem-solving: planning toward a solution 34; trying harder 9 / seeking or giving assistance: seek support from others 21.
Female: seeking or giving assistance: seeking support from others 21 / individual problem-solving: planning toward a solution 21; trying harder 15.

Greece: Male: individual problem-solving: planning toward a solution 38; trying harder 16 / disengagement: psychological distancing 7; escape-avoidance behavior 5 / seeking or giving assistance: seek support from others 6.
Female: individual problem-solving: planning to a solution 27; reframing 8; trying harder 7; mental preoccupation 5 / seeking or giving assistance: seek support from others 9 / disengagement: psychological distancing 9 / interpersonal interaction: assertive coping 4.

Table A2 (continued)

National background	Non-advantaged				Poverty				Non-classified	
	India		Venezuela		Brazil		England		Russia	
No of Ss	35	67	100	100	59	70	14	20	57	144
Gender	M	F	M	F	M	F	M	F	M	F
Coping strategies										
Seek/give aid	11.3	6.8	11.5	11.2	17.7	12.1	11.8	18.5	1.3	2.5
Interpersonal	6.2	9.6	10.9	15.8	5.2	10.2	2.9	13.0	5.7	14.0
Ind. Prob.-solve	58.8	55.9	56.3	43.9	34.4	38.2	20.6	27.8	44.9	47.6
Stress managmnt	2.1	6.8	0.5	8.7	7.3	2.5	5.9	0.0	6.5	11.0
Crying	0.0	0.0	0.0	0.0	0.0	5.1	0.0	3.7	0.0	2.4
Religious exp.	0.0	0.6	1.1	0.5	0.0	3.2	0.0	0.0	0.0	0.0
Resignation	17.5	15.3	8.7	10.2	27.1	21.7	14.7	16.7	2.2	0.0
Disengagement	3.1	4.5	10.9	9.7	8.3	7.0	38.2	20.4	18.7	16.6
Anti-social	1.0	0.6	0.0	0.0	0.0	0.0	5.9	0.0	2.2	0.0
Do nothing	0.0	0.0	0.0	0.0	0.0	0.0	0.0	0.0	18.6	6.0

India: Male: individual problem-solving: trying harder 21; planning toward a solution 13; mental preoccupation 7; accepting responsibility 7; anxiety without a plan for solution 7 / seeking or giving assistance: offer help to others 9.

Female: individual problem-solving: trying harder 28; planning toward a solution 16 / seeking or giving assistance: offer help to others 6 / stress management 6 / interpersonal interactions: assertive coping 5.

Venezuela: Male: individual problem-solving: trying harder 26; planning toward a solution 21; accepting responsibility 7 / interpersonal interactions: assertive coping 9 / disengagement: escape-avoidance behavior 7.

Female: individual problem-solving: planning toward a solution 20; trying harder 11; reframing 6 / interpersonal interactions: assertive coping 13 / seeking or giving assistance: seek support from others 8 / stress management 7 / disengagement: escape-avoidance behavior 5.

iic) Poverty subjects: categories of coping responses

Brazil: Male: individual problem-solving: planning toward a solution 24 / seeking or giving assistance: seek support from others 10; offer help to others 6 / disengagement: escape-avoidance behaviour 5 / resignation: give up 17; anger or depression 12.

Female: individual problem-solving: planning toward a solution 14; trying harder 9; anxiety without a plan for solution 5 / seeking or giving assistance: seek support from others 7 / crying 5.

England: Male: disengagement: escape-avoidance behavior 35 / individual problem-solving: planning toward a solution 12; trying harder 9 / seeking or giving assistance: seek support from others 12 / resignation: give up 9 / anti-social responding: steal.

Female: individual problem-solving: planning toward a solution 15; trying harder 9 / seeking or giving assistance: offer help to others 6 / resignation: anger 11 / disengagement: escape-avoidance behaviour 11.

iid) Non-classified subjects: categories of coping responses

Russia: Male: individual problem-solving: trying harder (study or work) 16; planning toward a solution (looking for work) 8 / disengagement: escape-avoidance behaviour 19.

Female: disengagement: escape-avoidance behaviour 17 / individual problem-solving: trying harder (study or work) 24; planning toward a solution (look for work) 4.

Table A3 1997 percentages of responses to classes and categories of desired helpers
ia) Advantaged subjects: classes of responses

National background	*Brazil*		*Canada*		*China*		*England*		*Greece*		*India*	
No. of Ss	*71*	*55*	*89*	*126*	*61*	*102*	*13*	*20*	*100*	*99*	*39*	*97*
Gender	*M*	*F*	*M*	*F*	*M*	*F*	*M*	*F*	*M*	*F*	*M*	*F*
Helper												
Family	30.6	26.6	34.1	38.2	13.1	24.5	23.3	30.6	36.8	48.7	37.6	39.2
Non-family	49.5	62.9	54.6	58.2	68.0	68.4	66.7	67.3	49.6	47.2	49.5	52.4
Offender	0.0	1.0	0.4	0.3	0.7	0.0	3.3	0.0	1.2	1.1	0.0	0.0
Supernat. being	1.8	0.0	1.7	0.0	0.0	0.0	0.0	0.0	0.0	0.0	3.7	1.1
Animate creatures/ inanimate objects	0.9	0.0	0.0	0.0	0.0	0.4	0.0	0.0	0.4	0.0	0.0	0.0
Non-specific	4.5	6.7	2.2	0.8	5.2	0.4	0.0	0.0	2.9	0.7	2.8	1.5
Nobody	12.6	2.9	7.0	2.5	13.1	6.3	6.7	2.0	9.1	2.2	6.4	5.9
No response	0.0	0.0	0.0	0.0	0.0	0.0	0.0	0.0	0.0	0.0	0.0	0.0

Advantaged subjects: categories of responses

Brazil: Male: non-family: personal friend 18; schoolmate or classmate 14; girlfriend or fiancée 11 / family: mother 10; father 10; sister 9.
Female: family:mother 19 / non-family: schoolmate or classmate: 19; boyfriend or fiancé 12; political leader 9.

Canada: Male: non-family: friend 10; girlfriend or fiancée 5; person possessing desired qualities for helping 5; nobody 7 / family: mother 13; other family member 9.
Female: non-family: personal friend 33; boyfriend or fiancé 6; counsellor 6; person possessing desired qualities for helping 6 / family: mother 17; other family member 6; sister 5.

China: Male: non-family: personal friend 32; schoolmate or classmate 16 / person possessing desired qualities for helping 15 / nobody 13.
Female: non-family: personal friend 42; schoolmate or classmate 13 / family: father 12; person possessing desired qualities for helping 10.

England: Male: non-family: personal friend 23; person possessing desired qualities for helping 10; other 10; girlfriend or fiancée 7; counsellor 7 / family: mother 13; brother 10.
Female: family: mother 25 / non-family: friend 25; boyfriend or fiancé 14; counsellor 8; other 14.

Greece: Male: non-family: personal friend 31 / family 15; father 9; girlfriend or fiancée 6 / nobody 9.
Female: non-family: personal friend 26; boyfriend or fiancé 8 / family: mother 17; sister 6; father 5; family member possessing desired qualities for helping 6.

India: Male: non-family: personal friend 36; girlfriend or fiancée 7 / family 6; mother 12; brother 8; father 6 / nobody 6.
Female: non-family: friend 41 / family 6; mother 15; sister 7; father 6 / nobody 6.

Table A3 (continued)

National background	*Israel*		*Japan*		*Philippines*		*USA*		*Venezuela*	
No. of Ss	*76*	*75*	*101*	*181*	*74*	*72*	*70*	*125*	*100*	*100*
Gender	*M*	*F*	*M*	*F*	*M*	*F*	*M*	*F*	*M*	*F*
Helper										
Family	33.3	34.2	21.9	20.9	19.0	28.1	35.3	39.6	33.5	44.3
Non-family	55.2	49.5	53.2	59.4	70.1	64.4	61.8	57.1	58.8	52.2
Offender	8.6	11.1	0	0.6	1.4	0.0	0.0	0.3	2.2	0.8
Supernat. being	0.0	1.6	0.7	0.0	1.4	1.0	0.0	0.3	0.0	0.0
Animate creatures/ inanimate objects	0.6	0.0	0.4	0.0	0.0	0.0	0.0	0.0	0.0	0.0
Non-specific	0.0	0.5	0.4	1.4	5.7	5.8	0.0	0.6	2.9	1.2
Nobody	2.3	3.2	23.4	17.7	2.4	0.6	2.9	2.1	2.6	1.6
No response	0.0	0.0	0.0	0.0	0.0	0.0	0.0	0.0	0.0	0.0

Israel: Male: non-family: personal friend 15; girlfriend or fiancée 14; counsellor 8 / family 9; father 10 / offender: source of problem 9.
Female: non-family: personal friend 21; counsellor 10; boyfriend or fiancé 6 / family: mother 16 / offender: source of problem 11.

Japan: Male: non-family: personal friend 34 / family 9; father 6; nobody 23.
Female: non-family: personal friend 47 / family 7; mother 8, nobody 18.

Philippines: Male: non-family: personal friend 47; girlfriend or fiancée 9 / family 5.
Female: non-family: personal friend 48; boyfriend or fiancé 6 / family: mother 10; sister 8.

USA: Male: non-family: personal friend 33; girlfriend or fiancée 11; schoolmate or classmate 7; instructor 6 / family 11; mother 12.
Female: non-family: personal friend 32; boyfriend or fiancé 12; schoolmate or classmate 5; instructor 5 / family 6: mother 22; sister 5.

Venezuela: Male: non-family: personal friend 33; girlfriend or fiancée 10 / family 11; mother 14.
Female: non-family: personal friend 25; boyfriend or fiancé 7; counsellor 6 / family 8; mother 22.

Table A3 1997 percentages of responses to classes and categories of desired helpers cont.
iia) Non-advantaged, poverty and non-classified subjects: classes of responses

	Non-advantaged									
National background	*Brazil*		*China*		*England*		*Ethiopia*		*Greece*	
No of Ss	60	61	81	76	22	39			100	100
Gender	*M*	*F*	*M*	*F*	*M*	*F*	*M*	*F*	*M*	*F*
Helper										
Family	33.9	27.9	10.0	21.1	32.7	30.6	13.2	20.3	44.3	42.9
Non-family	47.5	67.4	73.0	61.3	65.4	67.3	68.1	73.9	50.8	49.4
Offender	1.7	0.0	0.5	0.0	0.0	0.0	1.1	0.0	0.4	2.3
Supernat. being	0.0	2.3	0.0	0.0	0.0	0.0	3.3	0.0	0.0	0.0
Animate creatures/ inanimate objects	0.0	0.0	0.0	1.0	0.0	0.0	0.0	0.0	0.4	0.0
Non-specific	6.8	0.0	3.5	2.1	0.0	0.0	1.1	2.9	1.6	1.9
Nobody	10.2	2.3	13.0	14.4	1.9	2.1	13.2	2.9	2.5	3.4
No response	0.0	0.0	0.0	0.0	0.0	0.0	0.0	0.0	0.0	0.0

iib) Non-advantaged subjects: categories of responses

Brazil: Male: non-family: personal friend 22; instructor 7; girlfriend or fiancée 5; political leader 5 / family 10; father 10.
Female: family: mother 19 / non-family: schoolmate or classmate 19; boyfriend or fiancé 12; political leader 9.

China: Male: non-family: personal friend 24; schoolmate or classmate 22; teacher 8 / person possessing desired qualities for helping.
Female: non-family: personal friend 30; schoolmate or classmate 16 / family: parents 6; mother 5 / family member possessing desired qualities for helping 11.

England: Male: non-family: personal friend 27; other 21; instructor 6 / family: 8.
Female: non-family: personal friend 30; other 15; boyfriend or fiancée 11; schoolmate or classmate 5 / family: mother 16.

Ethiopia: Male: non-family 14; personal friend 26 / family: brother 7.
Female: non-family 9; personal friend 25; instructor 10; counsellor 10 / family 10.

Greece: Male: non-family: personal friend 27 / family 15; father 10; mother 8; brother 5; person possessing desired qualities for helping 9.
Female: non-family: personal friend 26; boyfriend or fiancé 8 / family: mother 17; sister 6; father 5; family member possessing desired qualities for helping 6.

Table A3 (continued)

National background	Non-advantaged				Poverty				Non-classified	
	India		Venezuela		Brazil		England		Russia	
No of Ss	35	67	100	100	59	70	14	20	57	144
Gender	*M*	*F*	*M*	*F*	*M*	*F*	*M*	*F*	*M*	*F*
Helper										
Family	41.2	32.4	30.4	47.7	26.7	24.7	20.6	15.4	36.2	53.4
Non-family	48.5	59.0	63.0	42.6	57.0	59.3	73.5	80.8	56.2	43.5
Offender	0.0	0.0	1.7	4.6	1.2	2.0	0.0	0.0	0.0	0.0
Supernat. being	1.0	0.5	0.0	0.0	1.2	9.3	0.0	0.0	0.0	0.0
Animate creatures/ inanimate objects	2.1	0.0	0.0	0.0	0.0	0.0	0.0	0.0	0.0	0.0
Non-specific	2.1	2.1	1.1	3.1	9.3	0.0	0.0	0.0	0.0	0.0
Nobody	5.2	5.9	3.9	2.1	4.7	4.7	5.9	3.8	0.0	0.0
No response	0.0	0.0	0.0	0.0	0.0	0.0	0.0	0.0	7.6	3.1

India: Male: non-family: personal friend 36 / family 5; mother 14; father 9; sister 7.
Female: non-family: personal friend 52 / family: mother 15; sister 6; father 6.

Venezuela: Male: non-family: personal friend 32; girlfriend or fiancée 11; schoolmate or classmate 5 / family 7; mother 13.
Female: non-family: personal friend 19; boyfriend or fiancé 6; schoolmate or classmate 5 / family 9; mother 12; sister 11.

iic) Poverty subjects: categories of responses

Brazil: Male: non-family: personal friend 21; political leader 8; employer 7; person possessing desired qualities for helping 6 / family: extended family member 12; mother 8.
Female: non-family 16; political leader 10; boyfriend or fiancé 6; counsellor 7 / family: extended family member 10; mother 6 / family member with desired qualities for helping 17.

England: Male: non-family: personal friend (or gangmate) 33; other 24; girlfriend or fiancée 12 / family: mother 6 / Nobody 6.
Female: non-family: personal friend 31; other 23; boyfriend or fiancé 14; schoolmate or classmate 6.

iid) Non-classified subjects: categories of responses

Russia: Male: non-family: personal friend 20; girlfriend or fiancé 10; official 8; teacher 6 / family: mother 10; father 10.
Female: non-family: personal friend 15; boyfriend or fiancée 10; teacher 6, counsellor or psychologist 6 / family: mother 14; sister 5; father 5.

Table A4 1997 percentages of responses to classes and categories of desired helper qualities
ia) Advantaged subjects: classes of responses

National background	*Brazil*		*Canada*		*China*		*England*		*Greece*		*India*	
No. of Ss	*71*	*55*	*89*	*126*	*61*	*102*	*13*	*20*	*100*	*99*	*39*	*97*
Gender	*M*	*F*	*M*	*F*	*M*	*F*	*M*	*F*	*M*	*F*	*M*	*F*
Helper quality												
Powerful	10.6	6.1	4.4	1.7	0.0	1.7	3.6	0.0	1.4	2.8	8.7	4.2
Knowledgeable	37.2	51.0	30.6	29.4	24.8	29.6	14.3	29.2	21.7	25.2	21.4	33.3
Available	2.1	1.0	1.5	0.0	2.9	0.4	10.7	6.3	22.6	16.9	0.0	0.0
Personal attrib.	33.0	26.5	33.5	41.8	48.9	33.8	53.6	29.2	29.4	28.0	35.9	35.6
Concern	13.8	14.3	29.6	26.5	19.0	32.9	14.3	33.3	18.6	25.2	28.2	22.6
Does not know	2.1	1.0	0.0	0.6	0.0	0.4	3.6	0.0	0.5	0.0	2.9	2.0
Nothing	0.0	0.0	0.0	0.0	0.0	0.0	0.0	0.0	0.0	0.0	0.0	0.0
No response	1.1	0.0	0.5	0.0	4.4	1.3	0.0	2.1	5.9	2.0	2.9	2.2

Advantaged subjects: categories of desired responses

Brazil: Male: knowledgeable: experience 18; similarity to subject 13 / appealing personal attributes: trustworthy 11 / powerful: can change situation 9 / concern for others: caring and loving 9.
Female: knowledgeable: experienced 17; similarity to subject 17; content area knowledge 6 / appealing personal attributes: good listener 12; trustworthy 6 / concern for others: understanding 7; caring 7.

Canada: Male: appealing personal attributes: approachable 18 / concern for others: understanding 18; supportive 7 / knowledgeable 8; similarity to subject 8; intelligent 5.
Female: appealing aersonal attributes: approachable 28; understanding 19 / knowledgeable 6; similarity to subject 5; experienced 5.

China: Male: appealing personal attribute: honesty 15; generous 9; approachable 7; loyalty 6 / knowledgeable: similarity to subject / concern for others: caring 9; understanding 5.
Female: concern for others: understanding 12 / appealing personal attributes: honest 9; caring 9; willing to help 6 / knowledgeable: similarity to subject 13; experienced 8.

England: Male: appealing personal attributes: good listener 39; trustworthy 7 / availability 7 / concern for others: understanding 27.
Female: concern for others 6; understanding 23; knowledgeable: similarity to subject 13; experience 8 / appealing personal attributes: good listener 13 / available 6.

Greece: Male: availability 23 / appealing personal attributes: trustworthy 18 / concern for others: caring 16; understanding 7 / knowledgeable 9; similarity to subject 9; experienced 4.
Female: availability 17 / knowledgeable 9; similarity to subject 8.

India: Male: concern for others: understanding 17 / knowledgeable: similarity to subject 10 / appealing personal attributes 8; good listener 7; patient 6; willing to help 6.
Female: concern for others: understanding 22 / appealing personal attribute: good listener 10 / knowledgeable 6; experienced 6; similarity to subject 6.

Israel: Male: knowledgeable 11; similarity to subject 15; experienced 15; intelligent 7 / concern for others: understanding 9; caring 5.
Female: knowledgeable 8; experienced 10; similarity to subject 10 / appealing personal attributes: sense of humor 8; patient 6 / powerful 7 / concern for others: supportive 6.

Table A4 (continued)

National background	*Israel*		*Japan*		*Philippines*		*USA*		*Venezuela*	
No. of Ss	*76*	*75*	*101*	*181*	*74*	*72*	*70*	*125*	*100*	*100*
Gender	*M*	*F*	*M*	*F*	*M*	*F*	*M*	*F*	*M*	*F*
Helper quality										
Powerful	6.9	9.7	19.7	13.9	0.4	1.5	1.8	3.0	7.3	4.4
Knowledgeable	51.4	37.8	27.0	35.3	24.0	22.0	38.4	32.9	31.3	30.0
Available	2.3	2.2	16.0	14.8	1.0	0.5	1.2	0.6	2.3	4.8
Personal attrib.	21.4	33.0	18.9	22.5	39.2	34.6	26.8	29.9	35.5	36.8
Concern	16.2	14.1	7.8	12.0	34.3	40.0	30.5	32.9	21.6	23.6
Does not know	1.7	2.2	7.0	0.9	1.0	1.5	0.6	0.6	1.9	0.0
Nothing	0.0	0.0	3.7	0.6	0.0	0.0	0.0	0.0	0.0	0.0
No response	0.0	1.1	0.0	0.0	0.0	0.0	0.6	0.0	0.0	0.4

Japan: Male: powerful: can exercise authority or change a situation 17 / availability 11 / knowledgeable: similarity to subject 9; experienced 5 / appealing personal attribute: trustworthy 8; good listener 6.

Female: knowledgeable: similarity to subject 18; content area knowledge 8 / availibility 15 / powerful: can exercise authority or change a situation 14 / appealing personal attribute: trustworthy 7 / concern for others: supportive 5.

Philippines: Male: concern for others: understanding 22; supportive 9 / appealing personal attributes: good listener 19; willing to help 7 / knowledgeable 6; similarity to subject 7; experienced 5.

Female: concern for others: understanding 29; supportive 10 / appealing personal attribute: good listener 20 / knowledgeable: similarity to subject 10.

USA: Male: knowledgeable 8; similarity to subject 17; experienced 6 / concern for others: understanding 17; caring 9 / appealing personal attributes: good listener 14.

Female: concern for others: understanding 23; supportive 6 / appealing personal attributes: good listener / knowledgeable 6; similarity to subject 4.

Venezuela: Male: knowledgeable: similarity to subject 22; experienced 7 / concern for others: understanding 15 / appealing personal attributes: trustworthy 15 / powerful 5.

Female: knowledgeable: similarity to subject 15; experienced 12 / concern for others: understanding 15; supportive 6 / appealing personal attributes: good listener 10; objective 7; trustworthy 6.

Table A4 1997 percentages of responses to classes and categories of desired helper qualities cont.
iia) Non-advantaged, poverty and non-classified subjects: classes of responses

	Non-advantaged									
National background	*Brazil*		*China*		*England*		*Ethiopia*		*Greece*	
No of Ss	60	61	81	76	22	39			100	100
Gender	*M*	*F*	*M*	*F*	*M*	*F*	*M*	*F*	*M*	*F*
Helper quality										
Powerful	13.2	0.0	1.7	0.6	7.8	2.6	22.4	21.9	3.9	2.4
Knowledgeable	32.1	13.8	35.0	22.7	25.5	25.0	30.3	21.9	33.6	28.1
Available	0.0	37.5	1.1	1.7	3.9	1.0	1.3	1.6	14.2	11.6
Personal attrib.	35.8	5.0	39.5	39.2	41.2	37.0	21.1	35.9	20.7	31.3
Concern	18.9	37.5	19.2	29.3	21.6	34.4	21.1	18.8	24.6	22.1
Uncertain	0.0	6.3	1.7	2.2	0.0	0.0	1.3	0.0	0.0	0.0
Nothing	0.0	0.0	1.7	4.4	0.0	0.0	2.6	0.0	0.0	0.0
No response	0.0	0.0	0.0	0.0	0.0	0.0	0.0	0.0	3.0	4.4

iib) Non-advantaged subjects: categories of responses

Brazil: Male: knowledgeable: experienced 15 / appealing personal attributes: trustworthy 10; loyal 9; willing to help 8 / powerful: can exercise authority or change a situation 11 / concern for others: caring 9; understanding 6.
Female: appealing personal attributes: trustworthy 15; loyal 6; good listener 5 / powerful: can exercise authority or change a situation 10 / knowledgeable: experienced 10; similarity to subject 10; content area knowledge 6.

China: Male: knowledge: similarity to subject 16; experienced 9 / appealing personal attributes; generous; honest 8 / concern for others: understanding 8; caring 7.
Female: concern for others: caring 13; understanding 12 / knowledgeable: experienced 9; similarity to subject 9 / appealing personal attributes: willing to help 7; honest 5.

England: Male: concern for others: understanding 20 / appealing personal attributes: good listener 16; trustworthy 14 / knowledgeable 6; gives advice 9 / powerful: can fulfill a material need 6.
Female: concern for others: understanding 28 / appealing personal attributes: good listener 20 / knowledgeable: similarity to subject 10.

Ethiopia: Male: knowledgeable: experienced 24 / powerful: can exercise authority or change a situation 16; can fulfill a material need 7 / appealing personal attribute 9; willing to help 7 / concern for others: caring 8.
Female: powerful: can exercise authority or change a situation 9 / knowledgeable: experienced 14 / appealing personal attributes:willing to help 11; good listener 9 / concern for others: understanding 9; caring 6.

Greece: Male: concern for others: caring 16 / understanding 7 / knowledgeable 6; similarity to subject 14 / appealing personal attribute: trustworthy 13 / available 11.
Female: appealing personal attribute: trustworthy 11 / concern for others: caring 14; understanding 8 / knowledgeable 14; similarity to subject 12 / available 12.

Table A4 (continued)

National background	Non-advantaged				Poverty				Non-classified	
	India		Venezuela		Brazil		England		Russia	
No of Ss	35	67	100	100	59	70	14	20	57	144
Gender	*M*	*F*	*M*	*F*	*M*	*F*	*M*	*F*	*M*	*F*
Helper quality										
Powerful	4.4	4.0	8.1	3.9	17.5	17.7	3.5	0.0	7.8	4.2
Knowledgeable	25.3	33.3	41.9	21.0	22.5	24.1	17.9	10.2	23.3	17.6
Available	1.1	0.0	0.0	3.3	0.0	2.8	10.8	6.1	11.9	2.8
Personal attrib.	41.8	35.6	33.1	35.9	37.5	31.2	39.3	51.0	22.0	18.8
Concern	20.9	22.6	15.7	34.8	20.0	12.8	28.6	30.6	28.0	56.0
Uncertain	1.1	1.7	0.0	0.0	0.0	0.7	0.0	0.0	0.0	0.0
Nothing	0.0	0.0	0.0	0.0	0.0	0.0	0.0	0.0	0.0	0.0
No response	5.5	2.8	1.2	1.1	2.5	10.6	0.0	2.0	6.9	0.7

India: Male: appealing personal attributes: willing to help 15; trustworthy 6 / concern for others: understanding 10; caring 6 / knowledgeable: gives advice 6.
Female: knowledgeable: gives advice 14; experienced 10 / concern for others: understanding 14 / appealing personal attributes: good listener 11; willing to help 9; patient 6.

Venezuela: Male: knowledgeable: experienced 20; similarity to subject 14 / appealing personal attributes: trustworthy 6; honest 5 / concern for others: understanding 8.
Female: concern for others: understanding 22; supportive 8; caring 6 / knowledgeable: experienced 11 / appealing personal attributes: good listener 11; trustworthy 9; willing to help 6; loyal 5.

iic) Poverty subjects: categories of responses

Brazil: Male: concern for others: understanding 14; good listener 6 / knowedgeable: experienced 11; similarity to subject 5 / appealing personal attributes: trustworthy 6; loyal 6; patient 5; willing to help 5; caring 5.
Female: concern for others: understanding 22; supportive 8; caring 6 / knowledgeable: experienced 11 / appealing personal attributes: good listener 11; trustworthy 9; willing to help 6; loyal 5.

England: Male: concern for others: understanding 29; good listener 21; objective 14 / knowledgeable 11 / available 7.
Female: concern for others: good listener 38; understanding 16; objective 10; caring 6; supportive 6 / available 6.

iid) Non-classified subjects: categories of responses

Russia: Male: knowledgeable: experienced 14; intelligent 7 / appealing personal attributes 13; good listener 8 / concern for others: understanding 10.
Female: concern for others: understanding 17 / knowledgeable: experienced 10 / appealing personal attributes: good listener 10.

Table A5 1997 percentages of responses to classes and categories of desired modes of helping
ia) Advantaged subjects: classes of responses

National background	*Brazil*		*Canada*		*China*		*England*		*Greece*		*India*	
No. of Ss	*71*	*55*	*89*	*126*	*61*	*102*	*13*	*20*	*100*	*99*	*39*	*97*
Gender	*M*	*F*	*M*	*F*	*M*	*F*	*M*	*F*	*M*	*F*	*M*	*F*
Helping mode												
Satisfy need	2.3	5.6	5.6	3.8	x	1.3	10.7	4.4	4.5	2.3	7.0	5.1
Exercise power	10.2	5.6	6.6	5.6	2.3	1.9	7.1	3.3	6.1	6.1	9.6	7.1
Intercede w/others	0.0	1.1	1.0	2.6	0.0	0.4	0.0	0.0	3.5	1.9	3.3	2.7
Counsel	38.6	40.4	39.9	40.5	40.8	47.7	21.4	27.9	55.1	47.0	43.0	41.7
Attend to	21.6	32.6	38.9	43.1	50.0	40.5	50.0	63.9	28.8	41.5	26.5	37.5
Evade problem	0.0	3.4	0.5	1.8	1.5	1.3	0.0	0.0	1.6	1.3	1.0	3.9
Uncertain	21.6	7.9	3.5	1.5	1.5	6.8	7.1	0.0	0.0	0.0	0.0	0.0
Nothing	0.0	0.0	0.0	0.0	0.0	0.0	0.0	0.0	0.0	0.0	0.0	0.0
No response	5.7	3.4	4.0	1.2	3.8	0.0	3.6	0.4	0.0	0.0	9.6	1.9

ib) Advantaged subjects: categories of responses

Brazil: Male: counsel: help subject to problem-solve 17; advise 14 / attend to: encourage 15 / exercise power: solve problem for subject 7.
Female: counsel: help subject to problem-solve 17; advise 16; share information 6 / attend to: encourage 15; comfort 7 / exercise power: give something 6.

Canada: Male: attend to: comfort 21; encourage 6; listen 5 / counsel: advise 20; help subject to problem-solve 14.
Female: attend to: comfort 22; encourage 7; listen 7 / counsel: advise12; help subject to problem-solve 15.

China: Male: attend to: encourage 23; reassure 21 / counsel: share information 20; help subject to problem-solve 13.
Female: attend to: reassure 19; encourage 16 / counsel: help subject to problem-solve 11; advise 11; share information 10; direct 9.

England: Male: attend to: comfort 18; listen 14; understand 7 / counsel: advise 14; help subject to problem-solve 7 / direct satisfaction of need: give something 11.
Female: attend to: comfort 26; understand 17 / counsel: help subject to problem-solve 15; direct 6.

Greece: Male: counsel: advise 30; help subject to problem-solve 14; direct 5 / attend to: care 7; comfort 7; encourage 9.
Female: counsel: advise 20; help subject to problem-solve 13; direct 7 / attend to: comfort 11; understand 7; care 7; listen 5; encourage 4 / exercise power: solve problem for subject 6.

India: Male: counsel: advise 30; direct 7 / attend to: encourage 11; agree 6 / exercise power: change the situation 5.
Female: counsel: advise 20; help subject to problem-solve 10 / attend to: encourage 11; agree 6 / exercise power: solve problem for subject 5.

Table A5 (continued)

National background	*Israel*		*Japan*		*Philippines*		*USA*		*Venezuela*	
No. of Ss	*76*	*75*	*101*	*181*	*74*	*72*	*70*	*125*	*100*	*100*
Gender	*M*	*F*	*M*	*F*	*M*	*F*	*M*	*F*	*M*	*F*
Helping mode										
Satisfy need	2.6	2.6	6.9	2.0	1.4	2.5	3.7	5.9	5.3	2.5
Exercise power	11.0	15.1	14.7	9.3	0.0	1.0	4.2	6.0	6.4	4.2
Intercede w/others	1.4	4.2	0.5	1.0	2.4	3.4	1.1	0.3	3.5	3.3
Counsel	42.2	37.8	24.9	32.5	28.8	27.5	52.0	33.7	58.6	53.3
Attend to	39.9	37.8	34.1	47.5	64.9	64.2	36.5	51.5	23.9	32.9
Evade problem	3.4	2.6	3.2	3.3	0.0	0.0	2.6	2.6	0.0	0.0
Uncertain	0.0	0.0	4.1	2.0	0.5	0.5	0.0	0.0	0.0	2.5
Nothing	0.0	0.0	0.0	0.0	0.0	0.0	0.0	0.0	0.0	0.0
No response	0.0	0.0	11.5	2.5	1.9	1.0	0.0	0.0	2.2	1.3

Israel: Male: counsel: share information 13; help subject to problem-solve 13; advise 9 / attend to: encourage 12; understand 8; listen 7; accept 5 / exercise power: solve problem for subject 6. Female: counsel: share information 14; help subject to problem-solve 10; advise 6 / exercise power: solve problem for subject 7; prevent problem 5 / attend to: listen 5.

Japan: Male: attend to: listen 16; understand 6 / exercise power: solve problem for subject 10; give 7 / counsel: direct 8; advise 7; help subject to problem-solve 6.
Female: attend to: listen 27; encourage 5 / counsel: share information 10; advise 8; direct 6; help subject to problem-solve 5 / exercise power: solve problem for subject 7.

Philippines: Male: attend to: comfort 29; encourage 19; listen 8 / counsel: advise 14; help subject to solve problem 8.
Female: attend to: comfort 27; encourage 20; listen 9 / counsel: advise 23.

USA: Male: counsel: advise 29; help subject to problem-solve 7 / attend to: comfort 11; encourage 9.
Female: attend to: comfort 25; encourage 7; listen 7 / counsel: advise 14; help subject to problem-solve 11.

Venezuela: Male: counsel: advise 22; help subject to problem-solve 13; direct 13; share information 10 / attend to: comfort 11; listen 6; encourage 5 / direct satisfaction of a need: give something 5.
Female: counsel: advise 20; help subject to problem-solve 15; direct 12; share information 6 / attend to: encourage 9; listen 6.

Table A5 1997 percentages of responses to classes and categories of desired modes of helping cont.
iia) Non-advantaged, poverty and non-classified subjects: classes of responses

	Non-advantaged									
National background	*Brazil*		*China*		*England*		*Ethiopia*		*Greece*	
No of Ss	60	61	81	76	22	39			100	100
Gender	*M*	*F*	*M*	*F*	*M*	*F*	*M*	*F*	*M*	*F*
Helping mode										
Satisfy need	7.5	6.4	0.6	0.6	17.6	5.7	8.0	4.4	5.0	4.8
Exercise power	5.7	15.4	1.1	2.2	17.6	4.6	20.0	20.6	6.8	5.2
Intercede w/others	0.0	0.0	0.0	0.0	0.0	1.1	1.3	4.4	1.3	2.0
Counsel	62.3	61.5	45.4	48.9	37.3	25.3	32.0	33.8	51.3	45.6
Attend to	20.8	15.4	46.0	37.6	27.5	62.1	28.0	36.8	27.7	36.0
Evade problem	0.0	1.3	1.7	0.6	0.0	0.0	0.0	0.0	1.6	0.8
Uncertain	3.7	0.0	1.7	3.9	0.0	1.1	8.0	0.0	2.9	3.2
Nothing	0.0	0.0	3.4	6.2	0.0	0.0	0.0	0.0	0.0	0.0
No response	0.0	0.0	0.0	0.0	0.0	0.0	2.7	0.0	3.4	2.4

iib) Non-advantaged subjects: categories of responses

Brazil: Male: counsel: advise 42 / help subject to problem-solve 13 / attend to: comfort 9; encourage 6 / exercise power: give 8.
Female: counsel: advise 40; share information 6; direct 5 / exercise power: change the situation 10; solve the problem for subject 5; other (refer to appropriate person for help) 6 / Attend to: encourage 6.

China: Male: attend to: encourage 25; reassure 15 / counsel: help subject to problem-solve 15; share information 11; direct 8; advise 6.
Female: attend to: 17; encourage 16 / counsel: help subject to problem-solve 15; share information 12; advise 10.

England: Male: exercise power: give 14; change the situation 8; solve the problem for subject 5 / counsel: advise 14; help subject to problem-solve 14 / attend to: comfort 10; listen 10.
Female: attend to: comfort 25; understand 9; listen 9; encourage 8 / exercise power: give 6.

Ethiopia: Male: counsel: advise 15; help subject to problem-solve 8; mediate 5; direct 5 / attend to: comfort 9; encourage 7 / exercise power: give 8; solve problem for subject 8; change the situation 5.
Female: attend to: comfort 15; encourage 12 / counsel: help subject to problem-solve 13; advise 8 / exercise power 6; solve problem for subject 10.

Greece: Male: counsel: advise 24; help subject to problem-solve 20 / attend to: encourage 14; comfort 8 / exercise power: solve problem for subject 6.
Female: counsel: advise 21; help subject to problem-solve 17 / attend to: encourage 19; comfort 11.

Table A5 (continued)

National background	Non-advantaged				Poverty				Non-classified	
	India		*Venezuela*		*Brazil*		*England*		*Russia*	
No of Ss	35	67	100	100	59	70	14	20	57	144
Gender	*M*	*F*	*M*	*F*	*M*	*F*	*M*	*F*	*M*	*F*
Helping mode										
Satisfy need	8.8	7.4	4.7	6.0	8.8	1.5	7.1	0.0	27.7	18.2
Exercise power	8.8	5.1	4.1	10.9	6.0	17.0	17.9	2.1	10.8	11.5
Intercede w/others	2.2	1.1	2.3	6.5	0.0	1.5	0.0	0.0	0.0	0.0
Counsel	56.6	58.4	63.2	45.1	48.5	31.9	32.1	14.9	45.8	55.7
Attend to	18.0	23.4	21.6	30.4	17.6	24.4	35.7	76.7	7.2	10.8
Evade problem	0.0	1.1	0.0	0.5	6.0	2.2	3.6	4.3	0.0	0.0
Uncertain	2.2	1.1	0.6	0.0	8.8	8.1	3.6	2.1	0.0	0.0
Nothing	0.0	0.0	0.0	0.0	0.0	0.0	0.0	0.0	0.0	0.0
No response	3.3	2.4	3.5	0.5	4.4	13.3	0.0	0.0	8.4	3.7

India: Male: counsel: advise 40; help subject to problem-solve 14 / attend to: encourage 14 / direct satisfaction of a need: give something 8.
Female: counsel: advise 39; help subject to problem-solve 13 / attend to: encourage 6

Venezuela: Male: counsel: advise 36; direct 13 / attend to: encourage 10; care 8.
Female: counsel: advise 25; direct 10; share information 7 / exercise power: solve problem for subject 7; other (intercede) 7; other (mediate) 7 / attend to: encourage 6 / direct satisfaction of need: give something 5.

iic) Poverty subjects: categories of repsonses

Brazil: Male: counsel: advise 25; help subject to problem-solve 19; direct satisfaction of a need: give something 9.
Female: counsel: advise 14; help subject to problem-solve 9 / exercise power: solve problem for subject 10 / attend to: encourage 10; reassure 6 / nothing 13.

England: Male: counsel: advise 11 / exercise power: change the situation 7 / attend to 7; encourage 7; understand 7; listen 7.
Female: attend to 8; listen 22; comfort 20; understand 12 / counsel: help subject to problem-solve 6.

iid) Non-classified subjects: categories of responses

Russia: Male: counsel: advise 28; help subject to problem-solve 28 / attend to: other (calm subject) 12; share information 11.
Female: counsel: advise 31; help subject to problem-solve 18; share information 12 / attend to: other (calm subject) 11; encourage 9.

Table B1 1989 percentages of responses to classes and categories of problems
ia) Advantaged subjects: classes of responses

National background	*Brazil*	*Greece*		*Israel*		*Japan*	*Philippines*		*USA*		*Venezuela*	
No of Ss	*53*	*100*	*100*	*71*	*72*	*59*	*100*	*100*	*42*	*52*	*100*	*100*
Gender	*M/F*	*M*	*F*	*M*	*F*	*M/F*	*M*	*F*	*M*	*F*	*M*	*F*
Problems												
Poverty	1.7	0.0	0.0	0.5	0.0	0.0	0.0	0.0	0.0	0.7	1.0	0.5
War	0.0	0.7	0.3	10.6	8.6	0.0	0.0	0.0	0.0	0.7	0.5	0.5
Catastrophe	0.8	0.3	0.7	2.4	2.9	0.0	0.0	0.0	0.0	0.0	0.5	0.0
Material desire	16.1	9.3	5.3	1.4	1.0	4.8	8.5	7.5	3.4	5.9	5.0	5.8
Family	12.7	13.0	17.0	14.0	16.2	0.0	14.3	16.2	4.2	7.2	7.0	11.1
Schooling	16.1	23.7	10.0	1.4	3.3	9.7	30.6	25.2	28	32	37.2	31.7
Identity	11.0	26.3	24.7	26.6	28.8	61.3	23.3	22.9	28	23.5	6.5	7.9
Sexuality	1.7	1.3	1.0	2.4	8.7	1.6	0.8	0.4	3.4	3.3	0.0	0.0
Courtship	4.2	6.7	10.3	5.8	7.6	9.7	9.3	12.4	11.6	8.5	5.5	2.4
Interpersonal	15.3	14	21.7	11.1	7.6	6.5	3.5	7.1	9.2	11.1	11.6	2.4
Emotional	4.2	1.3	6.0	10.1	5.3	0.0	3.9	4.1	4.2	0.9	1.5	3.3
Self-fulfilment	4.2	0.3	0.3	7.9	6.7	3.2	1.9	1.5	0.8	0.9	1.5	0.5
Altruism	11.9	3.0	2.7	5.8	3.3	3.2	3.9	2.6	7.6	5.3	8.0	12.2
No problem	0.0	0.0	0.0	0.0	0.0	0.0	0.0	0.0	0.0	0.0	14.1	22.0

iib) Advantaged subjects: categories of responses

Brazil: Male/Female: material desires: money 14 / interpersonal problems and socialization: employment 12 / schooling: academic achievement 9 / personal identity and self-concept: self-confidence 7 / altruism: justice and equality 7.

Greece: Male: personal identity and self concept: growing up (assuming adult roles) 14 / schooling: academic failure 9; teacher-related 6 / material desires: money 7 / interpersonal problems and socialization 7 / family issues: parental strictness 6.
Female: interpersonal problems and socialization: employment 12; friendship 7 / personal identity and self concept (assuming adult roles) 12 / family issues: parental strictness 7.

Israel: Male: personal identity and self concept: self-expectations 6; growing up (assuming adult roles) 6 / war 5.
Female: war 15 / personal identity and self concept: growing up (assuming adult roles) 6.

Japan: Male/Female: personal identity and self concept: growing up. (assuming adult roles) 50 / interpersonal problems and socialization: friendship 7.

Philippines: Male: schooling: academic failure 13; time pressures 8; inability to learn 5 / personal identity and self concept: self-confidence 7; growing up (assuming adult roles) 5 / courtship and dating 6 / material desires: money 6.
Female: schooling: academic failure 10 / material desires: money 7 / personal identity and self concept: growing up (assuming adult roles) 6.

USA: Male: schooling: academic achievement 14; academic failure 8; time pressures 5 / personal identity and self concept: growing up (assuming adult roles) 12 / courtship and dating: marriage restrictions 11.
Female: schooling: academic achievement 15; academic failure 9; time pressures 6 / personal identity and self concept: growing up (assuming adult roles) 19; physical appearance 7.

Venezuela: Male: schooling 17; academic failure 10; time pressures 10 / altruism 7 / interpersonal problems and socialization: friendship 5.
Female: schooling: academic failure 15; altruism 11.

Table B1 1989 percentages of responses to classes and categories of problems
iia) Non-advantaged, poverty and non-classified subjects: classes of responses

National background	*Non-advantaged*				*Poverty*		*Non-classified*			
	Greece		*Venezuela*		*Philippines*		*China*		*Russia*	
No of Ss	100	100	100	100	100	100	106	133	111	64
Gender	*M*	*F*	*M*	*F*	*M*	*F*	*M*	*F*	*M*	*F*
Problems										
Poverty	0.0	0.0	15.6	7.6	10.5	10.8	0.0	0.0	0.0	1.2
War	0.3	0.0	2.3	6.0	0.0	0.0	0.0	0.0	3.1	0.0
Catastrophe	0.0	1.3	0.4	0.0	0.0	0.0	0.4	0.0	0.3	0.0
Material desire	19.1	8.0	5.3	12.4	19.4	25.1	11.3	3.0	10.5	9.8
Family	6.4	22.8	15.3	29.3	18.1	23.5	2.9	6.7	4.1	6.1
Schooling	22.1	13.3	24.8	21.3	6.9	6.8	22.2	25.9	20.0	15.9
Identity	22.1	22.7	12.6	8.6	11.7	5.6	33.5	37.0	11.5	13.4
Sexuality	0.0	2.0	0.0	1.2	12.1	0.4	0.0	0.7	1.4	1.4
Courtship	10.4	8.0	2.3	3.6	0.0	8.0	7.1	5.1	3.8	7.9
Interpersonal	16.1	16.1	3.4	2.0	16.1	12.7	4.6	6.1	12.4	8.5
Emotional	1.0	3.7	1.5	1.6	2.4	2.4	7.5	2.7	3.1	3.0
Self-fulfilment	0.0	0.3	2.7	0.8	0.8	0.4	4.6	6.4	3.4	2.4
Altruism	2.3	1.7	10.7	3.2	2.0	4.4	4.2	3.4	22.3	29.1
No problem	0.0	0.0	3.1	2.4	0.0	0.0	1.7	3.0	3.1	1.5

iib) Non-advantaged subjects: categories of responses

Greece: Male: material desires: money 18 / schooling: time pressures 10; academic failure 8; extracurricular activities 7 / interpersonal problems and socialization: friendship 7; employment 5 / courtship and dating: not dating 6 / personal identity and self-concept: growing up (assuming adult roles) 6.

Female: personal identity and self-concept: growing up (assuming adult roles) 6; self-expectations 12 / material desires: money 7 / family issues: strictness 6 / interpersonal problems and socialization: employment 5.

Venezuela: Male: extreme poverty: unmet physical needs 15 / schooling: academic failure 9 / altruism 6 / personal identity and self-concept: self-confidence 6.

Female: schooling: academic achievement 12; academic failure 5 / material desires; money10 / war 6 / personal identity and self-concept: self-confidence 6 / family issues: domestic quarreling 5.

iic) Poverty subjects: categories of responses

Philippines: Male: material desires: money 19 / interpersonal problems and socialization: employment 12 / extreme poverty: unmet physical needs 11.

Female: material desires: money 24 / extreme poverty: unmet physical needs 10 / interpersonal problems and socialization: employment 8 / family issues: welfare of family 7.

iid) Non-classified subjects: categories of responses

China: Male: personal identity and self-concept 5: growing up (assuming adult roles) 17 / material desires: money 11 / schooling: academic failure 8.

Female: personal identity and self-concept 8; growing up (assuming adult roles) 19 / schooling: academic achievement 7; inability to learn 5.

Russia: Male: altruism 18 / material desire: money 11 / schooling: academic achievement 6 / interpersonal problems and socialization 5.

Female: altruism 26 / schooling: academic achievement 30.

Table B2 1989 percentages of responses to classes and categories of coping strategies
ia) Advantaged subjects: classes of responses

National background	*Brazil*	*Greece*		*Israel*		*Japan*	*Philippines*		*USA*		*Venezuela*	
No of Ss	*53*	*100*	*100*	*71*	*72*	*59*	*100*	*100*	*42*	*52*	*100*	*100*
Gender	*M/F*	*M*	*F*	*M*	*F*	*M/F*	*M*	*F*	*M*	*F*	*M*	*F*
Coping strategies												
Seek/give aid	3.8	11.7	10.4	16.1	15.2	2.0	8.8	11.0	7.5	8.4	4.3	14.4
Interpersonal	9.9	12.8	16.4	23.2	20.8	0.0	12.5	13.3	7.5	7.2	12.6	10.5
Ind.prob.-solve	65.9	54.8	47.9	43.4	46.3	96.0	46.8	48.7	52.7	49.4	38.2	50.3
Stress managment	2.2	1.0	1.7	6.6	4.3	0.0	1.8	1.4	3.2	5.5	9.7	4.4
Crying	1.1	0.3	0.3	0.3	1.5	0.0	0.3	0.8	0.5	3.4	0.0	2.8
Religious exp.	0.0	0.2	0.0	1.0	1.5	0.0	8.8	7.9	2.2	1.7	0.0	0.6
Resignation	17.0	9.1	9.7	5.9	7.2	2.0	10.6	9.3	8.1	7.2	17.9	10.5
Disengagement	0.0	10.0	13.6	2.8	2.5	0.0	9.1	7.1	18.3	17.3	15.9	6.6
Anti-social	0.0	0.0	0.0	0.8	0.8	0.0	1.2	0.4	0.0	0.0	1.4	0.0
Do nothing	0.0	0.0	0.0	0.0	0.0	0.0	0.0	0.0	0.0	0.0	0.0	0.0

ib) Advantaged subjects: categories of coping responses

Brazil: Male/Female: individual problem-solving: planning toward a solution 24; trying harder 21; reframing 7; mental preoccupation 6 / resignation: giving up, doing nothing 6.

Greece: Male: individual problem-solving: trying harder 22; planning toward a solution 19; mental preoccupation 6 / seeking or giving assistance: seek support from others 12 / interpersonal interactions: assertive coping 7.

Female: individual problem-solving: planning toward a solution 20; trying harder 16 / interpersonal interactions: assertive coping 11 / seeking or giving assistance: seek support from others 10 / disengagement: psychological distancing 8.

Israel: Male: seeking or giving assistance: seek support of others 12 / individual problem-solving: trying harder 12; accepting responsibity 9; planning toward a solution 7; mental preoccupation 7.

Female: seeking or giving assistance: seek support of others 12 / individual problem-solving: planning toward a solution 11; trying harder 11.

Japan: Male/Female: individual problem-solving: planning toward a solution 26; trying harder 17.

Philippines: Male: individual problem-solving: planing toward a solution 22; trying harder 15 / religious experience: prayer 9 / interpersonal interactions: assertive coping 9 / seeking or giving assistance: seek suppport from others 8.

Female: individual problem-solving: planning toward a solution 22; trying harder 17 / interpersonal interactions: assertive coping 11 / seeking or giving assistance: seek support of others 10 / religious experience: prayer 8.

USA: Male: individual problem-solving 17; trying harder 14; reframing 12; psychological distancing 12; planning 8 / seeking or giving assistance: seek support from others 5.

Female: individual problem-solving: planning toward a solution 16; trying harder 12; reframing 9; psychological distancing 8 / family issues 9.

Venezuela: Male: individual problem-solving: planning toward a solution 17; trying harder 10 / disengagement: psychological distancing 8 / stress management: relaxation 6 / interpersonal interactions: assertive coping 7; seek company 5.

Female: individual problem-solving: planning toward a solution 19; trying harder 17; reframing 5 / interpersonal interactions: assertive coping 7 / seeking or giving assistance: seek support from others 12.

Table B2 1989 percentages of responses to classes and categories of coping strategies
iia) Non-advantaged, poverty and non-classified subjects: classes of responses

National background	*Non-advantaged*				*Poverty*		*Non-classified*			
	Greece		*Venezuela*		*Philippines*		*China*		*Russia*	
No of Ss	*100*	*100*	*100*	*100*	*100*	*100*	*106*	*133*	*111*	*64*
Gender	*M*	*F*	*M*	*F*	*M*	*F*	*M*	*F*	*M*	*F*
Coping strategies										
Seek/give aid	5.8	12.4	17.3	11.1	12.8	13.8	1.9	1.5	3.1	1.9
Interpersonal	11.7	7.7	16.2	18.8	9.7	5.5	1.1	2.4	5.2	7.4
Ind.prob.-solve	59.0	54.5	47.3	43.3	50.5	42.9	63.2	68.2	46.7	48.8
Stress managment	0.5	1.2	5.3	5.4	1.7	4.2	8.4	4.8	5.2	6.8
Crying	0.0	0.5	0.3	3.0	0.0	2.0	0.0	0.0	0.0	0.6
Religious exp.	0.0	0.0	0.3	2.0	5.5	13.6	0.4	0.7	0.3	0.6
Resignation	13.2	10.3	6.2	7.0	10.0	11.4	13.8	18.5	24.6	25.9
Disengagement	9.8	13.4	7.3	9.4	9.7	6.5	11.1	3.9	13.5	7.4
Anti-social	0.0	0.0	0.0	0.0	0.0	0.0	0.0	0.0	1.4	0.6
Do nothing	0.0	0.0	0.0	0.0	0.0	0.0	0.0	0.0	0.0	0.0

iib) Non-advantaged subjects: categories of coping responses

Greece: Male: individual problem-solving: planning toward a solution 27 / trying harder 23 / interpersonal interactions: assertive coping 5 / seeking or giving assistance: seek support from others 5.

Female: individual problem-solving: planning toward a solution 24 / trying harder 17 / seeking or giving assistance: seek support from others 12 / disengagement: escape-avoidance behaviour 5 / resignation: do nothing 7.

Venezuela: Male: individual problem-solving: planning toward a solution 17; trying harder 17 / seeking or giving assistance: seek support from others 10; offer help to others 6 / interpersonal interactions: assertive coping 8.

Female: individual problem-solving: planning toward a solution 15; trying harder 12 / interpersonal interactions: seek company of others to solve problem 9; assertive coping 7.

iic) Poverty subjects: categories of coping responses

Philippines: Male: individual problem-solving: planning toward a solution 35; trying harder 8; interpersonal interactions: assertive coping 7 / seeking or giving assistance: seek support from others 13.

Female: individual problem-solving: planning toward a solution 32 / religious experience: prayer 14 / seeking or giving assistance: seek support from others 12 / interpersonal interactions: assertive coping 8.

iid) Non-classified subjects: categories of coping responses

China: Male: individual problem-solving: trying harder 27; planning toward a solution 25 / resignation 10 / disengagement: psychological distancing 5.

Female: individual problem-solving: trying harder 31; planning toward a solution 30 / resignation 11.

Russia: Male: individual problem-solving: trying harder 40 / disengagement: psychological distancing 8; escape-avoidance behavior 6.

Female: individual problem-solving: trying harder 34; accepting responsibility 7 / resignation: do nothing 20.

Table B3 1989 percentages of responses to classes and categories of desired helpers
ia) Advantaged subjects: classes of responses

National background	*Brazil*	*Greece*		*Israel*		*Japan*	*Philippines*		*USA*		*Venezuela*	
No of Ss	*53*	*100*	*100*	*71*	*72*	*59*	*100*	*100*	*42*	*52*	*100*	*100*
Gender	*M/F*	*M*	*F*	*M*	*F*	*M/F*	*M*	*F*	*M*	*F*	*M*	*F*
Helper												
Family	39.8	49.3	53.5	28.1	31.3	36.2	38.7	37.5	38.6	39.8	43.9	50.9
Non-family	55.2	50.0	46.1	68.0	61.1	63.8	54.5	51.8	59.1	56.4	47.3	39.8
Offender	0.0	0.1	0.3	1.5	4.4	0.0	0.2	0.3	0.0	0.0	0.0	1.7
Supernat. being	1.9	0.0	0.0	0.9	1.5	0.0	2.8	4.4	0.0	0.0	1.1	1.7
Animate creatures/ inanimate objects	0.0	0.0	0.0	1.0	0.3	0.0	0.0	0.0	0.0	0.0	3.7	0.0
Non-specific	0.4	0.4	0.0	0.5	0.5	0.0	2.3	4.4	0.0	0.0	1.1	2.4
Nobody	2.7	0.1	0.1	0.0	0.8	0.0	1.5	1.7	2.4	3.7	2.8	3.5
No response	0.0	0.0	0.0	0.0	0.0	0.0	0.0	0.0	0.0	0.0	0.0	0.0

iib) Advantaged subjects: categories of responses

Brazil: Male/Female: non-family: friend 18; schoolmate or classmate 14; boyfriend, girlfriend, fiancé or fiancée 11 / family: mother 10; extended family member 9; father 6.

Greece: Male: non-family: friend or gangmate 32; teacher 6 / family: family member 9; sister 7.
Female: non-family: friend or gangmate 30; boyfriend or fiancé 11 / family 7; mother 20; father 10; sister 9.

Israel: Male: non-family 6: personal friend 17; counsellor 14; girlfriend or fiancée 9 / family: father 7.
Female: non-family 6; counsellor 16; personal friend 14; boyfriend or fiancé 8; person with desired quality 5; family 6; mother 7.

Japan: Male/Female: non-family: friend 54 / family: mother 17; father 6.

Philippines: Male: non-family: friend 27; girlfriend or fiancée 6; schoolmate, classmate or gangmate 11 / Family 12; mother 7; brother 5.
Female: non-family: friend 26 / family 13; mother 8.

USA: Male: non-family: friend 36; girlfriend or fiancée 5 / family 9; mother 9; father 9; brother 6; sister 5.
Female: non-family: friend 32; counsellor 7 / family 13; mother 9 sister 8.

Venezuela: Male: non-family: friend 15; person possessing desired qualities for helping 11; girlfriend or fiancée 5 / family 8; mother 11; father 9; brother 7.
Female: family 9; mother 14; father 7; sister 6 / non-family: friend 11; instructor 6; person possessing desired qualities for helping 6.

Table B3 1989 percentages of responses to classes and categories of desired helpers
iia) Non-advantaged, poverty and non-classified subjects: classes of responses

National background	*Non-advantaged*				*Poverty*		*Non-classified*			
	Greece		*Venezuela*		*Philippines*		*China*		*Russia*	
No of Ss	*100*	*100*	*100*	*100*	*100*	*100*	*106*	*133*	*111*	*64*
Gender	*M*	*F*	*M*	*F*	*M*	*F*	*M*	*F*	*M*	*F*
Helper										
Family	53.8	60.0	49.4	52.1	39.3	42.4	20.8	33.2	22.5	28.4
Non-family	46.2	40.0	45.7	40.7	48.0	48.1	61.7	55.0	66.7	61.3
Offender	0.0	0.0	0.5	1.7	0.0	0.0	1.6	3.5	0.2	0.0
Supernat being	0.0	0.0	0.2	0.7	2.6	2.5	0.0	0.2	0.0	0.0
Animate creatures/ inanimate objects	0.0	0.0	0.0	0.0	0.2	0.0	0.3	0.6	3.6	2.5
Non-specific	0.0	0.0	3.6	1.7	9.0	6.2	4.7	3.7	0.0	0.0
Nobody	0.0	0.0	0.6	3.1	0.8	0.8	10.9	3.9	7.1	7.8
No response	0.0	0.0	0.0	0.0	0.0	0.0	0.0	0.0	0.0	0.0

iib) Non-advantaged subjects: categories of responses

Greece: Male: non-family: personal friend 23; schoolmate, classmate or gangmate 8; girlfriend or fiancée 5/ family 18; mother 10; father 10; sister 7.
Female: non-family: personal friend 21 / family 7; mother 20; father 10; sister 10.

Venezuela: Male: non-family: personal friend 16; schoolmate or classmate 5 / family: mother 13; father 11; brother 9.
Female: non-family: personal friend 19 / family: mother 16; father 10; sister 8; brother 6.

iic) Poverty subjects: categories of responses

Philippines: Male: non-family: personal friend 23; schoolmate, classmate or gangmate 6 / family 13; mother 8.

iid) Non-classified subjects: categories of responses

China: Male: non-family: personal friend 26; schoolmate14; teacher 6 / family 7 / person possessing desired qualities for helping 10.
Female: non-family: personal friend 26; schoolmate 13; teacher 7 / family 12; father 7; mother 7.

Russia: Male: non-family 12; personal friend 34; schoolmate or classmate 6 / family 7; mother 5.
Female: non-family 8; personal friend 32; boyfriend or fiancé 8 / family 6; mother 11.

Table B4 1989 percentages of responses to classes and categories of desired helper qualities
ia) Advantaged subjects: classes of responses

National background	*Brazil*	*Greece*		*Israel*		*Japan*	*Philippines*		*USA*		*Venezuela*	
No of Ss	*53*	*100*	*100*	*71*	*72*	*59*	*100*	*100*	*42*	*52*	*100*	*100*
Gender	*M/F*	*M*	*F*	*M*	*F*	*M/F*	*M*	*F*	*M*	*F*	*M*	*F*
Helper quality												
Powerful	1.7	2.3	0.6	1.5	3.7	2.5	3.2	2.8	1.6	2.3	13.4	6.8
Knowledgeable	20.3	23.3	29.4	31.8	31.0	60.0	27.4	23.7	36.7	36.9	39.5	32.6
Available	2.6	1.2	1.1	2.0	3.0	0.0	2.7	1.5	0.0	0.2	2.9	2.7
Personal attrib.	44.6	38.5	44.5	42.1	37.5	18.5	25.7	30.1	31.9	27.8	18.1	25.3
Concern	27.7	32.4	23.5	19.4	23.1	15.7	40.3	41.5	29.8	29.3	19.3	26.7
Uncertain	0.4	2.3	0.0	0.7	1.0	1.4	0.0	0.2	0.0	0.0	0.0	1.8
Nothing	2.6	0.0	0.8	0.2	0.5	1.4	0.0	0.0	0.0	2.4	0.0	0.0
No response	0.0	0.0	0.0	2.3	0.5	0.5	0.7	0.2	0.3	1.2	6.7	4.1

ib) Advantaged subjects: categories of responses

Brazil: Male/Female: appealing personal attributes: mature 9; stable 7; objective 6; trustworthy 5 / concern for others: understanding 13; supportive 10; caring 5 / knowledgeable: experienced.

Greece: Male: concern for others: caring 22;.understanding 8 / appealing personal attributes: trustworthy 20; willing to help 5.
Female: appealing personal attributes: trustworthy 19; willing to help 9; loyal 5 / concern for others: understanding 14; caring 9 / knowledgeable: similarity to subject 19; experienced 8.

Israel: Male: knowledgeable 7; experienced 10; intelligent 6; similarity to subject 5 / concern for others: understanding 9; supportive 5 / appealing personal attributes: objective 5.
Female: knowledgeable 5; experienced 12; similarity to subject 6 / concern for others: understanding 10; supportive 7; caring 7.

Japan: Male/Female: knowledgeable 16; experienced 26; intelligent 7 / concern for others: caring 10; understanding 6 / appealing personal attributes 6.

Philippines: Male: concern for others: understanding 20; caring 12; supportive 8 / knowledgeable: experienced 5 / appealing personal attributes: generous 5.
Female: concern for others 21; caring 12; supportive 9 / appealing personal attributes: approachable 11; generous 7 / knowledgeable: similarity to subject 6.

USA: Male: concern for others: understanding 15; caring 9 / appealing personal attributes 6; approachable 13 / knowledgeable: similarity to subject 12; experienced 11.
Female: concern for others: understanding 8; caring 8; supportive 5 / appealing personal attributes: approachable 12 / knowledgeable 9; experienced 10; similarity to subject 9.

Venezuela: Male: knowledgeable 7; experienced 14; similarity to subject 11; gives advice 5 / concern for others: understanding 13; supportive 5 / powerful: can exercise authority or change a situation 11.
Female: concern for others: understanding 17; caring 6 / appealing personal attributes: good listener 6; trustworthy 5 / powerful: can exercise authority or change a situation 6.

Table B4 1989 percentages of responses to classes and categories of desired helper qualities

iia) Non-advantaged, poverty and non-classified subjects: classes of responses

National background	*Non-advantaged*				*Poverty*		*Non-classified*			
	Greece		*Venezuela*		*Philippines*		*China*		*Russia*	
No of Ss	100	100	100	100	100	100	106	133	111	64
Gender	M	F	M	F	M	F	M	F	M	F
Helper quality										
Powerful	3.5	2.2	7.8	5.7	6.5	3.1	1.3	0.5	11.2	5.6
Knowledgeable	29.1	24.5	32.1	39.7	24.3	19.2	37.4	36.8	32.0	29.0
Available	0.0	0.6	4.0	2.8	3.4	1.9	4.2	4.4	0.4	0.6
Personal attrib.	29.7	38.1	29.4	27.6	30.0	30.3	28.2	29.2	21.9	21.0
Concern	37.8	33.7	23.1	21.6	35.3	45.4	18.9	27.2	30.9	43.2
Uncertain	0.0	0.0	1.0	1.3	0.0	0.0	4.2	0.0	2.9	0.6
Nothing	0.0	0.9	0.0	0.0	0.0	0.0	0.0	0.0	0.0	0.0
No response	0.0	0.0	2.7	1.3	0.5	0.0	5.9	1.8	0.7	0.0

iib) Non-advantaged subjects: categories of responses

Greece: Male: concern for others: caring 25; understanding 13 / knowledgeable: similarity to subject 20; experienced 7; appealing personal attributes: trustworthy 16; loyal 6.

Female: concern for others: caring 23; understanding 10 / appealing personal attributes: trustworthy 21; loyal 6; willing to help 6 / knowledgeable: similarity to subject 15; experienced 7.

Venezuela: Male: knowledgeable: experienced 10; gives advice 9; similarity to subject 7 / concern for others: understanding 10; caring 8; supportive 7; appealing personal attributes: honest 9; good listener 8; trustworthy 6.

Female: knowledgeable 7; experienced 10; similarity to subject 7; intelligent 5 / appealing personal attribute: trustworthy 5.

iic) Poverty: categories of responses

Philippines: Male: concern for others: understanding 20; caring 11 / appealing personal attributes: willing to help 16 / knowledgeable 7; gives advice13.

Female: concern for others: understanding 24; caring 15; supportive 6 / appealing personal attributes: generous 17 / knowledgeable: gives advice 10.

iid) Non-classified subjects: categories of responses

China: Male: knowledgeable: similarity to subject 13; experienced 8; gives advice 6 / appealing personal attributes 8; willing to help 8 / concern for others: caring 8; understanding 6.

Female: knowledgeable: similarity to subject 16; experienced 7; gives advice 7 / appealing personal attributes: trustworthy 8 / concern for others: understanding 14; caring 9.

Russia: Male: concern for others 8: understanding 16 / powerful: can exercise authority or change a situation 9 / knowledgeable: similarity to subject 8; experienced 8; intelligent 6.

Female: concern for others 9; understanding 25; caring 6 / knowledgeable: similarity to subject 10; intelligent 6.

Table B5 1989 percentages of responses to classes and categories of desired modes of helping
ia) Advantaged subjects: classes of responses

National background	*Brazil*	*Greece*		*Israel*		*Japan*	*Philippines*		*USA*		*Venezuela*	
No of Ss	*53*	*100*	*100*	*71*	*72*	*59*	*100*	*100*	*42*	*52*	*100*	*100*
Gender	*M/F*	*M*	*F*	*M*	*F*	*M/F*	*M*	*F*	*M*	*F*	*M*	*F*
Helper mode												
Satisfy need	4.4	4.5	2.3	2.3	1.5	4.0	4.4	2.1	0.7	1.9	6.0	4.8
Exercise power	6.3	6.1	6.1	9.4	12.1	0.0	3.5	4.2	5.3	4.9	16.3	9.7
Intercede w/others	1.3	3.5	1.9	2.0	3.0	0.0	3.5	2.7	0.0	0.0	4.3	2.8
Counsel	40.0	54.1	46.0	40.6	39.3	40.0	48.4	45.5	47.8	45.8	38.6	46.2
Attend to	43.1	27.7	40.5	41.6	40.1	28.0	31.9	38.7	42.4	46.9	20.7	28.3
Evade problem	1.9	1.6	1.3	3.3	3.0	2.0	3.5	3.0	1.5	0.6	0.5	0.7
Uncertain	2.6	2.2	0.0	0.8	1.0	26.0	2.2	2.1	2.4	0.0	0.0	2.1
Nothing	0.3	0.3	1.9	0.0	0.0	0.0	0.4	0.0	0.0	0.0	0.0	0.0
No response	0.0	0.0	0.0	0.0	0.0	0.0	2.2	1.8	0.0	0.0	13.6	5.5

ib) Advantaged subjects: categories of responses

Brazil: Male/Female: attend to: encourage 18; listen 8; care 6; comfort 5 / counsel: help subject to problem-solve 15; advise14.

Greece: Male: counsel: advise 30; help subject to problem-solve 14; direct 5 / attend to: encourage 9; comfort 7.
Female: counsel: advise 20; help subject to problem-solve 13; direct 6 / attend to: comfort 11; care 7; understand 7 / exercise power: solve problem for subject 6.

Israel: Male: counsel: help subject to problem-solve 11; share information 10; advise 6 / attend to: encourage 8; accept 8; understand 6; listen 5.
Female: counsel 13; advise 8; share information 7 / attend to: encourage 8; comfort 8; accept 5 / exercise power: change situation 5.

Japan: Male/Female: counsel: advise 14; help subject to problem-solve 14; share information 14 / attend to: encourage 6; understand 6; listen 6.

Philippines: Male: counsel: give advice 28; direct 6; help subject to problem-solve 12 / attend to: comfort 13; encourage 11; listen 6.
Female: counsel: advise 25; help subject to problem-solve 9; direct 7 / attend to: comfort 19; encourage 10; listen 6.

USA: Male: counsel: advise 27; share information 8; direct 7 / attend to: encourage 19; comfort 13.
Female: counsel: advise 28; direct 8 / help subject to problem-solve 5 / attend to: comfort 17; encourage 9; listen 7; understand 6.

Venezuela: Male: counsel: advise 7; direct 7; help subject to problem-solve 6 / exercise power: change situation 8; solve problem for subject 5 / attend to: comfort 8 / direct satisfaction of a need: give something 6.
Female: counsel: advise 17; direct 13; help subject to problem-solve 12 / attend to: encourage 9; comfort 6 / exercise power: change situation 5.

Table B5 1989 percentages of responses to classes and categories of desired modes of helping
iia) Non-advantaged, poverty and non-classified subjects: classes of responses

National background	*Non-advantaged*				*Poverty*		*Non-classified*			
	Greece		*Venezuela*		*Philippines*		*China*		*Russia*	
No of Ss	*100*	*100*	*100*	*100*	*100*	*100*	*106*	*133*	*111*	*64*
Gender	*M*	*F*	*M*	*F*	*M*	*F*	*M*	*F*	*M*	*F*
Helping mode										
Satisfy need	5.5	2.3	7.7	5.6	9.6	7.7	2.8	2.0	11.0	10.0
Exercise power	8.6	8.9	10.5	8.6	4.5	5.3	2.7	5.7	4.4	1.0
Intercede	0.0	0.7	4.3	10.1	3.4	4.7	0.4	0.0	1.1	1.0
Counsel	53.5	60.9	50.2	44.9	57.5	65.3	47.7	52.2	22.0	28.0
Attend to	31.3	23.2	22.6	27.7	17.5	14.7	32.6	34.0	17.6	30.0
Evade problem	0.3	2.3	0.9	1.1	5.1	1.7	3.2	2.0	2.2	3.0
Uncertain	0.0	0.0	0.6	0.7	1.4	0.3	10.3	3.9	29.7	15.0
Nothing	0.0	0.0	0.0	0.0	0.0	0.0	0.0	0.0	0.0	0.0
No response	0.7	1.7	3.1	1.1	1.0	0.3	0.2	0.2	12.1	12.0

iib) Non-advantaged subjects: categories of responses

Greece: Male: counsel: advise 32; help subject to problem-solve 20 / attend to: comfort 18; agree 5 / exercise power: solve problem for subject 9 / direct satisfaction of need: give something 5.
Female: counsel: advise 33; help subject to problem-solve 18 / attend to: encourage 11; comfort 10 / exercise power: solve problem for subject 9.

Venezuela: Male: counsel: advise 18; direct 13; help subject to problem-solve 11 / attend to: encourage 10; comfort 5 / direct satisfaction of a need: give something 8; exercise power: change situation 5.
Female: counsel: advise 16; direct 14; help subject to problem-solve 10; other (mediate) 9 / Attend to: comfort 7; encourage 6; understand 6.

iic) Poverty subjects: categories of desired ofresponses

Philippines: Male: counsel: advise 38; help subject to problem-solve 10 / attend to: comfort 10 / direct satisfaction of a need: give something 10 / evade: help subject escape problem 5.
Female: counsel: advise 42; help subject to problem-solve 13 / direct satisfaction of a need: give something 8 / attend to: comfort 6.

iid) Non-classified subjects: categories of responses

China: Male: counsel: advise 16; share information 13; help subject to problem-solve 7; direct 5 / attend to: comfort 16; encourage 7.
Female: counsel: advise 19; direct 10; help subject to problem-solve 10 / attend to: comfort 17; encourage 10.

Russia: Male: counsel: advise 12 / exercise power: give something 8.
Female: counsel: help subject to problem-solve 12; share information 8; advise 7 / attend to 5; encourage 7; comfort 7 / direct satisfaction of a need: give something 5.

Appendix IV
Statistical findings of the multinational study 1997 and 1989

	1997					*1989*		
	SES			*Gender*		*SES*		
	Adv	*Non-adv*	*Pov*	*M*	*F*	*Adv*	*Non-adv*	*Pov*
Problems								
Poverty	0.0	0.0	0.6	0.0	0.0	0.0	5.6	10.5
War	1.1	0.0	0.0	2.2	4.2	0.2	2.2	0.0
Catastrophe	0.0	0.0	0.2	0.0	0.0	0.0	0.2	0.0
Material desire	1.1	18.0	0.0	10.6	8.1	0.6	11.1	22.2
Family	7.5	8.5	27.8	9.9	17.5	13.1	18.4	20.6
Schooling	39.1	28.8	16.9	21.7	8.1	32.0	20.2	6.9
Identity	27.3	33.3	19.6	27.1	26.4	41.1	17.5	8.7
Sexuality	0.0	0.0	0.0	0.0	4.2	0.0	0.6	6.3
Courtship	6.4	0.0	0.0	6.5	10.4	3.5	6.1	4.4
Interpersonal	16.4	7.1	24.6	13.7	13.9	7.5	9.1	14.4
Emotional	0.0	0.0	0.0	0.5	0.0	0.0	2.2	2.2
Self-fulfilment	0.0	0.0	0.0	0.7	0.0	0.0	1.1	0.0
Altruism	1.1	4.4	10.2	7.2	7.3	2.0	4.3	3.2
No problem	0.0	0.0	0.0	0.0	0.0	0.0	1.4	0.0
Coping strategies								
Seek/give aid	13.1	11.1	8.1	10.1	12.4	11.9	12.2	6.6
Interpersonal	10.1	9.4	0.0	7.5	16.6	11.9	12.2	6.6
Ind.prob.-solve	47.8	51.2	65.4	62.8	52.6	54.2	54.2	73.5
Stress managment	0.0	1.1	0.0	0.0	0.0	0.0	0.0	0.0
Crying	0.0	0.0	0.6	0.0	0.0	0.0	0.0	0.0
Religious exp.	1.1	0.5	0.2	0.0	1.3	0.0	0.0	0.0
Resignation	10.9	13.6	8.4	10.1	9.5	9.9	9.2	6.6
Disengagement	17.1	13.1	17.3	9.6	7.5	12.2	12.2	6.6
Anti-social	0.0	0.0	0.0	0.0	0.0	0.0	0.0	0.1
Do nothing	0.0	0.0	0.0	0.0	0.0	0.0	0.0	0.0
No response	0	0	4.4	4.1	3.9	0	0	0

	1997					*1989*		
	SES			*Gender*		*SES*		
	Adv	*Non-adv*	*Pov*	*M*	*F*	*Adv*	*Non-adv*	*Pov*
Helpers								
Family	24.4	42.1	49.6	34.4	44.8	24.2	24.2	49.9
Nonfamily	60.2	57.9	49.6	58.2	49.7	60.6	60.2	47.9
Offender	4.2	0.0	0.0	1.3	0.0	8.7	4.2	0.0
Supernat being	0.0	0.0	0.2	0.0	4.2	1.3	1.1	0.0
Animate/Inanimate	0.0	0.0	0.0	0.0	0.0	0.0	0.0	0.0
Objects/creatures	1.3	0.0	0.0	0.0	0.0	0.0	0.0	0.0
Nonspecific	0.0	0.0	0.2	0.0	0.2	—	1.1	0.0
Nobody	9.9	0.0	0.3	6.1	1.1	5.1	9.1	2.2
No response	0.0	0.0	0.0	0.0	0.0	0.0	0.1	0.0
Helper qualities								
Powerful	0.0	4.1	14.8	7.4	5.1	0.0	0.0	0.0
Knowledgeable	32.1	33.3	22.2	36.4	26.3	49.9	50.0	33.3
Available	1.7	0.0	0.0	2.1	0.5	0.0	0.0	0.0
Personal attributes	42.1	43.3	44.2	33.8	39.3	37.9	38.0	37.8
Concern	24.1	19.3	18.7	19.4	27.6	12.2	12.0	29.0
Does not know	0.0	0.0	0.1	0.1	0.1	0.0	0.0	0.0
Nothing	0.0	0.0	0.0	0.0	0.0	0.0	0.0	0.0
No response	0.0	0.0	0.0	0.0	0.0	0.0	0.0	0.0
Helping mode								
Satisfy need	3.3	14.2	4.4	6.1	3.8	0.0	0.0	0.0
Exercise power	10.6	10.2	6.8	8.3	8.2	10.9	10.9	12.9
Intercede w/others	1.1	0.0	0.4	0.7	1.2	0.0	0.0	4.1
Counsel	40.0	33.1	34.2	43.2	36.1	51.3	51.3	49.5
Attend to	45.0	42.6	44.2	34.1	45.1	37.7	37.7	33.3
Evade problem	0.0	0.0	1.2	1.3	0.4	0.0	0.0	0.0
Uncertain	0.1	0.0	4.4	2.1	1.1	0.0	0.0	0.2
Nothing	0.0	0.0	0.0	0.1	0.2	0.0	0.0	0.0
No response	0.0	0.0	4.4	4.1	3.9	0.0	0.0	0.0

Note: By SES and Gender for 1997; by SES for 1989; includes classes only. Categories-within-classes were obtained by the researchers but not reported in this Appendix.

Index